THE

LIFE AND REVELATIONS

OF

SAINT GERTRUDE

ST. GERTRUDE THE GREAT.

Engraved from the Spanish miraculous Painting.

THE LIFE & REVELATIONS of
SAINT GERTRUDE

VIRGIN AND ABBESS · OF THE ORDER OF
ST. BENEDICT

ChristianClassics™

A DIVISION OF THOMAS MORE PUBLISHING

Allen, Texas

First Published in English, 1862.

Send all inquiries to:
CHRISTIAN CLASSICS™
a Division of Thomas More Publishing
200 East Bethany Drive
Allen, Texas 75002–3804

Printed in the United States of America

ISBN 0–87061–079–1

   9 10 11 12   00 99 98 97

Ad Mariam

Approbation of the Right Rev. Dr Moriarty.

THE PALACE, KILLARNEY, *Dec.* 17*th*, 1870.

MY DEAR SISTER IN CHRIST,—

I learn that you are issuing some new Works, and some new editions of those already published. Your literary labours reflect honour on your Convent, on your Order, and on this Diocese.

But I rejoice much more in this, that you are contributing to supply one of our greatest needs—a Catholic Literature. I know, too, that the funds realised by the sale of your works are exclusively devoted to the service of religion.

Praying God to bless you, and to preserve your health and strength,

Yours sincerely in Christ,

✠ D. MORIARTY.

TO SISTER M. FRANCES CLARE,
Convent of Poor Clares, Kenmare, Co. Kerry.

CONTENTS.

PART I.

CHAPTER I. PAGE 1.

The Saint's birth and parentage—Her early dedication to God—Intellectual gifts—Divine communications concerning her sanctity—Our Lord declares that He finds rest and repose in her heart—Desires a holy person to seek Him there.

CHAPTER II. PAGE 11.

St. Gertrude predicts the election of Adolphus of Nassau—Quiets the fears of the sisters, who expect to suffer a temporal loss—Her election as Abbess—Removal to Heldelfs—Revelations of her sanctity—Our Lord appears to her, bearing the house of religion—Her generosity of spirit.

CHAPTER III. PAGE 20.

The Saint obtains favourable weather—Miracles mentioned in her Office—Union of her will with God's—Counsels others—Desired to write her revelations—Her sanctity revealed to St. Mechtilde.

CHAPTER IV. PAGE 29.

She asks St. Mechtilde to pray for her—Our Lord is pleased with her patience and mildness—He declares that He dwells in her ; and hides her imperfections.

CHAPTER V. PAGE 32.

The Saint as Abbess—Tenderness towards others—Care of the sick—Her last illness—Value of suffering—She is forbidden to resign her office—Our Lord accepts as done to Himself what is done for her—St. Lebuin.

PART II.

PART III.

PART IV.

ADVERTISEMENT.

THE *Insinuationes Divinæ Pietatis* consist of Five Books. **The** Second only was written by the Saint : the remaining four were compiled from her papers, and from personal knowledge of her life, by a religious of her monastery. This religious,who carefully conceals her name, was probably the Sister whom St. Gertrude mentions herself, and in whom she evidently had the greatest confidence. As the object of the *Insinuationes* is manifestly to relate the supernatural favours bestowed on St. Gertrude, her personal history is but briefly adverted to, and only in connection with the graces bestowed on her by God. Hence but little is known of the Saint's early life. The first book of the *Insinuationes* contains some allusions to it ; but it consists principally of a panegyric and a formal enumeration of her virtues. To avoid needless and uninteresting repetition, this was omitted, and the substance of it carefully embodied in the life of St. Gertrude, for which we have endeavoured to collate materials from every possible source. The chronology of Campacci has been followed as the most reliable, and as highly esteemed by the learned Benedictines of Solesmes.

The second, third, fourth, and fifth parts of this work are translations of the second, third, fourth, and fifth books of the *Insinuationes*. The edition principally used has been the "*Insinuationes Divinæ Pietatis*, seu Vita et Revelationes S. Gertrudis, Virginis et Abbatissæ, Ordinis S. Benedicti. Amendis quibus scatebant expurgatæ studio et labore D[om] N[icolas] C[anteleu] B[enedictinus]. Parisiis apud Fredericum Leonard, Congregationis S. Mauri Ordinis S. Benedicti. Typogr. viâ

Jacobæa sub Scuto Veneto, M.DC.LXII. Cum privilegio et approbatione." The "Scuto Veneto" is duly represented on the title-page, and the winged lion of St. Mark holds an open Gospel, with the legend "Pax tibi Marce Evangelista meus." The motto, "Virtute invidiam vince," is engraved on a scroll above the emblem.

Dom Canteleu was a holy and learned priest. It is said that the hour of his death was revealed to him while he was occupied in preparing his edition of the *Insinuationes*. But he had commenced his work for God, and for Him also it was consummated. The last corrections were made the very day of his death ; and though he did not live to see his work issue from the press, surely his reward was not the less sure or magnificent.

This edition contains, first, a dedication of the work to the Maurist Fathers, by Leonard, the publisher ; secondly, a brief Prologue, by D. Canteleu, in which he explains the corrections and emendations which he has made in former editions ; and, thirdly, the well-known apology of Lanspergius, of which we have given a *résumé* in the Introduction. There are also extracts from Blosius's *Monili Spirituale*, and an important note, found in an old Codex of a Styrian monastery, which mentions that the convent of Helfide was destroyed in the year 1342, during the wars between the Duke of Brunswick and the Count of Mansfield ; but the holy virgins were saved by an evident protection of God, and removed to the suburbs of Eisleben.

It has been our earnest endeavour to render this translation as faithful and accurate as possible. One chapter has been omitted, and several passages, which could hardly be rendered in English with propriety ; and as the substance of several chapters from the fifth book are contained in the Life, they have also been passed over. We are privileged to say that we have been guided in the general arrangement of the work by the advice of the Right Rev. Dr Ullathorne, O.S.B., to whose paternal and most undeserved kindness on this, as on many other occasions, we owe a debt of affectionate gratitude. Nor can we omit most grateful mention of the invaluable assistance

obtained from the world-famed Abbayé of Solesmes, through
the Rev. Father Wilfrid Windham, O.S.B., to whose researches
and learning we owe many of the notes appended to this volume. We have also to acknowledge the charity of Dom
Wolter, O.S.B., Prior of Beuron, whose noble and successful
efforts to revive and extend the Benedictine Order in Germany
are too well known to need further comment.

The recently-published French translation of the *Insinuationes* is said to be a reprint of the translation made by Dom
Mege, from his Latin edition of 1664. In this edition many
passages are omitted, and others are rendered differently from
the editions of Canteleu and Tilmanni Bredenbachii, Coloniæ,
1563, which perfectly coincide. An Italian translation, which
purports to be a translation from the Latin of Lanspergius,
also corresponds with these works. The title-page runs thus :
" La vita della B. Virgine Gertruda, ridotta in v. libri, del
R. F. Geo. Lanspergio, Monaco della Certosa . . . Tradotta per
l'Eccel. Medico M. Vicenzo Buondi. Venetia, 1606." This
edition contains the *Exercises*.

Indeed, the Italian Benedictines have devoted themselves
with special fervour to producing editions or translations of
these Revelations ; but perhaps one of the most valuable works
on the subject is that of a secular priest, Gaspar Campacci, who
published the *Life of St. Gertrude*, in 4to, at Venice, in 1748.
His work is divided into two parts ; the first part contains the
Life of the Saint, the second part contains her Revelations.
At the end of the first part he has appended a valuable Chrono-
logical Discussion, in which he fixes the date of her birth, her
death, and the principal events of her life.

But one of the most interesting editions of the Life and
Revelations of this great Saint is the Spanish translation of
Leander, of Grenada, a copy of which is at present in the
Library of the British Museum, and is dated, Seville, 1606.

As the literary history of this work is one of more than
ordinary interest and edification, as well as a necessary explanation of the origin of the miraculous engraving, an account
of it is appended at considerable length ; and this account is

translated from the letter of the saintly Bishop Ypres, of Tarragona, to Dom Leander :—

"I cannot tell you with what joy and consolation I have
received the book of the Revelations of Gertrude, which you
have translated into Castilian. . . . I will now relate what
occurred regarding the Latin edition printed at Madrid.

"While I was Confessor to the King, I met with the works
of Blosius accidentally, and found so much pleasure therein,
that I read them repeatedly. Afterwards, when I mentioned
this to Dom Alphonsus Colone, now Archbishop of Carthagena,
he assured me that a translation was then in the press at
Seville ; and I requested him to send me the sheets as they
appeared. This was at the time when King Philip II. was
seized with his last illness. I considered the work so suitable
for his circumstances, that I read it to him frequently ; and
he found such consolation and sweetness therein, that in my
absence he caused it to be read to him by the Infanta Ma-
dame Elizabeth. I know well the profit he derived from it,
and it will be known to all in heaven.

"From this moment I conceived so strong an affection for
the Revelations of St. Gertrude, that I desired ardently to
know if they had been published."

The good prelate then relates how he found them, after
much research, in the library of St. Lawrence ; that the volume
had never been opened since it had been placed there ten
years before ; and details his many and unsuccessful attempts
to obtain a translation. After he had retired to Tarragona, he
commenced the undertaking himself ; but when he "had completed, corrected, and amended the first four books," he heard
that the work was already in the press at Salamanca.

"I desired some copies to be sent to me," he continues ;
"and when I had seen the translation, considered the diligence
with which it had been made, the grave, clear, eloquent style,
and the careful annotations, I was supremely delighted, because
the same thing had happened to me as to St. Bonaventure and
St. Thomas, in regard to the Office of the Most Holy Sacrament ; and I consider it a special favour that the Saint has so

ordered all, that my edition has been delayed, since the result will be a greater glory to her Sovereign Spouse. As for myself, I am persuaded that I have lost nothing thereby, and that she has received my labour and my good-will into her treasury. I must confess also that I have never in my life received a greater satisfaction in the perusal of any other work than this; for though I have read the Revelations so often in Latin that I know them almost by heart, I do not the less esteem this translation, and I will make it known to all my friends. Be assured, my father, that you have performed a great service to God, a great good to souls, and that you have thereby secured your salvation. May God fulfil in you all the privileges and promises which He has made to the clients of this sublime virgin !

" I have purchased an immense number of these volumes for the Discalced Carmelites, and all who are earnestly desiring a more perfect life ; and I would, were it possible, disseminate them throughout the entire world.

" If by chance you have met with the picture of this blessed Saint, I wish to tell you the origin of it, because I hope it will be a subject of consolation to you. The first picture, which was done in Spain, was copied, by my desire, from a portrait of a Religious of the same Order, which was in the royal cabinet at Madrid. To distinguish the copy from the original, I desired the painter to put an Infant Jesus in her heart, and a scroll with the words, *Invenies me in corde Gertrudis.* I also had seven rings put on the fingers of her right hand, that they might be a pledge of the promises which our Lord has made to favour her friends.

" The artist has declared to me that never in his life did such a thing happen to him as has happened in painting this virgin ; for though he had always succeeded in copying to the life, he now found that he could not succeed, with all his pains, in imitating the original ; and each time that he attempted to do so, he found he drew what far surpassed what he could have thought or imagined ; and so his picture in no way resembled the original, except in the habit. This picture has been circulated throughout Spain. I have had it painted in many places, in company with our holy mother Teresa of Jesus, whom you so often consoled by your discourses."

The saintly prelate concludes thus :—" God have you in His holy keeping. I hope that His Majesty will grant you the grace that you may be assisted at the hour of your death by His two faithful spouses, who during their lives were always so full of gratitude and courtesy.

　　　　　　　" FR. DIEGO, *Bishop of Tarragona.*
" *Given at Tarragona, Nov.* 15, 1603."

We can scarcely be surprised that a miraculous favour should be granted to one so profoundly humble, so deeply loving, and so rarely disinterested. Perhaps the annals of literature have seldom furnished so distinguished an example of courtesy as that given by the Bishop of Tarragona ; or rather, we should say, Christian charity has seldom shone forth so sweetly and so brightly as in his cordial desire for the success of another in a labour which he had all but accomplished himself.

A number of approbations follow that of the holy Bishop, notably one from Suarez, dated Salamanca, July 15, 1603, and another from the Father Prior of the Discalced Carmelites, who observes that an edition in the mother tongue is most useful and acceptable, even to the learned.

The miraculous picture was soon engraved, and its fame extended throughout Europe. The copy contained in this volume has been made from the edition of " P. F. Laurentii Clement, Monachi Ordinis S. Benedicti Congregationis Hispanicæ. Salisburgi, MDCLXII."

CONVENT OF POOR CLARES, KENMARE,
Feast of St. John before the Latin Gate,
　　May 6, 1865.

INTRODUCTION.

THERE is perhaps no Order in the Church which at once
commands our admiration and wins our love like that of
the great Order of St. Benedict. Even heresy has offered
its poor meed of praise, in attempting to transplant it to
a foreign soil; and is fain to shelter its feeble imitation of
religious life under the name of the great Patriarch of the
West, claiming a patron in the Church, because none
can be found outside its pale. It stands, like a primeval
forest, by the great river Time,—its roots extending deep
and wide, and forming an unshaken barrier to the ever-
surging waves : its branches extending far and high, and
affording shelter and protection in the wildest storms.

Peace and strength are the essential characteristics of
its Rule and its children ; prayer and love, the source and
the support of these, its most manifest glories. And of
this spirit St. Gertrude is the perfect realisation ; a *Pax
vobiscum* is breathed into the soul in every revelation and
in every action of that greatest of saints. Her strength
is the calm, beautiful strength of peace ; for perfect peace

alone can exist where the soul is stayed upon the Unchangeable, and thus can no longer be shaken by the
transitory blasts which disturb the less perfect.

This work has been undertaken with feelings of no ordinary affection.   There are few Orders in the Church which
are not indebted in some degree to the Benedictine : but
none more deeply than that of the poor one of Assisi, who
found in the Benedictines his first and kindest supporters ;
and when his second Order was established, it was they
who gave a temporary home and a holy example to the
gentle Clare de Scefi and her young sister Agnes.   We
can scarcely turn over a page in the history of the Friars
Minors or the Poor Clares without finding how this
kindness has been continued and increased.   May this
offering to the great Order of St. Benedict be accepted by
his devoted children as a humble though a poor return for
their unwearied love !

A recent review of the *Gertrudenbuch von P. Maurus
Wolter* which is attributed to a Father of the Order, enters
so fully into the peculiar merits and sanctity of St. Gertrude,
that we cannot forbear an extract.   Would that its eloquent
and spiritual words had found a less ephemeral resting-place
than the pages in which it is inserted !

"St. Gertrude, in the most extensive sense, was a
daughter of the cloister.   *Officium* and *sacrificium*, the
Scriptures and the Liturgy, are the two wings by which
pure souls fly to God in monastic life.   The Missal and
the Breviary are the two fountains of liturgical devotion
from which they may draw the pure waters of life.   These
waters and those wings were well understood and ap-

preciated in the Middle Ages ; and in the sixty thousand convents which sent up praise to God, *sicut incensum in conspectu ejus*, during the lifetime of St. Gertrude, there was not one being who more fully grasped these two means of perfection, or turned them to greater advantage, than our Saint. Through them she became the *grosse Aebtissinn ;* through them, directed by the tender, loving spirit of the Rule, she became the most perfect and striking exponent of the *spirit* of St. Benedict that can be found in the lives of the Saints of God."

Nor is he less eloquent in speaking of the great restorations, or rather, we should say, advancements, of his Order ; of St. Martin's, consecrated once more to its ancient uses, where, by the piety of the widowed Princess Catherine of Hohenzollern, the children of St. Benedict, with the special blessing of the Holy See, are leading lives of no ordinary fervour and devotedness, under the guidance of their holy Prior Dom Wolter ; where the ancient and miraculous image of the Mother of Sorrows is venerated once more by thousands of devout pilgrims ;—and of Solesmes with its Abbot, whose European fame for learning is only equalled by his cloistral fame for sanctity ; where "sixty God-praising monks chanted together the Gregorian choral song " in the curious old church of the monastery ; * " where

---

* This quaint and curious old church would require a volume of its own. It is chiefly remarkable for statuary of unusual size, in groups, representing various incidents in the life of our Divine Lord. One of these groups represents Jesus Christ giving Holy Communion to His Blessed Mother. A good prior of mediæval times considered this a grievous impiety, and accordingly chopped off the hands of our Lord

joyful obedience, brotherly love, and studious attention to
the never-wanting guest, are beautifully combined with,
and enhanced by, genuine and ardent zeal for ecclesiastical
discipline and authority, with a devotion to literature,
and an anxiety for its advancement, which can hardly be
surpassed."

The history of the labours of Abbot Gueranger would
almost require a volume. Perhaps his chiefest eternal
fame, and his brightest reward, will be, for the government
of his monastery; the foundations he has effected; and
his persevering efforts, in the face of opposition which
would have crushed any ordinary mind, in planting the
Roman Liturgy in France, in place of that which at least
bore a tincture of independence of the Holy See, and a
trace of rationalism.

We read in the Book of Genesis, that Adam and Eve
heard " the voice of the Lord God walking in Paradise at
the afternoon air." And we can scarcely doubt, that
had they preserved their original innocence, the Creator
would have found His delight in conversing with the
creature, and would have communicated Himself continually and familiarly to the beings to whom He had Himself
given existence. Sin prevented the continuance of that

---

with a hatchet! The Blessed Sacrament is reserved here in a golden
dove, according to an ancient custom. There is a very curious and
very ancient inscription, in the old Greek characters, which dates
from the end of the second century, over the altar of the Sacred Heart,
ΗΤΟΡΙ ΣΕΜΝΟΙ, "To the magnanimous Heart." It was found by
his Eminence Cardinal Petra, formerly monk of Solesmes, on a tomb-
stone near Autun.

which would have constituted man's highest felicity ; but where sin is subdued and banished from the soul by that all-victorious grace which has triumphed over man's perverseness, and made his very fall an occasion of mercy, there we might reasonably hope and expect that such favours would again be renewed. The artist loves to gaze upon the creation of his genius ; the poet, to muse upon the offspring of his fancy ; the philosopher, to ponder on the discoveries of his intellect ; the artificer, to admire the works of his hands ; the mother finds her joy in the simple affections of her children ; the bride, her only pleasure in the caresses of her bridegroom. Each loves with a special affection that which has emanated from his genius, or is so united to him by ties of consanguinity as to be a part of his being. And shall it be supposed that the great Father is less loving than His children ; that He who has hidden some, chosen amongst many, to be His brides, will love them less, and find less pleasure in converse with them, than those in whom He has Himself implanted the deep and ardent feelings of earthly love ?

We know how freely our Divine Lord conversed with His disciples when on earth ; and we may find a remarkable similarity between this converse, as recorded in the holy Gospels, and that which we find in the Revelations of St. Gertrude. He instructed them by parables ; and these parables were remarkable for their simplicity, and, if we may use the term, for their homeliness. The kingdom of heaven is likened to a householder : where shall we find a more ordinary comparison ? It is likened to leaven : what more familiar ? It is described as a treasure hidden in a field : what more simple ? And yet these ordinary, familiar and simple comparisons are explained in words as ordinary and simple. We shall find it so in the Revelations of this Saint ; and even as the instructions given to the Apostles were not intended solely for themselves, so also our loving Master permits us to know and to be instructed by what He vouchsafed to communicate to one of His most blessed Saints.

After His Resurrection, we find no change in His manner of addressing His disciples, unless, indeed, there be a deeper tenderness in His words and actions. He is anxious that they should dine when wearied with their long night's fruitless toil, and He Himself provides their meal; for when they come to land, they see "hot coals lying, and a fish laid thereon, and bread." Ah! who but Jesus would have had these "hot coals" ready, and provided not only necessary food, but even the luxury of fire? And so we find in the life of this dear Saint, that she also is invited many times to mystical repasts, wherein not her body, but her soul is fed, and not her soul only, but also the souls of all those who are privileged to read or hear of these mysterious banquets.

And yet in reading the lives of those Saints who have been favoured with intimate communications from their Spouse, there are few persons who do not select, on the most arbitrary principles—or rather, on no principles whatsoever—certain circumstances which they consider improbable, and certain communications which they think unlikely or even unreasonable ; and these they reject and condemn, while they believe and accept what seems to

their judgment possible or true. But who shall limit
the condescension of a God who has died of love? Who
shall say He may condescend so far to His creatures, but
no further? Who shall say He may communicate Himself
in this fashion, but not in that? Who shall venture to lay
down rules for the Spirit, which "breatheth where He
will?"* "Who among men is he that can know the
counsel of God? or who can think what the will of God
is? For the thoughts of mortal men are fearful, and our
counsel uncertain. For the corruptible body is a load
upon the soul, and the earthly habitation presseth down
the mind that museth upon many things. And hardly do
we guess aright at things that are upon earth: and with
labour do we find the things that are before us. But the
things that are in heaven, who shall search out? And
who shall know Thy thought, except Thou give wisdom,
and send Thy Holy Spirit from above?"†

Nay, rather let us listen in reverent awe when God
permits us the favour of hearing these blessed communications which He has been pleased to make to those whom
He has admitted to this singular intimacy with Himself.
If we are privileged to have patrons who hold high places
at court, let us thankfully avail ourselves of their condescension in admitting us to the intimacy of the King, in
allowing us the privilege of being sharers in His most
hidden counsels, and of knowing, as only His beloved can,
the secrets of His love. It is remarkable that those only
whom God has favoured with a more than ordinary inti-

---

* St. John iii. 8.   † Wisdom ix. 13–17.

macy, have invariably been distinguished for simplicity.
Whether it is that the Almighty wills to confound the
wisdom of the wise, by admitting those whom they might
contemn to a share in His most signal favours, or whether
it is that such are more peculiarly fitted to be recipients
of His grace, we would not even conjecture; yet such
appears to be the ordinary rule of spiritual life.   Perhaps
few, if any, were so favoured with the intimacy of our
Lord as the Saint of whom we write.   His absence was
an exceptional case, His presence her ordinary enjoyment.
The whispers of His love were heard alike in the stillness
of the night, in the psalmody of the choir, in the ordinary
duties of religious life, and in the less acceptable and more
trying moments spent in converse with strangers.   The
Dove seemed ever whispering in her inmost soul ;   or
rather, might we not say that she lay ever in the Wounded
Heart of her Spouse—the true home of His beloved
ones ; and there what other speech could fall upon her
listening ear, save the accents of that voice, whose lowest
murmur ravishes the very Seraphim in trance of ecstatic
praise ?

And when Jesus vouchsafes to speak as a friend to
his friend—nay, rather, as a spouse to his bride—why
should we be amazed that His converse should be of that
familiar and tender nature which characterises the human
love which He has sanctioned, and which has become
pure and holy since He, through His Church, has elevated it to the dignity of a Sacrament ?   Nay, long before
this elevation and dignity was vouchsafed to human
love, such intercourse—even in an inspired volume—is

taken to typify that which exists between the soul and God.

The words, " My love, My dove, My beautiful one ! " were addressed to the bride long before the Bridegroom had appeared as the Incarnate God. And why, when He has vouchsafed to become man, when He has participated in human griefs, and hallowed human affections—oh ! why should His accents be less loving, or His voice sound less sweetly in the ear ? When the day breaks, and the shadows pass away, shall we not also hear those accents, and behold that Face, and obtain some share in these favours, which even here are vouchsafed to more pure and saintly souls ?

The Revelations of St. Gertrude indeed differ from, or rather are distinguished above, those of other saints, in the familiarity and frequency of these heavenly communications. We shall not read of marvellous miracles, of ecstatic flights, of long-continued raptures, of prophetic announcements, though such events are recorded occasionally ; the Saint—if we may be permitted the expression— lived at home with her Spouse ; and hence her life was one continued and almost uninterrupted succession of the highest states of spiritual life.

Were an apology needed for the familiar terms in which this intercourse is described by herself in the one precious book in which she records these favours, or by others, in the continuation of the subject by one of her Religious, we might easily quote many passages, even from Scripture, where such expressions are used and therefore sanctioned. If it be objected that the frequent embraces

of love which she received from her Spouse are too
familiar a token of tenderness from a God to His creature,
let us remember that He permitted Magdalen to kiss
His feet, and the beloved Apostle to lie upon His bosom.
Is He not still Man, and does not His Human Heart still
love us with a human love? Why, then, may not the
condescension which the Son of God practised when on
earth be continued by Him when in heaven? Why, if
He were pleased that His Feet should be kissed and
anointed by a repentant sinner, should He not still accept
the love of those who perform spiritually a devotion which
they cannot perform corporally? And wherefore should
we suppose that the Fountain of Love should be less
loving than the poor little channels through which He
permits the impetuous torrent of His charity to flow,—
channels which only serve to chill that spring which at its
source has never ceased to burn?

If our love were purified,—if we had no carnal taint
in our affections,—if the slimy trail of the serpent had not
stained and darkened within us God's most precious gift,
that which He declares Himself to be,—we should not so
easily doubt or mislike these marvellous manifestations of
His most marvellous charity. Why should not the virgin
Gertrude rest in mystic rapture upon the bosom of Jesus,
when Jesus Himself every day permits those who are
incomparably less worthy to receive Himself within
them?

But enough of this. Let us rather apologise for our
own coldness in believing, than for God's love in giving;
and let us thank Him that He has found souls even upon

earth who will permit Him to love as He desires to love ;
who will, as far as creatures may, love as He asks to be
loved.

"I wish men could be persuaded to study St. Gertrude
more than they do," was the exclamation of one whose
own soul burned with no ordinary love. And why does he
desire this ? Because of her bright, free, joyous spirit ;
because she loved God so purely and so entirely, that the
narrow mistrusts of those who love Him less never for an
instant found place in her blessed soul. A loving heart
will always be a thankful heart ; and so the continual
incense of thanksgiving which ascended from the heart of
Gertrude before the Eternal Throne, was but the fragrant
aroma of the love which burned daily deeper and brighter
within her.

THE LIFE OF ST. GERTRUDE.

CHAPTER I.

The Saint's birth and parentage—Her early dedication to God—Intellectual gifts—Divine communications concerning her sanctity —Our Lord declares that He finds rest and repose in her heart —Desires a holy person to seek Him there.

THE thirteenth century was an eventful one for the world and the Church. Its commencement found the great orders of St. Dominic and St. Francis established in almost every city of Europe, already winning martyrs' crowns, and counting their trophies won for the Lamb by hundreds and by thousands. St. Elizabeth of Hungary had sanctified a palace, and edified a nation by her heroic virtue and her meek resignation in adversity. St. Thomas of Aquin and the seraphic St. Bonaventura had bequeathed such treasures to the Church, as had never before been confided to her keeping. St. Louis had died a victim to his love of Jesus crucified, and his grief that the land where his Lord had died should be despoiled by the heathen and defiled by the infidel. It was, in truth, a century of Saints, and of Saints of more than ordinary note; at the close of this cen-

tury, as a crowning gift, came the great and beautiful Saint
Gertrude, whose history has been too little known amongst
us, while her very name receives a continual homage of
reverent love.

The illustrious Benedictine Abbess was born at Eisleben,
a small town in the county of Mansfield, on the 6th of
January 1263 ;* and thus, as it has been happily remarked,
a star of no ordinary brilliancy was given to the Church on
the day on which that Church was mystically led by a star
to her Incarnate God. It is said that the family of the
Counts of Lachenborn were nearly related to the imperial
family of Germany ; but whatever their rank or dignity
may have been, all distinct remembrance of it has long
since passed away, and they are only now remembered as
illustrious because of the surpassing sanctity of their illustrious child. Bucelinus, in his *Aquila Imperii Benedictini*,
gives a genealogical tree of the family of the Counts of
Hackeborn, commencing with the father of the Saint, and
concluding with " Fredericus, Dominus et Comes in Hackeborn, familiæ suæ ultimus ;" but there is no date by which

* There has been much dispute as to the precise year in which the
Saint was born, though a circumstance which will be related hereafter
fixes the period with tolerable certainty. In the date, as also in the
etymology of her family name, we have followed the opinion of the
learned Abbot of Solesmes. In Coxe's *House of Austria* he mentions
the marriage of Anne, sister of Count Hohenberg, to the famous
Rodolph of Hapsburg ; Beetham, in his valuable *Genealogies*, calls
her Anne of Hochberg. The similarity of the name to that of
Hackeborn suggests a possibility that the connection with the imperial family may have been through this channel. The town of
Eisleben still exists, and has, it will be remembered, the unenviable
notoriety of being the birthplace of Luther. It is the capital of the
county of Mansfield : the tombs of the ancient Counts of Mansfield
are still preserved in the churches of St. Andrew and St. Ann. It
has also a ruined castle, but, alas ! no tradition of its Saint, though it
may be this ruin was once possessed by her noble family.

to determine when this Count, the "last of his family," passed away from earth. When the Saint had attained her fifth year, she was placed in the famous Benedictine Abbey of Rodersdorf, in the diocese of Halberstadt, where she was soon joined by her younger sister, Mechtilde.*

Here, under the careful training of the Benedictine Dames,—who then, as now, devoted themselves with unwearied solicitude, and more than ordinary intellectual abilities, to the education of those confided to their charge, —the young Countess of Lachenborn advanced in wisdom and learning, both human and divine.

The high intellectual gifts with which St. Gertrude was endowed had the most ample advantages for their development. At an early age she was sufficiently conversant with the Latin tongue to read and converse in that language; her reading was extensive for an age in which literature was confined to parchment manuscripts and oral instructions. Indeed, her devotion to literary pursuits—though these were of the best and purest kind, since the Scriptures, the Fathers, and other theological works, were her chief study — seemed at first likely to prove a hindrance to her spiritual advancement. Yet all was overruled by infinite love and infinite wisdom. Her writings were to be the Church's treasure in all ages, though, like stars in a stormy sky, their

---

* A special provision is made in the Rule of St. Benedict, ch. lix., to regulate this matter. The practice of offering very young children who were dedicated by their parents to the service of God in holy religion, was generally observed in the Order, until the custom was abolished by the authority of Pope Clement III. It is also expressly forbidden by the Council of Trent. (See Helyot, *Hist. Reg. Orders.*) When St. Benedict wrote his Rule, the Church had not legislated for religious orders. Had those regulations been enacted during his lifetime, he would have been the first to acknowledge their authority, and to require his spiritual children to submit to them.

light may be for a time concealed from men, only perchance
to shine more gloriously when they shall have emerged from
this passing obscurity.

Secular learning might encase the jewel, but it could not
produce it; it might enhance the beauty of the pure and
sparkling stream, by diverting its course through a more
cultivated channel, but it could not produce the stream itself. And now the Spouse of virgins began to speak to the
heart of His chosen one, and to withdraw her from those
exterior occupations, no longer necessary for mental cultiva-
tion, that she might listen without distraction or hindrance
to those whispers of His love which we also, despite our
unworthiness, are permitted to hear and to enjoy.

The Saint has informed us herself when and how the
first of these heavenly communications was vouchsafed to
her. It was on Monday, the 25th of January, "at the close
of day, the Light of lights came to dissipate the obscurity
of her darkness, and to commence her conversion." And
Jesus came, as He mostly comes to His beloved ones, as she
performed an act of humility and obedience—declining to
an ancient religious, to fulfil a conventual observance, and
doubtless from no mere habitual custom, but with deep and
lowly reverence for a spouse of Christ, whom she considered
incomparably her superior in virtue and sanctity.

Her sisters were not slow to perceive that their companion was specially favoured by Heaven. One religious,
who had long suffered from most painful temptations, was
warned in a dream to apply to Gertrude for relief, and to
recommend herself to her prayers. The moment she
complied with this injunction, the temptation ceased.
Another, who feared to communicate under a similar and
even more urgent trial, obtained a morsel of cloth which
had been used by the Saint, and placing it near her heart,

implored our Lord to deliver her by the merits of Gertrude. The favour was granted, and from that moment she never suffered from the same temptation. It would appear, indeed, that Gertrude was specially designed by Providence to assist others, even during her lifetime, by her merits and intercession, as well as by the gift of counsel with which she was singularly favoured.

A person, whose sanctity had been long manifest, and who was specially favoured by Divine communications, came to the monastery from a distant country, to obtain an interview with the Saint. As she knew none of the religious personally, she prayed that whoever would benefit her soul most by their conversation might be sent to her. It was then made known to her, that whoever should come and take their place beside her would be indeed the one most beloved by God, and the most holy amongst the religious. On her arrival, St. Gertrude came to her; but so well did she conceal any appearance of sanctity, and hide the supernatural light with which she was favoured, that the stranger imagined she had been deceived, and again prayed as she had done before. The same reply was once more vouchsafed to her; and she was assured that this was indeed the religious who was so dear to God. Shortly after, the visitor had a long interview with St. Mechtilde, whose conversation she greatly preferred, and whose sanctity was more apparent. Again she "inquired of God," and asked why St. Gertrude was preferred to her sister. Our Lord replied that He had indeed operated great graces in Mechtilde, but in Gertrude He had operated, and He would yet operate, far greater.

Another person of great sanctity, who was praying for the Saint, felt a singular impulse of affection for her, which she believed to be supernatural. "O Divine Love!" she

exclaimed, "what is it You behold in this virgin which
obliges You to esteem her so highly and to love her so
much?" Our Lord replied : "It is My goodness alone
which obliges Me ; since she contains and perfects in her
soul those five virtues which please Me above all others,
and which I have placed therein by a singular liberality.
She possesses purity, by a continual influence of My grace ;
she possesses humility, amidst the great diversity of gifts
which I have bestowed on her—for the more I effect in her,
the more she abases herself ; she possesses a true benignity,
which makes her desire the salvation of the whole world
for My greater glory ; she possesses a true fidelity, spreading abroad, without reserve, all her treasures for the same
end.   Finally, she possesses a consummate charity ; for she
loves Me with her whole heart, with her whole soul, and
with her whole strength ; and for love of Me, she loves her
neighbour as herself."

   After our Lord had spoken thus to this soul, He showed
her a precious stone on His heart, in the form of a triangle,
made of trefoils, the beauty and brilliancy of which cannot
be described ; and He said to her : "I always wear this
jewel as a pledge of the affection which I have for My
spouse.   I have made it in this form, that all the celestial
court may know by the brightness of the first leaf that
there is no creature on earth so dear to Me as Gertrude,
because there is no one at this present time amongst mankind who is united to Me so closely as she is, either by
purity of intention or by uprightness of will.   They will
see by the second leaf, that there is no soul still bound by
the chains of flesh and blood whom I am so disposed to
enrich by My graces and favours.   And they will observe
in the splendour of the third leaf, that there is no one who
refers to My glory alone the gifts received from Me with

such sincerity and fidelity as Gertrude ; who, far from wishing to claim the least thing for herself, desires most ardently that nothing shall be ever attributed to her." Our Lord concluded this revelation by saying to the holy person to whom He had thus condescended to speak of the perfections of our Saint : " You cannot find Me in any place in which I delight more, or which is more suitable for Me, than in the Sacrament of the Altar, and after that, in the heart and soul of Gertrude, My beloved ; for towards her all My affections, and the complacences of My Divine love, turn in a singular manner." *

On another occasion, a devout person, who was praying for the Saint, heard these words : " She for whom thou prayest is My dove, who has no guile in her, for she rejects from her heart as gall all the guile and bitterness of sin. She is My chosen lily, which I love to bear in My hands; for it is My delight and My pleasure to repose in the purity and innocence of this chaste soul. She is My rose, whose odour is full of sweetness, because of her patience in every adversity, and the thanksgivings which she continually offers Me, which ascend before Me as the sweetest perfumes. She is that spring flower which never fades, and which I take pleasure in contemplating, because she keeps and maintains continually in her breast an ardent desire not only for all virtues, but for the utmost perfection of every virtue. She is as a sweet melody, which ravishes the ears of the blessed ; and this melody is composed of all the sufferings she endures with so much constancy."

A little before Lent, as Gertrude was reading a lecture

---

* It is generally supposed, but without sufficient authority, that these words were addressed to St. Mechtilde. She *may* have been the " holy person " to whom the revelation was made ; but this opinion is merely conjectural.

for the community, according to the custom of the Order, she repeated these words twice : " Thou shalt love the Lord thy God with thy whole heart, and with thy whole soul, and with thy whole strength " (Deut. vi.)   The Saint lived in a community of saints, where more than one favoured soul was vouchsafed intimate and frequent communion with her Spouse.   A sister, who was touched by the devotion with which these words were uttered, prayed that He who so loved Gertrude, and had taught her to love Him so much, would vouchsafe to impart to her the same blessed lesson. Our Lord replied : " I have borne her in My arms from her infancy, I have preserved her in her baptismal purity and innocence, until she, by her own free choice and will, has given herself to Me entirely and for ever ; and as a recom- pense for the perfection of her desires, I, in return, have given Myself entirely to her.   So pleasing is this soul to Me, that when I am offended by men, I often enter therein to repose, and I make her endure some pain of body or of mind, which I inflict on her for the sins of others ; and as she accepts this suffering with the same thanksgiving, humility, and patience as she receives all that comes from Me, and offers it to Me in union with My sufferings, she appeases My anger, and obliges My mercy to pardon, for her sake, an immense number of sinners."

On another occasion, Gertrude having humbly asked the prayers of a sister, the religious complied with her re- quest, and while praying for the Saint, heard these words : " The faults which appear in Gertrude may rather be called steps in perfection ; for it would be almost impossible that human weakness could be preserved from the blasts of vain- glory, amidst the abundance of graces which I continually operate in her, if her virtues were not hidden from her eyes under the veils and shadows of apparent defects.

Thus, even as the earth produces a richer and more abundant harvest in proportion as the labourer has been careful in manuring it, so the gratitude of Gertrude bears Me richer fruit, the more I make her see her own weakness. It is for this reason that I permit different imperfections in her, for which she is in a state of continual humiliation, sending her a particular grace for each, with which she blots them all out from My sight; and the time will come when I will change these defects into so many virtues, so that her soul will shine before Me as a most glorious sun."

What these defects were, we are not told. The Saint's patience in sickness and in trial was unalterable; her charity to her sisters abounded with each necessity for its exercise; and her sanctity was apparent in every action of her holy life. A special gift of prophecy or foreknowledge enabled her to give advice with promptness, and the greatest wisdom, on the most important occasions. When these gifts became known, the monastery was frequently visited by all classes of persons, who came to converse with her on spiritual subjects, or to obtain counsel in difficulties. Her deep study of Holy Scripture and of the Fathers now bore abundant fruit, and it was observed that she had a singular, and no doubt a heaven-sent, felicity in applying what she had read and treasured in her memory to the spiritual necessities of those with whom she conversed.

God and the salvation of souls—this was the one object of her life, the one end of every action. From her humility, she had fully persuaded herself that the marvellous graces bestowed on her were given her merely for others. This holy delusion served two important ends—it saved her from every temptation to spiritual complacence, and it induced her to impart freely to others a knowledge of the revelations and other favours bestowed on her. She was simply, according to her own idea, a channel of divine grace to others; and believing this to be her end, she neither spared time nor labour for its accomplishment. Often her rest was shortened and her food forgotten, when souls demanded time or anxious thought. " Not satisfied even with this, she often deprived herself of the sweetness of contemplation, when it was necessary to succour the tempted, to console the afflicted, or, what she desired above all else, to enkindle and increase the fire of divine love in any soul. For as iron, when placed in the fire, becomes itself like fire, thus this virgin, burning with love, seemed to be all love, such zeal had she for the salvation of all."

She believed that God would indeed be glorified there-by, and that His gifts would thus be multiplied a hundred-fold ; " she was absolutely persuaded that she received nothing. for herself, but that all was for the salvation of others. She never beheld any one whom she did not con-sider better than herself, and it was on this account that she was so convinced that God would receive more glory by the communication of His graces to them. She believed that they merited more by a single thought, by their mere innocence, even by their purity of heart, than she could do by all her mental powers or spiritual gifts." Can we won-der that a vessel so emptied of self should have been filled to overflowing with God ?—that the " perfume of the oint-ment " should have lingered for so many hundreds of years in the house of God, and that it still affords refreshment and consolation to His chosen spouses, and to the most saintly souls ? May this poor effort to extend the sweet-ness of that perfume be for His honour and glory, for the honour of this blessed Saint, and for the refreshment of the little ones of Jesus !

CHAPTER II.

St. Gertrude predicts the election of Adolphus of Nassau—Quiets the fears of the sisters, who expect to suffer a temporal loss —Her election as Abbess—Removal to Heldelfs—Revelations of her sanctity—Our Lord appears to her, bearing the house of religion—Her generosity of spirit.

IN the year 1273, Rodolph of Hapsburg ascended the imperial throne as Emperor of Germany, though, as he was not crowned by the Holy See, he only bore the humbler title of King of the Romans. It is said that his election was predicted by a priest to whom he showed singular marks of reverence and respect while bearing the Holy Viaticum to a dying man.* Coxe, in his *House of Austria*, highly extols the character of this prince, but observes that he was raised to the imperial throne chiefly through the influence of the Archbishop of Mentz. Albert, the emperor's sole surviving son, succeeded to the hereditary dominions of his father. The electors would probably have

---

* This circumstance is so interesting, and so well authenticated, as to merit a passing notice. It is mentioned by Feller, Moreri, in Heiss's *History of Austria*, lib ii. c. 22, and in the *Acta SS. Maii*, tom. viii., where a somewhat similar act of devotion, performed by Charles II. of Spain, is related at length. The account given by Heiss is as follows : On one occasion, when Rodolph was engaged in the chase, it began to rain with such violence as to render the road extremely dirty ; when, chancing to meet a poor curate on foot, carrying the Host to a sick person, he was so much affected by the sight of this good priest labouring through the mire, that he immediately alighted, saying, it ill became him to ride on horseback while the priest who carried his Lord was walking on foot. He then made the priest mount his horse, attended him bareheaded to the sick man's house, and afterwards conducted him to his church, where the priest, amazed at his zeal, gave him his benediction, and, being inspired by the Holy Ghost, prophesied that he and his descendants would sit upon the imperial throne.

accepted him as their chief, had not his stern and uncon-
ciliating manners offended his best friends, and, contrary
to all expectation, Adolphus, Count of Nassau, was raised
to the vacant throne.

The nomination of Adolphus took place on the 10th
May 1292. How little did he imagine that his new dignity
and tragic end were at that very moment revealed to a nun
in a distant and lonely cloister ! The sisters were earnest
in their prayers for a worthy successor to their most
Christian king, and interceded, as true religious ever will,
with fervent supplications for the welfare of their country.
On the very day, and almost at the same moment, when
the important affair was decided, Gertrude told the Abbess
of her monastery what had occurred, and predicted the
terrible fate of the new monarch.*

The troubles of the times were not without their effect
upon the monastery of Rodersdorf. Once, when it was
threatened with a terrible calamity, which was considered
inevitable because of the menaces of those who had both
power and force on their side, the Saint went to her Superior, and assured her there was no longer any cause for
fear. Almost at the same moment, the person whose anger

---

* Adolphus, soon after his election, offended the Archbishop of
Mentz, to whom he owed his elevation, and alienated the electors by
arbitrary efforts to aggrandise his family. Albert, meanwhile, still
hoped by some happy chance to obtain his father's crown. In 1298 a
Diet was assembled at Mentz ; a long list of grievances was drawn
up ; Adolphus was cited to appear, and, on his refusal, deposed.
Albert was then raised to the imperial dignity. A civil war ensued.
The two armies met at Gellheim, between Spires and Worms, on the
2d July, and, being led by the rival sovereigns, fought with unusual
intrepidity. Here, by a clever stratagem, the soldiers of Albert
pierced through the guards who surrounded Adolphus, and dis-
mounted him. After a long defence, he attacked his rival once
more, but was slain by him with a lance.

had been so much dreaded came to the convent, and the religious found, to their joy and amazement, that the local judges had appeased all differences, and established peace even as Gertrude had predicted to the Abbess.

St. Gertrude was chosen Abbess of her monastery in the year 1294. The year following, the religious removed to Heldelfs. The Saint was elected to this important charge at the early age of thirty—no slight testimony to her singular prudence and extraordinary virtue. For forty years she continued to edify and guide her spiritual children, many of whom had attained a high degree of sanctity. As Superior, she was distinguished for charity and zeal. While others suffered, whether in body or in mind, she could not rest ; and where there was need of amendment, her tears and prayers brought repentance and renewed fervour, rather than any severity of reproof, which her very office might have more than sanctioned. The importance of her work, and its immense value in the eyes of her Divine Spouse, was manifested to her by a remarkable vision, which must ever be a special subject of instruction and consolation for those similarly circumstanced, and, indeed, for all religious.

Our Lord appeared to her, bearing on His sacred shoulders a vast and magnificent building.* "Behold," He said, "with what labour, care, and vigilance I carry this beloved house, which is none other than that of Religion. It is everywhere threatened with ruin, because there are so few persons who are willing to do or to suffer any-

---

* In the French translation this is rendered *maison de plaisance;* the idea is very beautiful, certainly, but then it is not in the original, where the term is simply *domum.* There is a remarkable coincidence between this vision and the command given to St. Francis of Assisi to repair the house of God.

thing for its support and increase. You, therefore, should suffer with Me in bearing it ; for all those who endeavour, by their words or actions, to extend religion, and who try to re-establish it in its first fervour and purity, are so many strong pillars which sustain this holy house, and comfort Me by sharing with Me the weight of this burden."

From this moment the Saint devoted herself, with all the sanctified energy of a naturally ardent temperament, to the work so dear to her Spouse. Her monastery became indeed a " pleasure-house " of delight to the Spouse of virgins. Under her guidance, the fervent increased in fervour, and the saintly advanced rapidly in perfection. Many were favoured with intimate and most blessed communications from heaven ; one at least,* her sister in the flesh as well as in the spirit, obtained even on earth a recognition of her sanctity, and ranks amongst those who are invoked upon the Church's altars.

But the life of the young Abbess was not to be devoted exclusively to active service ; and our Lord began now to teach her that exterior zeal should have its limits, however holy the end for which it laboured ; that contemplation was not only necessary for the individual soul, but also to promote the glory of God in others ; since prayer alone may effect conversions and sanctifications, while active exertion, without its vivifying influence, is of little avail. A person to whom our Divine Lord had revealed His designs in regard to the Saint wrote thus to her :—

" O blessed spouse of Christ, enter into the joy of your Lord ! His Divine Heart opens for you its fount of ineffable sweetness, as a reward for the fidelity with which

---

* St Mechtilde.

you have laboured for His glory and for the defence of the truth.   He desires now that you should rest in the shadow of His most peaceful consolations : * for as a good tree, planted by the river-side, takes root deeply and produces abundant fruit, so will you produce for your Beloved the fruit of your thoughts, words, and actions, which are most pleasing to Him, by His grace operating within you.   Do not fear that the heat of persecution will wither up your soul, for it is continually bedewed by the sacred waters of grace.   As you seek in all your actions the glory of God, and not your own, the fervour of your zeal increases a hundred-fold the fruits which you offer to your dear Spouse ; not only by the pious works which you actually accomplish, but even by those which you desire to do yourself or to see done by others, although it is not in your power to perform them.   Jesus Christ Himself will supply before His Father your needs and your defects, and those of others for whom you are solicitous ; therefore, do not doubt that He will equally reward all you desire to do as if you had accomplished it ; and know that the whole court of heaven rejoices in your advancement, and returns thanks and praise to God for love of you."

The union of the Saint with her Lord became now so intimate that even the apprehension of sudden death appeared unable to disturb her peace for a moment.   On one occasion, as she journeyed from one convent to another, she was suddenly precipitated down a steep mountain-path. "My sweet Lord," she exclaimed, "how happy should I have been if this fall had brought me sooner to Thee ! " Her companions inquired if she would not fear to die without the Sacraments.   "I desire most ardently," she replied,

---

* "Sub umbra tranquillissimæ consolationis suæ."

"to receive the support of the Sacraments before I die; but I prefer the providence and the will of my Lord and my God even to all the Sacraments, for I believe this is the best preparation for death. It is indifferent to me whether it be slow or sudden, provided that it is pleasing in His sight to whom I hope it will bring me; for I trust, in whatever manner I die, that I shall not be deprived of the mercy of my God, without which my eternal ruin would be inevitable, whether I die an unprepared death, or whether I have long anticipated my end."

The Saint's confidence in God was indeed an eminent characteristic of her sanctity, and one which obtained for her immense favours. How could the Heart of Jesus refuse anything to one who trusted Him so entirely? How pleasing this virtue was to her Spouse was revealed to one of her religious, who had long prayed in vain for a particular favour which she ardently desired. At last our Divine Lord vouchsafed to inform her of the reason of this delay, at which she had felt and expressed her profound amazement. "I have delayed answering your prayers, because you have not yet sufficient confidence in the effects which My mercy produces in you. Why do you not act like Gertrude, My chosen virgin, who is so firmly established on My Providence, that there is nothing which she does not hope for from the plenitude of My grace; therefore I will never refuse her anything, whatever she may ask Me."

A holy man once earnestly prayed that he might know what virtue was most pleasing to our Lord in His spouse. He was answered, that it was "her generosity of heart." *

---

* "Respondit Dominus : Libertas cordis ;" but the word "freedom" or "generosity" seems to give the idea more correctly in English. In this passage also the French translation is vague and incorrect.

But as this surprised him not a little, he ventured to reply:
" As for me, O Lord, I had imagined that what pleased
You most in this soul was the perfect knowledge she had
of herself, and the high degree of love to which, by Your
grace, she has attained." Our Lord replied : " This generosity of heart is of such value and so great a good, that
the height of perfection may be obtained through it. By
means of it My elect is prepared at all times for receiving
gifts of great value, which prevents her from attaching her
heart to anything which could either impede Me or dis-
please Me."

One happy effect of this liberty of spirit was, that the
Saint could not bear either to possess or retain anything
that was not absolutely necessary for use ; and yet we are
told that she had a sweet and holy attachment to such
things as were used for holy purposes—to the tablets on
which she wrote—and well might she love them, since her
writings were the special work for which Providence had
given her to the Church, and were begun by the express
command of her Divine Spouse ; for such spiritual works
as promised the greatest edification and proved most profit-
able to herself and to her sisters—and this because she
believed these inanimate things were used by her Lord to
render Him a special service, and to procure His greater
honour and glory.

The happy manner in which she combined the duties
of the active life with that unceasing union with her Beloved which so specially characterised her spiritual life
was shown to St. Mechtilde in a vision. On one occasion,
as she chanted, she beheld our Divine Lord seated on a high
throne, around which St. Gertrude walked without turning
her eyes from her Master even for a moment. At the
same time, she appeared to fulfil her exterior duties with

the most perfect exactness. As her holy sister mused in amazement on the vision, she heard these words : " This is an image of the life which My beloved Gertrude lives ; thus does she ever walk in My presence, never relaxing in her ardent desire to know and to do what is most pleasing to My heart. As soon as she has ascertained it, she executes it with care and fidelity, and then promptly passes to some other duty, seeking in her zeal always to find some new virtue to practise. Thus her whole life is a continuous chain of praise, consecrated to My honour and glory."

" But, Lord," replied St. Mechtilde, " if the life of St. Gertrude is so perfect, how is it that she cannot support the imperfections of others, and that they appear so great to her ? "

Our Lord replied, with admirable sweetness : " It is because she cannot endure that her own heart should be sullied with the slightest stain, and therefore she cannot see without emotion the least defect in the heart of another."

It was the custom of the Saint, when she was offered any choice in articles of clothing or other necessaries, to close her eyes, and then to put out her hand and take whatever she touched. Then she received whatever fell to her lot with the most lively gratitude, as a present from our Lord Himself. Indeed, her devotion to Divine Providence was a special feature in her sanctity, and one which procured her many favours. What could be refused to one who trusted so utterly to Eternal Love !

The sanctity of St. Mechtilde was well known to the Saint, and she frequently asked her advice and prayers. Once, as Mechtilde prayed fervently for her, in compliance with her desire, she beheld our Divine Lord attired as a Bridegroom, and clothed in a robe of green lined with gold.

His beauty surpassed that of millions of angels, and He tenderly embraced with His right arm her for whom she prayed. It appeared to her that Gertrude also embraced her Lord, and that her heart was attached to the wound in the side of Jesus. As she sought in amazement to comprehend this extraordinary vision, she heard these words: "Know that the green and gold of My vestments represent the operation of My Divinity, always new, and always acting by the influence of My love. Yes," He added, after again repeating the same words, "My operation is always new, and always in action in the soul of Gertrude; and the union which you behold of her heart with My side shows that she is attached so inseparably to Me, that she is in a condition to receive every moment the infusions of My Divinity."

St. Mechtilde then asked if St. Gertrude, who was so dear to God, never committed any fault; and why she appeared so ready at any moment to change her occupation, and to do, as if by chance, whatever came into her mind, her conscience appearing to be equally at rest whether she prayed, wrote, read, instructed, reproved, or consoled.

Our Saviour replied: "I have united My Heart so closely to her soul by the ties of My mercy, that she has become one spirit with Me. It is on this account she obeys so promptly all the desires of My will; so that the harmony and understanding which exist between the different members of the body and the heart is not greater than that which exists between the soul of Gertrude and Mine; and as the moment a man has willed in his heart a movement of his hands, they accomplish his desire, because they are entirely subject to the will of the heart; and as one desires in his mind that his eyes should look on any object, and his eyes immediately open to obey him,—so Gertrude is ever with Me, and at every moment is ready to obey the movements which I suggest."

A similar revelation was made about the same time to another holy person, to whom it was said, that the union of the Saint with her Spouse would become even yet more perfect, that she would receive the gifts of God with yet greater abundance, and that she would obtain so perfect a union with Him, that with her eyes she would only see what God willed her to see, with her ears only hear what He willed her to hear, and with her lips only speak what He willed her to speak.

CHAPTER III.

The Saint obtains favourable weather—Miracles mentioned in her Office—Union of her will with God's—Counsels others—Desired to write her revelations—Her sanctity revealed to St. Mechtilde.

THAT one so united to God should have been specially favoured with the gift of miracles, is but what we might expect in the ordinary course of spiritual life. Those who give themselves up without reserve to God, receive His gifts also without reserve. They do His will, and He accomplishes theirs : for the will of the Bridegroom and the bride is one. The Saint once obtained the cessation of a frost, which was so severe, that had it continued longer the fruits of the earth would have been utterly destroyed. Her petition was offered at the Holy Sacrifice ; and as she was about to approach the adorable Sacrament of the Altar, our Lord assured her that He had granted her request. With holy boldness, however, she asked that the hail which was then falling might instantly cease. Her petition was granted; but as she was absorbed in the greatness of the action she was about to perform, she thought no more of her request. It was only remembered as she left the church, and saw the thaw which had already commenced. Those who knew not of the prayer of the Saint were greatly amazed at the sudden change of weather, and feared it was but a passing cessation of the dreaded severity; but it was not so : the country was spared desolation and famine, though few knew to whom they were indebted for this favour.

Once also, when long and heavy rain threatened to destroy the harvest, all the sisters were constantly offering prayers and penances to avert the calamity. Gertrude at last, with the holy confidence of extraordinary sanctity, declared that she would not cease praying until she obtained fine weather. Immediately the sky became serene and fair, though a few moments before dark and heavy clouds had threatened a long continuance of rain.*

"One evening, after supper," says her biographer, "when the community went into the court to finish some work,

---

* This miracle is mentioned also in the Office for her Feast. The response after the vi. Lesson, ii. Nocturn, commences thus : "*Cum asperrimo gelu terra diu concreta,*" &c. "When the earth, hardened by severe frost, gave not its fruit, blessed Gertrude, touched with grief, prayed to her Spouse, when suddenly the ice thawed, and a joyful spring succeeded." The response after the vii. Lesson continues : "*Messis tempore,*" &c. "At harvest-time, when the fruits of the earth suffered from continued rain, Gertrude poured forth her heart as water in the sight of the Lord, and immediately there was a great calm."

As the Benedictine Breviary differs in many details from the Roman, a brief explanation of its arrangement may be necessary, as it will be so frequently referred to in this work. Matins commence, as usual, with the *Pater noster, Deus in adjutorium,* &c. ; then the *Domine labia* is repeated three times. The Psalm *Domine quid multiplicati sunt* (Ps. iii.) is recited before the *Venite.* There are usually twelve Lessons. These arrangements are expressly provided for in the Rule of St. Benedict, ch. viii. to xviii.

the sun, which was still above the horizon, was suddenly
covered with clouds, which threatened to fall in heavy rain.
Gertrude sighed deeply,—and I myself heard her,—speaking thus to God : ' O Lord my God, Creator of the universe, I do not pretend to constrain You to obey my sinful
will; on the contrary, if Your infinite mercy wills not to
oppose the degrees of Your justice, and prevent this rain,
except for my sake, I would rather that Your will, which
I adore, should be accomplished, and that it should rain,
if You have willed it thus.'   She said these things with a
perfect resignation to the will of God, having her mind
occupied solely with the consideration of Divine Providence, whose orders she desired to see executed.   But,
behold a marvel ! she had scarcely finished these words,
when a clap of thunder was heard, and large drops of
rain began to fall rapidly.   She, quite overcome, and
touched with compassion for the sisters, exclaimed again,
' Have pity on us, O God of clemency, at least for a
brief space, until we have finished the work which we
have been commanded to do.'   God, to show that He
refused nothing to her prayers, caused the rain to cease
until all was finished."   The community then returned
to their enclosure ; but they had scarcely reached the
door, when there came on so violent a storm of thunder,
lightning, and rain, that those who remained in the court
were perfectly deluged with it.   " It is thus," continues
the chronicler, " that God obeys the prayers of His elect,
who have entirely renounced their own desires for love of
Him."

It was the Saint's ordinary custom to have recourse to
her heavenly Spouse in every trial, whether of less or
greater import ; and her prayers were equally accepted
on all such occasions.   What, indeed, is little in His sight,

who so cares for His elect, that the very hairs of their head are numbered, and not one can fall without His knowledge ? Thus it is related of Gertrude, that even when she had lost a needle with which she had been working, and had sought it for some time in the straw where it had fallen, she turned to her Lord, for whose glory it had been used, and asked Him to help her in her search; even as she spoke, she put her hand once more into the straw, and found instantly what she had so long looked for in vain.   Indeed, so great was the power of the Saint over the Heart of her Spouse, that it appeared as if our Divine Lord Himself was pained to refuse her any request.   It happened on one occasion, that a long continuance of drought, combined with tempestuous weather, caused serious fears for the fruits of the earth.   St. Gertrude, as usual, had recourse to prayer.   It was not the will of God to grant her petition ; but with amazing condescension, He vouchsafed not only to inform her of His designs, but even, as it would appear, to excuse Himself to her for not complying with her request.

"The reason which obliges Me sometimes to grant the prayers of My elect does not exist between you and Me ; since our wills are so closely united by the sacred tie of grace, that you desire nothing but what I Myself desire. But because I design by the terrors of this tempest to conquer some who rebel against My will, and at least to oblige them to seek Me by prayer, since they only come to Me when they have no other resource, it is necessary that I should refuse you what you desire.   Nevertheless, that you may know that your prayers have not failed in their effect, I will grant you in return some other spiritual favour." What a revelation of the tenderness of the Father and the sanctity of the child !   Alas ! then, are there those to whom our dear Lord is obliged to grant the favours they ask because they cannot bear to be refused,—because, to prevent their murmurs, He gives that which, had they more faith, would be refused ! and, alas ! is it not too true that thousands seek Him only when all else has failed, and must be driven into the Arms which all day long are opened to welcome them with such ineffable tenderness !

As Gertrude was frequently consulted on all subjects, not only by those who had the happiness of living under her immediate guidance, but also by hundreds who came from afar, attracted by the fame of her sanctity, it happened more than once that she was seized with holy fear lest her words and her counsel should rather hinder than advance those who had recourse to her. As she prayed for light on this important subject, our Lord replied : " Fear nothing from henceforward ; be consoled, take courage, and be at rest. I am the Lord thy God ; I am thy Beloved, who has created thee by a pure effect of My love ; I have chosen thee to make thee My abode by My grace, and to take My delight in thee ; therefore, I will reply truly by thee to those who seek Me through thee with fervour and humility. I promise you also, that I will never permit any one whom I consider unworthy of receiving My Body and Blood to ask your advice on that matter. Therefore, send forward the scrupulous and timorous in the greatest security, because, for your sake, I will exclude none of them from My paternal affection ; but I will rather embrace them in the tenderest charity, and refuse them not My sweetest kiss of peace."

Once, as she prayed for a certain person, and felt ashamed that this person had not greater faith in obtaining even more than she had asked, our Lord said to her, with great kindness : " Whatever any person hopes to obtain through your intercession, they shall certainly receive from Me ;

and further, whatever you shall promise to any one in My name shall certainly be done for them; for though the suppliant, through human infirmity, may not perceive what I have done, I will nevertheless fulfil My promise, and produce the desired effect in his soul."

After some days, as the Saint reflected in amazement how such great promises could be made to one so unworthy, and inquired of her Spouse how He could bestow His graces on so vile a creature, He replied to her: "Does not the Universal Church allow that I formerly said to Peter alone, 'Whatever you shall loose on earth shall be loosed in heaven' (Matt. xvi.); and at the same time believe that the ministers of the Church exercise the same power now? Why, then, do you not believe that I can and will carry out whatever Divine love prompts Me to promise you?" He then touched her tongue, and said: "Behold, I have given My words in your mouth" (Jer. i. 9); "and I truly confirm whatever you may say to others at My suggestion and in My name: to whomsoever you shall promise any- thing through My goodness upon earth, I will make it sure, and ratify it in heaven." To these marvellous promises the Saint replied: "Lord, I would grieve were any one thus to incur eternal loss, as they would were I to say no crime would escape unpunished, or anything of that kind." He replied: "Whenever the love of justice or of souls shall prompt you so to speak, My clemency will previously admonish the sinner you thus address to repent of his sins, so that he may not deserve vengeance or punishment by making light of your instructions."* The Saint answered: "If it be really true, my God, that Thou, in Thy goodness, dost thus speak through me, how is it that my words have

---

* This passage is entirely omitted in the French translation.

so little effect on some persons, notwithstanding the ardent desire I have to lead them to glorify Thee and to save themselves ? "   Our Lord replied :   " Marvel not if your words are sometimes fruitless, and produce no effect, since, when I dwelt among men, My own words, though uttered with the fervour and power of the Godhead, produced not the fruit of salvation in the hearts of all.   It is through My Divine Providence that all things are arranged and perfected in the fitting time, as appointed by Me."

Soon after, having occasion to reprove a person for a fault, she feared she had acted indiscreetly, and with too much severity.   She turned immediately to her Spouse, and implored Him that she might never say anything to any one that would not be according to His heart.   " Fear nothing, My daughter," replied our Saviour, " but rather be filled with a holy confidence ; for I will give you this special grace, that when any one shall have recourse to you with faith and humility, in order to consult you on any subject whatsoever, the light of My truth shall discover to you the most hidden obscurities in the matter, and you will judge of them as truly as I Myself, according to the matter in hand, and the circumstances of the persons.   You will reprehend severely, from Me, those whose conduct I make known to you to have been guilty ; and, on the contrary, you will be sweet and affable to those whose faults have been less serious."   " King of heaven and earth," she exclaimed, " withhold the torrent of Thy mercies, for a fragment of dust and ashes such as I am is unworthy to receive such great favours."   " Why be so amazed, My daughter," replied our Lord, sweetly soothing her, " if I make you a judge of the causes of My enmities, when I have so often communicated to you the secrets of My friendship ? "   Then He added these words :   " All those who, when overcome with sadness, and having their hearts oppressed with any affliction, go with deep humility and true sincerity to obtain counsel and consolation from you, shall never be disappointed; for I the Lord, dwelling in thee, on the impulse of the exuberance of My love, desire to make you the medium of saving many; and it is certain that all the joy which your heart will experience in this is drawn from the fruitful source of My heart."

St. Mechtilde once beheld the heart of this Saint forming, as it were, a firm and stable bridge, the sides of which appeared to her to be bordered, the one with the Divinity of Jesus Christ, and the other with His holy Humanity, as with two walls.   After beholding this, she heard these words: "Those who come to Me by this bridge need have no apprehension of wandering or of falling; that is to say, all those who receive her counsels, and execute them faithfully, shall never wander from the right path, which leads to the life of a blessed eternity."

When our Divine Lord revealed to the Saint that it was His will she should commit her revelations to writing, her humility was exceedingly amazed.   But her heavenly Spouse thus instructed and consoled her: "For what purpose has it been committed to writing that I visited St. Catherine in her prison, and encouraged her by these words : 'Be firm and immovable, My daughter, for I am with you'?   What purpose does it serve that it should be known how I visited John, My favourite, and said to him, 'Come to Me, my beloved'?   What purpose does it serve that these and many other things concerning them and others of My Saints are known, unless it be to enkindle the zeal of those who read and hear them, and to manifest to all men the greatness of My love?   In this manner," added the Saviour, "the desire of obtaining the same favours as those which they shall see you have obtained from Me will produce devotion in the hearts of those who, considering the effusion of My grace and the excess of My mercy, shall endeavour to change their present life for one more perfect."

On another occasion, as the Saint marvelled why God urged her so strongly to make known her revelations, since He knew that the majority of mankind are so weak and unspiritual, that, far from finding in them any example for their edification, they would more probably find a subject of contempt and raillery, she heard the Lord saying to her: "I have so planted My grace in you, that I expect it will bear Me immense fruit; therefore it is My desire that all those who receive similar favours, and who despise them by their negligence, shall learn from you on what conditions I have given them these gifts, in order that My grace may be increased in them in proportion as their gratitude increases. But should there be any sufficiently malicious to defame the sanctity of these works, the penalty of their sin shall fall on themselves, and you will not be accountable for it. For the Prophet Ezechiel has said from Me: 'I will lay a stumbling-block before him' (Ez. iii.); that is to say, I dispose, permit, and even command many things for the salvation of My elect, although they are a subject of scandal to the reprobate."

From these words St. Gertrude understood that God often inspired His elect to do what was occasion of scandal to others, though not with the design of giving them scandal; and that we should never abstain from performing any good work in order to maintain a false peace with such persons: a lesson, indeed, worth treasuring and observing at every period of the Church's history; for what has the Church or the world ever gained by unholy compliances, by timid concealment of miraculous favours, or by the false shame of those who, through human respect, fear openly to confess their belief in supernatural occurrences, the truth of which they dare not altogether deny? If the world is scandalised, let it be scandalised, since even the Eternal Truth Himself was not spared its censures.

CHAPTER IV.

She asks St. Mechtilde to pray for her—Our Lord is pleased with her patience and mildness—He declares that He dwells in her; and hides her imperfections.

ON one occasion St. Gertrude implored St. Mechtilde to obtain by her prayers two graces, of which she believed herself to stand greatly in need. These graces were, patience and mildness. As St. Mechtilde prayed, our Lord spoke thus to her : " The sweetness which fills Gertrude with a perfect tranquillity, and which pleases Me infinitely, results from My making My abode in the peace of her heart ; * and because I dwell constantly in her, she of necessity must dwell in Me ; or if she is obliged sometimes to go out, let her do what the loving bride does when in the company of her spouse—if she is called away from him, she takes him by the hand and brings him with her : thus, if she judges it necessary to leave the sweet repose of contemplation, in order to labour for the salvation of her neighbour, let her make the saving sign of the Cross upon her heart ; let her utter My name once before she speaks ; and after that, let her say all that My grace inspires her with. In like manner, the patience of this Saint,

---

* " Mansuetudo quæ mihi in eâ placet nomen accipit a manendo."

to be agreeable to Me, must proceed from the peace and science* of her heart ; that is to say, she must be equally tranquil and enlightened ; and must have, on the one hand, such a care of possessing her peace, that no adversity may be able to deprive her of it ; and, on the other hand, let the motive for which she suffers be always present to her mind, and let her have no other motive in suffering but love alone, that she may give Me a proof of her perfect fidelity."

A person to whom the Saint was entirely unknown, but who had been asked to pray for her, received the following communication from our Lord : " I delight so much in her that I have chosen her as My abode. All that others see and love in her is My work ; and whoever loves My work in her, loves Me ; it is for this reason that those who are not capable of perceiving the interior gifts of her mind, admire her address, her eloquence, and all the other exterior qualities with which I have endowed her. And I desire that they should know that I have withdrawn her from her parents and all her friends, that none may love her from ties of consanguinity, but that I Myself may be the only cause of the love and esteem which they have for her."

When St. Gertrude was informed of these and other revelations which had been made concerning her, she exclaimed : " O my Beloved ! how is it that Thy mercy bears with my iniquity, for the sole reason that Thy providences and infinitely perfect and adorable works are always agreeable to me ?—since this does not result from my virtue, but from the attractions of Thy perfections and Thy adorable goodness, which does nothing unjust, nothing

---

* " Patientia nomen accepit a pace et scientiâ."

which is not perfectly good and perfectly adorable." The Lord made use of this simile in reply : " When a person cannot read some small writing, she uses glasses, in order to make the characters appear larger ; this is accomplished, not by any alteration in the writing, but by the quality of the glasses.* In like manner, My daughter, if I find any imperfections or defects in you, I efface them and repair them by the abundant liberality of My mercy."

As the Saint was deprived for some time of the accustomed visits of her Spouse, she ventured to inquire why the favour was withheld, though she neither fell into discouragement nor depression in consequence. " When a person looks at any one who is close to them," replied our Lord, " the too great proximity often prevents them from seeing distinctly ; as, for example, when a friend meets his friend and embraces him, this close union deprives him of the pleasure of looking at him. " St. Gertrude understood by these words, that we often merit more when deprived of sensible grace, provided that we do not become less fervent in the practice of good works.

In the early years of the Saint's spiritual life, our Lord often spoke to her in an audible voice ; but later these communications assumed a different character. The Saint inquired the reason, and received this reply : " In former years I oftener instructed you by giving you various answers that you might know, and that you might make known, the designs of My will to others ; but now I only make Myself known to you in spirit, and I give you inspirations by lights which would be difficult to express in words. For

---

* Reading-glasses had just then come into use. They are supposed to have been invented by Alexander de Spina, a monk of Florence, about 1285. The merit of the discovery is also claimed for our own Roger Bacon.

I have chosen you for this purpose that I may use you as
the repository of My treasures, wherein I may repose the
riches of My grace, providing that every one should find
whatever he needs in you, as in the spouse who knows all
the secrets of her Bridegroom, and, on account of her
Divine union with Him, acknowledges His wishes and His
will in all things." And it was even so. For when the Saint
prayed for anything, even if she received no reply from our
Lord, as she had done formerly, she nevertheless felt equal
consolation, and a certain assurance that her prayer was
heard. Also, when any one came to ask counsel or consolation of her, she at once felt her heart filled with the
necessary light, and inspired what to say, without a moment's reflection ; and this with so much assurance and
certainty, that she would have given her life for the truth
of the inspiration.

CHAPTER V.

The Saint as Abbess—Tenderness towards others—Care of the sick—
   Her last illness—Value of suffering—She is forbidden to resign
   her office – Our Lord accepts as done to Himself what is done for
   her—St. Lebuin.

ACCORDING to the calculations of Campacci, the Saint was
elected Abbess on the 3d of May 1294, and governed her
monastery for forty years, six months, and fourteen days.*
In the exercise of her charge she conducted herself with
great wisdom, sweetness, and prudence, coupled with a

---

* *Ins.* lib. v. : " Tandem exacto anno xl. et die xi. Heu ! heu!
infirmitatem incurrit, quæ dicitur apoplexia minor." The learned
Benedictine Fathers of Solesmes seem to prefer the reasoning of
Campacci ; but probably there is no discrepancy in the statement, as
he includes the time of her illness in the time of her continuance in
office.

marvellous discretion, and for the glory of God and the benefit of mankind; in charity and love towards God, in piety and vigilance towards her neighbour; in profound humility and mortification towards herself. The sick had special occasion to extol her charity and her care, for she visited them assiduously, supplied them with every necessary, and, far from contenting herself with consoling them merely by words, she served them with her own hands, comforting them in their necessities,* and providing even for their repose and recreation. Her religious, indeed, were often obliged to interfere in these exercises of devotion, lest their beloved Superior should exceed her strength, and exhaust an already enfeebled frame in these ministries of love. Even in her dying moments, her thoughts, as we shall see later, were constantly occupied with a sick sister; nor could she be satisfied until she was carried to her to console her. So true a mother was this blessed Saint to the children whom God had given her!

"While, then, she thus flourished in all kinds of virtue, and, like a mystic rose, emitted a sweet odour of sanctity, agreeable alike to God and man, when she had concluded the fortieth year and eleventh day of her administration of the charge of Abbess, she was attacked with an illness, usually called the little apoplexy. This illness was for her

---

* The 26th chapter of the Rule of St. Benedict provides especially for this important duty; and the Abbot is not only required "to take all possible care that nothing be neglected in the service of the sick," but is made responsible for the deficiencies of others in this matter: "Let the Abbot, therefore, be vigilant that the sick may suffer nothing by the negligence of procurators and servants, and remember that he shall be responsible for all the faults of his brethren." We see in the life of St. Gertrude, that even her own dangerous illness would not allow her to forget the sufferings of others. How, indeed, could a true spiritual mother allow any child to die alone and neglected?

a favourable touch of the Almighty Hand, who willed to free her from the ties of the flesh and the miseries of earth, and to draw to Himself this noble and generous soul, who, having nourished herself so long only with the fruit of the most excellent virtues, had acquired an extraordinary vigour and strength ; but for her religious, it was a dart which pierced their hearts, and filled them with exceeding sadness. They could not but be deeply moved and feel most acutely at beholding themselves on the point of losing so gifted a Superior, who, in their opinion at least, had no equal in the world ; such benedictions and favours had God poured forth on her, both in the order of nature and grace. She had brought up in the monastery, and received to profession, more than a hundred religious ; but of this great number we never knew one who had the same esteem and veneration for any person as for their incomparable Abbess. Her power of winning others was so great and so engaging, that even the young children who were placed in the convent conceived so tender and strong an affection for her, that as soon as they were instructed in the things of God, and learned that she was their spiritual mother, they would have considered it a fault and a disrespect to say that they loved either father or mother or any other relative more than the Saint.

"So dangerous an attack of illness made the religious fear that this star, which shone so brightly by the light of the Sun of Justice, was about to set ; and, as they apprehended, when they were no longer guided by the wisdom of so amiable and holy a mother, nor animated by the brilliancy and force of her example, that they might stray from the strictness of the narrow path of holy religion, they had recourse to the Father of Mercies, and addressed to Him their earnest prayers for her recovery. And He who is

sovereignly good despised not the sighs and tears of these
poor children, but, because it was not convenient that He
should grant them what was contrary to the immutable
decrees of His Providence, He heard them in another
manner, and in the way which was most useful and advantageous for their salvation ; since, by making them consider
the approaching decease of their mother as the commencement of her happiness, He filled them with consolation,
and enabled them to rejoice in her joy."

The religious of whom mention has already been made,
as one singularly favoured by Divine communications, now
prayed with great fervour for her dying Superior.   Our
Lord replied to her : " I have waited with inexpressible joy
for this moment, that I might lead My elect into solitude,
and there speak to her heart.   I have not been disappointed
in My expectation, for she conforms herself in all things
to My will, and obeys Me in the manner which is most
agreeable to Me."   The holy Benedictine understood that
by solitude our Lord meant the illness of the Saint, in
which He spoke to the heart of His beloved, and not to
her ear ; for His language is such as cannot be understood
in an ordinary manner, just as those things which are
spoken to the heart are rather felt than heard.   Tribulations
and afflictions of heart are the Lord's language to His elect ;
when one who suffers thus reflects that they are useless,
that they are spending their time uselessly,—that others are
labouring for them, and labouring in vain, inasmuch as
they are never to recover their health through this labour,
—the soul answers to such thoughts, that that which is
most pleasing to God is to maintain interior patience, and
to desire that the entire will of God may be accomplished
in them.   Such an answer does not reach heaven in the
usual manner of human communications, but resounds, as

it were, through that sweetest Divine organ, the Heart of Jesus, which is the ecstatic joy of the entire Trinity and the heavenly host. He continued thus: "My beloved affords Me the most intense and agreeable delight, because she despises not the afflictions of infirmity, as Queen Vasthi despised the orders of King Assuerus, when he commanded her to appear with a diadem on her head, that she might exhibit her beauty to his nobles. So, when I take pleasure in displaying the beauty of My chosen one in the presence of the ever-adorable Trinity and the heavenly host, I oppress her with sickness and infirmity; and she carries out My intentions to My perfect satisfaction, when, with all patience, she the more willingly and discreetly receives the relief and comfort I choose to give her body; and it adds to her glory that she sometimes does this with inconvenience to herself: but it should be her consolation to recollect that all things work together unto good to those that love God" (Rom. viii.)

On another occasion, while the same religious was praying for her, the Lord said to her: "It is a pleasure to Me to have My chosen one prepare a lodging for Me, and then to bestow on her pearls and flowers of gold. By pearls I mean her senses, by flowers of gold her leisure, with which, when she has time, and her strength is somewhat restored, she discharges her duty as well as she can, in preparing most becoming and acceptable ornaments for Me; being solicitous how she may so arrange everything that can tend to increase and preserve religion, so that after her death her rules and example may be as a firm pillar to support religion in eternal praise. But, in the height of her labours, if she feels that she is injuring her health, she immediately desists, and leaves Me to finish the work; for the real fidelity that moves My Heart consists in persons discharging their duty when they find themselves in good health, and immediately desisting and intrusting all to Me when they find themselves indisposed."

As the illness of the Saint increased, she became incapable of the least manual labour, and her tender conscience was filled with fear lest there should be any imperfection even in this compulsory inactivity ; she therefore requested the religious who had received so many revelations for her consolation to pray for her. Our Lord replied :

" A good king never takes it ill of his queen if she neglect bringing forward at a given hour the ornaments that he is most gratified at receiving ; but he is much more pleased at finding her always ready to comply with his wishes ; and the sweetness of My most benign Heart delights more in the patient endurance with which My chosen one bears her infirmity, on the relief of which she resumes her labours for the extension of religion, so far as she can do so without injuring her health."

As the Saint found herself daily more and more unequal to the important duties of her office, she became anxious to resign her charge ; but even this desire she was unwilling to put into effect, until assured that it was the will of God. Fearful lest her own inclination might deceive her, even in the interpretation of heavenly communications, she requested her favoured daughter to ask the counsel she needed from the Source of all wisdom. Our Lord condescended to reply,—may we not hope for the consolation and help of many of His chosen ones, as well as of the soul so singularly favoured thus specially to know His will ?—" By this illness I sanctify My chosen one, to make her a fit habitation for Myself—as a church is sanctified by the blessing of a bishop. In like manner as a church is secured with locks, to prevent the entrance of the unworthy, so I, by

that infirmity, seal her up so that her mind cannot be
occupied by externals, which tend to disturb the heart and
distract it from Me, and in which there is sometimes no
great utility.   Thus, as ' My delight is to be with the
children of men ' (Prov. viii.), as I have said in the Book of
Wisdom, I exercise and purify Gertrude by sickness, that
she may merit to become My dwelling and My temple;
according to the word of My Prophet : ' The Lord is nigh
unto those who are of a contrite heart ' (Ps. xxxiii.)   I
continue also to embellish and adorn her with the rich and
precious gifts of a good will and a right intention, which
produce and animate all her actions, that I may erect My
throne and repose in her, as a king who is seated on his
couch of justice, and that I may therein take My delight
as long as she is on earth, until I call her to abide with
Me in heaven, where I will share My eternal delights with
her; but in the meanwhile I have not entirely deprived
her of health, and I have left her the use of her exterior
senses, desiring still to employ her to make known My will
and My answers to the community which she governs, as
formerly I gave the people of Israel the Ark of the Covenant, where I delivered My oracles and received their
respect and adoration.   Therefore, as Gertrude is a spiritual ark, I desire that she should contain manna,—that is
to say, the sweetness and tenderness of charity to console
the souls under her guidance, and to solace their griefs as
far as she can.   I desire also that she should possess the
Tables of the Law,—that is to say, that she should declare
or forbid what should be done or not done, in order to
please Me, and that in so doing she should be guided by
the lights and discernment with which I have enlightened
her.   But I desire also that she should be the rod of Aaron,
—that is to say, the authority and zeal of justice, to correct

those persons who stray from their duty, to prescribe and impose salutary penances, and to decide and regulate everything with a fervent and even mind. She should consider that I could easily reform what needs reform, or what is ill-regulated, by simple inspirations, or by trials and disgraces; but I effect these things through her to increase her merit. And if any one fails to profit by her warnings and corrections, it shall be no prejudice to Gertrude, since she has done her duty and has employed all the care and vigilance possible to convert the sinner: Man may plant and water, but I only can give the increase (1 Cor. iii.)"

As the Saint now became troubled because she could not approach the Holy Communion as frequently as she had been accustomed to do, and also because she feared to approach it without her usual preparation, which her sickness rendered impossible, she made known her trial to the beloved companion who had so often obtained counsel for her. She was also grieved because the religious took so much trouble to serve her, and devoted so much time to her, since every effort to procure her recovery seemed of no avail. To the first difficulty the Lord replied : " When it is purely for Me that Gertrude abstains from communion, or from any other good work which she would willingly practise, if it could be accomplished without increasing her illness or injuring her health, then the liberality of My goodness will impart to her a share in all the good works which are done by the faithful ; for all the good which is done in the Church belongs to Me, and I dispose of it as I will ; and this because it is from a pure intention, and for Me only, that she has not participated in the graces of those holy exercises which she has omitted."

To the other inquiry our Lord answered : " You must serve her with respectful charity, cheerful and promptly, to love and honour Me, because I dwell in her, and I have made her the head of this community ; therefore let each assist her, as the members assist the head. Let her refer to My honour and glory the service which is rendered to her ; and rejoice that I employ her, as one who is united to Me by a constant and faithful friendship, to increase the merit of My elect ; for I will reward all the good that is done for her, not only in act, but by words of affection, as if it had been done to Myself."

On the feast of St. Lebuin,* as the sisters prayed in common, with special fervour, for the recovery of their beloved mother, the religious invoked the Saint with great earnestness ; and he replied : " When a king is engaged with his queen, do you not think that it would be most unbecoming in a private soldier to interrupt him, by asking him to give his family the pleasure and consolation of seeing her ?—thus, it is most unbecoming that any one should pray for the recovery of others, for their own views, when they are united by patience and good-will to the very King of heaven Himself." Whence we are to learn that when those who glorify God by sickness ask the prayers of the Saints, they merit thereby to become more patient and obtain more abundant and valuable fruit from their infirmity.

---

* St. Lebuin, Lebwin, or Liafwin, patron of Daventer. This Saint was English by birth ; after his ordination, he went to Germany, and there, under the direction of St. Gregory, built a church and founded a mission, near Daventer, in 772. He was not a martyr, though the term is used in the *Insinuations.* Butler says : " Being denied the more compendious sacrifice of himself, he finished his martyrdom, by labours and austerities, before the close of the eighth century." His feast is kept on the 12th of November—the date helps to fix that of St. Gertrude's death.

CHAPTER VI.

Her dying words—Devotion to the Divine Office—Tenderness to her spiritual children—Our Lord appears to her in her agony—Promises to receive her as He received His blessed Mother—Angels call her to paradise.

For several months before her death, St. Gertrude entirely lost the use of speech, and was only able to articulate the words " My spirit." * Those who attended her in vain endeavoured to ascertain what she meant ; indeed, it appeared almost miraculous that she was able to pronounce them, while otherwise totally deprived of utterance. As she repeated them constantly, the religious before mentioned inquired of her heavenly Spouse if they contained any spiritual signification. Our Lord replied : " Because I the Lord God, dwelling in her, have so drawn and united her spirit to Mine, that she sees Me alone in every creature, therefore, in her words, in her answers, and in her prayers, she makes mention of Me as the Person in whom her spirit lives. And whenever she acts thus, I intimate to the whole heavenly host that it is to Me alone she looks, and for this she will have everlasting glory in heaven."

The Saint still listened with the utmost attention when any one spoke to her of God ; and so great was her fervour, that she insisted on being brought daily to assist at the Adorable Sacrifice, although one of her limbs was perfectly useless, and the other in such a state that she could not bear it to be touched, even in the gentlest manner, without suffering most acute pain. Still she took the greatest care to conceal her real state, and avoided the least gesture of pain, lest she should be deprived of her highest consolation. Her

---

* " Spiritus meus,"

life-long devotion to the Office now manifested itself to all.
At the times at which she had been so long accustomed to
watch and pray, she remained wakeful and alert, although
even when taking necessary food she was constantly overcome by sleep, consequent on the languor of her disease.
It was remarked also that the last time she uttered the
words " My spirit," it appeared as if she intended it as an
offering of the Office of Compline, after which she fell into
her agony.

Her singular charity and tender affection were manifested
with peculiar sweetness during this long last illness. As she
could not speak to the sisters who visited her, she exerted
her failing strength to testify the pleasure she found in their
presence, and the depth of her maternal love, which could
not bear to leave one unconsoled. To each she would sweetly
use the one expression, " My spirit," and to each extend her
hand caressingly, though she could not move it without
severe pain : so like was she to her beloved Spouse, so
utterly regardless of her own suffering, when even a passing
consolation could be bestowed upon another. And each
time the religious left her, she again raised the suffering
hand in benediction, well knowing with what devotion that
favour had often been sought by her faithful children.

One sister, however, was unable to visit her dying Superior : she was herself confined to a bed of suffering ; but
she was not forgotten. The Saint made such earnest en-
treaties by signs to those who attended her, that at last they
complied with the request, and carried her to the religious.
She could only say the words so often uttered, but her
maternal heart was ingenious in its love, and she expressed
her sympathy and affection for the poor sister by·such
gentle and tender signs and caresses, that those who stood
by could not refrain from tears.

A month after the Saint had lost the use of speech, she appeared so ill that it was considered necessary to administer the last anointing without delay. As the religious were preparing for the holy rite, our Divine Lord appeared to St. Gertrude under the form of a Spouse of exceeding beauty, and extended His arms to her, as if to invite her to Himself, moving in whatever direction she turned her face. It was revealed to the religious before mentioned that our Lord had so much love for His faithful servant, that He ardently desired to receive her into the arms of His mercy, and to put her in possession of the glories of heaven. The religious inquired how it could be that her beloved mother equalled in merit those virgin Saints whom the Church had canonised because they had shed their blood for the faith. She received this reply : " Since the first year in which she held office as Abbess, she united and conformed her will so perfectly to Mine as to have merited an equal reward. But now that her virtues have increased with her years, I have given her a yet greater share of glory and merit."

When the happy day of release came, which the Saint had so long and so ardently desired, our Lord appeared to her with His Divine countenance radiant with joy. On His right hand stood His ever-blessed Mother, and on His left the beloved disciple John. An immense multitude of Saints attended the King of Saints, and amongst their glorious ranks were seen a band of virgins, who appeared to the religious of the monastery and joined themselves with them. Our Divine Lord approached the bed of the dying Saint, showing such marks of tenderness and affection as were more than sufficient to sweeten the bitterness of death. When the Passion was read, at the words, " *Et inclinato capite emisit spiritum*," * our Lord inclined to-

---

* " And bowing His head, He gave up the ghost " (John **xix.**)

wards His faithful spouse, and opened wide His adorable Heart, as if transported with love, pouring forth all its tenderness on her. It might have seemed enough ; but even on earth there was yet more consolation reserved for her who had been faithful *usque ad mortem*—even until death.

As the sisters prayed and wept around her bed, the religious so favoured by our Lord ventured to address Him thus : " O most sweet Jesus ! we beseech Thee, by the goodness which prompted Thee to give us so dear a mother, that, as Thou art about to take her from this world, Thou wouldst condescend to our prayers, and receive her with the same affection as Thou didst Thy Blessed Mother, when she went forth from the body. " Then our Lord, with exceeding clemency, turned to His blessed Mother, and said to her : " Tell Me, My Mother, what I did most pleasing to you when you were leaving the world ; for they ask Me to bestow a similar favour on their mother. " " My Son," replied the Holy Virgin sweetly, " my greatest joy was the grace which You showed me of receiving me in the secure asylum of Your holy arms. " Our Lord replied : " I granted this because My Mother, when on earth, ever remembered My Passion with such intense anguish. " Then He added : " I granted this favour to My chosen one in recompense for the care which you had, while yet on earth, to meditate often in your mind, and to revere by your grief and your tears, the mystery of My Passion. Gertrude must therefore render herself in some sort worthy of this favour, by the pain and difficulty which she will suffer to-day in breathing. The patience which she will thus be called to exercise will place her in a state somewhat similar to that to which you were often reduced by the recollection of My sufferings."

St. Gertrude accordingly continued in her agony the

entire day; but our Lord did not leave her to suffer alone. His Heart had already been opened to her, and from thence she drew the help and consolation she needed. Celestial spirits also surrounded her bed, and she beheld them inviting her to paradise, and heard their celestial harmony as they sung continually : "Come, come, come, O lady ! the **joys** of heaven await thee ! Alleluia ! Alleluia ! " *

CHAPTER VII.

Her death—Of her eternal joys—Our Lord consoles her religious —Revelations of her sanctity—Prays that her religious may be comforted at her tomb—Her obsequies—Our Lord blesses her tomb.

THE moment of release came at last, and Gertrude passed to the eternal embraces of her Spouse. The religious, whose revelations seemed scarcely less wonderful than those of her saintly Superior, heard our Divine Lord address her thus : "Behold, now, you are to be united to Me, and to become My own for ever, by the sweet embrace which I will give to your soul, and in which I will present you to My eternal Father by the close embrace of My Heart : " as if our Lord would say, that though His almighty power had detained her until that moment on earth in order that she might amass a greater fund of merit, His extreme goodness, and the impatience of His love, if we may be permitted so to speak, could no longer defer her happiness, or leave His treasure in the mire of earth ; but that He desired to transport her without delay to Paradise, and to

* *Ant. Mag.*, ii. Vespers of her Feast : " Apparuerunt cœlestes spiritus de cœlo descendentes in terram, qui Gertrudem ad paradisi gaudia modulatis vocibus invitabant : ' Veni, **veni, veni,** Domina, quia te expectant cœli deliciæ. All. All.' "

have the satisfaction of seeing her enjoy eternal blessedness.

" And now this happy and a thousand times blessed soul took her flight to heaven, and retired into the sanctuary of the Divinity—I mean, into the sweetest Heart of Jesus, the faithful and magnificent Spouse who had opened it to her by so great an excess of His bounty. Who can imagine the feelings which so extraordinary a favour excited in this holy soul, the wonders which she discovered, the glories with which she was enlightened, and the avidity with which she drank in the pure and holy delights which flowed upon her from the Divinity as from a fountain. We will not undertake to speak here of the welcome or of the caresses which she received from her Divine Spouse, which the excellence of His bounty and His infinite perfections rendered so amiable, nor of the joy and the thanksgivings with which the Angels and Saints attended her triumph, nor of the praise which they gave to her eminent virtue ; for our mind is too weak and our pen too poor in eloquence to relate such things ; and it is both more safe and more agreeable to our duty to content ourselves with sharing in the common joy of the blessed who assisted at her entrance into glory, and to sing canticles of thanksgiving to God, who, by His mercy, has raised her to such a high honour.

" This sun of the religious life, which had shed abroad so far the light of good example, shining no more on earth, and this soul, which was but as a little drop of water in comparison with God, having entered happily into the infinite ocean of the Divinity, from whence she had come forth by creation, the daughters of her monastery were at first quite cast down, and plunged into the obscurity of a dark sadness. They endeavoured, nevertheless, to rise from this depression, looking with the eyes of faith, as it were across little openings, at the sublime land of glory in which they believed their mother had been placed. But, on the other hand, as they considered the greatness of their loss, and that they had been deprived of so excellent an Abbess, whose like had never been nor could ever hope to be seen by them, they fell again into deep grief, and poured forth torrents of tears. But in the end, the hope of their mother's happiness increasing more and more in their souls, they began to rejoice with her, and to beseech her to console them herself with her maternal tenderness and affection ; and then they began to manifest their joy by singing the responsory *Surge, Virgo, et nostras*, which was commenced by that religious who had the greatest share in the confidence of St. Gertrude and in the favours with which heaven had honoured her, and who was therefore the more obliged to interest herself in her triumph.

" Thus this virginal body, which had been the temple of Jesus Christ, was borne by the hands of these virgins into the chapel, and placed before the altar. Then, all the community being prostrated in prayer round the corpse, they beheld the soul of the Saint, radiant with glory, standing before the throne of the most Holy Trinity, and praying for the salvation of all those who had been formerly under her guidance."

While the Mass was being said for the repose of her soul, the religious who had been so dear to her poured forth her heart to God, and represented the excess of her affliction to Him. Our Lord deigned to console her by this reply : " Why are you so afflicted for the death of Gertrude ? If I have taken her from you, am I not able to supply what is wanting to you ? If, after the decease of a gentleman, the lord to whom his lands belong takes possession of them, and unites them to his own domains by a just right, and if this lord has a high reputation for equity, there may well be confidence in him that he will not abandon the children of the deceased, and that he will give them what will be necessary for their subsistence,— how much more just is it, then, that you should confide in Me, who am goodness itself, and that you should hope firmly, if you turn to Me with your whole heart, that I will be to you all which she has been, and that I will give to each of you that which you think you have lost in her ?"

On the following day, when they were preparing to inter the body, before the first Mass, this servant of God offered the Heart of Jesus, with all its marvellous gifts and graces, for the repose of the soul so dear to her. Our Lord received this offering as a vase in the form of a human heart, filled with the most precious wines. Having placed it in His bosom, He called the Saint to Him thus : " Come to Me, My little one, and dispose of the goods which your children have sent you." Then the Saint turned to her Beloved, and found in His Heart treasures of all virtues and of all good ; she took several, as it were with her hand, and, moved by the tenderness and goodness with which God had filled her, she said : " O my beloved Lord, this grace would be most suitable for the Prioress, and this for another religious, and this for another ; " even as when on earth she had known the need of each, which now she desired to supply from the inexhaustible treasures of His Divine Heart.

Then our Lord, looking at her sweetly, said : " Come yet nearer to Me, My beloved." The Saint rose joyfully, and placed herself at the left side of our Lord, who made her look into His Heart, saying : " Behold Me now, as I behold you." * By this she learned that, in her desire to obtain graces and gifts for others, there had been formerly some natural affection; but this intimate communication with God changed her first desire into a perfect conformity to His will, for, though He loves men far more than they can possibly conceive, He nevertheless, in infinite wisdom, permits that many should continue in certain defects and imperfections, from which He could easily deliver them by His grace.

At the elevation of the Host, the same religious, in offering the Host conjointly with the priest, offered also for the deceased all the movements of filial affection which the Heart of Jesus Christ had for His holy Mother; then our Lord said lovingly to the soul: "Approach, O daughter, that I may manifest to you the filial affection of My most loving Heart." The Blessed Virgin then took this soul in her arms and brought her to her Son who inclined towards her, and testified a filial affection for her with the tenderest charity. The religious renewed the offering at other Masses; but as there were more than twenty celebrated, she desired to offer something still more precious, to increase the merit of her beloved mother. She therefore offered the filial affection which our Lord had for His Father in His Divinity, and for His Mother in His Humanity. When she made this offering, the Son of God arose, stood before His Father, and called the soul of the deceased to Him, saying: "Come hither, lady and queen; for now a greater offering is sent to thee." Then the Mother of God led her to a more sublime degree of glory, and the religious said to her: "O my venerable mother, I can no longer see you, nor can I know anything

---

* " Respice nunc, sicut ego respicio."

of the rank to which your merits have raised you." The Saint replied: "You can still ask me whatever you desire." The religious then said: "My good mother, why do you not pray to God that we may be able to restrain our tears, when you know that many of us have suffered in consequence of our grief, and you could never bear to see us afflicted when on earth?" The Saint replied: "My Lord has so tender and condescending an affection for me, that He makes even those things tend to my advantage and glory which would avail but little for others; and in recompense for the vigilance and discretion with which I formerly guided you, He permits me to present your tears to Him in a chalice of gold, and in exchange He gives me to drink of the living waters of His Divine sweetness. Therefore it is that, having tasted so agreeable a beverage, I sing to My Beloved a canticle of thanksgiving for my daughters and myself."

The religious then inquired if this favour was granted only for the tears they shed purely for God, and from their apprehension that regular observance should suffer by her decease. She replied: "For all tears, even when caused by human love and tenderness; but when these tears are shed for the glory of God, the Son of God Himself sings thanksgivings with me; and this affords me a joy as great as the difference between the creature and the Creator." Then, calling the religious by name, she said to her: "My daughter, I have received a particular recompense from God for the fidelity and zeal with which I led you to act for the glory of God in the matter you know of. For my beloved Lord Jesus sings continually in my heart a song of love, for which I am glorified by the whole court of heaven. My ears are entertained with a ravishing melody; my eyes behold a most glorious light; I inhale and taste a most sweet fragrance ; but there are other pleasures which I could have enjoyed, and of which I am deprived because I had been a little negligent in this affair, although I did all with a good intention and to promote peace."

When the bell was rung at the elevation of the Host, the religious offered It to supply the deficiencies of the deceased ; when she had done so, It appeared to the soul of the deceased in the form of a radiant sceptre, which seemed to move before her in a marvellous manner.   But when she desired to touch it, she was unable, because what is neglected in this life cannot be repaired or supplied perfectly in the other.   Nevertheless, as the Saint, by a special gift of God, excelled in gratitude and thankfulness, she prayed for all who had come to assist at her obsequies ; and she obtained for many the pardon of their sins, and an increase of grace to regulate their lives better and to perform good works.

When the priest was giving the Benediction at the end of Mass, the religious beheld her blessed mother standing before the throne of the most Holy Trinity, where she prayed thus : " Giver of gifts ! grant, I beseech Thee, that whenever any of my daughters shall go to my tomb to make known their griefs to me, or their imperfections and defects, that they may receive such consolation and support as to know that I am still their mother."   This prayer was heard ; for God, by His almighty power, His wisdom, and His goodness, granted special favours there to each religious.   When the body of the Saint was placed in the tomb, our Lord, to confirm His promise, was seen to make the sign of the cross on the body each time that earth was cast on it ; and after it was entirely covered, the Blessed Mother of our Lord also made the sign of the cross on the tomb, as a further assurance that her Son had granted this favour to the Saint.*

CHAPTER VIII.

Favours granted at the interment of the Saint—Souls released through her intercession—How our Lord gathered a lily—Of fear in the last agony—Purgatory in sickness—Efficacy of prayers for the dead.

AFTER the corpse had been interred, while the response *Regnum mundi* † was singing, wonderful signs of the beatitude of Gertrude were beheld in heaven, and the very walls and pavement of the monastery seemed to thrill with joy. The Saint appeared, with a troop of virgins of admirable beauty. She held a lily and other flowers in her right hand, and on her left conducted the religious of her community who had already attained eternal beatitude.

---

* We find the following passage in Père Baron's *Incendie,* vol. ii., lib. iii., c. 28 : " St. Gertrude, having made a donation of all her merits and good works to the souls in purgatory, the demon appeared to her at the moment of her death, and mocked her, saying : 'How vain thou art ! and how cruel thou hast been to thyself ! For what greater pride can there be than to wish to pay the debts of others without paying one's own ? Now—now we will see the result ; when thou art dead thou wilt pay for thyself in the fires of purgatory, and I will laugh at thy folly whilst thou weepest for thy pride.' Then she beheld her Divine Spouse approaching her, who consoled her with these words : ' In order that you may know how agreeable your charity for the souls of the departed has been to Me, I remit to you now all the pains of purgatory which you might have suffered ; and as I have promised to return you a hundred for one, I will further increase your celestial glory abundantly, giving you a special recompense for the charity which you have exercised towards My beloved souls in purgatory, by renouncing in their favour your works of satisfaction.'"

† "The kingdom of this world and all its ornaments I have despised for the love of my Lord Jesus Christ." *Ant. Com. Vid.*

In this glorious triumph they came before the throne of God; and when the words *quem vidi* were chanted, God the Father bestowed gifts on them; at the words *quem amavi*, God the Son bestowed His liberality on them; and at the *In quem credidi*, the Holy Spirit granted similar favours. When they sung *quem dilexi*, St. Gertrude turned towards her heavenly Spouse, and saluted Him with ardent love. As they chanted the response *Libera me, Domine*, many souls were seen entering heaven with great joy, who had been released through the Masses said that day, and by the merits of the Saint. Amongst others, a lay brother who had been somewhat negligent in spiritual things, but who had been much relieved by the intercession of the Saint.

On the thirtieth day St. Gertrude appeared again to this religious, but with a splendour which far surpassed the visions she had seen before. The reason of this was, that God willed that the merit which she had acquired by His grace in suffering her infirmities and sickness with so much patience, should appear exteriorly, and that the beauty of her soul should shine forth visibly. A book of gold, richly adorned, was seen before the throne of God, in which was written all the instructions she had given to those persons who had been under her guidance while she was on earth; to which was yet to be added all the advancement in virtue which they had attained either by her teaching or example.

At Mass, the religious prayed with great fervour that our Lord would reward her blessed mother for her maternal love and care. Our Lord replied: "I grant your prayer, and consent that each of you should make a similar petition to Me; for I have such a good will for this soul, that there is scarcely any gift or grace which I am not disposed to grant her." Then, looking at the Saint lovingly, He said : " You have bestowed your benefits well, since they are returned to you so gratefully." Gertrude then prostrated before the throne of His glory, to thank Him for the fidelity of those who had been formerly under her guidance, and said : " Eternal, boundless, and unceasing praise be to Thee, my sweetest Lord, for all Thy benefits ; and blessed be the moment in which Thou didst will to prepare and sustain me to receive such rewards. O God of my life, do Thou answer them for me." Our Lord replied : " I will fix the eyes of My mercy upon them." He then made the sign of the cross twice with His most holy hand ; and by this He gave to each member of the community the grace of giving good example, and the grace of having a pure intention of Divine love in their hearts.

Twelve days after the death of St. Gertrude, one of her spiritual daughters was also called to her eternal reward. Her death added much to the affliction of the religious, for her innocence and purity of heart had made her singularly beloved. As the favoured religious wept and prayed for her, and thought of how much her sisters had been deprived in losing her good example and her wise counsels, she ventured to exclaim : " Ah, my beloved Lord ! why have You taken her so suddenly from us ? " Our Lord replied : " While you were burying Gertrude, My beloved, I was taking My delight amongst your devoted community, where I had descended to feed upon the lilies ; and as I beheld this lily, which pleased Me exceedingly, I took it in My hand ; and as I held it therein for eleven days before breaking it from the stem, it increased marvellously in beauty and in the odour of sanctity ; and then I took it to Myself for My own special delight." He then added : " When any of you reflect on the pleasure you found in her society, and desire to enjoy it again, if you offer this desire to Me, it renews the pleasure I find in the fragrance of this lily, and I will return it a hundred-fold."

As the religious, like a faithful and loving sister, offered the Host at the Elevation for her soul, with all the fidelity of the Heart of Jesus, she saw her elevated to a higher and yet more sublime degree of glory, where her garments shone marvellously, and she was honoured by blessed spirits. And this she beheld whenever she made this offering for her.

Then, as she inquired of our Divine Lord why the sister had appeared in great fear and alarm during her agony, she received this reply : " It was for her good, and an effect of My mercy. For during her sickness she desired very much to be assisted by your prayers, so that she might be admitted into heaven immediately. I promised you this favour, which she believed she would obtain from Me. I was pleased with her confidence, and determined to do her yet more good than I had before purposed. But as young persons seldom purify themselves from slight negligences—such as seeking too much amusement, and taking pleasure in what is useless—and as it was necessary that she should be purified from these little stains by the inconveniences and pains of sickness, before I could bring her to heaven, I could not bear that, after having endured all with so much resignation and patience, she should still be unable to enjoy this blessedness. I therefore permitted her to be further tried by fear, caused by the sight of evil spirits ; and thus she became perfectly purified, and merited eternal glory." " But where wert Thou, then, O Lord ? " inquired the religious. Our Lord replied : " I was hidden on her left side ; and as soon as she was sufficiently purified, I showed Myself to her, and took her with Me to eternal rest and glory."

CHAPTER IX.

ANOTHER religious died soon after, who from her infancy had been specially devoted to the Mother of God. After she had received the last Sacraments, and when she appeared almost dead, she gave singular edification to the religious by the affection and compunction with which she kissed the wounds of a crucifix which was presented to her, addressing it in the tenderest words. After pouring forth the most ardent and fervent ejaculations for pardon of her sins, for the protection of her Spouse in her last moments, and for the assistance of the Blessed Virgin, the Angels, and Saints, her strength failed, and she passed, as in a quiet sleep, to her eternal reward. As the community were reciting the usual prayers for the repose of her soul, our Lord appeared to a religious with the deceased in His arms, saying to her, caressingly, " Do you know Me, My child ? " Then she who was favoured with this vision prayed that our Lord would specially reward that soul for her humble and efficacious charity in having served her on many occasions, and for having been specially earnest in doing service to those religious who were most holy and devoted to God, in order that she might share in their merits and graces. Our Lord therefore presented His deified Heart to her, saying : " Drink freely from Me a reward for all which thou didst when on earth for My elect."

On the following day, at Mass, the soul appeared as if seated in our Lord's bosom, and His Blessed Mother appeared to rejoice this soul by a communication of her merits. This was specially the case while the community recited the Psalter for her, with the *Ave Maria;* so that at each word the Mother of our Lord appeared to make presents to this soul, who received them to increase her merit before God. While they prayed thus, the religious desired much to know what faults the deceased had committed, from which it had been necessary to purify her before her death ; and she prayed God to make this known to her. As her prayer was the result of a Divine inspiration, and not of an idle curiosity, it was heard ; and our Lord replied : "She took some complacence in her own judgment ; but I purified her from this, by causing her to die before the community had finished the prayers which they were offering for her. This troubled her much, because she feared it would prove an obstacle to her happiness, by depriving her of the assistance which she hoped to derive from the prayers of others."

To this the religious replied : " Lord, could she not have been purified from this by the sentiments of compunction which she had in imploring pardon for all her sins at the last moment of her life ? " Our Lord replied : " This general contrition was not sufficient, because she still had some confidence in her own judgment, and was not perfectly docile to those who instructed her ; and therefore it was necessary that she should be purified by this suffering." He added : " She also needed purification, for having sometimes neglected the grace of confession ; but My goodness remitted this fault to her for the sake of some persons whom I honour with My friendship, and of others who had charge of her, and for the pain and mortification I caused her by obliging her to confess, against her inclination, on the day of her death ; and then I pardoned her all the omissions she had been guilty of in this matter."

At the Mass, when they sung at the offertory *Hostias ac preces,** our Lord elevated His right hand, and shed forth from it a marvellous light, which illuminated the whole heaven, but especially this soul, which was in the bosom of our Lord. Then the Saints approached, each according to their rank, and placed their merits as an offering on the breast of Jesus, to supply for the deficiencies of this soul. The religious knew that they acted thus because, when that soul was on earth, she had been accustomed to pray that the Saints would give this assistance to the souls of the deceased. The Saints then testified their affection for her by endeavouring to increase her happiness, and the virgins caressed her specially, as having, in common with them, the excellent grace of virginity.

On another occasion, when the religious prayed for this soul, with few but ardent words, it appeared to her that all her words were engraven on the bosom of Jesus, and formed there so many little windows, which opened into the Heart of Jesus. Then she heard our Lord say to this soul : " Look through heaven, and see if there is any grace in the Saints which you would desire to have, and draw it from My Heart through these little openings." The religious knew, further, that each prayer which was

---

* From the Offertory, *Missa Defu.* : "We offer to Thee, O Lord, sacrifices and prayers : do Thou receive them in behalf of those souls whom we commemorate," &c.

made devoutly for her produced the same effect.   At the elevation of the Host, our Lord appeared to present His sacred Body to this soul, under the form of a spotless lamb; having embraced it devoutly, she became entirely changed in this embrace, because she obtained new joys, and a more clear knowledge of the Divinity.   Then the religious begged her to pray for those who were under her guidance, and she replied : " I will pray for them, but I can desire nothing except what I see to be conformable to the will of my beloved Lord."   The religious replied : "Is it not advantageous to them to hope in your prayers ? "   She answered : " It will avail them much for our Lord to behold their earnest desire for our intercession."   " But," continued the religious, " can you not pray especially for your special friends, if they have not asked your prayers ?" She replied : " Our Lord, of His infinite charity, grants them particular favours for our sake."   " Since this is the case, pray specially for the priest who communicates for you."   The soul answered : " He will afford me a double advantage ; because, as the Lord receives it from him and returns it to me, so will He return to him what I have gained thereby ; as gold appears to greater advantage when contrasted with colours." *

"From what you say," continued the religious, "it would appear that it is more salutary to celebrate Mass for the dead than for any other intention ? "   She replied : " When this is done through charity, it is of more avail than if the mass were said merely as a sacerdotal duty." " And how know you all these things ?" inquired the religious, " since you appeared to know so little when on earth ? "   The soul replied : " I know it from the Source

---

* This passage is not very clear in the original.

of which St. Augustine speaks.   When God looks into the soul, it learns all things." *

Once, as the religious beheld this soul clothed with a scarlet robe, and in a high degree of glory, she inquired of our Lord how she had merited such favours.   He replied: " I have done for her what I promised through you, by clothing her with My Passion to reward her for an occasion on which her heart was greatly depressed, and yet she did not exempt herself from the ordinary duties of the order ; and although she had to do more than her strength allowed, she did not complain much of it."   He added : " And for the weakness and exhaustion which she suffered in her sickness, I have caused her to be accompanied by the princes of My kingdom, who make her find a special satisfaction in the glory which she enjoys ; and I have recompensed her so abundantly for what she endured, that she desires to have suffered a hundred times more."

The religious also beheld many souls kneeling before her to testify their gratitude for their deliverance from purgatory, through the prayers which had been offered for her, and which she had not needed.   She inquired if the community would obtain any advantage from this ; and they replied : " It is certainly very advantageous to you, for our Lord will pour forth grace on you for each." In another Mass, which was not for the dead, the religious inquired of this soul what fruit she could obtain thereby, as it was not for the dead.   The soul replied : " And what share has a queen in the possession of the king her lord ?   Know that I am so closely united to the King my Lord and my beloved Spouse, that I share in all His

* " Deum semel inspexisse, est omnia didicisse."

goods, as a queen is admitted to the table of the king ; for which, may the King of kings be eternally praised and glorified !"

CHAPTER X.

St. Gertrude not formally canonised—History of her *cultus*—Benedict XIV.—Her Office approved—Name inserted in Martyrology—Lanspergius—His history—Preface to *Insinuationes*—Plea for the female sex—Conclusion.

ST. GERTRUDE was never formally canonised. Benedict XIV. says,* that her *cultus* was first permitted on the 7th October 1606, four centuries after her death, when, by a decree of the Sacred Congregation of Rites, an office was granted to the nuns of the monastery of St. John Evangelist, of the city of Licia. On the 20th June 1609, the nuns of the Conception of the Blessed Virgin of Mexico obtained a similar favour, the Office being a double. The Benedictine monks and nuns of the Congregation of Cassiensis were granted a double, *ad lib.*, on the 19th December 1654. The beautiful Office of the Saint at present in use was composed by Dom G. H. Vaillant. †
In the *Bibliothèque Générale des Écrivains de l'Ordre de St. Benoît*, t. iii., p. 170, we find the following details : "Dom Bernard Audebert, Superior-General of the Congregation of St. Maur, having established the feast of St. Gertrude in 1673, whose *cultus* was already famous in Rome, Spain, and the Indies, Dom Vaillant, of the same

* *De serv. Dei can. et beat.*, lib. i., c. xli.
† In the Office for the Saint used by the Benedictines of the Most Holy Sacrament, we read that she was made Abbess of a monastery in the town of Delphos, and hence is called the Delphic Gertrude : "Deinde alterius in urbe Delphos, unde Gertrude Delphica dicitur." vi. Lesson, ii. Nocturn.

Congregation, composed the Office of the holy Benedictine
Abbess, which was chanted from this year in the monasteries of the congregation.   The author uses the most
tender expressions of the Canticle of Canticles—a language
which only suits a small number of holy souls, who are
elevated above earthly things."

It is more difficult to ascertain why the Office was
transferred to March.   The Maurist fathers made this
change in a general chapter, possibly because there are so
many feasts in November; but again the question arises
why they chose a day already occupied by St. Gertrude of
Nivelle.*   As far as we have been able to ascertain, the
feast is celebrated on the 15th November by the Benedictine Order, with the exception of this congregation.
The 17th November was the day first appointed for the
festival; but, as Benedict XIV. quaintly observes, it was
found that this day was already occupied by a Bishop and
Doctor of the Church, and as St. Gregory Thaumaturgus
had in his lifetime moved mountains from their place, it
was not seemly that after his death he should be removed
out of his place by a woman, or give precedence to a
virgin.   Moreover, the day of St. Gertrude's decease was
doubtful; it occurred soon after the feast of St. Lebuin
(November 12), and this was the only guide to a decision.
A decree was then published, *urbis et orbis.*   The Sacred
Congregation of Rites, at the instance of the King of
Poland, approved an Office conformable to the Roman
Breviary, for " Christians of both sexes, secular as well as
regular, who are bound to the Canonical Hours."   This
was authorised by his Holiness Clement XII. on the 9th
March 1739.

---

* Daughter of Pepin, duke of Brabant, A.D. 664.

The question of the Saint's canonisation had been raised previously. In the year 1677, the insertion of her name in the Roman Martyrology was proposed. Bothinius, Archbishop of Myra, then Promoter of the Faith, declared that there was no document warranting either her canonisation or beatification ; "However," Benedict XIV. adds, " I find the following note in his own handwriting : ' After writing the above, a plenary indulgence, authorised by a brief, was obtained on the feast of the Saint, which carries much weight with it ; because, according to the decrees of Alexander VII. of happy memory, such indulgence is not granted to any one not previously named in the Martyrology ; and at present (whatever may have been the case previous to the decree aforesaid) it is generally refused. But the official secretaries stated that they found St. Gertrude described in their books as *la magna*, and therefore entitled to be inserted in said Martyrology.' "

The name was therefore inserted on the 22d January 1678, but without any special eulogium. The words " who was remarkable for the gift of revelation " were added afterwards. It is generally believed that the five books known as the *Insinuationes Divinæ Pietatis* were first translated from the original German by Lanspergius. Benedict XIV. mentions a previous work by Lamberto Luscorino, written in 1390 ; " but this," he adds, "as far as I know, was never published." Lanspergius says, at the conclusion of his Preface, that after a most diligent search he could obtain only one copy in Latin, the first book of which was so torn and mutilated, that he was obliged to translate the same from the German into Latin, and adopt the Latin copy for the remainder. From this it may be reasonably inferred that the work had been already tran-

slated and edited ; but there is no doubt the edition of
Lanspergius was the first to bring the Revelations into
general notice.   How one longs to know if the "Teutonic"
copy which he used was the original manuscript of the
Saint, and where he obtained it !

Lanspergius wrote at the close of the fifteenth and at
the commencement of the sixteenth century.   He was
born at Lansberg, in Bavaria, and entered the Order of
Carthusians at Cologne while still young.   His piety and
devotion procured for him the distinctive appellation of
"the Just."   He died in 1539, before he had attained his
fiftieth year.   His works, which are principally ascetical,
breathe a singularly devout and pious spirit ; they were
published at Cologne, in five vols. 4to, 1693.

The Preface which he prefixed to the *Insinuationes* has
been republished by all who have since edited the work.
The title of *Insinuationes*, so expressive in the Latin, so
impossible to be translated into English, which he was the
first to prefix to the Revelations of St. Gertrude, has also
been retained.   Lanspergius commences his Preface by
observing, "that no one should be surprised if, in the
present day, when the Holy Scripture is inquired for by
all," he should have brought out a book of revelations ;
and he anticipates objections to the work by observing,
that even those who carp at such disclosures when made
to religious, cannot deny that the Old Testament itself is
entirely a volume of revelations.   He suggests that
objectors to such Divine manifestations must be of the
number of those from whom Christ Himself declares His
secrets to have been hidden by the Father, as being the
"wise and prudent" of the world.   It is for the "little
ones" that he uncovers his candle, which has been too
long hidden under a bushel ; but considering himself a

debtor to all, he feels bound to declare that nothing shall
be found in this volume which is contrary to Scripture, or
which may not be proved thereby. He continues :

" Let the reader further learn that we possess the pro-
foundest veneration for the Scripture, so that we do not
attribute equal authority to any other work, however
sublime ; but we must confess—such is the kindness and
profuseness of Divine love—that there is no sex, age,
condition, which it will not condescend to illuminate, or
entice, and invite, according to its capacity or its power of
being so attracted. And thus God has established in His
Church, not only various ecclesiastical writers, but also
various methods of teaching, of phrase, and of expression,
and that in both sexes ; so that every one may be instructed,
illuminated, and edified according to his taste.

" But some will perhaps object that these revelations
were made to a woman, and either despising or suspect-
ing the whole female race, will think that, no matter how
holy a virgin or a woman may be, she must of necessity
be frail and unstable, having nothing manly (which means
perfect) about her. As if holy women have not often
been more constant in virtue, more ready for martyrdom,
more chary of their chastity, more full of mercy, more intent
on averting God's anger, than many men ; and have given
us examples of virtue which are very often superior to those
of men. We men, therefore, should rather be confounded
when we reflect on them, and look up to the whole sex
with veneration.

" I will not deny that the same sex, that is, certain pious
virgins or women devoted to God, when left to themselves,
and unaided by any help from God, are by no means beyond suspicion ; for vain-glory, to which females are very
much exposed, or a vain complacency in themselves, leads

them to believe that what was entirely human was really
a Divine inspiration ; and at other times, delighted with
the applause and esteem of men, they have considered
themselves far better and superior to what they are in
reality.

"Such people, however, are easily detected. An im-
postor, especially a female one, cannot escape very long;
because, wherever the very deepest foundation of humility
is not laid, the whole edifice falls ignominiously. But
where real humility exists, such humility as those possess,
and as all should possess, who cling to God alone from
pure, simple, and chaste affection, whatever sex such belong to, they will neither be deceived nor will they wish
to deceive others ; for though they may feel some heavenly
motion, or receive some unusual celestial grace, it troubles
them, it raises much doubt in their mind, how such can
come from God—how such can happen to them, weak,
contemptible, mere nothings as they are—how God could
come to know them at all ; and they look upon it as nigh
absurd for God, by such singular gifts, to prefer them to
others, or to do any such thing for them in preference to
others."

He then speaks of the humility of the Blessed Virgin
when saluted by the Angel, and says that those who are
truly humble and holy will not believe any revelation or
vision until assured by those who direct them. God
speaks to whom He pleases, and makes no distinction
of sex, unless indeed it be to give more abundantly to
the weaker when they deserve it by humility and devotion. But though He chose to speak through Balaam's
ass, we are not therefore to call the ass blessed. But
we call St. Gertrude blessed, such was her sanctity, purity,
and sincerity in seeking God's glory and His will in all

things, as to merit being the medium of revealing His secrets to us.

Lanspergius then shows that the character of these Revelations is such as to make them of general utility to the Church, as there is " nothing obscure, nothing doubtful ; no prophecy of the future ; nothing but what we can desire and wish for,—namely, the extent of God's kindness, clemency, and compassion ; " and that " they show with what a most benign Providence He deals with His singular friends, who, renouncing their own desires, seek His will alone ; and how He promotes them to salutary, then to better, and then to the choicest gifts."

He then enumerates the various women mentioned in Scripture who have either prophesied or even had rule over God's people, commencing with Debbora* and ending with Elizabeth and Anna. " I say nothing of the Female, the Virgin Mary, the most worthy, not only of women, but of all created beings, for it is not seemly to compare her with any one, since she excels them all as the sun outshines the stars."

The good Carthusian returns again to what seems a favourite theme, and says he passes over the details which he might have given of the glorious triumphs, the constancy, and the endurance of female martyrs, and, with a brief condemnation of those ecclesiastics who, because they are, or think themselves, " men of great importance, and high in the esteem of the people, despise the weaker sex," and restrain the devout from communicating as frequently as they desire, passes on to a panegyric on the learning of the Saint and her sanctity : " As regards her sanctity, she so abounded in the virtues, that you could

---

* Is Father Faber's remark, *All for Jesus*, p. 333, a coincidence or a quotation?

not say which was most prominent. Look at her humility
— you can find nothing like it; at her chastity—you
would say she excelled in it; observe her mildness and
kindness—you would put them before the others : for she
was so advanced in each virtue, you would say each was
her principal one."

He next considers the practices of devotion which she
proposes, especially that of uniting all our actions, however trifling, to those of our Divine Lord : " Oh, the bar-
gain ! " he exclaims ; " would he not be considered a fool
who would not give a piece of copper for a heap of gold,
or a flint for a pearl ? " Thus are all our good actions
turned to immense account, and become of great value to
us, inasmuch as by our intention of uniting them with the
oblation of Christ they become part and parcel of His
merits. Further, if we do all this not merely for ourselves
but for others, and above all for Holy Church, our gain is
increased, God is more glorified, and the Church is
strengthened and supported : " for all property, the more
common it becomes, the more heavenly it becomes,"—
words surely worth noting and treasuring in every stage
of our spiritual life.

The testimonies of various divines and doctors who
had examined the Revelations are next adduced. The
most approved theologians amongst the Dominicans and
Franciscans were employed upon it ; amongst others,
Brother Henry of Mulhusen, and a certain Father called
a Burgo, belonging to the Friars Minors at Halbustat, a
person highly esteemed for his learning about the year
1300. He also observes : " There were many other
learned persons, especially among the Friars Preachers,
who conversed with her in her lifetime, and testified to
her learning and sincerity. The testimony of one who

sent the following, after a most accurate revision of the book, I cannot withhold : ' I consider that no one having the Spirit of God in him can either find fault with or impugn anything written in this book. Nerved by the Spirit of Truth, from whom all wisdom emanates, I offer and hold myself bound unto death to meet any one in defence of the holy and Catholic doctrine contained in it.' "

Such a testimony from a member of an Order ever distinguished for its theological learning and calm judgment, will carry a weight with it which renders further observation unnecessary ; and as the arrangement of the work has been fully explained elsewhere, we will conclude in the graceful and holy words of our author : " Farewell, therefore, courteous reader ; we ask your forgiveness for any oversight herein, for none certainly has been deliberate. Here look for and study what is right and perfect ; and may God, through the intercession of the same pious virgin and the prayers of all pious readers hereof, have mercy upon me."

PART II.

THE REVELATIONS OF ST. GERTRUDE.

WRITTEN BY HERSELF.

———————

CHAPTER I.

The Saint's thanksgiving to God for the first grace vouchsafed to her, by which her mind was withdrawn from earthly things and united to Him.

LET the Abyss of Uncreated Wisdom invoke the Abyss of Omnipotent Power to praise and extol the amazing charity which, by an excess of Thine infinite mercy, O most sweet God of my life and only Love of my soul, hast led Thee through a desert, pathless, and dry land—that is, through the many obstacles I have placed to Thy mercy—to descend into the valley of my miseries.

I was in the twenty-sixth year of my age when, on the Monday * before the Feast of the Purification of Thy most chaste Mother, in a happy hour, after Compline, at the close of day, Thou the true Light, who art clearer than any light, and yet deeper than any recess, having resolved to dissipate the obscurity of my darkness, didst sweetly

---

* "Secunda feria ante, &c., quæ fuit sexto kalendas Februarii." The French translation has : "Lundi vingt-cinquième janvier ; " the Italian, " Che fu alli 27 di Genaio."

and gently commence my conversion by appeasing the trouble which Thou hadst excited in my soul for more than a month, which Thou didst deign to use, as I believe, to destroy the fortress of vain-glory and curiosity which my pride had raised up within me, although I bore the name and habit of a religious to no purpose ; but Thou didst will to use this means, that Thou mightest thereby show me Thy salvation.

Being, then, in the middle of our dormitory, at the hour I have named, and having inclined to an ancient religious, according to our rule, on raising my head I beheld Thee, my most loving Love, and my Redeemer, surpassing in beauty the children of men, under the form of a youth of sixteen years, beautiful and amiable, and attracting my heart and my eyes by the infinite light of Thy glory, which Thou hadst the goodness to proportion to the weakness of my nature ; and standing before me, Thou didst utter these words, full of tenderness and sweetness : " Thy salvation is at hand ; why art thou consumed with grief ? Hast thou no counsellor, that thou art so changed by sadness ? " When Thou hadst spoken thus, although I knew that I stood corporally in the place I have mentioned, it seemed to me, nevertheless, that I was in our choir, in the corner * where I had been accustomed to offer up my tepid prayers, and that there I heard these words : " I will save thee, I will deliver thee ; fear not ;" and after I had heard them, I saw Thee place Thy right hand in mine, as if to ratify Thy promise.

Then I heard Thee speak thus : " You have licked the dust with My enemies, and you have sucked honey amidst thorns ; but return now to Me—I will receive you,

---

* " In angulo."

and inebriate you with the torrent of My celestial delights."
When Thou hadst said these words, my soul melted within
me ; and as I desired to approach Thee, I beheld between
Thee and me (I mean, from Thy right hand to my left
hand) a hedge of such prodigious length that I could see
no end to it either before or behind, and the top of it
appeared so set with thorns that I could find no way to
return to Thee, Thou only consolation of my soul. Then
I paused to weep over my faults and crimes, which were
doubtless figured by this hedge which divided us. In the
ardour of the desires with which I desired Thee, and in
my weakness, O charitable Father of the poor, " whose
mercies are over all Thy works," Thou didst take me by the
hand, and placed me near Thee instantly, without difficulty,
so that, casting my eyes upon the precious Hand which Thou
hadst extended to me as a pledge of Thy promises, I recognised, O sweet Jesus, Thy radiant wounds, which have
made of no effect the handwriting that was against us.*

By these and other illuminations Thou didst enlighten
and soften my mind, detaching me powerfully, by an interior
unction, from an inordinate love of literature and from all
my vanities, so that I only despised those things which
had formerly pleased me ; and all that was not Thee, O
God of my heart, appeared vile to me, and Thou alone wert
pleasing to my soul. And I praise, bless, adore, and thank
from my inmost soul, as far as I am able, but not as far
as I ought, Thy wise mercy and Thy merciful wisdom, that
Thou, my Creator and Redeemer, didst endeavour in so
loving a manner to submit my unconquerable self-opiniatedness to the sweetness of Thy yoke ; composing a beverage
suitable to my temperament, which has infused new light

An allusion to Col. ii. 14.

into my soul, so that I began to run after the odour of Thy
ointments, and Thy yoke became sweet and Thy burden
light, though a little while before they had appeared hard,
and almost unbearable.

CHAPTER II.

How the grace of God illuminated her interiorly.

HAIL, Salvation and Light of my soul! may all that is in
heaven, in earth, and in the abyss, return thanks to Thee
for the extraordinary grace which has led my soul to know
and consider what passes within my heart, of which I had
no more care formerly than (if I may so speak) of what
passes within my hands or feet.   But after the infusion
of Thy most sweet light, I saw many things in my heart
which offended Thy purity, and I even perceived that all
within me was in such disorder and confusion that Thou
couldst not abide therein.

Nevertheless, my most loving Jesus, neither all these
defects, nor all my unworthiness, prevented Thee from
honouring me with Thy visible presence nearly every day
that I received the life-giving nourishment of Thy Body
and Thy Blood, although I only beheld Thee indistinctly,
as one who sees at dawn : Thou didst endeavour by this
sweet compliance to attract my soul, so that it might be
entirely united to Thee, and that I might know Thee
better and enjoy Thee more fully.   And as I disposed
myself to labour for the obtaining of these favours on the
Feast of the Annunciation of Thy Mother, when Thou
didst ally Thyself with our nature in her virginal womb,
—Thou who saidest, " Here I am before I called Thee,"
—Thou didst anticipate this day by pouring forth on me

unworthy though I am, on the Vigil of the Feast, the sweetness of Thy benediction, at Chapter, which was held after Matins, on account of the Sunday following.

But since it is not possible for me to describe in what manner thou didst visit me, O Orient from on high, in the bowels of Thy mercy and sweetness, permit me, O Giver of gifts, to immolate a sacrifice of Thanksgiving to Thee on the altar of my heart, in order to obtain for myself and for all Thine elect the blessedness of experiencing frequently this union of sweetness and this sweetness of union, which before this time was utterly unknown to me; for when I reflect on the kind of life which I led formerly, and which I have led since, I protest in truth that it is a pure effect of Thy grace, which Thou hast given me without any merit of mine.

Thou didst give me from henceforward a more clear knowledge of Thyself, which was such that the sweetness of Thy love led me to correct my faults far more than the fear of the punishments with which Thy just anger threatened me. But I do not remember ever to have enjoyed so great happiness at any other time as during these days of which I speak, in which Thou didst invite me to the delights of Thy royal table; and I know not for certain whether it is Thy wise Providence which has deprived me of them, or whether it is my negligence which has drawn on me this chastisement.

CHAPTER III.

Of the pleasure which God took in making His abode in the soul of Gertrude.

WHILST Thou didst act so lovingly towards me, and didst not cease to draw my soul from vanity and to Thyself, it

happened on a certain day, between the Festival of the
Resurrection and Ascension, that I went into the court
before Prime, and seated myself near the fountain,—and I
began to consider the beauty of the place, which charmed
me on account of the clear and flowing stream, the verdure
of the trees which surrounded it, and the flight of the
birds, and particularly of the doves,—above all, the sweet
calm,—apart from all, and considering within myself what
would make this place most useful to me, I thought that it
would be the friendship of a wise and intimate companion,
who would sweeten my solitude or render it useful to others,
when Thou, my Lord and my God, who are a torrent of
inestimable pleasure, after having inspired me with the
first impulse of this desire, Thou didst will to be also the
end of it, inspiring me with the thought that if by continual
gratitude I return Thy graces to Thee, as a stream returns
to its source ; if, increasing in the love of virtue, I put forth,
like the trees, the flowers of good works ; furthermore, if,
despising the things of earth, I fly upwards, freely, like the
birds, and thus free my senses from the distraction of exterior things,—my soul would then be empty, and my heart
would be an agreeable abode for Thee.

As I was occupied with the recollection of these things
during the same day, having knelt after Vespers for my
evening prayer before retiring to rest, this passage of the
Gospel came suddenly to my mind : " If any man love Me,
he will keep My word, and My Father will love him, and
We will come to him and will make Our abode with him "
(John xiv. 23). At these words my worthless heart perceived Thee, O my most sweet God and my delight, present
therein. Oh, that all the waters of the sea were changed
into blood, that I might pass them over my head, and thus
wash away my exceeding vileness, which Thou hast chosen

for Thine abode! or that my heart might be torn this moment from my body and cast into a furnace, that it might be purified from its dross, and made at least less unworthy of Thy presence! for Thou my God, since that hour, hast treated me sometimes with sweetness and sometimes with severity, as I have amended or been negligent; although, to speak the truth, when the most perfect amendment which I could attain, even for a moment, should have lasted my whole life, it could not merit to obtain for me the most trifling or the least condescending of the graces which I have ever received from Thee, so great are my crimes and sins.

The excess of Thy goodness obliges me to believe that the sight of my faults rather moves Thee to fear Thou wilt see me perish than to excite Thine anger, making me know that Thy patience in supporting my defects until now, with so much goodness, is greater than the sweetness with which Thou didst bear with the perfidious Judas during Thy mortal life; and although my mind takes pleasure in wandering after and in distracting itself with perishable things, yet, after some hours, after some days, and, alas! I must add, after whole weeks, when I return into my heart, I find Thee there; so that I cannot complain that Thou hast left me even for a moment, from that time until this year, which is the ninth since I received this grace, except once, when I perceived that Thou didst leave me for the space of eleven days, before the Feast of St. John Baptist,—and it appeared to me that this happened on account of a worldly conversation the Thursday preceding; and Thy absence lasted until the Vigil of St. John, when the Mass *Ne timeas, Zacharia*,* is said.   Then Thy sweetest humanity

---

* " Fear not, Zachary; thy prayer is heard," &c. (Introit for Mass, Vigil of St. John Baptist.)

and Thy stupendous charity moved Thee to seek me, when I had reached such a pitch of madness, that I thought no more of the greatness of the treasure I had lost, and for the loss of which I do not remember to have felt any grief at that time, nor even to have had the desire of recovering it.

I cannot now be sufficiently amazed at the mania which possessed my soul, unless, indeed, it was, that Thou didst desire me to know by my own experience what St. Bernard said : " When we fly from Thee, Thou pursuest us ; when we turn our backs, Thou dost present Thyself before us ; when we despise Thee, Thou dost entreat us ; and there is neither insult nor contempt which hinders Thee from labouring unweariedly to bring us to the attainment of that which eye hath not seen, nor ear heard, and which the heart of man cannot comprehend."

And as Thou didst bestow on me Thy first graces without any merit on my part, so now that I have had a second relapse, which is worse than the first, and renders me yet more unworthy to receive Thee, Thou hast deigned to give me the joy of Thy presence without interruption, until this very hour : for which be praise and thanksgiving to Thee as the Source of all good ; and that it may please Thee to preserve this precious grace in me, I offer Thee that excellent prayer which Thou didst utter with such amazing fervour when sweating blood in agony, and which the burning love of Thy Divinity and Thy pure devotion rendered so efficacious; beseeching Thee, by virtue of this most perfect prayer, to draw and unite me entirely to Thyself, that I may remain inseparably attached to Thee, even when I am obliged to attend to exterior duties for the good of my neighbour, and that afterwards I may return again to seek Thee within me, when I have accomplished them for Thy glory in the most perfect manner possible, even as the winds, when agitated by a tempest, return again to their former calm when it has ceased ; that Thou mayest find me as zealous in labouring for Thee as Thou hast been assiduous in helping me ; and that, by this means, Thou mayest elevate me to the highest degree of perfection to which Thy justice can permit Thy mercy to raise so carnal and rebellious a creature ; so that Thou mayest receive my soul into Thy hands when I breathe my last sigh, and conduct it with a kiss of peace where Thou dwellest, who reignest indivisibly and eternally with the Father and the Holy Spirit for endless ages.   Amen.

CHAPTER IV.

Of the stigmatas imprinted in the heart of Gertrude, and her exercises in honour of the Five Wounds.

I BELIEVE it was during the winter of the first or second year when I began to receive these favours, that I met the following prayer in a book of devotions :

"O Lord Jesus Christ, Son of the living God, grant that I may aspire towards Thee with my whole heart, with full desire and with thirsty soul, seeking only Thy sweetness and Thy delights, so that my whole mind and all that is within me may most ardently sigh to Thee, who art our true Beatitude. O most merciful Lord, engrave Thy Wounds upon my heart with Thy most precious Blood, that I may read in them both Thy grief and Thy love ; and that the memory of Thy Wounds may ever remain in my inmost heart, to excite my compassion for Thy sufferings and to increase in me Thy love. Grant me also to despise all creatures, and that my heart may delight in Thee alone. Amen."

Having learned this prayer with great satisfaction, I repeated it frequently, and Thou, who despisest not the prayer of the humble, heard my petitions ; for soon after, during the same winter, being in the refectory after Vespers, for collation, I was seated near a person to whom I had made known my secret. I relate these things for the benefit of those who may read what I write, because I have often perceived that the fervour of my devotion is increased by this kind of communication ; but I know not for certain, O Lord my God, whether it was Thy Spirit, or perhaps human affection, made me act thus, although I have heard from those experienced in such matters that it is always better to reveal these secrets—not indifferently to all, but chiefly to those who are not only our friends, but whom we are bound to reverence ; yet, as I am doubtful, as I have said, I commit all to Thy faithful Providence, whose spirit is sweeter than honey. If this fervour arose from any human affection, I am even more bound to have a profound gratitude for it, since Thou hast deigned to unite the mire of my vileness to the precious gold of Thy charity, that so the precious stones of Thy grace might be encased in me.

Being seated in the refectory, as I said before, I thought attentively on these things, when I perceived that the grace which I had so long asked by the aforesaid prayer was granted to me, unworthy though I am ; for I perceived in spirit that Thou hadst imprinted in the depth of my heart the adorable marks of Thy sacred Wounds, even as they are on Thy Body ; that Thou hadst cured my soul, in imprinting these Wounds on it ; and that, to satisfy its thirst, Thou hadst given it the precious beverage of Thy love.

But my unworthiness had not yet exhausted the abyss of Thy mercy ; for I received from Thine overflowing liberality this remarkable gift—that each time during the day in which I endeavoured to apply myself in spirit to those adorable Wounds, saying five verses of the Psalm *Benedic, anima mea, Domino* (Ps. cii.), I never failed to receive some new favour. At the first verse, "Bless the Lord, O my soul," I deposited all the rust of my sins and my voluptuousness at the Wounds of Thy blessed Feet; at the second verse, "Bless the Lord, and never forget all He hath done for thee," I washed away all the stains of carnal and perishable pleasures in the sweet bath of Blood and Water which Thou didst pour forth for me ; at the third verse, "Who forgiveth all thine iniquities," I reposed my spirit in the Wound of Thy Left Hand, even as the dove makes its nest in the crevice of the rock ; at the fourth verse, "Who redeemeth thy life from destruction," I approached Thy Right Hand, and took from thence all that I needed for my perfection in virtue ; and being thus magnificently adorned, I passed to the fifth verse, "Who satisfieth thy desire with good things," that I might be purified from all the defilement of sin, and have the indigence of my wants supplied, so that I might become worthy of Thy presence,—though of myself I am utterly unworthy,—and might merit the joy of Thy chaste embraces.

I declare also that Thou hast freely granted my other petition—namely, that I might read Thy grief and Thy love together. But, alas ! this did not continue long, although I cannot accuse Thee of having withdrawn it from me ; but I complain of having lost it myself by my own negligence. This Thine excessive goodness and infinite mercy has hidden from itself, and has procured to me, without any merit on my part, the greatest of Thy gifts—the impression of Thy Wounds ; for which be praise, honour, glory, dominion, and thanksgiving to Thee for endless ages !

CHAPTER V.

Of the Wound of Divine Love ; and of the manner of bathing, anointing, and binding it up.

SEVEN years after, a little before Advent, by Thine ordinance, who art the Source of all good, I engaged a certain person to say this prayer every day for me before a crucifix, " O most loving Lord, by Thy pierced Heart, pierce her heart with the arrow of Thy love, so that nothing earthly may remain therein, and that it may be entirely filled with the strength of Thy Divinity." Being moved, as I believe, by these prayers, on the Sunday when they sang the Mass *Gaudete in Domino,** Thy infinite liberality having permitted me, by an excess of mercy, to approach the Communion of Thy adorable Body and Blood, Thou didst infuse a desire in me when I approached It, which broke forth in these words : " Lord, I am not worthy to receive the least of Thy gifts ; but I beseech Thee, by the merits and prayers of all here present, to pierce my heart with the arrow of Thy love." I soon perceived that my words had reached Thy Divine Heart, both by an interior effusion of grace, and by a remarkable prodigy which Thou didst show me in the image of Thy crucifixion.

After I had received the Sacrament of life, and had retired to the place where I pray, it seemed to me that I saw a ray of light like an arrow coming forth from the wound of the right side of the crucifix, which was in an elevated place, and it continued, as it were, to advance and retire for some time, sweetly attracting my cold affections. But my desire was not entirely satisfied with these things

* Introit for Third Sunday in Advent.

until the following Wednesday,* when, after the Mass, the faithful meditated on Thy adorable Incarnation and Annunciation, in which I joined, however imperfectly. And, behold,Thou camest suddenly before me, and didst imprint a wound in my heart, saying these words : " May the full tide of your affections flow hither, so that all your pleasure, your hope, your joy, your grief, your fear, and every other feeling may be sustained by My love !" And I immediately remembered that I had heard a wound should be bathed, anointed, and bandaged. But Thou didst not teach me then in what manner I should perform these things ; for Thou didst defer it, to discover it to me more clearly in the end by means of another person, who had accustomed the ears of her soul to discern far more exactly and delicately than I do the sweet murmurs of Thy love.

She advised me to reflect devoutly upon the love of Thy Heart when hanging on the cross, and to draw from this fountain the waters of true devotion, to wash away all my offences ; to take from the unction of mercy the oil of gratitude, which the sweetness of this inestimable love has produced as a remedy for all adversities, and to use this efficacious charity and the strength of this consummate love as a ligament of justification to unite all my thoughts, words, and works indissolubly and powerfully to Thee. May all the deprivation of those things which my malice and wickedness has caused be supplied through that love whose plenitude abides in Him who, being seated on Thy right hand, has become " bone of my bones, and flesh of my flesh !" As it is by Him, through the operation of the

* *Feria quartum.* The Annunciation is specially commemorated on the Wednesday in the third week in Advent. Formerly, feasts which fell on this day were transferred ; and in monasteries, the Abbot delivered a homily on the Gospel *Missus est.*

Holy Spirit, that Thou hast placed in me this noble virtue of compassion, humility, and reverence, to enable me to speak to Thee, it is also by Him that I present to Thee my complaint of the miseries I endure, which are so great in number, and which have caused me to offend Thy Divine goodness in so many ways by my thoughts, words, and actions, but principally by the bad use which I have made of the aforesaid graces, by my unfaithfulness, my negligence, and my irreverence. For if Thou hast given to one so unworthy even a thread of flax * as a remembrance of Thee, I should have been bound to respect it more than I have done all these favours.

Thou knowest, O my God, from whom nothing is hidden, that the reason why I have written these things, so much against my inclination, is, that I have profited so little by Thy liberality, that I cannot believe they were made known to me for myself alone, since thine eternal wisdom cannot be deceived. Grant, then, O Giver of gifts, who hast so freely and unreservedly bestowed them on me, that whoever reads these things may be touched with tenderness and compassion for Thee ; and, knowing that the zeal which Thou hast for the salvation of souls has induced Thee to leave such royal gems † so long in my defiled heart, they may praise, adore, and extol Thy mercy, saying with their lips, and with their hearts, " Praise, honour, glory, and benediction be to Thee, O God the Father, from whom all things proceed," thus to supply for my deficiencies. ‡

---

* " Filum de stupâ."
† " Tam regalem gemmam."
‡ The words, " *Hic distulit scribere usque in Octobrem,*" are at the end of chapter v. in the original, in italics.

CHAPTER VI.

Of the intimate union of the Infant Jesus with her heart.

O UNATTAINABLE height of surpassing excellence ! O profound abyss of inscrutable wisdom ! O immense extent of most desirable charity ! how powerfully and exuberantly are the most delicious torrents of Thy most sweet Divinity pouring themselves forth on me, vile worm that I am, crawling in my negligences and sins ; since it is permitted to me, even while wandering in exile, to speak, according to my poor capacity, of the ravishing sweetness and inconceivable delights by means of which those who unite themselves to God become one spirit with Him ; which blessedness is poured forth on me with such abundance, who am but a little dust. Since, after having permitted me to drink of this precious beverage, I am still privileged with the remembrance of it, I will use such words as I can to describe it.

It was on that most sacred night in which the sweet dew of Divine grace fell on all the world, and the heavens dropped sweetness, that my soul, exposed like a mystic fleece in the court of the monastery, having received in meditation this celestial rain, was prepared to assist at this Divine Birth, in which a Virgin brought forth a Son, true God and Man, even as a star produces its ray. In this night, I say, my soul beheld before it suddenly a delicate Child, but just born, in whom were concealed the greatest gifts of perfection. I imagined that I received this precious deposit in my bosom with the tenderest affection. As I possessed it within me, it seemed to me that all at once I was changed into the colour* of this Divine Infant, if we

* "In eumdem colorem."

may be permitted to call that colour which cannot be compared to anything visible.

Then I understood the meaning contained in those sweet and ineffable words : " God will (*erit*) be all in all " (1 Cor. xv. 28) ; and my soul, which was enriched by the presence of my Beloved, soon knew, by its transports of joy, that it possessed the presence of its Spouse.   Then it received these words with exceeding avidity, which were presented as a delicious beverage to satisfy the ardour of its thirst : " As I am the figure of the substance of God, My Father, in His Divinity, so also you shall be the figure of My substance in My Humanity, receiving in your deified soul the infusions of My Divinity, as the air receives the brightness of the solar rays, that these rays may penetrate you so intimately as to prepare you for the closest union with Me."

O most noble balsam of the Divinity, pouring Thyself out like an ocean of charity, shooting forth and budding eternally, diffusing Thyself until the end of time ! O invincible strength of the Hand of the most High, which causes so frail a vessel, and one which should be cast away in contempt, to receive within it so precious a liquor ! O evident testimony of the exuberance of Divine goodness, not to withdraw from me when I wandered in the devious ways of sin, but rather to unite me to itself as far as my misery would permit !

CHAPTER VII.

The Divinity is imprinted upon the soul of Gertrude as a seal upon wax.

THE day of the most holy Purification, as I was confined to bed after a severe illness, and as I was troubled in my mind about daybreak, fearing that my corporal infirmity would deprive me of the Divine visit with which I had been so often consoled,— on the same day the august media-trix, the Mother of God the true Mediator, consoled me by these words : "As you never remember to have endured more severe corporal sufferings than those caused by your illness, know also that you have never received from my Son more noble gifts than those which will now be given to you, and for which your sufferings have prepared you."

This consoled me exceedingly ; and having received the Food which gives life immediately after the Procession, I thought only of God and myself ; and I beheld my soul, under the similitude of wax softened by the fire, impressed like a seal upon the bosom of the Lord ; and immediately I beheld it surrounding and partly drawn into this treasure-house, where the ever-peaceful Trinity abides corporally in the plenitude of the Divinity, and resplendent with its glorious impression.

O ardent fire of my God, which contains, produces, and imprints those living ardours which attract the humid waters of my soul, and dry up the torrents of earthly delights, and afterwards soften my hard self-opinionated-ness, which time has hardened so exceedingly ! O con-suming fire, which even amid ardent flames imparts sweet-ness and peace to the soul ! in Thee, and in none other, do we receive this grace of being reformed to the image and likeness in which we were created. O burning furnace, in which we enjoy the true vision of peace, which tries and purifies the gold of the elect, and leads the soul to seek eagerly for its highest good, even Thyself, in Thy eternal truth.

CHAPTER VIII.

Of the admirable union of her soul with God.

ON the following Sunday, at the Mass *Esto mihi*,* Thou didst enkindle my spirit, and increase my desires to receive yet more noble gifts which Thou wert about to bestow on me ; especially by these two words, which moved my soul deeply, namely, the versicle of the first response : "*Benedicens*† *benedicam tibi*"—"With blessings I will bless thee," and the versicle of the ninth response : "*Tibi enim et semini tuo dabo universas regiones has*"—"To thee and to thy posterity I will give all these countries" (Gen. xxvi.). For then Thou didst show me what were these countries which Thy boundless liberality had promised. O blessed country, where blessings flow upon blessings ! O field of delights, whose least grain is capable of satisfying the hunger which any of the elect may have for those things which the human heart considers desirable, delightful, amiable, sweet, and joyful. While I attended to these things as well as I could, though not as well as I ought, the sweetness and charity of my Saviour and my God was made known to me ; not as an act of justice, for I was far from meriting such favours, but as an act of His ineffable mercy, fortifying me by an adoptive charity, and rendering my extreme vileness—all unworthy, miserable, and detestable as it is—capable of receiving a more supercelestial and superinestimable union with Him. But, my God, how have I merited this inestimable gift from Thy justice ? Surely it proceeds from this love, which observes no rule— this ardent love, which is not limited by reason, and which

* Introit of Mass for Quinquagesima Sunday.
† Response, i. Nocturn.

has inebriated Thee, my sweetest Lord, if I may dare say so—causing Thee, as if devoid of wisdom, to unite what is so dissimilar ; or, to speak more correctly, the tenderness of Thine essential goodness, and Thy nature, being inwardly moved by Thy sweetest charity (which causes Thee not only to love, but to be all love, and the torrent of which Thou hast turned towards the salvation of the human race), having inclined Thee to draw from the depths of misery the least of Thy creatures, deficient in all good, contemptible on account of her life and conduct, to elevate her to a share in Thy kingdom, or rather in Thy Divine Majesty, in order by this to confirm the confidence of all who are in the Church ; so that I have hope for all Christians, and can believe that there will not be even one who will abuse the gifts of God as I have done, or give such scandal to their neighbour.

But since we may understand the invisible things of God, in some measure, by those which are visible—as I have before remarked—I saw (to express as far as I can that which is inexpressible) that the part of His blessed Heart where the Lord received my soul on the Feast of the Purification, under the form of wax softened by the fire, was, as it were, dropping a sweat, which came forth with violence, even as if the substance of the wax was melted by the excessive heat hidden in the depth of this Heart. This sacred reservoir attracted these drops to itself with surprising force, powerfully and inexpressibly, and even so inconceivably, that one saw evidently that love, which could not be hindered from communicating itself, had an absolute power in this place, where it discovered secrets which were so great, so hidden, and so impenetrable.

O eternal solstice ! secure mansion, containing all that is desirable ! Paradise of unchanging delights, continual

fountain of inestimable pleasures, wherein there is eternal
spring-time, soothing by its sweet song, or rather by its
delicious and intellectual melodies, rejoicing by the odour
of its vivifying perfumes, inebriating by the soothing sweetness of its mystic liquors, and transforming by its secret
caresses !

O thrice blessed, thrice happy, and, if I may so speak,
a hundred times holy, is he who allows himself to be guided
by this grace ; and who, having clean hands, and a pure
heart, and spotless lips, merits to be thus united to and
incorporated with his God ! What does he not see and
hear and feel and taste ?   How can my stammering tongue
speak of it ?

For although the Divine mercy has made me experience
this by a particular favour, nevertheless the obstinacy of
my sins, and the thick covering of negligence with which
I am encompassed, hinders me from fully understanding
it.   For if all the science of men and angels were united
together, it would not be capable of making us understand,
even in the least degree, the sublime majesty of so high a
subject.

CHAPTER IX.

Of another admirable manner in which St. Gertrude was closely
united to God.

Soon after, during the fast * when I was confined to bed
for the second time by a severe sickness, and the other
sisters were occupied elsewhere, so that I was left alone one
morning, the Lord, who never abandons those who are deprived of human consolation, came to verify these words of

---

* Lent.

the prophet: "I am with him in tribulation" (Ps. xc.). He turned His right Side towards me, and there came forth from His blessed and inmost Heart a pure and solid stream, like crystal; and on His Breast there was a precious ornament, like a necklace, which seemed to alternate between gold and rose-colour. Then our Lord said to me : " This sickness which you suffer will sanctify your soul; so that each time you go forth from Me, like the stream which I have shown you, for the good of your neighbour, either in thought, word, or act, even then, as the purity of the crystal renders the colour of the gold and the rose more brilliant, so the coöperation of the precious gold of My Divinity, and the rose of the perfect patience of My Humanity, will render your works always agreeable to Me by the purity of your intention."

O greatness of this little bit of dust, which this celestial Lover has taken from the mire to encase in His jewels ! O excellence of this little flower, which the ray of the true Sun Himself has drawn from the marsh, to make it beautiful as Himself ! O happiness of this blessed and favoured soul, which the Lord of glory has esteemed so highly, that though He can create whatever He pleases, He attracts it so sweetly and beautifies it by uniting it to Himself ! This soul, I say, though it is adorned with His image and likeness, is, nevertheless, as far from Him as the creature from the Creator. Therefore is he blessed a thousand times who has received the grace to persevere in this state, to which, alas ! I fear I shall never attain, even for a single moment.

O gift surpassing all gifts, to be satisfied with the sweetness of the Divinity, and to be superabundantly inebriated with Divine charity in the cellar where it is reserved; so that our feet are no longer free to roam to any place where its Divine fragrance is not perceived : unless, indeed, they are led forth by charity, when they pour out on others the wealth of the Divine faithfulness, and enable them to partake of their surpassing sweetness.

I hope, my Lord and my God, that Thou, in Thy most benign love, wilt grant me this grace, which by Thine almighty power Thou canst impart to all Thine elect.   It is true Thine inscrutable wisdom alone knows how Thou canst do this, notwithstanding my unworthiness.   But I honour and I glorify Thy wise and merciful almightiness ; I glorify and magnify Thy almighty and all-merciful wisdom ; I praise and adore Thy wise and omnipotent mercy ; I bless and thank Thy omnipotent and wise kindness, O my God, because Thou hast bestowed on me graces so far beyond my deserts, notwithstanding all the obstacles I opposed to Thy bounty.

CHAPTER X.

How the Lord obliged her to write these things ; and how He illuminated her.

I CONSIDERED it so unsuitable for me to publish these writings, that my conscience would not consent to do so ; therefore I deferred doing it until the Feast of the Exaltation of the Holy Cross.*   On that day, having determined before Mass to apply myself to other occupations, the Lord conquered the repugnance of my reason by these words : " Be assured that you will not be released from the prison of the flesh until you have paid this debt which still binds you."   And as I reflected that I had already employed the

---

* September 14.   The words quoted in the following page are not in the present Office.

gifts of God for the advancement of my neighbour—if not by my writing, at least by my words—He brought forward these words which I had heard used at the preceding Matins : " If the Lord had willed to teach His doctrine only to those who were present, He would have taught by word only, not by writing. But now they are written for the salvation of many." He added further : " I desire your writings to be an indisputable evidence of My Divine goodness in these latter times, in which I purpose to do good to many."

These words having depressed me, I began to consider within myself how difficult and even impossible it would be to find thoughts and words capable of explaining these things to the human intellect without scandal. But the Lord delivered me from this pusillanimity by pouring out on my soul an abundant rain, the impetuous fall of which weighed me down like a young and tender plant—vile creature that I am !—instead of watering me gently, so as to make me increase in perfection ; and I could find no profit from it, except from some weighty words, the sense of which I was unable perfectly to penetrate. Therefore, finding myself still more depressed, I inquired what would be the advantage of these writings ; and Thy goodness, my God, solaced my trouble with Thy usual sweetness, refreshing my soul by this reply : " Since this deluge appears useless to you, behold, I will now approach you to My Divine Heart, that your words may be gentle and sweet, according to the capabilities of your mind." Which promise, my Lord and my God, Thou didst most faithfully fulfil. And for four days, at a convenient hour each morning, Thou didst suggest with so much clearness and sweetness what I composed, that I have been able to write it without difficulty and without reflection, even as if I had learned it by heart long before ; with this limitation, that when I had written a sufficient quantity each day, it has not been possible for me, although I applied my whole mind to it, to find a single word to express the things which on the following day I could write freely : thus instructing and refraining my impetuosity, as the Scripture teaches :* " Let none so apply himself to action as to omit contemplation."   Thus art Thou jealous for my welfare ; and whilst Thou givest me leisure to enjoy the embraces of Rachel, Thou dost not permit me to be deprived of the glorious fruitfulness of Lia.   May Thy wise love deign to accomplish in me these two things !

CHAPTER XI.

She receives the gift of tears, and is warned of the snares which the demon has laid for her.

SINCE, Lord, Thou hast so often diversified the salutary taste of Thy presence, and that Thou hast prevented my baseness so assiduously with the sweetness of Thy benedictions, especially during the first three years, and more especially when I was admitted to the participation of Thy adorable Body and Blood,—since I can make no return to Thee for this, even by a single thanksgiving for a thousand favours,— I remit the thanksgivings which I owe to that eternal, infinite, and incommunicable gratitude by which, O ever-peaceful and resplendent Trinity, Thou dost fully satisfy all our debts of Thyself, by Thyself, and in Thyself. And I, who am but dust, offer my thanksgivings to Thee, through Him who stands by Thee, clothed with my sub-

---

* " Sicut Scriptura docet."   The exact words are not in Scripture.

stance, through the operation of the Holy Spirit, for all the benefits which I have received from Thee, but principally, for having instructed my ignorance by so evident a sign, that Thou hast shown me clearly how I corrupt the purity of Thy gifts.

On one occasion, when I assisted at a Mass at which I was to communicate, I perceived that Thou wert present, by an admirable condescension, and that Thou didst use this similitude to instruct me, by appearing as if parched with thirst, and desiring that I should give Thee to drink ; and while I was troubled thereat, and could not even force a tear from my eyes, I beheld Thee presenting me with a golden cup with Thine own Hand. When I took it, my heart immediately melted into a torrent of fervent tears. Then I saw a certain despicable creature at my right hand, who was secretly putting something bitter and venomous into it, and inciting me to put it in this cup. But as this was followed by an instant motion of vain-glory, I easily understood that it was a stratagem of that ancient enemy, who turns against us all his rage when he sees us enriched with Thy gifts.

But thanks be to Thy faithfulness, my God, thanks to Thy protection, who art one and true God, Trinity in Unity, Unity in Trinity, who permittest not that we should be tempted beyond our strength, although Thou sometimes permittest us to be tempted for our advancement in virtue ; and when Thou seest that we confide in Thee, Thou undertakest our cause, and, with boundless generosity, dost win the victory for us, and then allow us the merit of it, if only we will to do right : and Thou dost procure us this advantage to increase our merit, that, as Thou dost not permit our enemy to interfere with our free will, so neither dost Thou interfere with it Thyself in any way.

Thou didst teach me also, on another occasion, that to yield easily to the enemy makes him insolent in attacking us again on the same subject; therefore Thy justice requires that Thou shouldst sometimes conceal the greatness of Thy mercy in pardoning our negligence, because we resist evil more certainly, more usefully, more efficaciously, and more happily, when we resist it with all our might.

CHAPTER XII.

With how much goodness God bears our faults.

I RENDER Thee thanks also for another revelation, which was no less advantageous and acceptable to me, by which I was shown with what benign patience Thou dost bear our defects, that, by correcting us thus, Thou mightest insure our happiness. For one evening, having allowed myself to give way to anger, and on the following morning, before break of day, finding myself disposed to pray, Thou didst present Thyself to me under so strange a form, that it seemed to me on beholding Thee that Thou wert not only deprived of all kind of good, but even of strength. Then, my conscience being touched for my past fault, I began to reflect with grief how improper a thing it had been for me to trouble the Supreme Author of peace and purity by my ill-regulated passion. I thought it would have been better that Thou shouldst have been absent from me when I failed to repel Thine enemy, while he solicited me to do that which was so contrary to Thy will.

Thou didst apply this to me: "Even as a poor invalid who has been brought out to enjoy the sunshine by the assistance of others, with much difficulty, when he sees a storm coming on, has no other consolation than the hope of soon seeing fine weather again,—thus, under the influence of your love, I prefer dwelling with you in all the tempests of vice, hoping to behold the calm of your amendment, and to see you enter the port of humility."

Since my tongue is too feeble to explain the abundance of the graces which thou didst pour forth on me during the three entire days in which this apparition lasted, permit, O my God, that my heart may supply for its weakness, and teach me how to render a thanksgiving of gratitude for the depth of the humility to which Thy love then abased itself for this charity, so amazing and so tender, which Thou hast for us.

CHAPTER XIII.

Of the necessity of exact vigilance over the senses and affections.

I CONFESS also before Thy goodness, God of mercy, that Thou didst use another means to animate my languor ; and though at first Thou didst commence Thy work by the intervention of a third person, Thou didst will nevertheless to consummate it Thyself with mercy and condescension. This person proposed to my consideration the Gospel which relates that after Thy Birth Thou wert found by shepherds ; she added, that Thou hadst made known to her that if I would truly find Thee, I must watch over my senses, as the shepherds over their flocks. I had some difficulty in believing this, and there seemed to me but little reason in it, knowing that Thou hadst given other capabilities to my soul than those of serving Thee as a hired shepherd would his master ; so that, from morning until evening, I was full of discouragement. After Compline, as I was in the place where I pray, Thou didst solace my grief by this comparison ; " If a bride prepare food sometimes for her bridegroom's falcons,* she will not on this account be deprived of his caresses ; so, if I occupied myself for love of Thee in watching over my affections and senses, I should not on this account be deprived of the sweetness of Thy graces."

Thou didst give me for this purpose the spirit of fear, under the figure of a green rod, in order that, remaining always with Thee, and never leaving the shelter of Thine embraces even for a single moment, I might without danger extend my care to all the windings and labyrinths in which human affection so often loses itself. Thou didst add, that when anything presented itself to my mind which sought to turn my thoughts to the right, as to joy or hope ; to the left, as to fear, grief, or anger,—that I should threaten them with the rod of fear ; and that afterwards, by the restraining of my senses, I should immolate this affection, like a new-born lamb, by the fire of my heart, and offer it to Thee as a feast.

But, alas ! how many times when the opportunity has come have I not snatched, as if from Thy very lips, by a malicious lightness, or by a passionate word or action, that which I had given Thee, and presented it to Thine enemy ! and even then Thou hast looked on me with tenderness and sweetness, as if Thou hadst not perceived my infidelity; and thereby Thou hast often excited transports of sweetness in my soul, which have served to make me correct and watch over myself far more than the threats and fear of Thine anger.

---

* *Accipitribus ;* lit. birds of prey.

CHAPTER XIV.

Different exercises by which the soul is purified.

THE Sunday before Lent, while they chanted the *Esto mihi*,* Thou didst make me understand by the words of this introit, O only Object of my love, that, being wearied by the persecutions and outrages which so many persons inflict on Thee, Thou didst ask for my heart, that Thou mightest repose therein. Therefore, each time that I entered therein during these three days, Thou didst appear to me as if lying down there like a person exhausted by extreme languor, and I could find no greater solace of Thy woe during this period than to pray, keep silence, and perform other exercises of mortification in Thine honour for the conversion of worldly persons.

Thy grace makes me know further, by frequent revelations, that the soul, dwelling in the body of frail humanity, is darkened in the same manner as a person who stands in a narrow space, and is surrounded on all sides by a vapour exhaling from a cooking vessel. And when the body is afflicted by any evil, the part which suffers is to the soul as a beam from the sun which enlightens the air, and from which it receives marvellous clearness; therefore the heavier one's sufferings are, the purer is the light the soul receives. But afflictions and trials of the heart in humility, patience, and other virtues impart the greatest lustre to the soul, as they touch it more keenly, efficaciously, and intimately; works of charity, above all, give it an admirable serenity and brightness.

Thanks be to Thee, O Lover of men, that Thou hast sometimes led me by this means to patience! But, alas!

---

* Introit for Quinquagesima.

—and a thousand times, alas !—how seldom have I listened
to Thy counsels, or rather, how seldom have I done what
I ought to have done ! O Lord, Thou knowest the grief,
the shame, and the dejection of my soul for this ; Thou
knowest the desire of my heart to apply to Thee for my
deficiencies.

On another occasion, when I was about to communicate
at Mass, being filled abundantly with Thy Spirit, and seeking within myself what I could do in return for so great a
favour, Thou didst propose to me, as a Master full of wisdom, these words of the Apostle : " I wish myself to be an
anathema for my brethren" (Rom. ix.).   And although Thou
hadst taught me before that the soul had its abode in the
heart, Thou didst make me know also that it resided in the
brain ; and this truth, of which I had been ignorant until
then, was confirmed to me afterwards by a testimony of
Scripture.   Thou didst teach me also, that the great perfection of a soul consists in relinquishing the pleasure which
it finds in the affections, in order to occupy itself, for the
love of Thee, in watching over its exterior senses, and in
labouring in works of charity for the salvation of its neighbour.

CHAPTER XV.

How agreeable works of charity are to God ; and also meditations
on holy things.

The day of Thine adorable Nativity, I took Thee from the
crib, wrapped in swathing-clothes, like a little infant newly
born, and placed Thee in my heart, that I might make a
bouquet of myrrh of all thy infant sufferings and incom-
modities, to place it in my breast, that I might drink there-

from a libation * of Divine sweetness. But as I considered this the greatest favour Thou couldest bestow on me, Thou, who, when we least expect it, accompaniest Thy first graces by others yet more precious, didst will to diversify the abundance of Thy graces in this manner.

For on the same day, the following year, as the Mass *Dominus dixit* † was said, I received Thee, coming forth from the virginal womb of Thy Mother as a feeble and delicate Infant, and carried Thee for some time in my arms. It seemed to me that the compassion which I had shown before the Feast, by some special prayers for a person in affliction, had obtained this favour for me ; but, alas ! after having obtained it, I did not receive it with the devotion I ought. I know not if it were an act of Thy justice, or a chastisement of my negligence ; I hope, nevertheless, that Thy justice, by the intermission of Thy mercy has so ordered it, to make me know more clearly the greatness of my unworthiness, and to make me less negligent in putting away idle thoughts. But it is for Thee, O Lord, to say to which of these causes I ought to refer this effect.

Nevertheless, as I gathered up all my strength to make a last effort to gain Thee by my loving caresses, I perceived that all this was of no avail, until I commenced praying for sinners, for the souls in purgatory, or for those who were in any affliction, when I knew that I was heard ; but still more one evening, when I formed the resolution of commencing the prayers which I say for the deceased, offering them for those most beloved by Thee, with the

---

* *Botrus*, a Hebrew word, translated "the grape," Mich. vii. 1 ; in Greek βοτρυς ; and hence Latinised *botrus* or *botrys*. Used also tropically for a draught or medicament.

† Introit, First or Midnight Mass at Christmas.

Collect, *Omnipotens, sempiterne Deus, cui nunquam sine spe,** instead of commencing, as I had been accustomed to do, by praying for those related to me, with the Collect, *Deus, qui nos patrem et matrem ;* and it seemed to me that this change was very pleasing to Thee.

I believe also that it pleased Thee much, when I chanted as loud as I could, and at each note fixed my intention on Thee, as one fixes his eye on his book, who has not yet learned the chant perfectly. Still I know that I have been negligent in this and in other things which concern Thy glory ; and I confess it to Thee, Father of mercy, asking pardon through the bitter Passion of Thy blameless Son Jesus Christ, in whom Thou didst declare Thyself well pleased, saying : "This is My beloved Son, in whom I am well pleased " (St Matt. xvii.) ; through Him I ask the grace of amendment and atonement for my negligences.

CHAPTER XVI.

Of the inconceivable tenderness which the most glorious Virgin has for us.

On the Feast of the Purification, at the Procession, when Thou, our Salvation and Redemption, wert borne as an offering to the Temple, at the Antiphon, *Cum inducerent,*†

---

* Not in present office : *Deus qui*— Collect, Mass for Deceased Parents.

† "When His parents brought in the Child Jesus," &c., Versicle at Procession, Feast of the Purification. This procession is very ancient. It is mentioned by Pope Gelasius I. St. Bernard's sermons on such occasions are full of singular unction and sweetness. He says : "The procession was first made by the Virgin Mother, Simeon, and Anna, to be afterwards performed in all places and by every nation. The concurrence of many in procession symbolises our union

Thy Virgin Mother told me to give her her Child, the blessed Fruit of her womb; and she demanded Thee again from me with a severe countenance, as if she was not pleased with my care of Thee, who art the honour and joy of her spotless virginity.

Then, remembering the grace which she had received from Thee of being the hope of the despairing and the reconciler of sinners, I exclaimed : " O Mother of mercy ! was not the Fount of forgiveness given to thee as thy Son, that thou mightest obtain all grace for us from Him, and that the multitude of our sins and our deficiencies might be covered by thy abundant charity ?" Then she looked on me once more with a serene and loving countenance, so that I might know that if my fault obliged her to appear severe to me, she was, nevertheless, full of the most con-summate tenderness, and penetrated to her inmost heart with the most sweet and Divine charity. I soon beheld the tokens of it, since a few words removed her anger, and her sweetness shone forth resplendently. May this abundant tenderness of Thy Mother intercede with Thee, and obtain pardon for my faults !

And I know, by a testimony clearer than light itself, that no obstacle could have arrested the torrent of Thy sweetness, when, on the Feast of Thy Nativity, the preceding year, Thou didst grant me a yet greater favour, though in a similar manner, as if I had merited it by the fervour of my zeal the year before, when, far from meriting a new grace, I was justly worthy of chastisement for having lost the first.

For when these words of the Gospel were read, " *Peperit*

---

and charity ; our walking, advancement in virtue ; the lights we carry, Christ, the true Light."

filium suum primogenitum," Thy spotless Mother presented Thee to me with her pure hands. And Thou, O amiable Infant, didst endeavour to embrace me with all Thy might ; I, though utterly unworthy, received Thee, and Thou didst put Thy little arms round my neck, exhaling on me from Thy mouth a breath so full of sweetness, that I was nourished and abundantly satisfied therewith. For this, O Lord my God, may my soul and all that is within me adore and bless Thy Holy Name ! And when Thy Blessed Mother sought to wrap Thee in Thy swathing-clothes, I desired to be wrapped up in them also, for fear of losing the company of One whose smiles and favours exceed the sweetness of honey and the honeycomb. Thou wert then clothed in the fairest robe of innocence, and cinctured with the golden cincture of love ; and I felt that if I wished to be so clothed and so cinctured, I should seek to have more purity of heart, and to abound more in love.

CHAPTER XVII.

Of the garments with which we should clothe Jesus and His Mother.

I GIVE Thee thanks, Creator of the firmament, Fashioner of its celestial lights and of the flowers of spring, because, although Thou needest not my goods, Thou, for my instruction, didst order me to clothe Thee with the garments of an infant on the day of Thy Purification, before Thou

---

* " She brought forth her first-born Son," &c. (Luke ii.), Gospel for Midnight Mass. What follows is omitted in the French translation.

wert carried into the Temple. And this is the manner in which Thou dost desire me to draw from the hidden treasures of Thy love—namely, to extol with all my powers the innocence of Thy Holy Humanity, but with such faithfulness and devotion, that if I could receive in my own person all the glory due to Thy blessed innocence, I would, nevertheless, freely renounce it, in order to enhance thereby the praise of Thy innocence. It seemed to me that this pure intention clothed Thee with a White robe, such as infants wear: Thou whose omnipotence " calleth those things that are not as those that are " (Rom. iv. 17).

So also, when I endeavoured to penetrate devoutly into the abyss of Thy humility, I saw thee clothed in a green tunic, as a sign that Thy grace is ever flourishing, and that it never withers in the valley of humility. Then contemplating the fire of Thy love, which has made Thee produce all which Thou hast produced, I beheld Thee clothed in purple, to indicate that charity is truly a royal mantle, without which none can enter into the kingdom of heaven.

As I admired the same virtues in Thy glorious Mother, she appeared to me clothed in the same manner ; and as this Blessed Virgin flourishes like a rose without thorns, and a lily without spot, being adorned with the flowers of all virtues, I besought this most benign Mother to intercede continually with Thee for our necessities.

CHAPTER XVIII.

How God bears with our defects—Instruction on humility.

ONE day, after I had washed my hands, and was standing round the table with the community, perplexed in mind, considering the brightness of the sun, which was in its full strength, I said within myself: " If the Lord, who has created the sun, and whose beauty is said to be the admiration of the sun and moon,—if He, who is a consuming fire, is as truly in me as He shows Himself frequently before me, how is it possible that my heart continues like ice, and that I lead so evil a life ? "

Then Thou, whose words, though always sweet, were now much sweeter, and therefore the more necessary for my heart in its state of agitation,—Thou, I say, didst reply thus to me : " In what should My omnipotence be extolled, if I could not contain Myself within Myself wherever I am, so that I am only felt or seen as is most suitable for the time, place, and person ?   For since the creation of heaven and earth I have worked for the redemption of all, more by the wisdom of My benignity than by the power of My majesty. And this benignity of wisdom shines most in My tolerance towards the imperfect, leading them, even by their own free will, into the way of perfection."   Seeing also, on a certain feast-day, that many who had recommended themselves to my prayers were going to Communion, and that I was deprived of It by sickness—or rather, prevented on account of my unworthiness—and reflecting in my mind on the numerous benefits I had received from God, I began to fear the wind of vain-glory, which might dry up the waters of Divine grace ; and I desired to have some reflection in my mind that might prevent its recurrence.   Then Thy paternal goodness instructed me thus : that I should consider Thy affection towards me under the similitude of a father of a family, who, being delighted at seeing so many beautiful children receiving admiration from his neighbours and servants, had, amongst others, a little one who was not so beautiful as his companions, whom he, nevertheless, often took in his bosom, moved by paternal tenderness, and consoled him by gentle words and kind gifts ; and Thou didst add, that if I had this humble esteem of myself, so as to believe myself the most imperfect of all, the torrents of Thy celestial sweetness would never cease to flow into my soul.

I give thanks to Thee, most loving God, Lover of men, by the merit of the reciprocal gratitude of the adorable Trinity, for this and for many other salutary instructions by which Thou hast instructed my ignorance so many times as the best of masters,—I offer my sighs to Thee through the bitter Passion of Jesus Christ Thy Son ; I offer to Thee His pains and tears and dolors, in expiation of all the negligences by which I have so often stifled the Spirit of God in my heart. I beseech Thee, in union with the efficacious prayer of this Thy beloved Son, and by the grace of the Holy Ghost, to amend my life, and to supply for my deficiencies. This I beseech Thee to grant by that love which arrested Thine anger when Thy only Son, the object of Thy complacence, was reputed a criminal.

CHAPTER XIX.

How God is pleased to condescend to His creatures ; and what glory
God derives thence from the blessed.

I give thanks to Thy loving mercy and to Thy merciful love, most loving Lord, for the revelation by which Thy

goodness satisfied my weak and wavering soul when I so
ardently desired to be released from the chains of the flesh :
not that I might suffer less, but that I might release Thy
goodness from the debt which Thy exceeding love has undertaken for my salvation ; although Thy Divine omnipotence
and eternal wisdom were not obliged to grant me this
favour,—but Thou didst bestow it on my unworthiness
and ingratitude of Thy superabounding liberality.

When, therefore, I desired to be dissolved, Thou, my
God, who art the honour and glory of heaven, didst appear
to me, descending from the royal throne of Thy majesty,
and approaching to sinners by a most obliging and favourable condescension ; and then certain streams of precious
liquor seemed to flow through heaven, before which all the
saints prostrated themselves in thanksgiving ; and having
satisfied their thirst with joy in this torrent of delights,
broke forth in canticles of praise for all Thy mercy towards
sinners.   Whilst these things happened I heard these words :
" Consider how agreeable this concert of praise is, not only
to My ears, but even to My most loving Heart ; and beware
for the future how you desire so importunately to be separated from the body, merely for the sake of being delivered
from the flesh, in which I pour forth so freely the gifts of
My grace ; for the more unworthy they are to whom I
condescend, the more I merit to be glorified for it by all
creatures."

As thou didst give this consolation at the moment
when I approached Thy life-giving Sacrament, as soon as
I had recollected myself and formed my intention, as I
was bound to do, Thou didst make known to me further
in what manner, and with what intention, each one should
approach to unite themselves to Thy sacred Body and
Blood ; so that, even if this Sacrament served for our con-

demnation, were it possible, the love of Thy love and of
Thy glory would cause us to think nothing of this, provided
that thereby Thy mercy shone forth still more in not refusing to give Thyself to those who are so utterly unworthy.
Then I inquired concerning those who, from a consciousness
of their unworthiness, abstain from Communion, fearing
to profane by a presumptuous irreverence the sanctity of
this Sacrament ; and I received this blessed answer from
Thee : " He who communicates from a pure desire of My
glory, as I have said, can never communicate with irreverence." For which may eternal praise and glory be given
to Thee for endless ages !

CHAPTER XX.

Of some considerable privileges which God granted to this virgin, and
of the grace which He promised to her clients.

MAY my heart and my soul, with all the substance of my
flesh, all my senses, and all the powers of my body and my
mind, with all creatures, praise Thee and give Thee thanks,
O sweetest Lord, faithful Lover of mankind, for Thy signal
mercy ; which has not only dissimulated the utterly unworthy preparation with which I have not feared to
approach the supercelestial banquet of Thy most sacred
Body and Blood, but has added this gift to me, the most
utterly vile and perfectly useless of Thy creatures.   First,
of having been assured by Thy grace that all who desire
to approach this Sacrament, and who are restrained by fear
from a timid conscience, who come to me, who am the least
of Thy servants, led by humility, to seek consolation,—
that Thy exceeding mercy will judge them worthy, in re-

compense for this humility, to receive this Sacrament with fruit to eternal life. Thou hast also added, that Thou wilt not permit any one, whom thy justice deems unworthy, to abase themselves to ask counsel of me, O Supreme Ruler, "who, though Thou dwellest on high, regardest the humble" (Ps. cxii.).

What prompted Thy mercy, when Thou sawest me approach so often unworthily, to suspend Thy judgment, and not to inflict on me the punishment I deserve? Thou willest to make others worthy by the virtue of humility; and though Thou couldst do so more effectually without my assistance, Thy love, looking upon my misery, made Thee effect this through me; so that thus I may be a sharer in the merits of those who, through my admonitions, enjoy the fruits of salvation.

But, alas! this is not the only remedy which my misery requires; nor will one remedy satisfy Thy mercy, O most kind Lord! For Thou didst assure my unworthiness that Thou wouldst consider whoever should expose their defects to me, with a contrite and humble heart, guilty or innocent, as I had declared them more or less guilty; and from henceforward Thy grace would so sustain them that They should never again be in such danger from their faults as they had been previously. And thus Thou hast relieved my indigence, which is so great that I have never even for a single day corrected myself as I ought, and yet Thou dost permit me to participate in the victories of others, when Thou, my good God, dost condescend to make use of me, as a most unworthy instrument, to give the grace of victory to Thine other more deserving friends through my words.

Thirdly. The abundant liberality of Thy grace has enriched my poverty of merit by this assurance,—that when-

ever I promise a favour to any one, or the pardon of any
fault, through confidence in Thy mercy, Thy benign love
will ratify my words, and execute my promise as faithfully
as if it had been confirmed by an oath of the Eternal Truth.
Thou didst add further, that if any one found that the
salutary effects of my promises were deferred, they should
continually remind Thee that I had promised this grace
from Thee. Thus dost Thou provide for my salvation
according to the words of the Gospel : " With what measure
you mete, it shall be measured to you again " (Matt. vii. 2).
And as I, alas ! continually fall into the greatest faults, Thou
desirest by this means to remit the punishment I deserve.

Fourthly. To solace my miseries, Thou hast assured me,
amongst other things, that whosoever recommend themselves humbly and devoutly to my prayers will certainly
obtain all the fruit which they hoped to obtain by the
intercession of any other person : in which Thou hast provided for my negligence, which prevents me from satisfying,
not only for the prayers which are made gratuitously for
the Church, but also for those of obligation ; and thou hast
found the means of applying the fruit of them to me, according to the words of David : " My prayers shall be
turned into my bosom " (Ps. xxxiv.) ; making me participate
in the merits of Thine elect, who shall ask these graces of
Thee through my intermission, although I am utterly unworthy of it, and granting me a share in them to supply for
my indigence.

Fifthly. Thou hast further promoted my salvation by
conferring these special favours on me, that whosoever,
with a good will, a right intention, and a humble confidence, shall come to speak to me upon their spiritual advancement, should never leave me without being edified or
receiving spiritual consolation. In this also thou hast

most suitably supplied for my indigence ; for, alas ! I have
wasted the talent Thou didst so liberally bestow on me by
my useless words ; but now I may gain some merit by
what I confide to others.

Sixthly. Thy liberality, O Lord, has bestowed on me
this gift, more necessary than all,—certifying to me, that
whoever, in their charity, will either pray for me—the
vilest of God's creatures—or perform any good works,
either for the amendment of my life,—or the forgiveness of
the sins of my youth, or the correction of my iniquity and
malice, shall receive this reward from Thy abundant
liberality—namely, that they shall not die until, by Thy
grace, their lives have become pleasing to Thee ; and that
Thou wilt dwell in their souls by a special friendship and
intimacy.

And this Thou hast granted of Thy paternal tenderness,
to assist my extreme indigence ; as thou knowest how
many and how great corrections are needed for my innu-
merable sins and negligences. Thus, as Thy loving mercy
will not permit me to perish, and, on the contrary, by
reason of Thy justice, will not permit me to be saved with
all my imperfections, Thou hast provided for me by means
of the gains and merits of others.

Thou hast added to all these favours, my kind God, by
an abundant liberality,—that if any one, after my death,
considering with how much familiarity Thou didst communicate with my unworthiness while in this life, should recommend themselves humbly to my prayers, Thou wouldst
hear them as willingly as if they invoked the intercession
of any other person, provided that they had the intention
of repairing their faults and negligences, and that they
humbly and devoutly thanked Thee for five special benefits
which Thou didst grant me.

First. For the love by which Thou didst freely choose me from all eternity, and which I declare to be the greatest of all the benefits which Thou hast bestowed on me ; for as Thou wert not ignorant of, or rather didst foresee, the corrupt life which I should lead, the excess of my ingratitude, and how I should abuse Thy gifts, so that I deserve to have been born a pagan, and not an enlightened human being,—Thy mercy, which infinitely exceeds our crimes, has chosen me, in preference to many other Christians, to bear the holy character of a religious.

Secondly. Because Thou hast drawn me blessedly to Thee ; and I acknowledge it to be an effect of the clemency and charity which is natural to Thee, who hast won, by the attractions of Thy caresses, this rebellious and stubborn heart, which deserves to be loaded with fetters and chains ; and it has seemed as if Thou hadst found in me the faithful companion of Thy love, and that Thy greatest pleasure was to be united to me.

Thirdly. Because Thou hast united me so intimately to Thee ; and I declare, as I am bound, that I am indebted for this only to Thy signal liberality, as if the number of the just was not great enough to receive the immense abundance of Thy mercies ; not that I had better dispositions than others, but, on the contrary, that Thy charity might be the more signalised in me thereby.

Fourthly. That Thou hast taken pleasure and delight in dwelling in my soul ; and this, if I may so speak, proceeds from the ardour of Thy love, which has deigned to testify, even by words, that it is the joy of Thy all-powerful wisdom to stoop to one so dissimilar to Thee, and so utterly ungrateful.

Fifthly. That it has pleased Thee to accomplish Thy work happily in me ; and it is a favour which I have hoped with humble confidence from the tenderness of Thy most benign charity, and for which I adore Thee with gratitude; declaring, O sovereign, true, and only treasure of my soul, that I have in no way contributed to it by my merits, but that it is a pure gift of Thy liberality.

All these benefits coming from Thine immense charity, and being so far above my nothingness, I am unable to give thanks for them worthily; but Thou hast further assisted my misery, in exciting others, by the most condescending promises, to render thanksgivings to Thee, the merit of which may supply my deficiencies. For which may all creatures in heaven, on earth, and under the earth, glorify Thee and thank Thee continually!

CHAPTER XXI.

Thanksgivings for the confirmation of the aforesaid favours.

AMONGST other things, it has pleased Thee, my Lord, in the abundance of Thine inestimable charity, to ratify and confirm these favours. On a certain day, as I meditated on and compared Thy mercy and my malice, I was filled with extreme joy, even to such presumption, as to complain that Thou hadst not assured me of these favours by solemn contract; * when Thy sweet and affable charity agreed to satisfy my objection, saying to me: "Do not complain of this; approach and receive the confirmation of My promises." And immediately Thou didst open to me, with both hands, the ark of Thy Divine love and infallible truth, namely, Thy Deified Heart; and Thou didst command me

* " Manu ad manum non firmasse."

to extend my hand,—I, perverse creature as I am, seeking, like the Jews, for a sign ; and then, drawing back Thy Sacred Heart, with my hand enclosed therein, Thou saidst : " Behold, I promise to preserve inviolate the gifts which I have bestowed on thee ; however, if I suspend their effects for a time, by way of dispensation, I oblige Myself, by the omnipotence, wisdom, and love of the Trinity, in which I live and reign true God through all ages, to recompense thee afterwards threefold."

After these most sweet words, as I withdrew my hand, I perceived thereon seven golden circlets, in the form of rings,* one on each finger, and three on the signet finger ; which indicated that the seven privileges were confirmed to me, as I had asked. Then Thy loving mercy added these words : " Each time that you acknowledge your unworthiness of My gifts, and confide fully in My mercy, each time you acquit yourself of the debts you owe Me for these benefits."

Oh, how ingenious is Thy Paternity in providing for Thy children, notwithstanding their vile degeneracy, and the manner in which they have squandered Thy substance, falling from innocence, and depriving Thee of Thy rightful worship ! yet hast Thou deigned to accept as an offering the reflection I make on my miseries. Do Thou, the Giver of gifts, the Source of all good, without whom nothing is good and nothing is holy,—do Thou, for Thy glory and the salvation of my soul, grant me grace to know my un-

---

* This favour is commemorated by the Church in her Office, 3d Ant. at Lauds, " Annulis septem," &c. ; " My Lord Jesus has espoused me to Him with seven rings, and crowned me as a bride." A similar Antiphon may be found in the Office of St. Agnes, V. M. ; " My Lord Jesus Christ hath espoused me with His ring," &c. (Vespers, 3d Ant.)

worthiness of all Thy gifts, whether great or little, whether
exterior or interior, and in all things to have the most
perfect confidence in Thy mercy.

CHAPTER XXII.

How St. Gertrude was admitted to the vision of God—Of the kiss
of peace, and other similar favours.

I SHOULD be unjust, in recalling the gratuitous gifts which
I have received from Thy charitable clemency, if I ungrate-
fully passed over what was granted to my unworthiness, by
Thy most loving clemency, during a certain Lent.   For on
the second Sunday, as they sang at Mass before the procession, the response which commences *Vidi Dominum
facie ad faciem,** a marvellous and inestimable coruscation
illuminated my soul with the light of Divine revelation,
and it appeared to me that my face was pressed to another
face, as St. Bernard says : " Not a form, but forming ; not
attracting the bodily eye, but rejoicing the heart ; giving
freely gifts of love, not merely in appearance but in
reality."

In this most enchanting vision, Thine eyes, bright as
the solar rays, appeared opposite to mine, and Thou alone
knowest how Thou, my dearest Lord, affected not only my
soul, but even my body and all my strength.   Grant, therefore, that as long as I live I may prove myself Thy humble
and devoted servant.

---

* Loquebar Christus : " Christ spoke to His beloved Gertrude face
to face, as a man speaks in secret to his friend " (i. Ant. ii. Vespers).
See also x. Response, 3 Nocturn., Benedictine Breviary, Office for
second Sunday in Lent.

But even as the rose is more beautiful and gives forth a sweeter fragrance in the spring, when it flourishes, than in the winter, when it is dried up, and, like the remembrance of a joy that is past, rekindles in us some pleasure to think of it, so I desire, by some comparison, to declare what I felt in this most joyful vision, to extol Thy love, so that if those who read this receive similar or even greater favours, they may thereby be excited to acts of thanksgiving; and I myself, by recalling them frequently, will inflame the negligence of my gratitude beneath the rays of this burning-glass. When Thou didst display Thy most adorable Face,— the source of all blessedness, as I have said, embracing me, unworthy,—a light of inestimable sweetness passed through Thy Deified eyes into mine, passing through my inmost being, operating in all my members with admirable power and sweetness : first, it appeared as if the marrow were taken from my bones ; then, my flesh and bones appeared annihilated ; so much so, that it seemed as if my substance no longer had any consciousness save of that Divine splendour, which shone in so inexplicable and delightful a manner that it was the source of the most inestimable pleasure and joy to my soul.

Oh, what shall I say further of this most sweet vision, if I may so term it? For all the eloquence in the world, if employed daily to persuade me, could never convince me that I should behold Thee more clearly even in glory, O my God, the only salvation of my soul, if Thou hadst not taught me by experience. I will dare to say that if anything, human or Divine, can exceed the blessedness of Thy embrace in this vision, as I consider, I may truly say that, unless thy Divine virtue possessed that person, the soul would never remain in the body after a momentary taste of this blessedness.

I render thanks to Thee, through the union of mutual love which reigns in the adorable Trinity, for what I have so often experienced, and that Thou hast deigned to favour me with Thy caresses ; so that while I sat meditating, or reading the Canonical Hours, or saying the Office of the Dead, Thou hast often, during a single Psalm, embraced my soul many times with a kiss, which far surpasses the most fragrant perfumes or the sweetest honey ; and I have often observed Thou didst look on me favourably in the condescending caresses Thou didst give to my soul. But though all these things were filled with an extreme sweetness, I declare, nevertheless, that nothing touched me so much as this majestic look of which I have spoken. For this, and for all the other favours, whose value Thou alone knowest, mayest Thou rejoice for ever in that ineffable sweetness surpassing all comprehension, which the Divine Persons communicate mutually to each other in the bosom of the Divinity !

May a like thanksgiving—or, if possible, one even greater—be rendered to Thee, for an extraordinary favour Thou hast granted me, of which Thou alone knowest, and which is so great, that I can neither fully express it by my feeble words, nor altogether pass it over in silence ; and, lest I should lose the remembrance of it through my frailty, I write this to recall it to my memory and to excite my gratitude. But, my God, do not allow the meanest of Thy servants to be guilty of such an excess of madness as voluntarily to forget, even for a single instant, the gratitude which she is bound to have for the visits with which Thou hast honoured her of Thy pure and gratuitous liberality, and which she has received for so many years without meriting them. For, although I am the most unworthy of all creatures, I declare, nevertheless, that these visits with which Thou hast favoured me far surpass anything that could be merited during this life.   I, therefore, implore Thy sweetest mercy to preserve this gift to me for Thy glory, with the same goodness with which Thou hast so liberally bestowed it, without any merit on my part, so that all creatures may glorify Thee eternally for it; since the more my unworthiness is made known, the more resplendently Thy mercy will shine forth.

CHAPTER XXIII.

Recapitulation of the gifts already mentioned—The Saint complains of her infirmity and ingratitude.

MAY my soul bless Thee, O Lord God, my Creator, from the inmost depths of my heart ; and let it declare the mercies with which Thy charity has abounded, and encompassed me, O my sweetest Love !   I give thanks, as far as I am able, to Thine immense mercy ; I praise and glorify the longanimity of Thy patience, which has borne with me, while I passed the years of my infancy, childhood, and youth, even until my twenty-fifth year, in such blindness and folly, that if Thou hadst not preserved me, either by the natural dread which Thou didst give me for evil, and an inclination for good, or by the reproofs of others, and by so many aids, and if Thou hadst not saved me by Thy pure mercy, it appears to me that I would have sinned at every opportunity, either by my thoughts, my words, or my actions, even as if I had been an infidel in the midst of infidels, and as if I had not known, my God, that Thou wert the rewarder of good and the avenger of evil, although Thou didst choose me even from my infancy—that is, from the age of five years—to live in the bosom of holy religion, amongst Thy most faithful friends.

Although Thy felicity, O Lord, can neither increase nor diminish, and Thou needest not our goods,* nevertheless, neither my negligences nor my faults have diminished Thy praises, if I may so speak,—I who am so justly bound to glorify Thee continually, with all creatures, and with all the powers of my soul. Thou alone knowest what I feel concerning this matter, and how profoundly my soul is touched by Thy condescension towards it.

Therefore, O loving Father, I offer thee, for the remission of my sins, all the sufferings which Thy beloved Son endured, from the hour when He wept on straw in a manger,—all the sufferings of His Infancy, the privations of His Childhood, the griefs of His Youth, and the bitter sufferings of His Manhood, —until the hour when He bowed His head upon the Cross, and gave up the ghost with a loud cry. Furthermore, in satisfaction for all my negligences, I offer to Thee, O loving Father, the life of Thy Divine Son, which was so perfect in every thought, word, and action, from the time when He came down from Thy celestial throne to The Virgin's womb, and thence came forth into this world, until the hour when He presented to Thy Fatherly regard His victorious and glorified Body.

And because it is just that the heart which loves Thee should compassionate all Thy afflictions, I beseech Thee, for the love of Thy only Son, and by the virtue of the Holy Spirit, that whoever, by my request, or from any other motive, shall desire to supply for my deficiencies, either during my life or after my death, for Thy glory, even by a sight† or by a good work, that Thou wilt receive for them

---

* Psalm xv. 2.   † " Etiam uno gemitu."

also, and for the remission of their sins and negligences, the offerings which I make Thee of the conversation and sufferings of Thy Divine Son ; and that I may effectually obtain my request, I conjure thee to perpetuate my desire to all eternity, and even when I shall reign, by Thy grace, with Thee in heaven.

I adore and bless with thanksgiving, and with all humility, Thy ineffable charity, O Father of mercies, by which, notwithstanding the disorders of my life, Thou hast had thoughts of peace towards me, and not of severity, overwhelming me with the greatness and multitude of Thy benefits, even as if I had led the life of an angel amongst men. Thou didst commence this work in me during Advent, before I had attained my twenty-fifth year, and consummated it on the Epiphany by a certain fear, by which I was so agitated that I began to have a distaste for all the pleasures of youth, so that thus my heart became in some sort prepared to receive Thee.

Having entered on my twenty-sixth year, the second feria before the feast of the Purification, at the close of day, after Compline, Thou, Lord, who art the true Light shining in darkness,—Thou didst put an end to my spiritual obscurity and darkness, and to my youthful vanities. For at this time Thou didst give me evident tokens of Thine amazing charity and of Thine amiable presence ; and Thou didst teach me, by a loving reconciliation, to know Thee and to love Thee ; and having made me enter into my interior, which was until then unknown to me, Thou didst act towards me in marvellous and hidden ways, so that thou didst seem to take the same delight in dwelling in my soul as a friend in living with his friend or a bridegroom with his bride.

Thou didst visit me, then, at different times, and in

different ways, to preserve this commerce of charity; but
especially on the Vigil of the Annunciation, and before the
Ascension, commencing Thy work on that day in the morning, and completing it after Compline, by granting me that
favour which ought to be a subject of admiration and
reverence to all creatures,—namely, that from that hour
until now I never found Thee absent from my heart for a
single instant when I entered therein, except once, when
Thou wert absent for eleven days.

As I cannot express by my words either the number or
the value of the gifts Thou hast bestowed on me, permit
me, O Giver of gifts, to offer Thee in thanksgiving a sacrifice of joy in a spirit of humility, especially for having prepared a dwelling in my heart, according to Thy desire and
mine; so that I have neither heard nor read anything of
the Temple of Solomon or the palace of Assuerus which
seemed to me preferable to the delights which, thanks to
Thy grace, have been placed in me, and which Thou hast
permitted my unworthiness to share with Thee, as a queen
with the king.   But there are two favours which I especially esteem.   The first is, that Thou hast imprinted on
my heart the glorious marks of Thy saving Wounds, and
that Thou hast truly and deeply pierced this same heart
with the wound of Thy love; so that even if Thou hadst
never granted me a greater consolation, either exteriorly or
interiorly, Thou hast conferred such happiness on me by
these two alone, that even if I lived for a thousand years I
should find each hour more consolation, thanksgiving, and
instruction than I could possibly contain.

Besides these things, Thou hast also granted me Thy
secret friendship, by opening the sacred ark of Thy Divinity
—I mean Thy Deified Heart—to me in so many manners,
as to be the source of all my happiness; sometimes impart-

ing it freely, sometimes as a special mark of our mutual friendship, exchanging it for mine. Thou hast also revealed to me hidden mysteries concerning Thy judgments and Thy beatitudes ; and Thou hast so often melted my soul by Thy loving caresses, that if I did not know the abyss of Thy overflowing condescensions, I should be amazed were I told that even Thy Blessed Mother, who reigns with Thee in heaven, had been chosen to receive such extraordinary marks of tenderness and affection.

By all these marks of Thy gentle love Thou hast led me to a salutary knowledge of my faults, and at the same time spared my shame with so much charity, that—pardon me for saying it—it would seem as if the loss of half Thy kingdom were less to Thee than to cause me a momentary confusion for my imperfections. Therefore, in order to make them known to me, Thou didst use this wise expedient, —discovering to me the defects which displeased Thee in others, and of which, when I entered into myself, I found I was more guilty than they were, although Thou didst not give me the least sign of having perceived them in me.

Further, Thou hast won my soul by Thy faithful promises of benefits at my death and after it ; and if I had only obtained this favour from Thee, it would be sufficient to fill my heart with the most lively hope and desire. But the ocean of Thy infinite mercy was not yet exhausted, for Thou hast heard the frequent prayers which I addressed to Thee for sinners for their souls, or for other considerations ; and so great have been these favours, that I have not yet found one to whom I could discover them, as I know them myself, on account of the pusillanimity of the human heart, which is slow of belief. To crown all these benefits, Thou hast given me Thy sweetest Mother, the Blessed Virgin, for my advocate, and Thou hast lovingly recommended me to her many times with the same ardour as a faithful bridegroom would recommend his beloved bride to his own mother. Thou hast also often sent the princes of Thy court to minister to me ; not only from the choirs of angels and archangels, but even those of higher rank, as Thy kindness, my God, judged it expedient for my advancement in spiritual exercises. But when, for my soul's good, Thou hast deprived me for a time of some of Thy delights, I have yielded to a weak and shameful ingratitude, and have forgotten Thy gifts, as if they had been of no benefit to me ; and if by Thy grace I discovered what I had lost, and asked Thee to restore it, or to grant me some other favour, Thou didst immediately give me all, as if it had been a deposit which I had entrusted to Thy keeping.

Besides these favours, Thou didst grant me others of the utmost value, especially on the day of Thy Nativity, the Sunday *Esto mihi ;* and also another Sunday after Pentecost Thou didst elevate me, or rather Thou didst ravish me, to so close a union with Thyself, that I marvel more than at a miracle how I have lived since then as a creature amongst creatures ; and am even more amazed, and even horrified, that I have not amended my faults as I was bound to do. Nevertheless, the fountain of Thy mercy has not dried up for me, O Jesus, of all lovers the most loving, —or rather, the only One who loves the ungrateful truly and disinterestedly. For after a time, having forgotten my vileness, unworthy that I am, and having begun to disrelish those things which are the joy and praise of heaven and earth,—if it were only because an infinite God had abased Himself unreservedly towards a vile and abject worm,—Thou, the Giver, Renovator, and Preserver of every good,—Thou didst arouse me from my torpor, and excite me to gratitude, by revealing to a certain person, who was very devout to Thee and familiar with Thee, some particulars of the gifts which Thou hast bestowed on me, which they could not have known by human means, since I had not revealed them to any human being; so that I heard from their lips what was only known to my secret heart.

As I recall these words and others, the glory of which is due to Thee alone, I will sing a canticle on a harmonious instrument, which is none other than Thy Divine Heart, by the virtue of the Spirit of consolation. Eternal Father, may all that is in heaven, on earth, or in the deep—may all things which have been, which are, or which will be—render Thee thanks and praise ! Even as gold shines most clearly when surrounded by various colours,—even as black appears darker by contrast with them,—so is the blackness of my ungrateful life, when compared with the splendour of the Divine benefits so abundantly bestowed on me. For as Thou couldst not grant any favours that were not commensurate with Thy royal liberality, I have only received them in my boorish ignorance, and as an unfortunate abuser of thy graces. This Thou didst, as it were, dissimulate by an effect of Thy natural clemency, so that it appeared as if Thou never didst more for me than when I did least for Thee. And even when Thou didst seek hospitality in my poor dwelling,—Thou, who reposest in the loving bosom of thy celestial Father,—I have been so negligent and so careless in entertaining Thee, that I should, even from natural humanity, have been bound to tend a leper with more care who had asked a shelter under my roof, after overwhelming me with outrages and injuries. Far, O Lord, who adorned the stars with beauty— far from recognising the graces Thou didst bestow on me —whether by filling me with interior consolation, or by imprinting on me Thy sacred Wounds, or by revealing to me Thy secrets, and even those of Thy friends, or by giving me marks of Thy friendship and tenderness greater than could have been found had the earth been traversed from east to west—I have been so ungrateful as to outrage Thee by despising these things, by seeking strange pleasures, and by preferring the bitterness of exterior things to the sweetness of Thy celestial manna. I have distrusted Thy promises, O God of truth, as if Thou wert a man who couldst lie, or fail in Thy fidelity !

Alas ! I have also offended the goodness with which Thou hast heard my unworthy prayers so favourably, by hardening my heart against Thy will, and, as I ought to declare with tears in my eyes, sometimes pretending not to understand Thy will, lest the reproaches of my conscience should oblige me to obey it.

I have also despised the aid of Thy most glorious Mother, and that of the blessed spirits whom Thou hast sent to me ; and I have been so unhappy as to prove an obstacle even to my earthly friends, on whom I have leant, instead of relying on Thee alone ; and far from increasing my gratitude and my vigilance over my faults, on seeing that Thy charity continued Thy favours, notwithstanding my negligence, I, on the contrary, returned Thee evil for good, like a tyrant, or rather like a demon, and had the hardihood to live even more carelessly.

But my greatest fault is, that after the incredible union which I have had with Thee, and which is known to Thee alone, I have not feared to sully my soul again with the same defects, which Thou hast permitted to continue in me in order that I might conquer them, and thus obtain greater glory with Thee in heaven. I have sinned also, in that when Thou didst discover to my friends Thy hidden

favours, to excite my gratitude, I failed in accomplishing
Thy designs therein, by rejoicing in a human manner, and
neglecting to correspond with Thy designs by the duty of
gratitude.

And now, O adorable Creator of my soul, permit the
groans of my heart to rise even to heaven in expiation of
all these faults, and of others which Thou mayest yet bring
to my recollection. Accept my grief for the immense
number of offences which I have committed against the
nobleness of Thy Divine goodness. I offer it to Thee, with
all the gratitude and all the reverence which Thou hast
enabled me, for all in heaven, on earth, and in the deep,
through the merit of Thy beloved Son, and by the power
of the Holy Spirit.

Since, then, I am altogether incapable of producing
worthy fruits of penance, I implore Thy mercy, O my
sweetest Love, to inspire those hearts which have sufficient
fidelity and zeal to appease Thee by a sacrifice of propitiation, to repair for my defects by their sighs, their prayers,
and other good works, and to pay the debt of praise which
I owe to Thee alone, O Lord my God ; because, as Thou
seest the bottom of my heart, Thou knowest that I have
only written these things from a pure love of Thy glory,
in order that many who shall read them after my death
may be touched by Thy sweetness and clemency, considering the greatness of Thy love, which has abased itself so
low for the salvation of mankind as to permit such numerous and precious gifts to be abused, as I, alas ! have abused
them.

But I give thanks with all my might, O Lord, my
Creator and re-Creator, to Thine infinite mercy, that, from
the abyss of Thy overflowing goodness, Thou hast made
known to me that whosoever shall remember me as I have

said above, for Thy glory, either by praying for sinners, or by giving thanks for the elect, or by any other good works, shall not leave this world until Thou hast granted him the grace to become pleasing to Thee, and so order his heart that Thou mayest find joy and pleasure therein. For which may eternal praise be given to Thee, which shall return without ceasing to the uncreated Love whence it proceeded.

CHAPTER XXIV.

Conclusion of this Book.

BEHOLD, O loving Lord, I offer Thee the talent of Thy con-descending intimacy, which Thou hast confided to me, vile creature that I am. I have traded with it for love of Thy love in that which I have written, or which I may yet write. And I can boldly declare, by Thy grace, that I have had no other motive in saying or writing these things, except that of obeying Thy will, of promoting Thy glory, and of zeal for the salvation of souls. I desire, therefore, that all should praise Thee and give Thee thanks, that my un-worthiness has not caused Thee to withdraw Thy mercy from me. I desire also that Thou shouldst be praised for those who, reading these things, are charmed with the sweet-ness of Thy charity, and inwardly drawn to desire the same ; and also for those who, studying them as students, commence with the alphabet, and attain to philosophy,—thus being led by the perusal of these things, as by pic-tures and images, to search for the hidden manna, which in-creases the hunger of those who partake of it, and which is not found in corporal substances.

Therefore, since Thou, the Almighty Dispenser of all

good things, dost vouchsafe to pasture us during our exile, until, "beholding the glory of the Lord with unveiled countenance, we are transformed into His image, and from glory to glory by the power of the spirit of love" (2 Cor. iii. 18); meanwhile, according to Thy faithful promises and the humble desire of my heart, grant, I beseech Thee, to all who read these writings with humility, the peace of Thy love, compassion for my miseries, and a salutary compunction for their furtherance in perfection; so that, elevating their hearts towards Thee with burning love, they may be like so many golden censers, whose sweet odours shall abundantly supply all my negligence and ingratitude.   Amen.

PART III.

THE REVELATIONS OF ST. GERTRUDE.

COMPILED BY THE RELIGIOUS OF HER MONASTERY.

CHAPTER I.

Our Lord gives His Blessed Mother to St. Gertrude to be her mother, in order that she may have recourse to her in all her afflictions.

ST. GERTRUDE having learned by Divine revelation that she was about to endure some trial * for the increase of her merit, began to fear through human weakness; but the Lord had compassion on her infirmity, and gave her His most merciful Mother, the Empress of Heaven, for her mother and for her dispenser; so that, when the burden of her grief appeared beyond her strength, she might always have recourse to this Mother of mercy, and by her intervention obtain relief.

Some time after, as she was much grieved because a devout person obliged her to reveal the singular favours

---

* The French translations here have "quelque disgrâce;" the Latin, "adversitatis." The passage which follows has also been translated very loosely, and two sentences inserted which are not in the original.

with which God had honoured her on the preceding feast,
she had recourse to the Mother of the afflicted, in order
to learn from her what she ought to do on this occasion.
" Give freely what you possess," she replied ; " for my
Son is rich enough to repay all that you expend for His
glory." But as the Saint desired to conceal as much as
possible the great favours granted to her, even while she
partly revealed them, she desired to know from her
heavenly Spouse how far her conduct was agreeable to
Him. Prostrating herself at His feet, she implored Him
to make known His will to her, and to give her the desire
of accomplishing it. Her confidence merited for her this
reply, which she received from the Divine Mercy : " Give
My money to the bank, that when I come I may receive
it with usury " (Luke xix. 23). And thus she learned
that the reasons which she had considered good, and even
inspired by the Spirit of God, were merely human ; so
that from henceforth she imparted more freely what was
revealed to her, and not without reason ; for Solomon has
declared : " It is the glory of God to conceal the word
and the glory of kings to search out the speech " (Prov.
xxv. 2).

CHAPTER II.

Adversity is the spiritual ring with which the soul is betrothed
to God.

As Gertrude offered to God in her prayers all that she
suffered in body and mind, and all the pleasures of which
she had deprived herself, whether in the flesh or the spirit,
our Lord appeared to her, and showed her the pleasures
and the pains which she had offered to Him under the
form of two rings, enriched with precious stones, which He

wore to adorn His hands. The Saint, perceiving this, repeated the offering frequently; and when suffering a corporal affliction some time afterwards, she beheld Jesus her Lord touch her left eye with the ring which He carried in His left hand, and which represented corporal afflictions and sufferings; and from this moment she felt extreme suffering in this eye, which she had beheld our Lord touch in spirit, and this pain was never entirely removed.

She knew from this that, as the ring is the sign of espousal, so also sufferings in body or mind are testimonies of the spiritual espousal of the soul with God; so that whoever suffers may say confidently, with all truth: "My Lord Jesus Christ has espoused me to Him with His ring;" and if he recognises in those afflictions the graces which he has received, and returns thanks, he may add: "He has adorned me with a crown as His spouse;" because thanksgiving in tribulation is a crown of glory more brilliant than gold, and incomparably more precious than topaz.

CHAPTER III.

Human consolation weakens that which is Divine.

GERTRUDE received another plain testimony, although she did not understand it very well at first, that contradictions and privation of consolation in suffering greatly increase merit. On a certain day, about the Feast of Pentecost, as she suffered such severe pain in her side that those who were present feared her last hour had arrived, her Beloved, the true Consoler of her soul, retired from her, and thus increased her suffering, although the cares and attentions of those who surrounded her were redoubled; whereas, when she was less carefully attended, this loving Lord remained near her, to solace the severity of her pain by His presence; thus making her understand, that when we are deprived of human consolation, the Divine Mercy regards us most favourably.

Towards evening, as the Saint was worn out by acute suffering, she sought to obtain some mitigation of it from our Lord; but He raised His right arm, and showed her the pain she had endured all day as a precious ornament on His bosom. As this ornament appeared so perfect and so complete in every part, she rejoiced, hoping that her suffering would now cease; but our Lord replied: "What you suffer after this will add brightness to this ornament." And certainly, although it was garnished with precious stones, the gold appeared dark and dull. What she suffered afterwards was not so grievous in itself; but she was more tried by being deprived of consolation, than by the acuteness of the pain.

CHAPTER IV.

How vile and despicable are all transitory pleasures.

ABOUT the Feast of St. Bartholomew,* Gertrude felt herself overwhelmed with an exceeding sadness and a temptation

---

* August 24. This Saint was martyred in Armenia. It is related in the *Life of St. Elizabeth of Hungary*, that when the Blessed Virgin appeared to her during the vigil of Christmas, she mentioned the blessed Bartholomew, with St. John and St. Lawrence, as special "lovers of Jesus." She added : " If thou wilt consent to be deprived of all that is dear to thee, and even of thy own will, I will obtain for thee the same reward that Bartholomew received when his skin was flayed off. If thou endurest insults patiently, thou wilt be like unto

to impatience. This caused such darkness in her soul, that she appeared insensible to all the pleasures which the presence of God imparted to her, and light was not restored to her until the following Saturday through the intercession of the Mother of God, when they sang in her honour the Antiphon which commences "Mary, Star of the sea." * The following day, as she rejoiced inwardly at the sweetness and tenderness with which God treated her, she began to reflect on her late impatience and her other faults ; then, feeling exceedingly displeased with herself, she prayed to God for her amendment, but with such discouragement, that, beholding the enormity and the multitude of her faults, she cried out in despair : "God of mercy, set bounds to my malice, since I place neither end nor measure to it ! 'Deliver me, O Lord, and set me beside Thee, and let any man's hand fight against me'" (Job xvii. 3).

Our Lord, compassionating her extreme affliction, showed her a small, narrow garden, filled with many beautiful flowers, but surrounded with thorns, through which a little stream of honey flowed. He said to her : "Would you prefer the pleasure which you might enjoy here to Me?" She replied : "Assuredly not, O Lord my God." Then He showed her another little garden, filled with mire and dirt, but covered with some verdure, and containing a few common flowers. Being asked likewise if she would prefer this, she turned away from it to show her aversion, and exclaimed : "May I never prefer the fearful illusion of an apparent good, which conceals a real evil, to Him who is the only sovereign, true, unchangeable, and eternal Good !"

Lawrence when he suffered martyrdom. If thou keepest silence when reproached and offended, thou wilt merit as John did when the wicked sought to poison him."

    * *Stella Maria maris ;* probably *Ave maris stella.*

Our Lord replied : " Why, then, do you mistrust, as one deprived of charity ; since the favours with which I overwhelm you are a proof that you possess it ? And why do you speak despairingly because of your sins, since Scripture testifies that charity covers a multitude of sins, when you do not prefer your will to Mine, although by following it you might live without trouble, and in honour, in the esteem of men, and with a reputation for sanctity ? I have represented this self-will to you under the figure of a garden filled with flowers, and the pleasures of a sensual life by the verdure which covered the mire." She replied : " Oh, would to God a thousand times that, by the contempt of the garden of flowers, which Thou hast shown me, I may have altogether renounced my own will ! but I fear the insignificance of the place disposed me to do so more easily." " It is thus," our Lord replied, " that, in guiding the consciences of My elect, I only let them see temporal advantages to a small extent, in order to avoid exposing their weakness to great temptation, and to inspire them more easily with contempt for the false pleasures of earth."

Then Gertrude renounced entirely all the pleasures of heaven and earth, and cast herself with such constancy and fervour into the bosom of her Beloved, that she believed no creature would now be able to remove her for a single moment from His arms, where she tasted with joy that life-giving draught which flowed from the wounded Side of her Lord, and whose sweetness infinitely surpassed that of the most precious balm.

CHAPTER V.

The perfect resignation of St. Gertrude into the hands of God in all
adversities, and what merit she acquired thereby.

On the Feast of the Apostle St. Matthew,* our Lord having
prevented her by the sweetness of His frequent benedictions,
she offered the chalice in thanksgiving at the Elevation;
and having reflected that her oblation would be of little
value if she did not willingly offer to bear all kinds of suffering for the love of Christ, she rose, in the fervour of her
zeal, from the bosom of her Spouse, in which was all her
delight, and threw herself on the ground as a vile carcass,
exclaiming : "I offer myself to Thee, O Lord, to endure
all that may promote Thy glory." Then the Lord hastened
quickly to her, and placed Himself on the ground beside
her, as if to support her, saying : "This is Mine." " Yes,"
exclaimed the Saint, turning towards God, and animated
with fresh courage ; " I belong to Thee—I am the work of
Thy hands." "It is true," replied our Lord ; " but this
grace is singularly yours, that I am so closely united to
thee by love, that I would not willingly enjoy beatitude
without thee."

Being amazed at the exceeding condescension of these
words, she exclaimed : " Why dost Thou speak thus to me,
O Lord, since Thou hast such an infinite number of friends
in heaven and on earth, with whom Thou couldst share
Thy happiness, even had I never been created ? " Our Lord
replied : " He who has always wanted a limb does not feel
the same privation as one who loses it in advanced years ;
in like manner, I have so placed My love in thee, that I
could not bear that we should be separated from each other."

* September 21.

CHAPTER VI.

ON the Feast of St. Maurice,* as the celebrant pronounced the secret words of consecration, St. Gertrude said to our Lord : " Lord, the mystery which Thou dost now operate is so tremendous and so great, that I scarcely dare to breathe or speak ; it is enough for me to hide myself in the deepest valley of humility which I can find, expecting my share in the salvation which Thou dost there impart to Thine elect."   Our Lord replied : " When a mother wishes to do some work with pearls and precious stones, she sometimes places her child in an elevated place to hold her thread or her pearls, or to do her some other service ; so I have placed you in an eminent position to dispose of the merits of this Mass ; and if you elevate your will even to desire willingly to suffer all kinds of labour and pain, in order that this sacrifice, which is so salutary for all Christians, whether living or dead, may be fully accomplished in all its excellence, you will then have contributed, according to the extent of your ability, to the accomplishment of My work."

Once, when the Saint was confined to bed, and unable to assist at Mass, at which she had hoped to have communicated, she said to God with a troubled spirit : " To

---

* September 22. St. Maurice was a commander, if not chief captain, of the famous Christian Theban legion, which was first decimated, and then cruelly martyred in cold blood, by the command of the Emperor Maximinian, for refusing to join the army in sacrificing to the gods for the success of his expedition into Gaul.

what must I attribute my hindrance from assisting to-day at the Holy Mysteries, if not to Thy Divine Providence, my Beloved?—and how shall I prepare myself to receive the Communion of Thy adorable Body and Blood, since my intention at Mass always seemed to me my best preparation?" "Since you attribute the cause to Me," replied our Lord, "to console you, I will make you hear the songs of joy with which heaven resounds when I espouse a soul.

"Hear, then, from Me, that my Blood is your redemption; meditate on those three-and-thirty years during which I laboured for you in exile, and sought only to ally Myself with you; and let this serve for the first part of Mass.

"Hear me telling you how I have dowered you with the riches of My Spirit, and that even as I endured so much bodily labour during the three-and-thirty years in which I sought you, so also My soul feels an ineffable joy at the union and spiritual marriage which we have contracted; and let this be your consolation during the second part of Mass.

"Listen, then, to Me, while I tell you how you are replenished with My Divinity, which has the power to make you taste the purest delights and the most ravishing sweetness inwardly, whilst exteriorly you are suffering the severest pain. This will serve for the third part of Mass.

"Hear, further, how you are sanctified by My love; know that you have nothing of yourself, and that all which renders you agreeable to Me comes from Me. Occupy yourself with these thoughts during the fourth part of Mass.

"Lastly, hear that you have been united * to Me in the sublimest manner; and know that, as 'all power has been given to Me in heaven and on earth,' I cannot be hindered

* "Conglutinatione."

from exalting you, as a king exalts his queen to his throne, and consequently renders her an object of respect. Rejoice, then, in reflecting on these things, and do not complain again that you have been deprived of hearing Mass."

CHAPTER VII.

With what confidence we should have recourse to God in all our needs and temptations.

As Gertrude prepared herself for Communion on the Feast of the Holy Innocents, she found herself distracted by a crowd of importunate thoughts ; and having implored the Divine assistance, our Lord, in His exceeding mercy, spoke thus to her : " If any one, when encompassed by temptation, throws himself on My protection with a firm hope, he is of the number of those of whom I can say : ' One is My dove, chosen amongst a thousand ; he has pierced My Divine Heart with one glance of His eye ; ' so that if I thought I could not assist him, My heart would be so desolate that even all the joys of heaven could not alleviate my grief, because he is a part of My Body, and is united to My Divinity ; and I am ever the advocate of My elect, full of compassion for their every need."

" Lord," replied St. Gertrude, " how is it that Thy immaculate Body, in which Thou never hadst any contradiction, enables Thee to compassionate our many weaknesses ?" He replied : " You may easily convince yourself of this. Has not My Apostle said : ' It behoved Him in all things to be made like unto His brethren, that He might be able to succour them also that are tempted?' " * He added:

* Heb. ii. 17, 18.

"This eye of My beloved, which pierces My heart, is the confidence which she ought to have in Me,—that I know, that I am able, and that I am willing to assist her faithfully in all her miseries ; and this confidence has such power over My goodness, that it is not possible for Me to abandon her." "But, Lord," replied the Saint, "since confidence is so great a gift that none can have it unless Thou dost bestow it, what merit have those who are deprived of it?" He replied : "Each can at least overcome his diffidence, in some degree, by the testimony of Scripture, and say, if not with his whole heart, at least with his lips : 'If I should be cast into hell, Thou, O Lord, wilt deliver me ;' and again, 'Although He should kill me, I will trust Him.'"

CHAPTER VIII.

Of the efficacy of prayers for others.

God having revealed to a certain person that He willed to deliver a great number of souls from purgatory, through the prayers of the community, a general prayer was enjoined for all the religious. As St. Gertrude prayed, one Sunday, in the manner prescribed, she pleaded most fervently with God for the deliverance of these souls, and, being rapt in spirit, she beheld the Lord, like a king in the midst of His glory, occupied in distributing rewards and gifts ; not being able to discern exactly why He was thus so greatly occupied, she said to Him : "Most loving Lord ! since you made known to me last year, on the Feast of St. Mary Magdalen, notwithstanding my unworthiness, that Thine own goodness had obliged Thee to grant mercy to those who approached Thy sacred Feet, since so many persons prostrated themselves before Thee on this day, to imitate the blessed sinner, Thy faithful lover, do me the further grace to discover to the eyes of my soul the meaning of Thy present employment, which I do not understand."

Our Lord replied : " I am distributing gifts." The Saint knew by these words that God was applying the prayers of the community to the souls, whom, however, she was not permitted to see, although they were present. Then He added : " Will you not offer Me your merits to increase My gifts ? " At these words she was deeply moved ; and not knowing that the community were then occupied in the same way, she was filled with gratitude, believing that something special was required of her, and replied joyfully : " Yes, Lord ; I offer Thee not only my merits, which are worth nothing, but I offer Thee all the good done by my community, which I attribute entirely to the union which I have, by Thy grace, with my sisters ; and I offer it to Thee of my free will, and most gladly, for the honour of Thy majesty and Thine infinite perfection." And the Lord graciously accepted her offering.

Then our Lord appeared as if disengaged, and, covering Himself and Gertrude with a light cloud, He inclined lovingly towards her, and said : " Listen to Me only, and taste the sweetness of My grace." She replied : " My God and my Beloved ! why hast Thou deprived me of the favour Thou hast bestowed on another, of revealing to her with so much clearness the mercy which Thou didst desire to exercise towards those souls, since Thou hast discovered to me so many secrets ? " He replied : " Reflect frequently, that My graces usually serve to humble you, because you believe yourself unworthy of them, and that you believe that they are only given to you as to a servant who is engaged for daily labour, and as if you could not be faithful

to Me without this reward ; and hence you prefer others
who serve Me faithfully without these favours.   And I
have willed to render you like them in this ; so that while
you did not know more than others of the mercy which I
desired to exercise towards those souls, you laboured for
them with equal zeal ; therefore you are not deprived of
an advantage you value so much for others."

At these words she was exceedingly moved ; marvelling
at the amazing and ineffable condescension of the Divine
goodness towards her, in pouring forth on her such abundant
favours ; and, when giving less, acting thus to preserve that
humility which is the foundation of all graces.   She learned
then how God arranges, for the good of those whom He
loves, the bestowal or the refusal of His favours ; and being
ravished out of herself in an excess of adoration and gratitude for the infinite goodness of God towards her, she cast
herself, fainting away in utter self-annihilation, into the
arms of her Lord, saying to Him : " My God, my weakness
is unable to bear the excess of Thy mercy."   Then the
Lord moderated in her a little the overwhelming power of
this great thought, and, as she recovered her strength, she
said to Him : " Since Thy inexplicable and incomprehensible wisdom wills that I should be deprived of this gift, I
will desire it no longer.   But, my God, wilt Thou not hear
my prayers for my friends ? "   Then our Lord confirmed His
words as with an oath, replying : " I will, by My Divine
power."   The Saint replied : " Hear, then, my petition for
the person so often recommended to my prayers."   And
immediately she beheld a stream, pure as crystal, flowing
forth from the Heart of the Lord into the person for whom
she prayed.   She then asked : " Lord, what will this person gain by this, since she does not see it flowing into her ? "
He replied : " When a physician gives a draught to a sick

person, those who are present do not see him recover his health the moment he takes the remedy, nor does the sick man himself feel cured; nevertheless, the physician knows well the value of the remedy, and how salutary it will prove to the patient." "But why, Lord, dost Thou not deliver her from the ill-regulated habits and the other defects from which I have implored Thee so many times to deliver her?" He replied: "It is said of Me, when I was in My Childhood, that I 'advanced in wisdom, and in age, and in grace with God and man.' So will this person advance from hour to hour, changing her faults into virtues; and I will deliver her from all the infirmities of nature, so that after this she may possess the blessedness which I have prepared for man, whom I have exalted above the angels."

As the hour at which the Saint was to communicate was now near, she prayed God to show mercy to as many sinners as would be saved (for she dared not pray for the reprobate) as He had that day delivered souls from purgatory by the merit of the prayers which had been offered. But our Lord reproved her timidity, saying: "Is not the offering of My spotless Body and My precious Blood sufficient merit to recall even those who walk in the ways of perdition to a better life?" Then Gertrude, reflecting on the infinite goodness testified by these words, exclaimed: "Since Thine ineffable charity will condescend to my unworthy prayers, I beseech Thee, uniting my petitions to the love and desire of all creatures, that it may please Thee to deliver as many persons who live in sin and are in peril thereby as Thou hast delivered souls from purgatory, without preferring those who are my friends either by consanguinity or proximity." Our Lord accepted this petition graciously, and certified its acceptance to her. "I would know further,

O Lord," she continued, " what I shall add to these prayers to make them yet more efficacious ?" Then, as she received no answer, she continued : " Lord, I fear that my unfaithfulness does not merit a reply to this question, because Thou, who seest the hearts of all, knowest that I will not comply with Thy command." Then our Lord, turning towards her with a countenance full of sweetness, replied : " Confidence alone can easily obtain all things ; but if your devotion urges you to add anything further, say the Psalm *Laudate Dominum, omnes gentes*, three hundred and sixty-five times, in order to supply for those praises which men fail in offering to Me."

CHAPTER IX.

Of the admirable effects of Communion, and that we should not lightly abstain from It, even for our unworthiness.

ON the Feast of St. Mathias * Gertrude resolved, for many reasons, to abstain from Holy Communion. But as her mind was occupied with God and herself during the first Mass, our Lord presented Himself to her, with such marks of affec tion as a friend might manifest to his friend. Nevertheless, as the Saint was accustomed to such favours, she desired yet more, and wished to pass entirely into her Beloved, so that she might be wholly united to Him and consumed in the fire of His love. But as she could not obtain this, she began to occupy herself with the Divine praises, which was one of her ordinary exercises. First, she glorified the goodness and mercy of the ever-adorable Trinity, for all the graces which had flowed forth from its deep abyss for

* February 24.

the salvation of all the elect; secondly, she returned thanks for all the favours which had been bestowed on the august Mother of God; thirdly, for all the graces infused into the sacred Humanity of Jesus Christ; imploring all the saints in general, and each in particular, to offer individually in sacrifice to the effulgent and ever-peaceful Trinity, in satisfaction for her negligence, all the dispositions and zeal with which they were adorned on the day of their elevation into glory, and the consummation of their perfection, and of their eternal reward. For this intention she said the Psalm *Laudate Dominum* thrice: first, in honour of all the saints; secondly, in honour of the Blessed Virgin; and thirdly, in honour of the Son of God.

Our Lord then said to her : " How will you recompense My saints, who have made such offerings to Me for you, since you intend to omit your usual offering of thanksgiving for them ? " The Saint did not reply. At the oblation of the Host she desired greatly to know what offering of eternal praise she could make to God the Father. " If you prepare yourself to approach the life-giving Sacrament of My Body and Blood to-day," said our Lord, " you will obtain this triple favour which you have desired during Mass—namely, to enjoy the sweetness of My love, and to become united to Me by the power of My Divinity, even as gold is united to silver, and thus will possess a precious amalgam, which will be worthy to offer to the eternal praise of God the Father, and acquit yourself of the gratitude which you owe to all the saints."

These words kindled in her so ardent a desire for Communion, that even if she had to force her way to it across drawn swords, it would have appeared little to her. Afterwards, when she had received the Body of the Lord, as she made her thanksgiving, this Lover of men spoke thus to her: "You have resolved of your own will to serve Me to-day with others by brick, straw, and stubble; but I have chosen to place you amongst those who are replenished with the delights of My royal table."

On the same day another person abstained from Communion without any reasonable cause. She said to her Lord: "Most merciful God, why have You permitted her to be thus tempted?" "What can I do for her," He replied, "since she has herself so covered her eyes with the veil of her unworthiness, that she cannot possibly see the tenderness of My paternal Heart?"

CHAPTER X.

The indulgence which our Lord granted to St. Gertrude—Her ardent desire to be conformed in all things to the will of God.

As the Saint learned that an indulgence of many years was published on condition of the usual offerings, she said, with her whole heart: "Lord, if I were rich I would willingly give a large sum of gold and silver, that by this means I might be absolved by these indulgences for the praise and glory of Thy Name." To this the Lord replied lovingly, saying: "I grant you, by My authority, a full remission of all your sins and negligences;" and at the same moment she saw her soul without spot, and as white as snow.

But some time after, entering into herself and finding her soul still adorned with the same purity, she feared what she had seen before had been an illusion, as it seemed impossible that it had not been in some degree tarnished by the negligences and faults into which her weakness caused her to fall so often. But the Lord consoled her affliction by these words: "Dost thou think that I possess less power than I have bestowed on My creatures? If I have given to the material sun such virtue, that if a discoloured garment is exposed to its rays it will recover its former whiteness, and even become brighter than before, how much more can I, who am the Creator of the sun, by directing My looks upon a sinner, remove all his stains, purifying him, by the fire of My love, from every spot?"

On another occasion she was so discouraged by her unworthiness and weakness, that she seemed to have no power to praise God, nor to taste the sweetness of contemplation. But the Lord, by a pure effect of His mercy, so restored her courage, by communicating to her the most holy conversation of Jesus Christ, that all her desires were satisfied, and she seemed to be presented to the King of kings, her Spouse, with the same beauty as Esther was presented to Assuerus. As she appeared so adorned, the Saviour, in loving condescension, addressed her thus: "What dost thou desire, O queen?" "I beseech and implore Thee, O Lord," she replied, "with all my heart, that Thy adorable and Divine will may be accomplished in me, according to Thy good pleasure." Our Lord then named different persons who had recommended themselves to her prayers, and asked what she desired for each individually. "Lord," she replied, "I only ask that Thy most peaceful will may be perfectly accomplished in them." Our Lord inquired further: "And what do you desire that I should do for you?" "I have no other joy," she answered, "than to desire that Thy amiable and peaceful will may always be accomplished in me, and in all creatures; and I am ready, for this end, to offer every member of my body to be exposed, one after the other, to the acutest suffering." God, who had granted her the grace to speak these words, rewarded her for them afterwards, saying to her : " Since you have desired with such ardour to see the designs of My will executed, I will reward you with this recompense, that you shall appear as agreeable in My eyes as if you had never violated My will, even in the most trifling matter."

CHAPTER XI.

How the soul may seek God, and transfigure itself into Him, in four ways.

WHILE the Antiphon *In lectulo meo* * was chanted, in which the words *quem diligit anima mea* are repeated four times, she reflected on four different manners in which the faithful soul may seek God.

By the first words, " By night I sought Him whom my soul loveth," she understood the first way of seeking God, by the praises and blessings which are offered to Him on the sacred couch of contemplation.   Hence the words, " I sought Him, and found Him not," follow immediately ; because while the soul is imprisoned in the flesh she cannot praise God perfectly.

She understood the second manner of seeking God in the words, " I will rise, and will go about the city : in the streets and the broadways I will seek Him whom my soul loveth ; " because the various thanksgivings which the soul renders to God for all the gifts with which He enriches His creatures are expressed by the words, " the streets and broadways."   And as we cannot praise God in this world

* "In my bed, by night, I sought Him whom my soul loveth " (Cant. iii. 1) ; commencement of i. Lesson, i. Nocturn, Feast of St. Mary Magdalen, but not used as an Antiphon.

as He should be praised for all His gifts, the words, " I
sought Him, and I found Him not," are added.

By these words, " The watchman found me," she understood the justice and mercy of God, which cause the soul
to enter into herself, and then to compare her unworthiness
with the benefits which she has received from God ; so that
she begins by her grief and repentance for her faults to
seek His mercy, saying : " Have you seen Him whom
my soul loveth ? " And thus, as she has no faith in her
own merits, she turns with humble confidence to the
Divine mercy, and by the fervour of her prayers, and the
inspiration of grace, she at last finds Him whom the faithful soul seeks.

This Antiphon being concluded, she felt her heart deeply
moved by all the sweetness with which the Divine mercy
had filled it during this time, and with many other graces
which it would be impossible to describe, so that even her
bodily strength failed her. Then she said to God : " It
seems to me that I can truly say to Thee now, ' Behold !
my beloved Lord ! not only my inmost soul, but every part
of my body is moved towards Thee ! ' "—" I know and feel
it perfectly," replied our Lord, " because these graces have
flowed from Me and returned to Me. But as for you, who
are held captive in the chains of mortality, you can never
understand all the reciprocal sweetness which My Divinity
feels towards you." He added : " Know, however, that this
movement of grace glorifies you, as My Body was glorified
on Mount Thabor in presence of My three beloved disciples ; so that I can say of you, in the sweetness of my
charity : ' This is My beloved daughter, in whom I am
well pleased.' For it is the property of this grace to communicate to the body as well as to the mind a marvellous
glory and brightness."

CHAPTER XII.

Reparation for the fall of a Host, which it was feared had been consecrated.

IT happened one day that, in preparing for Mass, a Host fell from some fold, and all were in doubt whether it had been consecrated or not. The Saint had recourse to God; and having learned that the wafer had not been consecrated, she rejoiced much that no irreverence had been committed. Yet, as all her care was to promote the glory of God, she said to Him : " Although Thy infinite goodness has not permitted that Thou shouldest receive so great an outrage in this place, and in the Sacrament of the Altar,—nevertheless, O Lord of the Universe, because Thou wert treated with a like indignity and irreverence, not only by Thy enemies the heathen and the Jews, but, alas ! even by Thy most faithful friends, whom Thou hast redeemed by the price of Thy most precious Blood, and, I weep to say it, sometimes even by priests and religious, I will not make it known that this host was not consecrated, in order that Thou mayest not be deprived of the satisfaction that will be offered to Thee." Then she added : " O Lord my God ! make known to me what satisfaction is most agreeable to Thee for each offence which is committed against Thee ; because I will try to accomplish it for love of Thy honour and glory, even if I consume my whole strength in doing it." Our Lord then made known to her that He would accept the recital of the Lord's Prayer two hundred and twenty-five times, in honour of His sacred Limbs ; and of as many acts of charity towards her neighbour, in thanksgiving to Him who has said : " So long as you did it to one of these My least brethren,

you did it to Me " (Matt. xxv.), and in union with that
love which made God become Man for us ; and that she
should deprive herself as many times of the vain and useless pleasures of earth, and occupy herself only with the
real and true pleasures of the Divinity.

Oh, how great and ineffable is the mercy and kindness
of our most loving God, which accepts and rewards as
offerings what we should deserve most just punishment
for if we omitted !

CHAPTER XIII.

Of the value and efficacy of Confession—How we should conquer the
difficulties we feel in approaching the Sacrament of Penance.

THE Lord, who is ever jealous of the salvation of His elect,
sometimes makes the most trifling thing appear full of
difficulty, for the increase of our merit.   It was with this
intention that He once allowed St. Gertrude to feel the
duty of confession so burdensome, that it seemed as if she
could never perform this duty by her own strength.   She
therefore addressed herself to God with all the fervour she
could command, and He replied : " Why do you not confide this confession to Me, with such confidence that you
need think no more of your own labour or exertion to
make it perfect ? "   She replied : " I have a full and superabundant confidence in Thy mercy and omnipotence,
my loving Lord ; but I think it is only just, as I have
offended Thee by my sins, that I should give Thee some
tokens of my amendment, by reflecting on the disorders of
my life in the bitterness of my soul."   Our Lord having
manifested to her that her design was agreeable to Him,
Gertrude occupied herself entirely with the recollections
of her sins, and it appeared to her as if her skin were torn

in several places, and as if it had been pierced with thorns; then, having discovered her wounds and miseries to the Father of Mercies as to a wise and faithful Physician, He inclined lovingly towards her, and said : " I will warm the bath of confession for you by My Divine breath ; and when you have bathed yourself in it, according to My desire, you will appear without spot before Me." Then she prepared in all haste to plunge into this bath, saying : "Lord, I renounce every sentiment of human respect for love of Thee ; and even should I be obliged to publish my crimes to the whole world, I am ready to do so." Then our Lord covered her with His mantle, and allowed her to repose upon His bosom until this bath was prepared for her.

When the time came for confession, she was more tried than before. "Lord," she exclaimed, " since Thy paternal love knows all I suffer about this confession, why dost Thou permit me to be weighed down by this trial ? " "Those who take a bath," replied our Lord, " are accustomed to have themselves rubbed, in order to purify themselves more completely : thus the trouble of mind which you suffer will serve to purify you." Then, having perceived on the right side of her Spouse a bath which exhaled a thick vapour, she saw on the other side a delicious garden, enamelled with flowers, of which the most remarkable were roses without thorns, of rare beauty, which emitted a sweet and vivifying odour, attracting all who approached thither. The Lord made a sign to her to enter this garden, if she preferred it to the bath which she feared so much. "Not this, O Lord," she exclaimed, " but the bath which Thou hast warmed for me by Thy Divine breath." Our Lord replied : " May it avail for your eternal salvation ! "

Gertrude then understood that the garden represented the interior joys of Divine grace, which expose the faithful soul to the south wind of charity, water it with the loving dew of tears, and in an instant make it whiter than snow, assuring it not only of a general pardon of all its faults, but even of a new increase of merit. But she doubted not God was better pleased that for love of Him she had chosen what was painful, and refused what was consoling. Then, having retired to pray after her confession, she felt a most powerful assistance from God in this exercise; so that what He had formerly made so painful to her now appeared light and easy. It must be observed here that the soul is purified from the stain of sin principally in two manners; first, by the bitterness of penance, which is represented under the figure of a bath; and secondly, by the sweet embrace of Divine love, which is figured by the garden. Before confession, the Saint had occupied herself in contemplating the Wound of the Left Hand, so that after this bath she might rest therein until she could accomplish the penance enjoined by the priest. But as it was such that she was obliged to defer it for some time, she was extremely afflicted that she could not converse familiarly and freely with her faithful and amiable Spouse until she had paid this debt. Therefore, during Mass, as the priest immolated the Sacred Host, which truly and efficaciously blots out all the sins of men, she offered to God thanksgiving for all that He had done for her in the bath of penance, and in satisfaction for her faults. This the Eternal Father accepted, and received her into His bosom, where she learned that "this Orient from on high" had visited her in the plenitude of mercy and truth.

CHAPTER XIV.

The different effects of charity are explained by the comparison of
a tree covered with leaves, flowers, and fruit.

ON the following day, as the Saint heard Mass, she was
overcome by weariness ; but the sound of the bell aroused
her, and she beheld Jesus Christ, her Lord and King, holding a tree in His hand, which appeared to have been just cut
from the root, but which was covered with the most beautiful fruit, and whose leaves shone like so many stars,
shooting forth rays of admirable brightness ; and having
given of these fruits to the Saints who composed His
celestial court, they found a marvellous sweetness therein.
Soon after, our Lord planted this tree in the garden of
her heart, that she might make it more fruitful by cul-
tivation, that she might repose under it and be refreshed
there.   Having received this deposit, she began to pray
for a person who had persecuted her a short time before,
asking, to increase its fruitfulness, that she might suffer
again what she had already suffered, to draw down more
abundant grace on this person.   At this moment she beheld a flower, of a most beautiful colour, burst forth on the
top of the tree, which promised to change into fruit if she
executed her good intention.   This tree was the symbol of
charity, which bears not only the abundant fruit of good
works, but also the flowers of good-will, and the bright
leaves of holy desires.   Therefore, the citizens of heaven
rejoice greatly when men condescend towards their brethren,
and endeavour with all their power to solace them in their
needs.   At the moment of the elevation of the Host, our
Lord adorned the Saint with the various graces which He
had communicated to her on the preceding day.

On the same day, at noon, our Lord appeared to her under the form of a beautiful youth, and asked her to gather nuts for Him from the tree before mentioned ; and for this purpose He raised the tree up, that she might place herself in the branches. "But, my sweet Lord," * she replied, "why do You ask me to do that which is far beyond the weakness of my virtue and my sex, and which Thy condescension would rather incline Thee to do for me?" "By no means," He replied ; "should not the spouse act more freely in her own house, amongst her friends and domestics, than a respectful bridegroom who only enters occasionally to pay her a visit? But if she grant any-thing to the timidity of her bridegroom while he is with her, he will not fail to have the same consideration for her when she visits him." By this she understood what un-reasonable excuses persons make when they say : "If God wills me to do this or that, He will give me the grace necessary to do it ; " whereas it is only just that men should bend their wills entirely to God's, and never seek their own convenience on any occasion, and then they will enjoy here-after an eternal recompense.

As Gertrude now desired to present her Divine Spouse with the nuts for which He had asked, He ascended the tree, and seated Himself near her, commanding her to peel them, and prepare them for eating ; teaching her by this parable, that it is not sufficient for us to overcome our aversion to do good to our enemies, if we do not also seek to do so in a perfect manner. He thus deigned to teach her, by ordering her to pull and prepare those nuts, that we should do good to our persecutors ; and it is for this reason that nuts, whose shell is hard and bitter, were

---

* "O dulcissime juvenis!"

mingled with the soft and delicious fruit of this tree, in order that we might understand that charity towards our enemies should be seasoned with the sweetness of Divine grace, which makes men ready to endure death itself for Jesus Christ.

CHAPTER XV.

How afflictions unite the soul to Jesus Christ; and of the effect of an unjust excommunication.

WHILE the Mass, *Salve, Sancte Parens,** was said in honour of the Mother of God, being the last day on which the Holy Sacrifice was allowed to be celebrated, on account of an interdict, St. Gertrude addressed God thus : " How wilt Thou console us, most kind Lord, in our present affliction ?"   He replied : " I will increase My joys in you ; for as a spouse entertains himself more familiarly with his bride in the retirement of his house than in public, so will I take My pleasure in your retreat.   My love will increase in you, even as a fire which is enclosed burns with great force ; and the delight which I will find in you, and the love which you will have for Me, will be like a pent-up ocean, which seems to increase by the impediments placed to its progress, until at last it breaks forth impetuously." " But how long will this interdict continue ?" inquired the Saint.   The Lord replied : " The favours which I promise you will last as long as it does."   She replied : " It appears a degradation to the great ones of earth to reveal their secrets to those beneath them ; is it not, then, unworthy of

---

* "Hail, holy Parent."   Introit of Mass of the Blessed Virgin, from the Purification to Advent, composed by Sedulius.

Thy Majesty, who art the King of kings, to discover the secrets of Thy Divine Providence to me, who am the shame and rebuke of all creatures? It is on this account, doubtless, that Thou dost not make known to me when this interdict will terminate, although Thou knowest the end of all things before they have commenced." "It is not so," replied the Lord; "I conceal the secret from you for the furtherance of your spiritual welfare; for if I sometimes admit you to My secrets in contemplation, I exclude you from them also to preserve your humility, that by receiving this grace you may know what you are in Me; and by being deprived of it, you may know what you are of yourself."

At the offertory of the Mass, *Recordare, Virgo Maria,** as the words *ut loquaris pro nobis bona* were repeated, the Saint raised her heart towards the Mother of all grace, and the Lord said to her: " Even should there be none to speak good things for you, I am already prepared Myself to favour you." But as Gertrude reflected on the multitude of her own faults, and those of some others, she was doubtful whether she was entirely reconciled with God; but He said to her tenderly : " My natural goodness obliges Me to have regard to those amongst you who are most perfect; and as all are encircled by My Divinity, the perfections hide the imperfections." " O bountiful Lord !" inquired Gertrude, " how canst Thou give graces so full of consolation to one so unworthy to receive them?" He replied : " My love compels Me." " Where, then," she inquired, "are the stains which I contracted lately by my impatience, and which I manifested by my words?" "The fire of My love," He replied, " has consumed them entirely;

---

* Now offertory for the Mass of the Seven Dolors.

for I efface all the stains which I meet with in the souls whom I visit by My free and loving grace."

"O God of mercy!" continued Gertrude, "since Thou hast so often assisted my misery with Thy graces, I desire to know if my faults, such as my late impatience and other similar ones, will be purified in my soul before or after my death?" Then, as our Lord lovingly made as though He heard her not, she added: "If Thy justice demanded it, I would freely and willingly descend even into hell, to make a more condign satisfaction to Thee. But if it is more glorious to Thy natural goodness and mercy to consume my imperfections by the fire of Thy love, I will venture to implore Thee that this same love may efface all the stains from my soul, and make it purer than I could merit." And this appeared agreeable to our Lord in His goodness and tenderness.

On the following day, as Mass was celebrated for the people in the parish church, she said to God at the time of Communion: "Dost Thou not compassionate us, most loving Father, for being deprived, on account of these goods, of this most precious good, the Sacred Food of the Body and Blood?" "How can I feel it more?" replied the Lord; "if I conduct My spouse to a banquet, and I perceive, before she enters, that her attire is disarranged, will I not draw her aside to a retired place, and arrange it with My own hands, that I may introduce her with honour?" "But, my God," she inquired, "how can they have this grace who suffer this evil through us?" He replied: "Do not think of them; I will settle this matter with them."

Then, at the oblation of the Host, as she offered It to the Lord for His eternal praise and the welfare of her community, the Lord received It in her, communicating to her its vivifying sweetness, and saying: "I will nourish them with this Divine Food." "Wilt Thou not communicate Thyself, my God, to all the community?" she inquired. "No," He replied: "only to those who have the desire of communicating, or the will to desire it; but for the rest who belong to the community, they shall have the advantage of feeling themselves excited to partake of this celestial food, even as persons who have no thought of eating are attracted by the odour of some viand, and begin to desire to partake of it."

On the Feast of the Assumption she heard our Lord say, at the elevation of the Host: "I am going to immolate Myself to God My Father for My members." She said: "Most loving Lord, wilt Thou permit us, who are cut off from Thee by the anathema of those who would take our goods from us, to be joined to them?" The Lord replied: "If any one could take away from you the intimate union by which you are united to Me, then indeed you would be separated from Me. But as for the excommunication which is inflicted on you, it will make no more impression on you than a blunt knife would upon a tree, which it could not penetrate, and at best could but mark slightly." She replied: "My Lord and my God, who art the infallible Truth, Thou hast made known to me, although unworthy of such a revelation, that Thou wouldest increase Thy consolations in us and redouble Thy love; and yet there are some amongst us who complain that their charity is becoming cold." "I contain all good in Myself," replied our Lord; "and I distribute to each in season what they need."

CHAPTER XVI.

A vision in which St. Gertrude beheld our Lord communicating the sisters.

On a Sunday on which fell both the Feast of St. Lawrence and that of the dedication of the church of the monastery,* the Saint, having begun to pray during the first Mass for some persons who had recommended themselves to her prayers, perceived a green vine-branch which came forth from the throne of God, and descended to the earth ; and by its foliage, as by steps, one could ascend from the bottom to the top. She understood that this mystic ladder was a symbol of faith, by which the elect mount up to heaven ; and as she saw many of her sisters assembled at the summit of this vine, on the left side of the throne of God, amongst whom Jesus Christ stood with extreme pleasure in presence of His heavenly Father, the hour approached at which the community would have communicated, if they had not been hindered by the interdict ; and she desired ardently that she and those present might receive this life-giving Sacrament, which, by an incomprehensible secret of the Divine goodness, gives life to men, despite all the obstacles which are opposed to it.

After this, she saw Jesus Christ holding a Host in His hand, which He plunged into the Heart of God His Father ; and when He drew it forth, it seemed as if coloured vermilion or tinged with blood. Gertrude was amazed at this, and marvelled much what it might signify, the more so because red is a symbol of the Passion, and the Eternal Father could never have any marks of suffering. Being thus entirely absorbed in meditating on what she saw, she

* August 10.

forgot to ask for the accomplishment of her desires; but soon after she knew, without perceiving in what manner it was effected, that the Lord had chosen for the place of His dwelling and repose the hearts and souls of all her sisters whom she had seen assembled around the throne of God. The Saint now remembered a person who had recommended herself to her prayers before Mass with great humility and devotion, and she prayed God to grant her a share in these favours. He replied, that no one could ascend thus unless she was elevated by confidence, of which the person for whom she prayed had but little. The Saint replied : " It seems to me, my God, that the want of confidence in this person proceeds from a humility, on which Thou dost usually pour forth Thy most abundant graces." Our Lord answered : " I will descend now, and communicate Myself to this soul and to all who are in the valley of self-abasement." Then the Son of God, the Lord and Master of all virtues, appeared to descend suddenly by a crimson ladder, and soon after she beheld Him at the altar of the church of the monastery, clothed with pontifical vestments, and bearing in His Hands a pix like those in which the consecrated Hosts alone are reserved, and He remained seated before the priest until the Preface of the Mass.

A multitude of angels attended Him, so that the whole church on the northern side, which was to the right side of the Lord, seemed filled with them ; and these blessed spirits testified a particular joy in visiting the place where their fellow-citizens,[*] the religious of the monastery, had so often addressed their prayers to God. On the left—that is, on the south side—there was but one choir of angels, who were followed by a choir of apostles, a choir of martyrs, a

---

[*] " Concivibus suis."

choir of confessors, and a choir of virgins, each apart.
Gertrude, beholding so august an assembly, and reflecting
that, according to Scripture, it is purity which brings us
nearest to God, perceived between the Lord and the choir
of virgins rays of light, shining like snow, which united
these holy virgins more closely than the other saints to
their Spouse, by the ravishing sweetness of His caresses
and intimacy.

She also perceived rays of a most brilliant light, which
were shed upon some members of the community, as if there
were no obstacle between them and God ; although they
were materially separated from the church where she
beheld this mysterious apparition.   And though the Saint
was filled with an extreme joy during this rapture, she was
still solicitous for the sisters, and said to God : " Lord, since
Thou hast been pleased to pour forth on me the free gifts
of Thine ineffable love, what wilt Thou give to those who
are engaged in exterior duties ? "   He replied : " I will
anoint them with balsam, though they seem to sleep."
Gertrude was surprised at this, and could not understand
how those who did not give themselves to a contemplative
life should receive nevertheless the same reward as those
who were entirely devoted to it.   Then, as she began to
examine into the quality of these perfumes of which the
Son of God had spoken, by comparing them to balm and
aromatic ointments,—a small portion of which will suffice
to preserve the body from corruption, whether it is em-
balmed before or after the sleep of death, so that it has
received this unction,—she was enlightened in her difficulty
by this familiar comparison : namely, that when any one
partakes of food, every member of his body is strengthened
and nourished by it, although the mouth alone perceives
the delicacy of the viand : so when God, by an excess of

His mercy, grants any special grace to one of His elect, all participate in it ; and principally those who are united by the ties of community, where they receive an increase and superabundance of merit; and they only are excluded from this benefit who exclude themselves by their jealousy or ill-will.

Then, as the *Gloria in excelsis* was intoned, the Sovereign Pontiff, our Lord Jesus Christ, breathed towards heaven, to the honour of His Eternal Father, a breath like a burning flame.   And at the words : *Et in terrâ pax hominibus bonæ voluntatis,* He breathed upon those who were present a white light, bright as snow.   At the words of the Preface, *Sursum corda,* the Son of God arose, and by an efficacious attraction drew towards Himself all who were present.   Then turning towards the east, assisted by an infinite number of angels, He stood and raised His hands, and offered to God His Father, through the words of the Preface, the prayers of the faithful.   After this, when they began the *Agnus Dei,* the Lord rose before the altar, with all the power of His majesty ; communicating Himself, at the second *Agnus Dei,* by an impenetrable effect of His wisdom, to the souls of all the assistants ; at the third *Agnus Dei,* withdrawing into Himself, He offered in His own person to God His Father all their prayers and desires.   Then pouring forth again His sweetness, He gave the pax with His own blessed lips to all the saints who were present ; honouring with singular favour the company of virgins, offering this kiss both to their lips and their hearts.

After this, pouring forth the torrents of His love, He gave Himself to the community, with these words : "I am all yours ; therefore, let each enjoy Me as she desires." Then Gertrude replied to her Spouse : "Lord, now that I am satiated with Thy incredible delights, it seems to me

that Thou art still too far from me when Thou reposest on
the altar; therefore, for the benediction of this Mass, unite
my soul so to Thee that I may feel it is bound to Thee."
This the Lord accomplished in such a manner that she
knew by her union with her Spouse how pleasing her
desire was to Him.

CHAPTER XVII.

How we should prepare ourselves to receive the Body of Jesus Christ
— Different exercises of piety which St. Gertrude practised towards
this august Sacrament.

§ 1. *The Three Persons of the Blessed Trinity communicate
Their sanctity to Gertrude, that she may communicate
more worthily.*

As the Saint approached to receive the Sacrament of Life—
when they sang the *Sanctus, sanctus, sanctus,* in the Antiphon *Gaude et lætare*—she prostrated herself on the ground,
praying to God with her whole heart that He would be
pleased to prepare her worthily to participate in the celestial Food, for His glory and for the advantage of others.
The Son of God then abased Himself quickly towards her,
and, embracing her soul while they sang the word *sanctus,*
said : " At the word *sanctus,* which is referred to My
Person, I will give you all the sanctity of My Divinity and
My Humanity, as a worthy preparation to approach these
Holy Mysteries."

The following Sunday, as she returned thanks to God
for this favour, she beheld the Son of God, more beautiful
than a million of angels, presenting her condescendingly to
God His Father, clothed with His own holiness, which He
had given to her.   The Eternal Father took such great

pleasure in the soul, for the sake of His only Son, that, not being able to refrain from pouring forth His graces, He granted to her, with the Holy Spirit, the sanctity, which is attributed to Them as holy (*sanctus*), that she might obtain the full blessing of all sanctity, as well of that which emanates from Omnipotence as of that which emanates from wisdom and love.

§ 2. *St. Gertrude, preparing for Communion, receives the assurance from Jesus Christ that He will never depart from her, and that for her sake He will do good to others.*

On another occasion, when she was about to communicate, and perceived that many were abstaining from it for different reasons, she rejoiced in spirit, and being touched to the heart, said to God : "I give Thee thanks, my most loving Love and my God, that Thou hast placed me in this happy state, in which neither my relations nor any earthly consideration can prevent me from approaching Thy banquet of delights." To which the Lord replied, with His usual sweetness : "Since you have declared that there is nothing which can separate you from Me, know also that there is nothing in heaven or earth, neither judgment nor justice, which can hinder me from doing all the good for you which My Divine Heart desires."

On another occasion, as Gertrude approached the Holy Communion, and desired ardently that the Lord would prepare her worthily, this sweet and loving Lord consoled her by these tender words : "I will clothe Myself with your person, in order that I may be able to extend My Hand *
to do good to sinners without being wounded by the thorns

` "Delicatam mauum . . . inter hispidos peccatores."

which surround them. And I will also clothe you with
Myself, in order that all those whom you remember before
Me, and even those who are naturally like you, may be
raised to this high dignity, that I may do good to them according to My royal munificence."

§ 3. *St. Gertrude is presented to the Holy Trinity by Jesus
Christ. She obtains joy for the blessed, grace for the just,
repentance for sinners, and release for the souls in purgatory.*

One day when the Saint was about to partake of the
Divine Food, she reflected on the graces which God had
bestowed on her, and recalled this passage in the Book of
Kings: "Who am I, and what is my father's family?"
(1 Kings xviii.) Then, turning from these last words, as
only proper for those who had always served God, she considered herself as a little plant, which, on account of its
proximity to the inextinguishable fire of the Divine Heart,
received its benefits; and she saw that she wasted it, hour
after hour, by her faults and negligences; and that, being
reduced as it were to ashes, she resembled a burned-out
coal, which had been cast away. Therefore she turned
towards Jesus Christ, her beloved Mediator, and besought
Him to present her to God the Father, and to reconcile her
to Him; and it appeared to her that her dear Spouse drew
her to Him by the vapour of the love which came forth
from the Wounds of His Heart, and that He washed her
in the water which flowed from it, watering her with the
life-giving Blood which was contained therein; so that, by
degrees, she was transformed from the burned-out coal to a
tree covered with verdure, whose branches were divided
into three parts, like a lily; and the Son of God, having
taken it, presented it, with marks of honour and thanks-

giving, to the most holy and adorable Trinity; who received it with such love and tenderness, that the Eternal Father, by His omnipotence, attached to the highest branches of this tree all the fruit which the soul of the Saint might have produced if she had corresponded as she ought with the commands of the Divine Omnipotence. The Son of God and the Holy Spirit, in like manner, placed on two other parts of its branches the fruits of wisdom and charity.

Having, therefore, received the Body of Jesus Christ, and contemplating her Lord, as we have said, under the similitude of a tree, whose root was in the Wound of the Side of Jesus Christ, it seemed to her that a kind of sap, formed of the Humanity and Divinity of Jesus Christ, came forth in a miraculous manner from this sacred Wound, and passed through the stem of this tree into all its branches, producing flowers and fruit, which appeared as bright, in comparison with her ordinary life, as gold exceeds crystal in its brightness. This gave pleasure and an indescribable joy, not only to the Most Holy Trinity, but even to all the blessed, who, having risen out of respect, presented their merits to her individually, in the form of crowns, and suspended them on the branches of this tree, to His praise and glory who had given them new joy through her merits.

Then Gertrude prayed to God that all who were in heaven, on earth, or in purgatory, and who ought without doubt to have reaped some fruit from her works, had she not been so negligent, might at least receive some advantage from the graces which His Divine goodness had communicated to her. Then these good works, which were figured by the fruit of the tree, began to distil a liquor of extraordinary virtue: a part of which evaporated on high, filling the blessed with joy; another portion flowed down into purgatory, soothing the pains of those who suffered there ; and part, spreading itself forth upon the earth, augmenting the sweetness of grace in the just, and in sinners the bitterness of penance.

§ 4. *How advantageous it is to hear Holy Mass.*

As Gertrude offered the adorable Host to the Eternal Father, at the moment of the Elevation, in satisfaction for all her sins, and in reparation for all her negligences, she beheld her soul presented before the Divine Majesty with the same sentiments of joy in which Jesus Christ—who is the splendour and living image of the glory of His Father, and the Lamb of God without spot—offered Himself on the altar to God His Father for the salvation of the whole world ; because the Eternal Father considered her as purified from all sin by the merit of the spotless Humanity of Jesus Christ, and enriched and adorned with all the virtues which, through the same Holy Humanity, adorned the glorious Divinity of His Son.

As the Saint returned thanks to God for these graces with all her power, and took pleasure in considering the extraordinary favours which He had communicated to her, it was revealed to her that whenever any one assists at Mass with devotion, occupied with God, who offers Himself in this Sacrament for the whole world, he is truly regarded by the Eternal Father with the tenderness merited by the sacred Host which is offered to Him, and becomes like to one who, coming out of a dark place into the midst of sunlight, finds himself suddenly surrounded by brightness. Then the Saint made this inquiry of God : " Is not he who falls into sin deprived of this good, even as one who goes from light into darkness loses the favour of beholding the

light ?"   The Lord replied : "No ; for although the sinner
hides My Divine light from him, still My goodness will
not fail to leave him some ray to guide him to eternal life ;
and this light will increase whenever he hears Mass with
devotion or approaches the Sacraments."

§ 5. *The spiritual vestments with which the soul should be
adorned to receive the Holy Communion, and of the necessity of sanctifying the tongue which has touched the Body
of Christ.*

As Gertrude was about to communicate, and feared she
was not sufficiently prepared, though the moment was at
hand, she addressed her soul thus : "Behold, thy Spouse
calls thee : and how canst thou dare to appear before Him
without being adorned as thou shouldst be?"   Then, reflecting more and more on her unworthiness—entirely dis-
trusting herself, and placing her confidence in the mercy of
God alone—she said to herself: "Why defer longer ? since,
even had I a thousand years, I could not prepare as I
ought, having nothing which could serve to promote the
right dispositions in me.   But I will meet Him with con
fidence and humility ; and when my Lord beholds me from
afar, He can fill me with all the grace and the attractions
with which His love desires that I should appear before
Him."   And, approaching the Holy Mysteries in this
disposition, she thought only of her negligences and imperfections.   But as she advanced, she perceived our Lord
regarding her with an eye of compassion, or rather of love,
and sending her His innocence, that she might be adorned
therewith as with a white garment.   He gave her His humility, which made Him converse with creatures so utterly unworthy of such a favour ; and this served her for a purple
tunic.   He filled her with that hope which would make

her sigh ardently for Him whom she loved, to add the beauty of green to her garments. He presented her with His love of souls for a vestment of gold. He inspired her with the joy which He takes in the hearts of the faithful for a crown of precious stones. And, lastly, He gave her for sandals that confidence with which He deigned to rest on the inconstancy of human frailty, and which made Him find His delights with the children of men. And thus she was worthy to be presented to God.

After her Communion, as she recollected herself interiorly, our Lord appeared to her under the form of a pelican, as it is usually represented, piercing its heart with its beak. Marvelling at this, she said : " My Lord, what wouldst Thou teach me by this vision ? "—" I wish," replied our Lord, " that you would consider the excess of love which obliges Me to present you with such a gift ; for after having thus given Myself, I would rather remain dead in the tomb, so to speak, than deprive a soul who loves Me of the fruit of My liberality. Consider also, that even as the blood which comes from the heart of the pelican gives life to its little ones, so also the soul whom I nourish with the Divine Food which I present to it, receives a life which will never end."

On another occasion, after Communion, as the Saint was considering with what circumspection she should use that tongue, honoured above all the members of the body in being the depository of the most precious mysteries of Jesus Christ, she was instructed by this comparison : That one who does not abstain from vain, idle, or sinful discourse, and who approaches the Holy Communion without repentance, is like a person who gathers a heap of stones at the threshold of his door to throw at his guest when he comes to visit him, or beats him cruelly on the head with a rod

§ 6. *Of the ineffable love of God in the Sacrament of the Altar.*

Gertrude, having one day heard a sermon on the justice of God, was so overcome by fear, that she dared not approach this Divine Sacrament; but God, in His mercy, reassured her by these words: "If you will not look with the eyes of your soul on the many mercies which I have bestowed on you, open at least the eyes of your body, and behold Me before you enclosed in a little pix, and know assuredly that the rigour of My justice is even thus limited within the bounds of the mercy which I exercise towards men in the dispensation of this Sacrament."

On a similar occasion, the sweetness of Divine goodness urged her to a participation in the Holy Mysteries, by these words: "Consider in how small a space I give you My entire Divinity and My Humanity. Compare the size * of this with the size of the human body, and judge then of the greatness of My love. For as the human body surpasses My Body in size—that is to say, the quantity of the species of bread under which My Body is contained—so My mercy and charity in this Sacrament reduce Me to this state, that the soul which loves Me is in some sort above Me, as the human body is greater than My Body."

On another day, as she received the saving Host, our Lord addressed her thus: "Consider that the priest who gives you the Host touches it directly with his hands, and that the vestments with which he is clothed, out of respect, do not reach beyond his arms; this is to teach you, that although I regard with pleasure all that is done for My glory, as prayers, fasts, vigils, and other like works of

---

* "Quantitatem."

piety, still (those who have little understanding will not comprehend it) the confidence with which the elect have recourse to Me in their weakness touches Me far more sensibly ; even as you see My flesh is nearer to the hands of the priest than his vestments."

§ 7. *That humility is more agreeable to God than sensible devotion ; and how much our Lord desires to give Himself to the soul who loves Him.*

Once, when Gertrude heard the bell which called her to Communion, and the chant had already commenced, as she felt that she was not sufficiently prepared, she said to our Lord : "Behold, Lord, Thou art coming to me ; but why hast Thou not granted me the grace of devotion, so that I might present myself before Thee with a better preparation ?" He replied : "A bridegroom admires the personal beauty of his bride more than her ornaments ; and in like manner I prefer the virtue of humility to the grace of devotion."

Once, when many of the religious had abstained from Communion, Gertrude returned thanks to God, saying, " I thank Thee, O Lord, that Thou hast invited me to Thy sacred Banquet." To which our Lord replied, with words full of sweetness and tenderness : " Know that I have desired thee with My whole heart." " Alas, Lord ! " she exclaimed, " what glory can accrue to Thy Divinity when I touch this Sacrament with my unworthy lips ?" He replied : " Even as the love which we have for a friend makes us take pleasure in hearing him speak, so also the charity which I have for My elect makes Me sometimes find satisfaction in that in which they find none."

Once, as the Saint ardently desired to see the sacred

Host as the priest communicated the people, but could not do so on account of the crowd, she heard our Lord saying to her : " A sweet secret shall be between us, which is unknown to those who absent themselves from Me ; but thou, if thou wouldst enjoy it, approach ; and thou shalt not see, but taste and prove, the sweetness of this hidden manna."

§ 8. *That it is not wrong to abstain from Communion through reverence.*

As Gertrude saw one of her sisters approaching the Holy Eucharist with extreme emotions of fear, she turned from her with a feeling of indignation ; but the Lord charitably reproved her by these words : " Do you not know that I am honoured by reverence as well as by love ? But as human weakness is not able to combine the two at one moment, and as all are the members of one body, those who have less should take from those who have more.   For example, let her who is more moved by the sweetness of My love think less of the duty of respect, and be thankful that another supplies for her deficiency, by being more exact in testifying her reverence ; and let that other desire that she should obtain the joy and consolation that a soul possesses who is full of the Divine unction."

Once also, as Gertrude prayed for a sister under similar circumstances, our Lord replied : " I would that My elect should not consider Me so severe, but rather believe that I receive as a benefit the least service they render Me at their own expense.   For example, she makes a sacrifice to God at her own expense who, although she finds no sweetness in devotion, never omits the service of God, either by prayers, prostrations, or other acts of devotion, still hoping, in His mercy, that He will accept the fulfilment of these auties."

§ 9. *Whence it is that we sometimes feel less fervour at the moment of Communion than at any other time.*

As Gertrude prayed for a person who complained of having less devotion on the days on which she communicated than on others, our Lord said to her : " This has not happened by chance, but by a particular Providence, which inspires feelings of devotion at unexpected times, to elevate the heart of man, which is so enslaved by the body ; but on festivals and at the time of Communion I withdraw this grace, preferring to occupy the hearts of My elect with good desires or humility ; and this may be more advantageous to their welfare than the grace of devotion."

§ 10. *God permits the just to fall for their humiliation.*

As the Saint prayed for a person who had abstained from receiving the Body of the Lord, fearing to be an occasion of scandal, our Lord made known His will by this comparison : " As a man who washes his hands to remove a stain, removes at the same time not only what he has seen, but also cleanses his hands perfectly, so the just are allowed to fall into some trifling faults, that they may become more agreeable to Me by their repentance and humility ; but there are some who contradict My designs in this, by neglecting the interior beauty which I desire to see after their penance, thinking of the exterior, and of the judgment of men ; and this they do, when they deprive themselves of the grace which they might receive in the Sacrament, from the fear of scandalising those who do not think them sufficiently prepared."

§ 11. *Jesus Christ Himself prepares the Saint for Communion.*

As the Saint was about to receive Holy Communion, she felt herself invited by Jesus Christ Himself. It appeared to her that she was in the celestial kingdom, and that she was seated in glory near the Eternal Father, to eat with Him at His table. But as she considered that she was neither properly attired nor sufficiently prepared, she endeavoured to withdraw. Then the Son of God came to her, and led her to a retired place to prepare her for this banquet. And first, He remitted her sins by washing her hands; offering His Passion for her amendment. Then He gave her a necklace, bracelets, and rings; and having thus adorned her, He desired her to walk discreetly, as one so adorned should do, and not like a foolish person, who, even when thus attired, would be despised rather than honoured.

She understood by these words, that they walk like fools who, after they have been cured of their defects, are as pusillanimous as ever, because they have not an entire confidence that Jesus Christ will supply for their defects.

§ 12. *Of the value of communicating for the souls in purgatory.*

One day, after Communion, the Saint offered the Host which she had just received for the souls in purgatory; and perceiving the great benefit they obtained thereby, she was amazed, and said to her Spouse: "My God, since I am obliged to declare for Thy glory that Thou dost honour me continually with Thy presence, or rather, that Thou abidest in my soul, unworthy as I am, how is it that Thou dost not work through me as Thou hast done to-day after I have received Thy adorable Body?" He replied: "It is not easy for every one to approach a king who remains always in his palace; but when his love for his queen induces him to go forth, then all may behold, through her kindness, his pomp and magnificence; thus, when, moved by My love, I visit one of the faithful (who is free from mortal sin) in the Sacrament of the Altar, all who are in heaven, on earth, or in purgatory, receive immense benefits thereby."

On another occasion the Saint humbled herself deeply before approaching the Holy Communion, in honour and in imitation of the humility of the Son of God in descending into limbo. Then, uniting herself with His descent, she found herself descending to the very depths of purgatory; and humbling herself still lower, she heard our Lord say to her: "I will draw you to Me in the Sacrament of the Altar in such a manner that you will draw after you all those who shall perceive the odour of your desire."

Having received this promise from our Lord, she desired after Communion that He would release as many souls as she could divide the Host into particles in her mouth; but as she tried to effect this, He said to her: "In order that you may know that My mercy is above all My works, and that the abyss of My mercy cannot be exhausted, I am ready to grant you, through the merit of this life-giving Sacrament, more than you dare to ask Me."

CHAPTER XVIII.

The devotion of St. Gertrude to the Mother of God—She is taught to invoke her as the white lily of the adorable Trinity, and the vermilion rose of heaven.

As Gertrude offered herself to God during her prayer, and inquired how He desired her to occupy herself at this time,

He replied : " Honour My Mother, who is seated at My side, and employ yourself in praising her." Then the Saint began to salute the Queen of heaven, reciting the verse, *Paradisus voluptas*, &c.—" Paradise of delights ; " and extolling her because she was the abode full of delights which the impenetrable wisdom of God, who knows all creatures perfectly, had chosen for His dwelling ; and she besought her to obtain for her a heart adorned with so many virtues that God might take pleasure in dwelling therein. Then the Blessed Virgin inclined towards her, and planted in her heart the different flowers of virtue— the rose of charity, the lily of chastity, the violet of humility, the flexibility of obedience, and many other gifts ; thus showing how promptly she assists those who invoke her assistance.

Then the Saint addressed her thus : *Gaude, morum disciplina*—" Rejoice, model of discipline ; " praising her for having ordered her desires, judgment, and affection with more care and circumspection than the rest of mankind, and for having served the Lord, who dwelt in her, with such respect and reverence, that she had never given Him the least occasion of pain in her thoughts, words, or actions. Having besought her to obtain for her also the same grace, it appeared to her that the Mother of God sent her all her affections under the form of young virgins, recommending each in particular to unite her dispositions to those of her client, and to supply for any defects into which she might fall. By this also she understood with what promptitude the Blessed Virgin assists those who invoke her. Then the Saint besought our Lord to supply for her omissions in devotion to His Blessed Mother, which He was pleased to do.

The following day, as Gertrude prayed, the Mother of God appeared to her, in the presence of the ever-adorable

Trinity, under the form of a white lily, with three leaves, one standing erect, and the other two bent down. By this she understood that it was not without reason that the Blessed Mother of God was called the white lily of the Trinity, since she contained in herself, with more plenitude and perfection than any other creature, the virtues of the Most Holy Trinity, which she had never sullied by the slightest stain of sin. The upright leaf of the lily represented the omnipotence of God the Father, and the two leaves which bent down, the wisdom and love of the Son and the Holy Spirit, to which the Holy Virgin approaches so nearly. Then the Blessed Virgin made known to her that if any one salutes her devoutly as the white lily of the Trinity and the vermilion rose of heaven, she will show her how she prevails by the omnipotence of the Father, how skilful she is in procuring the salvation of men by the wisdom of the Son, and with what an exceeding love her heart is filled by the charity of the Holy Ghost. The Blessed Virgin added these words : " I will appear at the hour of death to those who salute me thus in such glory, that they will anticipate the very joys of heaven." From this time the Saint frequently saluted the Holy Virgin or her images with these words : " Hail, white lily of the ever-peaceful and glorious Trinity ! hail, effulgent rose, the delight of heaven, of whom the King of heaven was born, and by whose milk He was nourished ! do thou feed our souls by the effusions of thy Divine influences."

CHAPTER XIX.

How the praises offered to the Saints may be referred to God.

As St. Gertrude was accustomed to refer all that was sweet
and agreeable to her Beloved, when she heard or read the
praise of the Blessed Virgin or of the Saints, and was more
than usually moved thereby, she raised her heart to God,
so that she thought more of Him than of the Saint whose
memory was honoured ; and as she heard a sermon on the
Feast of the Annunciation, in which the Blessed Virgin was
spoken of exclusively, and no mention was made of the
Incarnation of the Son of God, she was so grieved, that as
she passed the altar of the Blessed Virgin, returning from
the sermon, she did not salute her with her usual devotion,
but rather offered her salutation to Jesus, the blessed Fruit
of her womb.   But afterwards she feared she had displeased
this august queen, until our Lord consoled her by these
loving words : " Fear not, Gertrude, My beloved ; for although you have referred the honour and praise which you
usually render to My dear Mother exclusively to Me, it will
not be the less agreeable to her."

CHAPTER XX.

How God desires to be sought for by the soul that loves Him ; and
how He loves us when we suffer.

On one occasion, when the Saint was prevented from
assisting at Vespers, by some infirmity, she exclaimed :
" Lord, wouldest Thou not be more honoured if I were in
choir with the community, engaged in prayer, and fulfilling
the duties of my Rule, than by my being here, passing my
time uselessly, in consequence of this illness ? "   Our Lord

replied : " Be assured that the bridegroom takes more pleasure in conversing with his bride familiarly in his house, than when he displays her before the world, adorned with her richest ornaments." By these words she understood that the soul appears in public, and clothed with all her state, when she occupies herself in good works for the glory of God ; but that she reposes in secret with her Spouse, when she is hindered by any infirmity from attending to those exercises, for in this state she is deprived of the satisfaction of acting according to her own inclination, and she remains abandoned entirely to the will of God ; and therefore it is that God takes most pleasure in us when we find least occasion of pleasing and glorifying ourselves.

CHAPTER XXI.

The Saint receives a triple absolution and benediction from the
Blessed Trinity, through the merits of Jesus Christ.

As the Saint heard Mass one day with the greatest fervour, it appeared to her that her guardian angel took her in his arms as if she were a little child, at the *Kyrie Eleison,* and presented her to God the Father, to receive His benediction, saying : " Eternal Father, bless Thy little child." And because for a time He replied not, as if He would testify by His silence that so miserable a creature was unworthy of this favour, she began to enter into herself, and to consider her unworthiness and nothingness with extreme confusion. Then the Son of God arose, and gave her the merits of His most holy life to supply her defects, so that she appeared as if clothed with a rich and shining robe, and as if she had attained to the full age and strength of Jesus Christ.

Then the Eternal Father inclined lovingly towards her, and gave her His absolution thrice, as a sign of the triple remission of all the sins which she had committed against His omnipotence in thought, word, or deed. The Saint offered in thanksgiving the adorable life of His only Son ; and at the same time the precious stones with which her garments were adorned emitted a harmonious concert to the eternal glory of God, which testified how agreeable it is to Him to offer Him the all-perfect and holy life of His Son. The same angel then presented her to God the Son, saying : " Bless Thy sister, O King of Heaven ; " and having received from Him a triple benediction, to efface all the sins she had committed against the Divine Wisdom, he then presented her to the Holy Spirit, with these words : " O Lover of men, bless Thy spouse;" and she received from Him also a triple benediction, in remission of all the sins which she had committed against the Divine Goodness. Let those who read this reflect on these three benedictions at the *Kyrie Eleison.*

CHAPTER XXII.

Favours granted to the Saint during the recital of the Divine Office.

ONCE, as the Saint was reciting the Divine Office with extraordinary fervour, on the Feast of a Saint, each word which she uttered appeared to dart like an arrow from her heart into the Heart of Jesus, penetrating it deeply, and filling it with ineffable satisfaction. From one end of these arrows rays of light shot forth like stars, which seemed to fall on all the saints, but especially on the one whose festival was celebrated ; from the lower end of the arrows drops of dew flowed forth, which fertilised the souls of the living, and refreshed the souls in purgatory.

As the Saint endeavoured on another occasion to attach some particular intention to each note and each word of her chant, she was often hindered by the weakness of nature, and at last exclaimed, with much sadness : "Alas! what fruit can I obtain from this exercise, when I am so unstable?" But our Lord, who could not endure to behold the affliction of His servant, with His own hands presented her with His Divine Heart, under the figure of a burning lamp, saying to her: "Behold, I present to the eyes of your soul My loving Heart, which is the organ of the Most Holy Trinity, that it may accomplish all that you cannot accomplish yourself, and thus all will seem perfect in you to My eyes ; for even as a faithful servant is always ready to execute the commands of his master, so, from henceforth, My Heart will be always ready, at any moment, to repair your defects and negligences."

Gertrude wondered and feared, because of this amazing goodness of her Lord, thinking that it was not becoming for the adorable Heart, which is the treasure-house * of the Divinity, and the fruitful source of every good, to remain continually near so miserable a creature, to supply for her defects, even as a servant attends on his master. But the Lord consoled and encouraged her by this comparison: "If you have a beautiful and melodious voice, and take much pleasure in chanting, will you not feel displeased if another person, whose voice is harsh and unpleasant, and who can scarcely utter a correct sound, wishes to sing, instead of you, and insists on doing so? Thus My Divine Heart, understanding human inconstancy and

---

* "Gazophylacium."

frailty, desires with incredible ardour continually to be invited, either by your words, or at least by some other sign, to operate and accomplish in you what you are not able to accomplish yourself ; and as its omnipotence enables it to act without trouble, and its impenetrable wisdom enables it to act in the most perfect manner, so also its joyous and loving charity makes it ardently desire to accomplish this end."

CHAPTER XXIII.

Of the abundant virtue which flows from the Heart of Jesus into the faithful soul.

SOME days after, as the Saint reflected upon this stupendous favour with singular gratitude, she anxiously inquired of the Lord how long it would be continued to her.   He replied : " As long as you desire to have it , for it would grieve Me to deprive you of it."   She answered : " But is it possible that Thy Deified Heart is suspended like a lamp in the midst of mine, which is, alas ! so unworthy of its presence, when at the same time I have the joy of finding in Thyself this very same source of all delight ? "   " It is even so," replied the Lord ; " when you wish to take hold of anything, you stretch forth your hand, and then withdraw it again after you have taken it; so also the love which I bear towards you causes Me to extend My Heart to draw you to Me, when you are distracting yourself with exterior things ; and then, when you have recollected yourself, I withdraw My Heart, and you along with it, so that you may enter into Me ; and thus I make you taste the sweetness of all virtues."

Then, as she considered on the one hand, with exceeding wonder and gratitude, the greatness of the charity which

God had for her, and, on the other, her own nothingness
and the great number of her faults, she retired with profound self-contempt into the valley of humility, esteeming
herself unworthy of any grace ; and having remained
therein hidden for some time, He who loves to pour forth
His gifts on the humble seemed to make a golden tube *
come forth from His Heart, which descended upon this
humble soul in the form of a lamp, making a channel
through which He poured forth on her the abundance of all
His marvels ; so that when she humbled herself at the
recollection of her faults, our Lord poured forth on her
from His sacred Heart all the virtue and beauty of His
Divine perfection, which concealed her imperfections from
the eyes of the Divine Goodness. And further, if she
desired any new ornament, or any of those things which
appeared attractive and desirable to the human heart, it
was communicated to her, with much pleasure and joy, by
this same mysterious canal.

When she had tasted the sweetness of these holy
delights for some time, and was adorned with all virtues,—
not her own, but those given her by God,—she heard a
most melodious sound, as of a sweet harper harping upon
his harp, and these words were sung to her : " Come, O
Mine own, to Me : enter, O Mine own, into Me : abide, O
Mine own, with Me." † And the Lord Himself explained
the meaning of this canticle to her, saying : " Come to Me,
because I love you, and desire that you should be always
present before Me, as My beloved spouse, and therefore

---

* " Fistulam."

† " Audivit quandam vocem dulcissimam, tanquam cytharistæ
suaviter demulcenti melodiâ cytharizantis in cythara sua, hæc verba :
Veni mea ad me : Intra meum in me : Mane meus mecum." Had
she, then, indeed heard that ineffable song which will be the joy and
the eternal consolation of the redeemed ?

I call you ; and because My delights are in you, I desire
that you should enter into Me. Furthermore, because I
am the God of love, I desire that you should remain
indissolubly united to Me, even as the body is united to
the spirit, without which it cannot live for a moment."
This rapture continued for an hour, and the Saint was
drawn in a miraculous manner into the Heart of Jesus,
through this sacred channel of which we have spoken, so
that she found herself happily reposing in the bosom of
her Lord and Spouse. What she felt, what she saw, what
she heard, what she tasted, what she learned of the words
of life, she alone can know, and they who, like her, are
worthy to be admitted to this sublime union with their
Spouse Jesus, their soul's true love, who is God, blessed
for ever. Amen.

CHAPTER XXIV.

Of the sepulchre of Jesus Christ in the faithful soul, and how to
make a spiritual cloister in the Body and Heart of Jesus.

On Good Friday, as they made a commemoration of our
Lord's burial, after the Office, Gertrude implored Him to
bury Himself in her soul, and to abide therein for ever.
Our Lord replied, with infinite charity ; " I will serve as
a stone to close the gates of your senses ; I will place My
affections there as soldiers to guard this stone, to defend
your heart against all hurtful affections, and to work in
you My Divine power, for My eternal glory."

Then, fearing that she had judged a person harshly for
something which she had seen her do, she said to God :
" Lord, Thou hast placed soldiers to guard the entrance of
my heart ; but, alas ! I fear they have withdrawn, since I

have judged my neighbour so harshly." "How can you complain that they have withdrawn," replied our Lord, "when at this moment you experience their assistance?—for it is a sign that one desires to be united to Me when they cannot take pleasure in what displeases Me."

While they sang the Antiphon at Vespers, *Vidi aquam egredientem*—"I saw water springing forth"—the Lord said to Gertrude: "Behold My Heart,—let it be your temple; then go through the other parts of My Body, and arrange for the other parts of a monastery wherever it seems best to you; for I desire that My sacred Humanity should henceforth be your cloister." "Lord," replied the Saint, "I know not how to seek or choose, because I have found such sweetness in Thy Heart, which Thou hast deigned to give me for a temple, that I can find neither repose nor rest out of it,—two things which are absolutely necessary in the cloister." "If you desire it," said the Saviour, "you can still find these two things in My Heart; for have you not heard that there are persons who never leave My house even for food or rest, like St. Dominic? Nevertheless, choose in the other parts of My Body the places which you have need of for this spiritual monastery."

Then Gertrude, obeying the commands of God, chose the Feet of her Spouse for her lavatory; His Hands for her work-room; His Mouth for her reception-room, or chapter-room; His Eyes for her school, in which she could read; and His Ears for her confessional. Then the Lord taught her that whenever she committed any fault, she should ascend to this sacred tribunal by the five degrees of humiliation, which are expressed in those five words: "I come to Thee vile, sinful, poor, wicked, and unworthy, O Abyss of overflowing goodness, to be cleansed from every stain, and purified from all sin."

CHAPTER XXV.

Of the union of the soul with Jesus Christ, and how she is prepared, by the merits of the Saints, to be an agreeable abode for
her God.

As Gertrude reflected on different instances of instability,
she turned to God, and said : " It is my only good to be
united to Thee alone, my Beloved." The Lord, inclining
towards her and embracing her tenderly, said : " And it is
always sweet to me to be united to thee, My beloved." As
He said these words, all the saints arose and offered their
merits before the throne of God for her soul, that it might
become more worthy of being His abode. Then she knew
how prompt God is in inclining towards the soul that calls
upon Him, and with what joy all the blessed contribute
their merits to supply for our unworthiness.

The Saint then exclaimed, in the fervour of her desires :
" I salute Thee, my most loving Lord, although I am but a
vile and abject creature." And she received this reply
from the sweetest mercy of God : " And I salute you also in
return, My beloved spouse." By this she knew that each
time a soul says to God, " My Beloved, my most dear
Lord, my sweetest Jesus," or any other words which express her ardent devotion, He often replies to her in a
manner which obtains for her a special privilege of grace
in heaven ; like the special glory which St. John the Evangelist obtained on earth, of being called " the disciple
whom Jesus loved."

CHAPTER XXVI.

Of the merit of a good will, and instructions on some words of the Divine Office.

At the Mass *Veni et ostende*,* the Lord appeared to St. Gertrude, full of sweetness and grace, breathing forth a holy and vivifying odour, and pouring forth from the august throne of His glory the influences of His love for the sweet Feast of His Nativity.

Then, the saint having prayed Him to enrich all who had been recommended to her prayers with special grace, He said to her : " I have given to each a tube of pure gold ; of which such is the virtue, that by it they may draw forth all they need from My sacred Heart." By this mystic tube she understood that good will by which men may acquire all the spiritual riches which are in heaven and on earth. For example : if any one, burning with the fire of pure and holy desires, endeavours to give God as much thanks and praise and as many testimonies of service and fidelity as certain of His saints have rendered to Him, the infinite goodness of God regards this good will as if it had really been effected. But this tube becomes more brilliant than gold when men thank God for having given them so noble and elevated a will, that they might have acquired infinitely greater advantages by it than the whole world could bestow.

She knew, also, that all her sisters who surrounded Jesus Christ received Divine grace by similar tubes. Some appeared to receive it directly from the Heart of Jesus

---

* Introit for Saturday in Ember Week ; Advent, " Come, O Lord, and show unto us Thy face," &c.

Christ, others from His Hands; but the farther from His
Heart they drew these graces, the more difficulty they had in
obtaining them; whereas those who drew them from His
Divine Heart obtained them more easily, more sweetly,
and more abundantly. ' Those who drew directly from His
sacred Heart represented those persons who conform themselves entirely to the Divine will, who desire above all
things that this will should be accomplished in them, both
in regard to spirituals and temporals. And these persons
touch the Heart of God so powerfully, and render it so
favourable to them at the time that God has determined, that
they receive the torrent of Divine sweetness with as much
abundance and pleasure as they have abandoned themselves
perfectly to His holy will. But those who endeavoured to
draw their graces from the other members of the Body of Jesus
Christ, represent those persons who endeavour to acquire virtue according to their natural inclinations ; and the fear and
difficulty they experience is proportionate to the extent to
which they have relied on their own judgment, and have
failed to abandon themselves to Divine Providence.

§ 1. *Of the most perfect manner of offering our hearts to
God.*

As Gertrude offered her heart to God in the following
manner,—" Lord, behold my heart, which is detached from
all creatures ; I offer it to Thee freely, beseeching Thee to
purify it in the sanctifying Waters of Thy adorable Side,
and to adorn it with the precious Blood of Thy sweetest
Heart, and to unite it to Thee by the odours of charity,"—
our Lord appeared to her, and offered her heart to His
Eternal Father, united to His own, under the form of a
chalice, the two parts of which were joined together by
wax. The Saint, perceiving this, said, with extreme fer-

vour: "Grant me the grace, most loving Lord, that my heart may be always before Thee like the flasks * which princes use, so that Thou mayest have it cleansed and filled and emptied, according to Thy good pleasures, whenever and however Thou willest." This request being heard favourably by the Son of God, He said to His Father: "Eternal Father! may this soul pour forth for Thy infinite glory what Mine contains in My Humanity!" And from that moment, whenever the Saint offered her heart to God, saying the words above mentioned, it seemed to her so filled, that it poured itself forth in thanksgiving and praises, augmenting the joy of the blessed in heaven, and contributing to the adornment of the just on earth, as will be seen hereafter. From this moment the Saint knew that God willed her to commit to writing what He had revealed to her, that it might be for the benefit of many.

§ 2. *Of confidence in God, and of reparation for the contempts offered to Him.*

In Advent, by the response *Ecce venit*,† she knew that if any one formed in their heart, with a firm purpose, a perfect desire of submitting in all things to the adorable will of God, alike in prosperity as in adversity, they would, by His grace, render the same honour to God by this thought as if they crowned Him with a royal diadem.

And by these words of the Prophet Isaias: "Arise, arise! stand up, O Jerusalem;" she understood the advantage which the Church militant receives from the devotion of the elect. For when a soul, full of love, turns to God

* "Flasconum, qui ad refectionem dominorum deferuntur."

V. Response, ii. Nocturn, 2d Sunday in Advent: "Behold, the Lord our Protector cometh, the Holy One of Israel."

with her whole heart, and with a perfect will of repairing, were it possible, all the dishonour done to Jesus Christ, she appeases His anger by her loving charity, so that He is willing to pardon the sins of the whole world.

By the words, "That hast drunk the cup of His wrath even to the bottom" (Isa. li.), may be understood how she has averted the severity of Divine justice. But by the following words, "That hast drunk even to the dregs," she knew that the reprobate have the dregs of this chalice for their portion, and can never obtain redemption.

§ 3. *Of refraining from useless words.*

By these words of Isaias, "Thou dost not thy own ways, and thy own will is not found to speak a word" (lviii. 13), she knew that he who regulates his words and actions thoughtfully, and abstains even from those that are lawful when they are not necessary, will obtain a triple advantage: first, he will find a greater pleasure in God, according to these words, "Thou shalt be delighted in the Lord;" secondly, bad thoughts will have less power over him, for it is said, "I will lift thee above the high places of the earth;" and thirdly, in eternity the Son of God will communicate the merits of His most holy life more abundantly to him than to others, because by it he has been victorious over every temptation, and gained a glorious victory, as these words express: "I will feed thee with the inheritance of Jacob thy father."

God made known to her also by these words, "Behold, his reward is with him" (Isa. xxxix.), that our Lord Himself, by His love, is the reward of His elect; and He insinuates Himself into their souls with such sweetness, that they may truly say they are rewarded beyond all their deserts. "And his work is before him;" that is to say, when we abandon ourselves entirely to Divine Providence, and seek only the accomplishment of the will of God in all things, grace has already rendered us perfect in the sight of God.

By the words, " Be ye holy, children of Israel," Gertrude learned that those who repent promptly of the sins they have committed, and set themselves with a sincere heart to keep the commandments of God, are as truly sanctified and as promptly cured as the leper to whom our Lord said : "I will : be thou made clean." By the words, "Sing ye to the Lord a new canticle" (Ps. cxlix.), she knew that he sings a new canticle who sings with devotion ; because, when he has received the grace from God to understand what he sings, his chant becomes agreeable to God.

§ 4. *God sends afflictions to cure our souls.*

By the words, "The Spirit of the Lord is upon me ; He hath sent me to heal the contrite of heart" (Isa. lxi.), she understood that the Son of God, having been sent by His Father to heal contrite hearts, was accustomed to send some affliction to His elect, even should it be only exterior, in order to heal them. But when this happens, He does not always deliver them from the affliction which has made them contrite, because it is not hurtful to them ; for He prefers to cure that which might cause them eternal death.

By the words, *In splendoribus sanctorum* *—" In the brightness of the saints " (Ps. cix.), she knew that the light of the Divinity is so great and so incomprehensible, that even if each saint who has lived or who will live, from the

---

* Antiphon at ii. Vespers of the Nativity, from the first Psalm at Vespers for Sundays and Festivals. These revelations were probably made during Advent, when the prophecies of Isaias are read at Matins.

time of Adam to the end of the world, were given a special knowledge of it, as clear, as elevated, and as extended as could be given to any creature, so that none should be able to explain it to the other, nor to share in their knowledge,— even should the number of saints be a thousand times greater than it is,—the Divinity would still remain infinitely beyond their conception.   Thus it is not written *splendore*, but *in splendoribus*—"In the brightness [plu.] of Thy saints; from the womb, before the day-star, I begot Thee."

§ 5. *How we must carry our cross after Jesus Christ, and how the mercy of God chastises the elect.*

At the Antiphon *Qui vult* *—"If any man will come after Me, let him take up his cross and follow Me" (Matt. xvi.), Gertrude beheld our Lord walking on a road which seemed pleasant because of the beauty of the verdure and flowers which covered it, but which nevertheless was narrow, and rough with thorns.   Then she beheld a cross which went before Him, and separated the thorns from one another, making the road wider and more easy; while the Saviour turned to those who came after Him, and encouraged them, looking at them with a sweet and loving countenance, and saying: "Let him that will come after Me, take up his cross, and deny himself, and follow Me." By this she knew that our temptations are our crosses. For example : it is a cross to one person to be obliged by obedience to do what she dislikes; to another, to be restrained.   Now, each ought so to carry his cross as to be willing to suffer with a good heart all that crosses him, and yet to neglect nothing which he thinks may be for the glory of God.

---

* Ant. at Magnificat of ii. Vespers, Com. of one Martyr.

As they chanted this verse,* "The words of the wicked have prevailed over us" (Ps. lxiv.), she knew that when any one who has sinned through human frailty is too severely reprehended for it by another, this excessive severity draws down the mercy of God on him, and increases his merit.

As they sung the *Salve Regina*, at the words, "Turn on us those merciful eyes of Thine," as the Saint desired that our Lord would cure her of a bodily infirmity, He said to her, with sweet familiarity : " Do you not know that I look on you with eyes of mercy whenever you suffer any pain of body or mind ?"

On another occasion, as they sung the words *Gloriosum sanguinem*,† on the Feast of some Martyrs, she knew that even as blood, which naturally inspires a feeling of horror when considered in itself, is nevertheless praised in Scripture when it is poured forth for Jesus Christ, so omissions of religious duties, from charity or obedience, are so agreeable to God, that they may be justly termed glorious. She knew also, on another occasion, that God, by a secret dispensation of His judgments, sometimes permits sinners to receive a reply which serves only to harden them in their obstinacy, when they seek by artifice to ascertain from the elect what is hidden from them. Even as the Prophet Ezechiel writes : " He that shall place his uncleannesses in his heart, and set up the stumbling-block of his iniquity before his face, and shall come to the prophet, inquiring of Me by him ; I, the Lord, will answer him according to the multitude of his uncleannesses " (Ez. xiv.)

---

* " *Verba iniquorum prævaluerunt super nos*," 2d Ps. at Lauds, *feria quarta*, and in the Office of the Dead.

† Response after ii. Lesson in the Common of many Martyrs.

§ 6. *That without the consent of the will we do not sin, and
how we are obliged to reprove evil-doers.*

As they sung these words in honour of St. John, *Haurit
virus hic letale,** she understood, that as the virtue of faith
preserved John from the poison, so the action of the will
which resists sin preserves the soul pure, however mortal
the venom may be which glides into the heart against its
will.   By the versicle *Dignare, Domine,*† she knew that
when man has recourse to God, and beseeches Him to preserve him from sin, even though he should seem afterwards,
by a secret permission of Providence, to fall into some considerable fault, his fall nevertheless will not be nearly so
great as it would otherwise have been, and the grace of
Jesus Christ will so sustain him that he will easily repent.

When they chanted the Response *Benedicens,*‡ she stood
demanding the benediction in the person of Noah.   On
receiving it, the Lord in His turn seemed to ask hers.   By
this she understood that man blesses God when he repents
for having offended his Creator, and when he asks His help
to avoid sin for the future.   By the words, *Ubi est* § (Gen.
iv.), she knew that the Lord would demand an account
from every religious of the sins which her neighbour had
committed, and which she might have prevented, either
by warning the person herself or by informing her superior ; and that the excuse of those who say, " It is not

---

* " This Saint took poison without harm."   Not in either of the
Offices of St. John ; probably from a hymn.

† " Vouchsafe, O Lord, to keep us this day without sin," at Prime,
and in the *Te Deum.*

‡ ix. Response, iii. Nocturn, Sexagesima Sunday.   But the word
there is *Benedixit*—" God blessed Noah and his sons," &c.

§ i. Nocturn, ii. Lesson, v. Feria after Septuagesima—" Where is
thy brother Abel ? "

my place to correct others;" or, "I am as bad as they are," will be no more accepted by God than the words of Cain : "Am I my brother's keeper ? "

For each is obliged before God to turn his brother from sin, and to assist him to advance in virtue ; and he who neglects this duty against his conscience offends God. It is useless for him to pretend that he has received no commission, for his own conscience will teach him that God requires it from him ; and if he neglects it, God will demand an account from him even more strictly than from a superior who was absent when the evil was committed, or who did not notice it when present. Thus we find these words in Scripture : " Woe to him who sins, but a double woe to him who assists in sin." We make ourselves guilty of the sin of others, if we consent to it by concealing it when we might procure glory to God by discovering it.

§ 7. *They who labour for the advancement of religion are rewarded as if they had clothed the Saviour—Angels encompass the blest.*

By the Response which commences *Induit me*,* Gertrude learned that he who labours by his works and by his words for the advancement of religion and the defence of justice, acts as if He clothed God Himself with a magnificent and sumptuous garment ; and the Lord will recompense him in the life eternal, according to the riches of His royal liberality, by clothing him with a robe of gladness, and crowning him with a diadem of glory ; but, above all, that he who suffers for the promotion of good, or for religion, is as agreeable to God as a garment which warmed

---

* "The Lord hath clothed me," Common of Virgins, **xi. Response.** iii. Nocturn.

and covered him would be to a poor man; and that if he
who labours for the good of religion makes no progress on
account of the obstacles he meets with, his reward will not
be the less for this before God.

While they chanted the Response *Vocavit angelus,**
she knew that the choirs of angels, whose assistance is so
powerful, surround the elect to defend them. But God, by
His paternal Providence, sometimes suspends the effect of
this protection, and permits the just to be tempted, that He
may recompense them gloriously when they have gained a
victory with less help from on high and from their angels.

At the Response *Vocavit angelus Domini Abraham,* she
learned that as Abraham satisfied the claims of obedience
by raising his arm, and merited to be called by an angel,
so, when the elect bend their minds and their wills to perform any painful work for the love of God, they merit to
taste at that moment the sweetness of grace, and to be consoled by the testimony of their own conscience. And this is
a favour which the infinite liberality of God bestows even
before those eternal recompenses which shall be given to
each according to the measure of his works. As the Saint
reflected on some trials which she had formerly suffered,
she inquired of God why she had been thus tried by these
persons. "When the hand of a father wills to chastise his
child," replied our Lord, "the rod cannot oppose itself.
Therefore, I desire that My elect should never attribute
their sufferings to those whom I make use of to purify
them; but rather let them cast their eyes on My paternal
love, which would not allow even a breath of wind to
approach them unless it furthered their eternal salvation;

---

* "The Angel of the Lord called Abraham," Quinquagesima Sunday,
Response, ii. Nocturn.

and therefore they should have compassion on those who stain themselves to purify them."

§ 8. *Of offering our actions through the Son to the Eternal Father.*

One day the Saint offered a painful duty to the Eternal Father, saying : " Lord, I offer Thee this action through Thy only Son, in the power of the Holy Spirit, for Thy eternal glory." And it was made known to her that this intention gave an extraordinary value and price to her work, and elevated it above a mere human action ; and that this offering was very agreeable to God the Father. And even as objects appear green when seen through green glass, or red when seen through red glass, so all that is offered to the Eternal Father through His only Son becomes most pleasing and acceptable to Him.

§ 9. *Of the utility of prayer when it does not produce sensible fruit.*

Gertrude inquired of God what advantage some of her friends had gained by her prayers, since they did not seem better for them. The Lord instructed her by this comparison : " When a child returns from visiting an emperor, who has enriched him with vast possessions and an immense revenue, those who behold him in the weakness of childhood little imagine the treasures of which he is in possession, although those who have been present are well aware how powerful and important his wealth will render him hereafter. Do not, therefore, be surprised if you do not see the fruits of your prayers with your bodily eyes, since I dispose of them, according to My eternal wisdom, to greater advantage. And know that the more you pray for any one, the happier they will become, because no prayer of faith can remain unfruitful, although we do not know in what manner it will fructify."

§ 10. *Of the eternal recompense of directing our thoughts to God.*

Gertrude desired to know what advantage there was in referring our thoughts to God, and she received this instruction : that when man raises his mind to heaven by meditation or reflection, he presents, as it were, before the throne of God's glory a bright and shining mirror, in which the Lord beholds His own image with pleasure, because He is the Author and Dispenser of all good. And the more difficulty any one finds in this elevation of soul, the more perfect and agreeable this mirror appears before the Most Holy Trinity and the saints, and it will remain for the eternal glory of God and the good of this soul.

§ 11. *That adversity prevents occasion of sin, and of the good effects of a good will.*

On a fast-day, when the Saint was unable to chant from severe indisposition and headache, she inquired of God why He so often permitted these infirmities to visit her on festivals. Our Lord replied : " It is to prevent you from dissipating yourself by the pleasures of the harmony of the chant, and so being less disposed to receive grace." "But," she inquired, " could not Thy grace prevent this misfortune ?" To this our Lord answered : " It is a greater advantage to men to turn away occasions of falls by trials, because then they have a double merit—that of patience and that of humility."

Once also the Saint exclaimed with ardour : " O my Saviour ! why have I not a fire sufficiently strong to melt my heart, so that I might pour it forth entirely into Thee ?"

"Your will," replied the Lord, " will be to you the fire which you desire." And from this she knew that by the effort of his will man may fully accomplish all that he desires to do for the glory of God.

As the Saint often sought by her prayers to obtain the extinction of all vices, both in herself and in others, it appeared to her that this favour could only be obtained by the removal of inclination to evil, so that the soul should be enabled to resist evil as easily as she is inclined to it. But she perceived the admirable wisdom of Divine Providence for the salvation of mankind, which, for the increase of our eternal glory, permits us to combat with our vices, that we may be crowned more gloriously in heaven.

§ 12. *Of the effects of Divine love.*

Having heard a preacher declare that no person could be saved without the love of God, and that all must at least have so much of it as would lead them to repent and to abstain from sin, the Saint began to think that many, when dying, seemed to repent more from the fear of hell than from the love of God. Our Lord replied : " When I behold any one in his agony who has thought of Me with pleasure, or who has performed any works deserving of reward, I appear to him at the moment of death with a countenance so full of love and mercy, that he repents from his inmost heart for having ever offended Me, and he is saved by this repentance. I desire, therefore, that My elect should acknowledge this mercy by thanksgivings, and that they should praise Me for this amongst the great number of benefits which they receive from Me.

Once also, as Gertrude meditated on her own sinfulness and depravity, she began to marvel how she could be agreeable in the sight of God, who must behold a thousand

imperfections where she saw only one.   But our Lord consoled her by this reply : " Love makes all agreeable." *
And she learned that if on earth love has such power that
it makes even deformity pleasing, how much more easily
can that God who is Love render those pleasing to Himself
by love whom He loves !

§ 13. *The merit of conforming one's will to God for life or death.*

As the Saint desired, like the Apostle, to be dissolved
and to be with Christ, and poured forth many sighs to God
for this end, she was consoled by this reply : " Whenever
any one desires with all their heart to be delivered from the
prison of the body, and yet, at the same time, is perfectly
willing to remain therein so long as it shall please God,
Jesus Christ unites the merit of His adorable life to theirs,
which renders them marvellously perfect in the sight of the
Eternal Father."

§ 14. *That God does not always expect a full return for the graces He bestows, and of the value of fervent desires.*

As the Saint reflected on the little profit she had gained,
either for herself or for others, from the many graces which
had been bestowed on her, she was consoled by this assurance : " That God does not bestow His graces on His
elect in such a manner as to expect a perfect return, as
human frailty often prevents this ; but His excessive liberality cannot contain itself, though He knows that man cannot exercise himself in all ; nevertheless, He continually
communicates new graces of supererogation, in order to raise

* " Amor facit placentiam."

him thereby to the highest blessedness in the world to come. And even as wealth is bestowed on a child so that he may profit by it hereafter, though he knows not as yet the value of it, so the Lord communicates His grace to His elect in this life, that He may amass treasures for them, the enjoyment of which will render them happy in heaven."

§ 15. *Our Lord prefers suffering without devotion to devotion without suffering.*

On another occasion, as the Saint grieved in her heart that she could not form as ardent desires for the glory of God as she wished to do, she was taught by God that He is perfectly satisfied with our desires when we are not able to do more ; and that they are great in proportion to our desire that they should be great. When, therefore, the heart forms a desire, or wishes to have a desire, God takes the same pleasure in abiding therein as men do in dwelling where flowers are budding forth in the spring-time. Once also, when she found herself negligent and distracted from infirmity, and, entering into herself, began to confess her fault to our Lord with humble devotion,—though she feared that it would be long before she should recover the sweetness of Divine grace of which she had been deprived,—the infinite mercy of God was moved towards her, and He said to her : " My daughter, thou hast been always with Me, and all that I have is thine." Then she knew by these words, that when, through frailty, we fail to refer our intentions to God, His mercy still esteems our will worthy of eternal recompense, provided only that our will has not strayed from Him, and that we often make acts of contrition for our sins.

As the Saint felt an illness coming on her immediately before a festival, she desired that our Lord would preserve her health until it was over, or at least permit her to have sufficient strength to assist at it; still, she abandoned herself entirely to the will of God.   Then she received this reply from the Lord : " In asking Me these things, and at the same time in submitting entirely to My will, you lead Me into a garden of delights, enamelled with flowers, which is most agreeable to Me.   But I know that if I grant what you ask, and allow you to assist at these services, I shall be obliged to follow you into the place which pleases you ; whereas, if I refuse you this, and you still continue patient, you will follow Me into the place which I prefer, because I find more pleasure in you if you form good intentions in a state of suffering, than if you have devotion accompanied by pleasure."

§ 16. *The pleasure of the senses deprives of spiritual pleasures.*

As the Saint one day reflected on the arrangements of Providence, by which some are filled with consolation, while others experience only dryness, God made known to her that He had created the human heart to contain pleasure, as a vase contains water.   But if this vase lets out the water by little holes, it soon becomes empty ; or if any water remains, it will eventually dry up.   So, if the human heart, when filled with spiritual delights, pours itself out through the bodily senses, by seeing, hearing, &c., it will at last become empty, and incapable of tasting the pleasures which are found in God, as each may know by his own experience.   If we give a glance or say a word without reflection, it passes away like water emptied from a vessel.   But if we do ourselves violence for the love of God, celestial sweetness will so increase in our hearts that they will seem too small to contain it.   Thus, when we learn to restrain the pleasures of the senses, we begin to find pleasure in God, and the more this victory costs us, the more joy we find in God.

Once, as the Saint was exceedingly troubled about a matter of little consequence, and offered her trouble to God, for His eternal glory, at the moment of the Elevation, it seemed to her that our Lord drew her soul by the Host as if by a ladder,* until He made it repose on His bosom, and then He spoke thus lovingly to her : " In this sacred couch you shall be exempt from every care ; † but whenever you leave it, your heart will be filled with a bitterness as an antidote against evil."

§ 17. *Of the caresses with which God favours a faithful soul, and of the esteem we ought to have for patience.*

Gertrude, finding herself one day depressed by weakness, said to God : " Lord, what will become of me, and what dost Thou design to do with me ?"   " I will comfort you," He replied, " even as a mother comforts her child." He added : " Have you never seen a mother caress her child ?"   As she did not reply, because she did not remember a circumstance of the kind, our Lord showed her a mother whom she had beheld caressing a little child about six months before, and He made her remark three things which she had not observed.

First, that this mother often offered to embrace this child, and that the child rose up to come to her, though still weak and frail. He added, that thus she ought to rise up by the love of contemplation to the enjoyment of the Adorable Object of her love.

Secondly, that the mother often tried her child, asking

---

* " Cancellum."   † " Respirabis ab omni molestia."

him would he have this or that, and yet not giving him what she offered. Thus God sometimes tempts man by allowing him to fear afflictions which never happen ; and yet, if he submits freely, God is satisfied with his resignation, and it obtains an eternal reward for him.

Thirdly, that none of those who were present, except the mother, understood what the child said, because he could not yet speak plainly. Thus God alone knows and understands the intentions of men, and judges them accordingly ; in which He acts very differently from their fellow-creatures, who only consider the exterior.

Gertrude inquired one day of our Lord how He desired her to employ her time at that hour. " I will that you should learn patience," He replied ; for at the time she was very much disquieted. " But," she replied, " how, and by what means, can I learn it ? " Then our Lord, like a charitable master who takes up his little scholars in his arms, began to teach her three different letters by which she might learn patience. " Consider," He said, " in the first place, how a king honours those who are most like him with his friendship ; and learn from this how the love which I bear you is increased when, for love of Me, you suffer contempts like those which I endured. Secondly, consider how much the court respects him who is most like the king, and is most intimate with him : and judge from this what glory is prepared for you in heaven as the reward of your patience. Thirdly, consider what consolation the tender compassion of a faithful friend gives to his friend, and learn from this what compassion I feel in heaven for even the least thought which afflicts you here."

CHAPTER XXVII.

Why God is pleased by images of Jesus crucified.

On the return of the community from a procession which had been ordered for fine weather, Gertrude heard the Son of God speak thus to His Father from a crucifix which had been carried before the procession : " Eternal Father, I come with My whole army to supplicate You, under the same form in which I reconciled You to the human race." And these words were received by the Eternal Father with as much complacence as if a satisfaction had been offered to Him which surpassed a thousand times all the sins of men. Then she beheld God the Father taking up the image of the crucifix into the clouds with these words : " This is the sign of the covenant which I have made with the earth " (Gen. ix.)

On another occasion, when the people were suffering exceedingly from the inclemency of the weather, the Saint often implored the mercy of God with others, but without effect. At last she addressed her Lord thus : " O charitable Lord, how canst Thou so long resist the desires of so many persons, since I, who am so unworthy of Thy goodness, have often obtained much more considerable favours merely by the confidence I have in Thee ? " " Why be surprised," replied our Lord, " that a father should allow his son to ask him repeatedly for a crown, if he laid by a hundred marks of gold for him each time the request was made ? Neither should you be surprised if I defer answering your petition ; because each time that you implore My aid by the least word, or even in thought, I prepare a recompense for you in eternity of infinitely greater value than a hundred marks of gold."

CHAPTER XXVIII.

Of spiritual thirst for God, and of the utility of sufferings.

WHILE the Psalm *Sicut cervi* * was chanted in the Office for the Dead, Gertrude, hearing these words, " My soul thirsteth," endeavoured to re-animate her fervour, and said to our Lord : " Alas, Lord ! how feeble are the desires I have for Thee, who art my true and only Good ! and how seldom I can say to Thee, ' My soul thirsteth for Thee '!" " You tell Me," replied our Lord, " not seldom, but without ceasing, that your soul thirsteth after Me ; for the exceeding love which makes Me seek the salvation of men obliges Me also to believe that in all the good which My elect desire, they desire Me, because all good proceeds from Me. For example : if any one desires health, rest, wisdom, conveniences, or any other advantages, My goodness often makes Me believe it is Me whom they seek in these things, that I may give them a greater reward ; unless they deliberately turn their intention from Me, as by desiring wisdom that they may satisfy their pride, or health that they may commit some sin.   And it is for this reason that I am accustomed to afflict those who are dearest to Me with corporal infirmities, with mental depression, and other trials. so that when they desire the goods which are opposed to these evils, the ardent love of My Heart may reward them with greater profusion."

Gertrude also learned that " He whose delight is to be with the children of men " (Prov. viii.), when He finds nothing in them worthy of His presence, sends them sufferings either of body or mind, that He may be able to abide with them, as Holy Scripture says : " The Lord is nigh

* Ps. xli. ; in the Office for the Dead, 3d Ps. in iii. Nocturn.

unto those that are of a contrite heart" (Ps. xxxiii.) ; and, " I am with him in tribulation" (Ps. xc.) Let such considerations excite our gratitude, and teach us to exclaim, with the Apostle, and with the whole affection of our souls : " Oh, the depth of the riches of the wisdom and the knowledge of God ! How incomprehensible are His judgments, and how unsearchable His ways !" (Rom. xi.)—which He has discovered to save men.

One night, while the Saint was sleeping, our Lord visited her with so much sweetness, and she felt so consoled with His Divine presence, that it seemed to her as if she had been refreshed by some delicious feast. When she awoke, she returned thanks to God, exclaiming : " How have I merited this, my Lord and my God, more than others, who are so often tormented by horrible dreams, that their very cries terrify those who hear them ? " Our Lord replied : " When those persons whom I have determined to sanctify by suffering seek bodily comforts while they are awake, and thus deprive themselves of occasions of merit, I, in My love, send them sufferings during their sleep, that they may have an opportunity of acquiring merit." " But, Lord," replied the Saint, " how can they merit by this when they suffer without any intention, and against their will ? " " It is an effect of My mercy," replied our Lord ; " for the same thing happens to these persons as to those who adorn themselves with waxen ornaments, and who appear well attired, although those who wear gold and precious stones are esteemed more wealthy."

CHAPTER XXIX.

How insidious are the snares of the demon, and especially when we chant.

As Gertrude recited her Hours without much attention, she perceived our ancient enemy mocking her at the Psalm *Mirabilia*,* cutting each word short, and then exclaiming : " Your Creator, your Saviour, and your Redeemer has well bestowed on you the gifts of speech, since you can recite so glibly that even in a single Psalm you have omitted so many letters, so many syllables, and so many words ! " She knew from this, that if this treacherous enemy had counted so exactly even the least letter or syllable of the Psalm which she had omitted or uttered carelessly, what terrible accusations he would bring after death against those who were in the habit of reciting their Office hurriedly, without any intention.

On another occasion, as the Saint was occupied in spinning wool, she allowed some little tufts to fall on the ground, thinking only of recommending her work to God with great fervour. In the meanwhile she perceived the demon busily occupied in gathering up the tufts, as if for a testimony of her fault ; but the Saint invoked the assistance of the Lord, who chased away the evil spirit with indignation, for daring to interfere in a work which had been recommended to God at its commencement.

* " Thy testimonies are wonderful : " the last portion of Psalm cxix., which is recited at None.

CHAPTER XXX.

That our prayers are certainly heard, even though we do not perceive their effect ; and how to supply for our unworthiness in
approaching Holy Communion through the merits of Jesus
Christ and His saints.

ONE day, as Gertrude felt herself enkindled with extraordinary desires, she said : " Lord, may I pray to Thee now ? "
" You may, My beloved one," [*] He replied tenderly, " because I will comply with your will in all things, as a
servant would obey the commands of his master." " I am
well assured," replied the Saint, " O God, full of charity,
that Thy words are always true ; but since Thou dost manifest such condescension towards me, although I am so unworthy of it, whence comes it that my prayers so often
remain without effect ? " Our Lord replied : " If a queen
desires her servant to give her some thread,[†] which she
supposes, because she is unable to see behind, is hanging
from her left shoulder, and he finds it at her right, does he
not equally fulfil her intention, if he hands it to her from
the place he finds it in, as if it were from the place she
supposed it to be ? So also, if in My inscrutable wisdom
I do not hear your prayers exactly as you desire, I do so
in a manner more useful for you, though human frailty
prevents you from seeing this."

As the Saint was about to communicate on one occasion,
she felt grieved that she had not made sufficient preparation,
and she besought the Blessed Virgin and all the saints
to offer to God for her all the dispositions which each had
entertained in receiving the various graces which had been
granted to them. She then besought our Lord Jesus Christ

---

[*] " Domina regina."   [†] " Filium."

that He would be pleased also to offer for her the perfection
with which He appeared on the day of His Ascension, when
He presented Himself to God the Father and entered into
eternal glory. Afterwards she desired to know of what
avail this prayer had been to her, and our Lord replied :
"It has enabled you to appear before the whole court of
heaven with all the ornaments you have desired." He
added : " Why should you distrust Me, who am all-powerful and all-merciful, since there is not one upon earth
who could not clothe his friend in his own ornaments and
garments, and thereby make him appear as gloriously attired
as himself ? "

As she remembered afterwards that she had promised to
communicate that day for some persons who had recommended themselves to her prayers, she besought God with
great fervour to grant them the fruit of this Sacrament, and
received this reply : " I will grant them this favour ; but
I leave it to their free will to avail themselves of it as
they wish." She then inquired how these souls should be
prepared to receive this grace, and our Lord answered :
" Whenever, from this time, they turn to Me with a pure
heart and a perfect will, invoking the assistance of My
grace, if only by a single word or the least sigh, they will
immediately appear clothed with the ornaments that you
have obtained for them by your prayers."

CHAPTER XXXI.

Of the advantages of frequent Communion, and of receiving the holy
Viaticum.

ONCE also, as the Saint was about to communicate, she
said : " O Lord, what wilt Thou give me ? "   " I will give
Myself to thee entirely," He replied, " with all the virtue
of My Divinity, even as My Virgin Mother received Me."
" But what shall I gain by this ? " inquired Gertrude,
" more than those persons who received Thee yesterday
with me, and who will not receive Thee to-day, since Thou
dost always give Thyself entirely and without reserve ? "
Our Lord replied : " If people in the world honour one who
has been a consul twice more than a person who has only
once filled that office, how shall he fail of greater glory in
eternity who has received Me more frequently on earth ? "
Then she exclaimed, sighing : " How far above me in
beatitude will those priests be who communicate every day
to fulfil the duties of their ministry ! "   " It is true," replied
our Lord, " that those who celebrate worthily shall shine
in great glory ; but the love of him who communicates
with pleasure should be judged of very differently from the
exterior magnificence which appears in this mystery.   There
will be one reward for him who has approached with desire
and love ; there will be another for him who approaches
with fear and reverence ; and another for him who is very
diligent in his preparation.   But those who habitually
celebrate through custom only, shall have no share in My
gifts."

As the Saint prayed that God would permit her to
receive the holy Viaticum as her last nourishment immediately before her death, she was informed interiorly that

her desire was not a good one ; for the effect of the Sacrament could not be lessened by the trifling refreshment taken in sickness, merely to preserve life, for the glory of God. Everything good in man is ennobled by participation in the Sacrament which unites him to God ; but particularly at the moment of death, after he has received the Bread of Life, he may merit by all that he does with a pure intention, such as performing acts of patience, eating, drinking, &c., by which he accumulates eternal beatitude from his union with the Body of Christ.

CHAPTER XXXII.

How God corrects the past negligences of a soul who loves Him, and remedies those which may occur in future.

ON a Feast of the Blessed Virgin, on which Gertrude had received some special and admirable gifts, she began to enter into herself, and considering her ingratitude and negligence, she became dejected, because she had shown so little devotion towards the Mother of God, and the Saints who were honoured on that day, on account of the singular favours which they had received.   But our Lord, desiring to console her, with His ordinary goodness, said to His Blessed Mother and the Saints : " Have I not satisfied for her by communicating Myself to her with all the sweetness of My Divinity in your presence ? " They replied : " The goodness with which Thou hast supplied what she owed to us truly surpasses all our merits."   Then our Lord conversed sweetly with this soul, and said : " Are you satisfied with this reparation ? " " I should be so indeed, my God," she answered ; " but one thing is wanting to me ; I fear, now my past negligences are effaced, that I shall begin to commit new ones,—I am so inclined to evil." He replied : " I will give Myself to you in so efficacious a manner, that I will efface entirely, not only the faults which you have committed, but even those which you may commit ; only be careful to preserve yourself from any stain of sin after you have received the most holy Sacrament." As He said these things, she replied : " Alas, Lord ! I fear that I shall not even fulfil this duty as I ought : therefore, O most charitable of all Masters, teach me, I beseech Thee, how I may purify myself from the stains which I may contract." He replied : " Do not allow them to remain long in you, but as soon as you perceive them say, with all the fervour of your heart : ' Lord, have mercy on me ! ' or, ' Jesus Christ, who art my only hope, grant that all my sins may be effaced by the merit of Thy saving Death ! ' "

The Saint then approached to receive the Body of Christ, and she perceived that her soul had become as clear as transparent crystal, and that the Divinity of Jesus Christ, whom she had just received, was miraculously encased therein like gold shining through the crystal, and producing such sweet, amazing, and inconceivable effects, that the adorable Trinity and all the saints were thereby filled with joy. From this we may know that every spiritual loss can be repaired by worthily receiving the Body of Christ. For in truth the effects produced in her soul by God were so excellent, that it appeared as if the whole celestial court testified that their greatest delight was to behold a soul in whom such marvels were performed.

The promise which God made her in regard to her future faults must be understood thus : that as one sees equally well on every side an object which is contained in crystal, so also the Divine operations were seen in this soul, unless they were obscured by the cloud of sin, for this alone could prevent their being discerned.

CHAPTER XXXIII.

Of the value and importance of spiritual Communion.

THIS holy spouse of Jesus Christ had usually an extreme and ardent desire to receive the Body of Christ, and it happened that once, when she prepared for Communion with more than ordinary devotion, she found herself so weak on Sunday night, that she feared she would not be able to communicate ; but, according to her usual custom, she consulted her Lord, to know what would be most pleasing to Him. He replied : " Even as a spouse who was already satisfied with a variety of viands would prefer remaining near his bride to sitting at table with her, so would I prefer that you should deprive yourself of Communion through holy prudence, on this occasion, rather than approach it." " And how, my loving Lord, can You say that You are thus satiated ? " The Lord replied : " By your moderation in speech, by your guard over your senses, by all your desires, by all your prayers, by all the good dispositions with which you have prepared to receive My adorable Body and Blood—these are to Me as the most delicious food and refreshment."

When she came to Mass, though still in a state of extreme weakness, and had prepared for spiritual Communion, she heard the sound of a bell announcing the return of a priest who had gone to a village to give communion to a sick person. " O Life of my soul ! " she exclaimed ; " how gladly would I receive Thee spiritually, if I had time to prepare myself worthily ! " " The looks of

My Divine mercy," replied the Lord, " will impart to you
the necessary preparation ; " and at the same time, it seemed
to the Saint that the Lord cast a look upon her soul like a
ray of sunlight, saying : "I will fix my eyes upon thee " (Ps.
xxxi.) From these words she understood that the look of
God produces three effects in our souls, similar to those that
the sun produces in our bodies, and that the soul ought
to prepare in three ways to receive it. First, the glance
of Divine mercy searches the soul, and purifies it from
every stain, making it whiter than snow ; and we obtain
this favour by a humble acknowledgment of our defects.
Secondly, this look of mercy softens the soul, and prepares it to receive spiritual gifts, even as wax is softened by the heat of the sun, and becomes capable of
receiving any impression ; and the soul acquires this by
a pious intention. Thirdly, the glance of Divine mercy
on the soul makes it fruitful in the different flowers of
virtue, even as the sun produces and ripens different sorts
of fruit ; and the third effect is obtained by a faithful
confidence, which causes us to abandon ourselves entirely
to God, confiding assuredly in the superabundance of His
mercy, believing that all things will contribute to our
eternal welfare, whether they appear favourable or adverse.
Then, as some of the community communicated at Mass,
our Divine Lord appeared to give Himself to each with His
own Hand, making the sign of the cross as the priest does ;
the Saint, marvelling at this, said to Him: "Lord, have not
those who have received Thee in this Sacrament obtained
greater grace than I, whom Thou hast gratuitously favoured
with so many benefits ? " " Who is esteemed most worthy,"
replied our Lord, " he who is adorned with pearls and precious stones, or he who has an immense treasure of pure
gold hidden in his house ? " making her understand by

these words, that while he who communicates sacramentally receives without doubt immense grace, both spiritually and corporally, as the Church believes, still, he who abstains from receiving the Body of Christ through obedience and holy discretion, and purely for the glory of God, and who, being inflamed with Divine love, communicates spiritually, merits to receive a benediction like that given to the saint, and obtains from God more abundant fruit, although the order and secret of this conduct is entirely hidden from the eyes of men.

CHAPTER XXXIV.

Of the utility of meditating on the Passion of our Lord, and how He offers Himself to the Eternal Father in satisfaction for our sins.

ON a certain Friday, in the evening, Gertrude cast her eyes on a crucifix, and, being penetrated with grief, she exclaimed : " Ah, my Creator and my Beloved ! what cruelties hast Thou not suffered on this day for my salvation ! while I, alas ! have been so occupied that I have not devoutly recalled what Thou didst suffer for me each hour, when Thou, who art the Life which vivifies all things, didst will to die for love of me." To which our Lord answered from the cross : " I have supplied what you neglect, for I have accumulated each hour in My Heart what you ought to have accumulated in your heart ; in consequence, it is so inflamed with love, that I have ardently desired this hour in which you have addressed this prayer to Me, in union with which I will offer to God my Father all that I have done for you during this day, and without which even that could not be so advantageous for your salvation."

We may learn from this the faithful love of God towards man, since He satisfies His Eternal Father by a single intention which He excites in them, and this in so sublime and excellent a manner that it merits the everlasting praises of men.

As this Saint touched the crucifix devoutly, she learned that if any one only looks on the image of the cross of Jesus Christ with a holy intention, God regards him with such goodness and mercy, that he receives in his soul, as in a spotless mirror, an image which is so agreeable that the whole court of heaven delights therein ; and this serves to increase his eternal glory in the life to come in proportion as he has practised this act of devotion in this life.

On another occasion she learned that when any one turns towards a crucifix, he ought to persuade himself that our Lord speaks thus lovingly to his heart : " Behold how, for your love, I have been fastened to this cross,—naked, despised, torn and wounded in My Body, and in all My members ; and still My Heart has such tender charity for you, that were it necessary for your salvation, and were there no other means of saving you, I would even at this moment suffer for you alone all that I have suffered for the whole world." By this reflection man ought to excite himself to gratitude, because it never happens that any one looks at a crucifix without a particular providence. There is no Christian, therefore, who is not guilty, if he is so ungrateful as to neglect the adorable price of his salvation, since we can never look at a crucifix thoughtfully without receiving great benefit thereby.

On another occasion, as she was occupied in considering

the Passion of our Lord, it was made known to her that there is infinitely more merit in meditating attentively on the Passion of Jesus than in any other exercise. For as it is impossible to handle flour without attaching it to yourself, so also is it impossible to meditate devoutly on the Passion of the Lord without deriving great fruit thereby. And when any one reads anything concerning the Passion, they at least dispose their souls to receive the fruit of it, as it is more meritorious to meditate on it than on any subject. Let us, then, endeavour to reflect constantly on it, that it may be honey to our lips, music to our ears, and joy to our hearts.

As the Saint endeavoured to choose, amongst the different favours which our Lord had bestowed on her, the graces which would be most for the benefit of others, if revealed to them, our Lord spoke thus to her : " It is most advantageous to men to make known to them that it would be of extreme utility to remember constantly that I, who am the Son of a Virgin, stand before God the Father for the salvation of the human race, and that whenever they commit any fault in their hearts through human frailty, I offer My spotless Heart to the Eternal Father in satisfaction for them ; when they sin by their actions, I offer My pierced Hands ; and so in regard to the other faults that they commit. Thus My innocence appeases Him, and disposes Him to pardon those who do penance for their faults. And therefore it is that I desire My elect should return Me thanks whenever they have obtained pardon for their faults, because it is through Me that they have obtained it so easily."

CHAPTER XXXV.

Of the bundle of myrrh, and how we should practise patience in
adversity, according to the example of Christ.

ONE night a crucifix, which the Saint had near her bed,
seemed to bow down towards her, and she exclaimed : " O
my sweet Jesus ! why dost Thou thus abase Thyself ? " He
replied : " The love of My Divine Heart attracts Me to you."
Then she took the image and placed it on her heart, caressing it tenderly, and saying : " A bundle of myrrh is
my Beloved to me " (Cant. i.) ; to which our Lord replied,
interrupting her : " I will carry Him in my bosom ; "
making her to understand by this that we ought to hide in
His adorable Passion all the pains we suffer, whether of
body or mind, as we would place a prop * in a bundle of
sticks.   Thus those who are tempted to impatience by adversity should recall to mind the adorable patience of the
Son of God, who was led like a meek lamb to the slaughter
for our salvation, and never opened His mouth to utter the
least word of impatience.   And when any one is disposed
to revenge the ill that has been done to him, either in word
or deed, he should endeavour to recall to himself with
what peace of heart his beloved Jesus suffered, not rendering evil for evil, nor testifying the least resentment by His
words, but, on the contrary, rewarding those who made
Him suffer by redeeming them by His sufferings and His
death : and thus let us endeavour, according to the example of our Lord, to do good for evil.   So also, if any one
entertains a mortal hatred towards those who have offended
him, he ought to remember the exceeding sweetness with

---

* " Sudem. '

which the Son of God prayed for His executioners, even when enduring the very torments of His Passion, and in the agony of death praying for His crucifiers with these words: "Father, forgive them," &c. (Luke xxiii.); and, in union with this love, let us pray for our enemies. Our Lord then said : " Whosoever hides his sufferings and adversities in the bouquet of My Passion, and joins them on to such of My sufferings as they seem most to resemble, he truly reposes in My bosom, and I will give him, to augment his merits, all that My singular charity has merited by My patience and by My other virtues."

The Saint inquired : " How, O Lord, do You receive the special devotion which some have for the image of Your cross ? " Our Lord replied : " It is very acceptable to Me ; nevertheless, when those who have a special devotion to these representations of My cross fail to imitate the example of My Passion, their conduct is like that of a mother who, to gratify herself and for her own honour, adorns her daughter with different ornaments, but refuses her harshly what she most desires to have. While this mother deprives her child of what she wishes for, the child cares little for all else that is given to her, because she knows it is done through pride, and not from affection. So all the testimonies of love, respect, and reverence which are offered to the image of My cross will not be perfectly acceptable to Me unless the examples of My Passion are also imitated."

CHAPTER XXXVI.

That devotion to the Passion of our Lord promotes union with God.

As Gertrude once sought, with some anxiety, for an image of the holy cross, that she might often honour it for love of her Lord, she began to fear that this exterior exercise might hinder her from enjoying the interior favours of God. But our Lord said to her: " Fear not, My beloved ; for this cannot hinder your spirituality, since I alone will occupy you ; for I am not a little pleased with those who honour the image of My crucifixion very devoutly ; and as it often happens that, when a king has a spouse with whom he cannot always remain, he leaves one who is most dear to him to take charge of her in his absence, and regards all the duties of friendship and affection which she renders to him as if they had been offered to himself, because he knows that this proceeds from her love for him,—so I take pleasure in the veneration offered to My cross, when it is offered purely for My love,—when the cross is not desired for itself, but that it may serve to renew the memory of the love and fidelity with which I endured the bitterness of My Passion, and when there is an ardent desire to imitate the example of My Passion."

One night, as the Saint was occupied in meditating on the Passion, she found that the fervour of her zeal had affected her body, and caused an inflammation in the side ; when she addressed herself thus to God : " Most sweet Love ! if some persons knew what I now suffer, they would think that I ought to interrupt this exercise, in order to recover my bodily health ; although Thou knowest—Thou who beholdest clearly that which is most hidden within me

—that all my strength and my senses could not resist the most passing movement of Thy grace." To which our Lord replied : " Who could be ignorant of this, without being altogether insensible that the sweetness of My Divinity surpasses incomparably all the pleasures of the flesh and the senses ? since all earthly and corporal pleasure is but as a drop of dew to this great ocean. And yet these sensible pleasures often draw men away irresistibly, though they know how they endanger, not only their bodies, but even their souls. How, then, should a soul penetrated with the sweetness of My Divinity be able to hinder itself from being carried away by the attractions of a love which will constitute its eternal felicity ?"

She replied : " But perhaps they would say that, as I am professed in a religious order, I ought so to moderate the ardour of my devotion that it may not prove a hindrance to my observance of rule." Then the Lord deigned to instruct her by this comparison : " If a chamberlain had been placed at the table of a king, in order to serve his majesty with the respect due to him, and if this king, from age or infirmity, required one who stood by to support him, would it not be an extreme incivility if this chamberlain rose hastily and allowed his master to fall, because he had been also specially chosen to stand and serve at his table ? So would it be far more uncourteous if one whom I called in My gratuitous mercy to the enjoyment of My contemplation should withdraw from it to satisfy the requirements of the order in which he was professed ; since I, the Creator and Framer of the universe, take infinitely more pleasure in loving souls, than in any labours and corporal exercises performed without love and without a pure intention. But if any person is not really called by My Spirit to the repose of contemplation, and yet neglects the observance of his

Rule to occupy himself therein, he is like those who place themselves at the table of the king without being invited, although they were only destined to serve at it. And, as a servant who sat at the king's table without being asked would receive contempt instead of honour, so he who neglects his Rule, and endeavours in his own strength to obtain the gift of contemplation—which none can obtain without a special gift from Me—would receive more disadvantage than profit ; making no progress in what he had undertaken, and becoming tepid in his duty. But as for him who, without any necessity, and merely for his bodily convenience, neglects the exercises of his Order, and seeks satisfaction in exterior things, he acts as one would do who, being destined to serve at the king's table, should go out to his stables and defile himself shamefully in cleansing them."

CHAPTER XXXVII.

Of the nails of sweet-smelling cloves * which the Saint, moved by love, put into the wounds of the crucifix instead of the iron nails, and of the gratitude which our Lord testified for this.

ONE Friday, when the Saint had spent the whole night in meditation, and had been prevented from sleeping by the ardour of her love, she remembered with what tenderness she had snatched the iron nails from a crucifix which she always kept near her, and replaced them by nails of sweet-smelling cloves, and she said to God : " My Beloved, how didst Thou accept my drawing the iron nails from the sacred Wounds of Thy Hands and Feet, to place these cloves therein, which give an agreeable odour ?" Our Lord replied : "It was

---

* " Gariofilis. "

so agreeable to Me, that in return for it I poured forth the noble balsam of My Divinity into the wounds of your sins. And for this all the saints will praise Me eternally; for your wounds, by the infusion of this liquor, will become agreeable." "But, Lord," inquired the Saint, "wilt Thou not grant the same grace to those who perform the same action?" "Not to all," He replied; "but those who do it with the same fervour will receive a similar reward; and those who, following your example, do likewise with all the devotion of which they are capable, will receive a lesser recompense."

Gertrude then took the crucifix and clasped it in her arms, kissing it tenderly, until she felt herself growing weak from her long vigil, when she laid it aside, and taking leave of her Spouse,* asked His permission to go and rest, that she might recover her strength, which was almost exhausted by her long meditation. After she had spoken thus, she turned from the crucifix and composed herself to sleep. But as she reposed, our Lord stretched forth His right Hand from the cross to embrace her, and whispered these words to her: "Listen to Me, My beloved; I will sing you a canticle of love." And then He commenced, in a tender and harmonious voice, to sing the following verse to the chant of the hymn *Rex Christe, factor omnium:*—

> " Amor meus continuus
> Tibi languor assiduus :
> Amor tuus suavissimus
> Mihi sapor gratissimus." †

---

* "Vale dilecte mi, et habe bonam noctem."

† The hymn *Rex Christe* may be found in Gerbert's *Monumenta veteris Liturgiæ Alemannicæ*. It was composed by St. Gregory the Great, and was formerly chanted at Tenebræ after the *Benedictus.*

Having finished the verse, He said : " Now, My beloved, instead of the *Kyrie eleison*, which is sung at the end of each verse of the hymn *Rex Christe*, ask what you will, and I will grant it to you." The Saint then prayed for some particular intentions, and her prayers were favourably heard. Our Lord again chanted the same verse, and at the end again exhorted Gertrude to pray. This He repeated many times, at different intervals, not allowing her a moment's rest, until she became completely exhausted. She then slept a little before daybreak ; but the Lord Jesus, who is always near those who love Him, appeared to her in her sleep. He seemed to prepare a delicious feast for her in the sacred Wound of His adorable Side, and He Himself placed the food in her mouth in order to refresh her ; so that when she awoke, she found that she had been marvellously strengthened during her sleep, for which she returned most humble and ardent thanks to God.

CHAPTER XXXVIII.

How we may remember the Passion of Christ, and proclaim the praises of the Virgin Mother of God, in reciting the Seven Canonical Hours.

ONE night, as Gertrude kept vigil, and was occupied with the remembrance of the Lord's Passion, as she felt much

---

The verse sung to this chant is extremely difficult to render in English :

> " The more I love thee, yet the more
> Thou seek'st this burning fire ;
> While thy dear love is still to me
> Sweetness I still desire."

fatigued, although she had not yet recited Matins, she said
to God : " Ah, my Lord ! since Thou knowest that my
weakness requires rest, teach me what honour and what
service I can render to Thy Blessed Mother, now that it is
not in my power to recite her Office." *   " Glorify Me," replied our Lord, " through My loving Heart, for the innocence of that spotless virginity by which she conceived Me,
being a virgin; brought me forth, being a virgin ; and still
remained a pure and spotless virgin after childbirth ; imitating thus My innocence when I was taken at the hour
of Matins for the redemption of the human race, and was
bound, struck with rods, buffeted, and overwhelmed piti-
lessly with every kind of misery and opprobrium."   While
she did this, it appeared to her that the Lord presented His
Divine Heart to the most holy Virgin His Mother, under
the figure of a golden cup, that she might drink from it ;
and that, being satiated with this sweet beverage,—or rather
abundantly inebriated thereby,—her very soul might be
filled with exceeding gladness.

Then Gertrude praised the Blessed Virgin, saying to her :
" I salute thee, most Blessed Mother, august Sanctuary of
the Holy Spirit, through the sweetest Heart of Jesus Christ,
thy beloved Son and the Son of the Eternal Father, beseeching thee to assist us in all our necessities, both now
and in the hour of our death.   Amen."   She knew, when
any one glorified our Lord in these words, and added,
in praise of the Blessed Virgin, " I praise and salute thee,
O Mother," &c., that each time He presented her His

---

* ' Not of obligation, but recited by some religious who are not
bound to recite the Divine Office, and also by several of the contemplative Orders, as a matter of devotion, after they have recited
their Office of obligation.

Divine Heart to satisfy her thirst in the manner above described, it gave exceeding satisfaction to the Queen of Virgins to be saluted thus; and that she would recompense it according to the extent of her liberality and maternal tenderness.

Our Lord then added: "At the hour of Prime, praise Me, through My sweetest Heart, for the most peaceful humility with which the immaculate Virgin disposed herself more and more to receive Me, and imitated the humility with which I, who am the Judge of the living and the dead, willed at the same hour to submit Myself to a Gentile, to be judged by him for the redemption of mankind.

"At Tierce, praise Me for the fervent desires by which the Blessed Virgin drew Me down into her virginal womb from the bosom of My Eternal Father, and imitated Me in the ardour and zeal with which I desired the salvation of men, when, being torn with whips and crowned with thorns, I bore, at the third hour, a shameful and infamous cross on My shoulders with extreme meekness and patience.

"At Sext, praise Me for the firm and assured hope with which this celestial Virgin thought only of glorifying Me by the purity of her intentions; in which she imitated Me when I, being suspended on the tree of the cross, in all the bitterness and anguish of death, longed with My whole soul for the redemption of the human race, crying out, 'I thirst!' —that is, for the salvation of men; so that, had it been necessary for Me to suffer more bitter or cruel torments, I would willingly have borne them for their redemption.

"At None, praise Me for the ardent and mutual love which united My Divine Heart to that of the spotless Virgin, and which united and inseparably conjoined My all-glorious Divinity with My Humanity in her chaste womb, imitating Me in My mortal life until I expired on the cross at the ninth hour for the salvation of men.

"At Vespers, praise Me for the constant faith of My Blessed Mother at My death, during the desertion of My Apostles, and the despair of all; in which she imitated the fidelity with which I descended into limbo after My death, that I might withdraw those souls by My all-powerful hand and mercy, and bring them to the joys of paradise.

"At Compline, praise Me for the incomparable perseverance with which My sweetest Mother persevered in every virtue even to the end, and imitated Me in the work of man's redemption, which I accomplished with so much care, that after I had obtained their perfect redemption by a most cruel death, I nevertheless allowed My incorruptible Body to be laid in the tomb, to show that there is no degree of contempt or humiliation to which I would not submit for the welfare of man."

CHAPTER XXXIX.

That we should give some token of our love to God after exterior occupations.

IT was always a trial to the Saint to be obliged, even for a time, to occupy herself with exterior things; and often when this occurred she would rise suddenly in the fervour of her spirit, and, hastening to the place where she was accustomed to pray, would exclaim: "Behold, Lord, how I am wearied with creatures! I would have no other companionship and no other conversation except Thine,—I leave them all to seek Thee, sole and only Good, and delight of my heart and soul." Then, kissing the Wounds of Christ five times, she would say each time: " Hail, Jesus, my loving Spouse!—I embrace Thee respectfully in the joy of the Divinity, with the whole universe, and with all the affection of which I am capable ; and I embrace Thee in the Wounds of Thy love." Thus did she pour forth all her griefs into the Wounds of her Lord, and find therein all her consolation and all her joy.

As she frequently acted thus, she inquired one day of our Lord if it was agreeable to Him, because it only occupied her for a few moments. Our Lord replied : " Each time that you turn thus to Me, I accept it as a friend would accept the kindness of his friend, who frequently through the day endeavoured to show him the greatest hospitality by word and act. And even as such a person would consider how he could repay this kindness when his host came to his house, so do I reflect continually, with the greatest pleasure, how I shall repay you, and recompense you in glory, according to the royal liberality of My omni-potence, of My wisdom, and of My mercy, by testimonies of charity and sweetness multiplied a hundredfold, for each offering that you have made Me on earth."

CHAPTER XL.

Of the effects of prayer in adversity.

ONCE, as the community feared an armed attack upon their monastery, they recited the entire Psalter, and at the end of each Psalm, the verse, " *O Lux beatissima*," * with the

---

* " O most blessed Light :" the commencement of a verse of the Sequence in the Mass for Whit-Sunday.

Antiphon, "*Veni, Sancte Spiritus.*" Gertrude, who was praying fervently with her sisters, knew interiorly that our Lord, by this prayer, had moved the souls of some by the Holy Spirit to perceive their negligences, and to repent. As they felt these movements of compunction, the Saint saw a kind of vapour exhaling from the hearts of those who were thus moved, which covered the monastery and the places around it, and drove away every enemy. And in proportion as the heart of each was moved to compunction and inclined to good, the vapour appeared more powerful in expelling evil. Thus she knew that this fear was designed by the Lord to draw to Himself the hearts of His elect congregation, that, being proved by affliction and purified from their negligences, they might take refuge under His paternal protection, and find more abundant succour and consolation. Having perceived this, she said to the Lord: "Whence comes it, my loving Lord, that the revelations which Thou hast made to me in Thy gratuitous mercy are so different from those which Thou hast made to others, that persons may often know them, although I so much desire to conceal them?" Our Lord replied: "If a master, when questioned by persons who speak different languages, answered each in the one tongue, his discourse would only profit those who understood it; but if he speaks to each in his own tongue—in Latin to him who understands Latin, and in Greek to him who understands Greek—then each can comprehend what is said. Thus the greater the diversity with which I communicate My gifts, the more My impenetrable wisdom is displayed, which replies to each according to their comprehension and the understanding with which I have gifted them,—speaking to the simple by plain and sensible parables, and to the enlightened in a more sublime and hidden manner."

CHAPTER XLI.

Prayer composed by our Lord Jesus Christ Himself, which He promised to hear favourably.

On a similar occasion, as the community recited the Canticle *Benedicite*,* adding to each verse prayers proper for the occasion, Gertrude perceived our Lord standing before her; and at each verse which they recited, prostrate and imploring pardon, He appeared to raise His left arm, and offer her the Wound of His adorable Side to kiss. As the Saint embraced it several times, our Lord testified that this mark of her love was extremely agreeable to Him. Then she said to Him : " Since I perceive, my most loving Lord, that Thou art pleased with this devotion, do me the favour of teaching me some little prayer which Thou wilt receive with a like charity, when it shall be addressed to Thee devoutly by any one." Then she knew by inspiration, that if any one shall say these words five times with devotion : " Jesus, Saviour of the world, have mercy on me !—Thou to whom nothing is impossible, save to refuse mercy to the wretched ; " or, " O Christ, who by Thy Cross hast redeemed the world, hear us ! " or, " Hail, Jesus, my loving Spouse ! I salute Thee in the ineffable joys of Thy Divinity ; I embrace Thee with the affection of all creatures, and I kiss the sacred Wound of Thy love ; " or, " The Lord is my strength and my glory : He is my salvation,"—if these words are recited in honour of the Five Wounds of the Lord, kissing them devoutly, adding some prayers or good works, and offering them through the sweetest Heart of Jesus Christ, which is the organ of the most Holy Tri-

---

* " All ye works of the Lord, bless the Lord : " Canticle of the Three Children, said at Lauds on Sundays and festivals.

nity, they will be as acceptable to God as the most arduous devotion.

On another occasion, also, when they recited the same Canticle, our Lord appeared to her, making burning flames to pour forth from the crucifix which was usually exposed before the community, and sending them up to God for them ; manifesting to her the excessive love and ardent desire of His Heart, when He interceded with His Father for the welfare of this congregation.

CHAPTER XLII.

How the just delight in God, and how God takes pleasure in them, especially when they commit all their good desires to Him.

ON one occasion, when the Saint was prevented by illness from communicating, and she felt her devotion also languishing, she addressed herself thus to God : " O Sweetness of my soul! knowing—alas! only too well—how unworthy I am to approach the Sacrament of Thy Body and Blood, I would abstain from Communion, if I could find consolation in any creature out of Thee; but since I can behold nothing from east to west, nor from north to south, in which I can find any consolation or pleasure, either for body or soul, except in Thee alone, and as I am parched and thirsty, and breathless from desire, I come to Thee, the Fountain of living water."   Our Lord, in His benign love, replied thus : " As you assure Me that you can find no pleasure apart from Me, so I assure you also that I do not wish to find pleasure in any creature apart from you."   But as the Saint reflected, that although the Lord had promised this at that time, still at some future period it might be otherwise,

He answered her thoughts thus : " My will is the same as
My power, and therefore I can do nothing except what
I will." " But, O most loving Lord," replied the Saint,
" what subject of complacence canst Thou find in one who
is the repulse and shame of all creatures ? " " The Eye of
My Divinity," He replied, "takes extreme pleasure in regarding you, on account of the various great gifts which
I have bestowed on you. Your words are as a concert of
sweet music to My Divine ears, whether you utter them to
offer Me your love, to pray for sinners or for the souls in
purgatory, to instruct or to correct others, or when you
speak in any manner for My glory ; and though men may
obtain no advantage from your words, and they may remain
without effect, still the good intention which prompted
them, and which has Me only for its object, makes them
resound sweetly in My ears, and will cause them to touch
even My very inmost heart. The hope with which you
sigh after Me ascends as a fragrant odour before Me ; your
prayers and desires are sweeter to Me than any perfume ;
and in your love I find the greatest pleasure."

Then the Saint began to desire ardently a restoration of
her former health, that she might be able to observe the
austerities of her Order with more exactness. But our Lord
replied lovingly : " Why does My spouse become importunate
to Me, as if she would oppose My will?" "What, Lord!" she
replied ; " how can a desire, which seems to me to be only
for Thy glory, be so opposed to Thy will ? " " From the
manner in which you ask it," replied our Lord, " I consider it only as the desire of a child ; but if you should ask
it more earnestly, I should not be pleased at your request."

From these words the Saint knew that the desire of
health, from a pure intention of serving God, is indeed
good ; but that it is far more perfect to abandon oneself

entirely to the Divine will, and to believe that all which God ordains for us, whether of prosperity or adversity, cannot but be for our advantage.

CHAPTER XLIII.

Of two pulsations of the Heart of Jesus.

As Gertrude saw one of her sisters hastening to the sermon, she said to God complainingly : " Thou knowest, my Beloved, with what pleasure I would now hear this sermon, were I not hindered by sickness." Our Lord replied : " Wilt thou, My dear spouse, that I should preach to thee Myself ? " and she answered : " Very willingly." Then our Lord made her rest on His Heart, so that her soul touched it ; and as she remained there some time, she felt two most sweet and admirable movements therein. Then the Lord said to her : " Each of these movements operates the salvation of man in three different manners. The first operates the salvation of sinners ; the second, that of the just. By the first, I converse continually with my Eternal Father—I appease His anger against sinners, and I incline Him to show them mercy. By the second, I speak to My saints, excusing sinners to them, and urging them, with the zeal and fidelity of a brother, to intercede with God for them. By the third, I speak to sinners themselves, calling them mercifully to penance, and awaiting their conversion with ineffable desire.

" By the second movement of My Heart, I invite My Father to rejoice with Me for having poured forth My precious Blood so efficaciously for the just, in whose merits I find so many delights. Secondly, I invite all the heavenly host to praise My providences, that they may return Me thanks for all the benefits which I have granted them, and that I may grant them more for the future.   Thirdly, I speak to the just, giving them many salutary caresses, and warning them to profit faithfully by them, from day to day, and hour to hour.   As the pulsations of the human heart are not interrupted by seeing, hearing, or any manual occupation, but always continue without relaxation, so the care of the government of heaven and earth, and the whole universe, cannot diminish or interrupt for a moment these two movements* of My Divine Heart, which will continue to the end of ages."

CHAPTER XLIV.

Of the manner in which we should ask our Lord for rest or sleep.

It happened some time after, that Gertrude passed an entire night without sleeping, which so weakened her that her strength entirely failed ; and she offered her prostration, as usual, for the glory of God and the salvation of men. Then our Lord, charitably compassionating her weakness, taught her to invoke Him by these words : " I beseech Thee, O most merciful God, by the most tranquil sweetness with which Thou hast reposed from all eternity in the bosom of the Father, by Thy peaceful abode of nine months in the womb of a virgin, and by all the holy delights which Thou hast ever enjoyed in souls filled with Thy love, to grant me some rest,—not for my own satisfaction, but for Thy eternal glory,—in order that the strength of my wearied body may be restored, and that I may be able to fulfil my duties."

* "Binos pulsus."

And as she said these words, she saw herself coming nearer to God, as if she ascended by steps. Then our Lord showed her a place at His right hand, and said to her : " Come, My beloved, repose on My Heart, and see if My anxious love will permit you to rest without anxiety." * As she reclined thus on the loving Heart of Jesus, and felt its sweet pulsations more sensibly, she said to Him : " O my Beloved ! what wouldest Thou say to me by those pulsations ?" He replied : " I would say, that when any one finds herself exhausted and deprived of strength by long wakefulness, and addresses to Me the prayer with which I have just inspired you, that I may grant them the strength they need for My service,—if I do not hear them, and they bear their weakness with patience and humility, I will console them with the same tenderness and charity as a friend would his friend, who rose from his bed with alacrity, although overpowered with sleep, merely for the sake of enjoying the pleasure which he found in his conversation. And as this compliance would be even more agreeable to him than if it were offered by a person who usually passed the night without sleeping much, so also is he infinitely more pleasing to Me who, having exhausted all his strength by vigils, offers Me his weakness, and bears it with humility and patience, than he who, being more robust, is able to remain entire nights in prayer, without suffering much inconvenience."

* " Et proba utrum inquietus amor meus te quiescere sinat."

CHAPTER XLV.

Of perfect resignation of ourselves to the Divine will.

GERTRUDE being once ill of a fever, which sometimes increased after perspiration and sometimes diminished, finding herself one night bathed in perspiration, began to desire very anxiously to know if she would be better or worse after it. Then our Lord Jesus Christ appeared to her radiant with beauty, and bearing health in His right hand and sickness in his left : He presented them to her, that she might choose whichever she preferred. But the Saint refused both, and, casting herself into the arms of her Lord, she approached His loving Heart, in which the plenitude of all good abides, that she might learn His adorable will. Our Lord received her with much sweetness, and embraced her lovingly, allowing her to rest on His bosom ; but she turned her face away from Him, and, inclining her head backwards, exclaimed : "I turn my face from Thee, and I entreat Thee with my whole heart not to consider my inclination in anything, but to accomplish Thy adorable will in all that concerns me."

From this we may learn that the faithful soul ought to confide all that concerns her to God with perfect confidence, and that she should prefer being ignorant of His designs towards her, so that His will may be more fully accomplished in her.

The Lord then poured into the bosom of the Saint two streams of living water, which came forth from the two sides of His Heart, as from a mystic vessel, and said to her : " Since you have turned your face from me, and renounced your own will in all things, I will pour forth on you all the sweetness of My Divine Heart." " My sweet

Lord," replied Gertrude, "since Thou hast so often, and in such different ways, bestowed Thy Deified Heart on me, I desire to know what I shall gain from this new gift." He replied: "Does not the Catholic faith teach you that I bestow Myself, with all the riches that are contained in the treasures of My Divinity and My Humanity, for the salvation of those who communicate even once?—and that the oftener men communicate, the more their beatitude is increased and perfected?"

CHAPTER XLVI.

Of the sensible pleasure which the soul finds in God.

As many persons advised the Saint to refrain from meditation until she recovered her health, she complied with their desire, being always anxious to do the will of another rather than her own; but on condition that she should be allowed to occupy herself in adorning the crucifixes and other holy images, so that she might at least preserve a perpetual remembrance of Jesus crucified by these exterior representations. One night, as she was occupied in thinking how she could arrange some straw * as a sepulchre for the crucifix, on Friday evening, at the commemoration of the Passion after Vespers, the God of love, who regards the intention rather than the works of those who love Him, insinuated Himself into her thoughts thus: "Rejoice in God, My beloved, and He will give you all your heart's desires." By these words she understood, that when we take pleasure in such things for the love of God, His Divine Heart is pleased thereby; even as the father of a

* "Paliis."

family engages an excellent concert of music, which entertains those who are seated at table with him as well as
himself.

"But, my most loving God," inquired the Saint, "what
glory can this exterior satisfaction give Thee, which satisfies
the senses more than the soul?" He replied : "Even as
an avaricious usurer would be sorry to lose the opportunity
of gaining a single penny, so I, who find all my joy in you,
do not intend to allow even your least thought, nor a single
movement of your finger, which you have done for love of
Me, to pass by without using it for My glory and your
eternal welfare." She replied : "If Thine immense goodness can find pleasure in this, what dost Thou say of the
verses in which all Thy passion is commemorated?" "I
take the same pleasure in them," replied our Lord, "as a
person would who was conducted by his friend, with marks
of tenderness and friendship, to an agreeable garden, where,
while breathing the fresh air and sweet odour of the place,
he would also have the pleasure of admiring its beautiful
flowers, hearing a concert of exquisite music, and of refreshing himself with the rarest and most exquisite fruits.
And I promise you, My beloved, recompense for the satisfaction you have given Me by your verses, and also those
who read them often with devotion, while they live in this
life of sorrow, which leads to the life eternal."

CHAPTER XLVII.

Of the languor caused by Divine love.

SOON after, during the seventh illness of the Saint, as her
mind was occupied with God, on a certain night our Lord
approached her, and said to her, with extreme sweetness

and charity : " Tell Me, My beloved, that you languish for love of Me." She replied : " How can I, a poor sinner, presume to say that I languish for love to Thee?" Our Lord answered : " Whoever offers himself willingly to suffer anything in order to please Me, he truly glorifies Me, and, glorifying Me, tells Me that he languishes for love of Me ; provided that He continues patient, and that he never turns his eyes away from Me." " But what advantage canst Thou gain from this assurance, my beloved Lord?" inquired the Saint. The Lord answered : " This assurance imparts joy to My Divinity, glory to My Humanity, pleasure to My eyes, and satisfaction to My ears. Further, the unction of My love is so powerfully moved thereby, that I am compelled to heal the contrite heart—that is to say, those who desire this grace ; to preach to those who are in captivity —that is, to pardon sinners ; to open the door to those who are in prison—that is, to release the souls in purgatory."

Gertrude then said to the Lord : " Father of mercies ! after this sickness, which is the seventh that I have had, wilt Thou not restore me to my former health?" Our Lord replied : " If I had made known to you at the commencement of your first illness that you would have to endure seven, perhaps you would have given way to impatience through human frailty. So, also, if I now promised you that this would be the last sickness, the hope with which you would look forward to its termination might lessen your merit. Therefore the paternal providence of My uncreated wisdom has wisely ordained that you should remain ignorant on both subjects, that you might be obliged to have recourse to Me continually with your whole heart, and to commend your troubles, whether exterior or interior, to My fidelity ; since I watch over you so faithfully

and lovingly, that I would not permit you to be tried beyond your strength, knowing how much your patience can
bear. This you can easily understand, if you remember
how much weaker you were after your first sickness than
you are now after your seventh ; for although human
reason might have considered this impossible, yet nothing
is impossible to My Divine omnipotence."

CHAPTER XLVIII.

That the faithful soul ought to abandon herself to the will of God, for life and death.

As the Saint offered various testimonies of her love to God
during the night,—asking Him, amongst other things, how
it happened that she had never wished to know whether
her sickness would end in life or death, though it had
lasted so long ; and how it was that she felt equally indifferent to either,—our Lord answered her thus : " When a
bridegroom conducts his bride into a garden of roses, to
gather them for a bouquet, she takes so much pleasure in
his sweet conversation, that she never pauses to inquire
which of the roses he would wish her to gather, but she takes
whatever flower her bridegroom gives her, and places it in
her bouquet. So also the faithful soul, whose greatest
pleasure is the accomplishment of My will, and delights in
it as in a garden of roses, is indifferent whether I restore
her health or take her out of the present life, because,
being full of confidence, she abandons herself entirely to
My paternal care."

One night also, when the Saint was much exhausted by
her spiritual exercises, and by the interior converse she

had had with her Lord, she took a few grapes, with the intention of refreshing her Spouse in herself.   The Lord received them with much gratitude, and said to her: "I am
now compensated for the bitter draught offered me in a
sponge as I hung on the cross for your love, because I
taste now in your heart an ineffable sweetness ; and the
more purely you recreate your body for love of Me, the
sweeter is the refreshment I find in your soul."

As she had thrown from her the skins and stones of the
grapes which she had in her hands, she saw the devil—the
persecutor of all good—trying to gather them up, as if to
reproach her for the dispensation which her infirmity had
made her take, by eating after Matins, contrary to the
Rule.   But the moment he attempted to touch one of the
skins, he was so scorched and burned, as if by devouring
flames, that he fled from the house, uttering fearful cries,
and taking care for the future how he touched anything
that could cause him such frightful torments.

CHAPTER XLIX.

Of the benefit we may derive from our faults.

One night, as Gertrude was occupied in examining her
conscience, she remarked that she had a habit of saying
"God knows," without reflection and without necessity ;
and having blamed herself very severely for this fault, she
besought the Divine Majesty never to permit her to use
His sweet name lightly again.   Our Lord replied lovingly
to her: "Why would you deprive Me of the glory and
yourself of the immense reward which you acquire every
time you perceive this fault, or any similar one, and seriously endeavour to correct it ?   For when any one exerts

himself to overcome his faults for love of Me, he offers Me the same testimony of fidelity and respect as a soldier would do to his captain when he courageously resisted his enemies in battle, overcoming them all, and casting them to the ground with his own arm."

After this, as the Saint rested on the bosom of her Lord, she felt a great weakness of heart, which she offered thus to Him : " My beloved Spouse ! I offer Thee this debilitated heart, with all its affections and desires, that Thou mayest take pleasure therein according to Thy will." He replied : "I accept your offering of this weak heart, and prefer it to a strong one ; even as the hunter prefers what he has taken in the chase to tame animals."

Although the infirmities of the Saint prevented her from assisting in choir, still she often went to listen to the Office, in order thus to exercise her body in some manner in the service of God ; and reflecting that she was not as attentive or recollected as she desired, she manifested her grief to her Divine Spouse, saying to Him, with a dejected heart : " What glory canst Thou receive, my loving Lord, from my sitting here in this idle and negligent manner, paying so little attention to what is said or chanted to Thy glory ? " Our Lord replied : " And what satisfaction would you not have if your friend presented you with a draught of newly-made and delicious mead, which you thought would strengthen you ? Be assured, then, that I find infinitely more pleasure in every word, and even every syllable, to which you listen attentively for My glory."

At the Mass which was celebrated after, Gertrude felt unable to rise at the Gospel, and she doubted whether to spare herself or not on such occasions, as she had no hope of her recovery ; but she asked God, according to her custom, what would be most for His glory. He replied :

" When, for love of Me, you do anything with difficulty, and which is beyond your strength, I receive it even as if I had an absolute need of it; but when you omit anything to take due care of your body, referring all to My glory, I consider it in the same manner as an infirm person would consider some relief that it was impossible for him to do without: thus I will recompense you for both according to the greatness of My Divine munificence."

CHAPTER L.

Of the renewal * of the Seven Sacraments in her soul, and of fraternal charity.

As Gertrude examined her conscience one day, she discovered some faults which she was extremely anxious to confess; but as she could not have recourse to her confessor at the time, she began as usual to discover her grief to our Lord, who consoled her thus: " Why," He inquired, " are you troubled, My beloved, since I am the sovereign Priest and true Pontiff, to whom you can have recourse; and I can renew in your soul with greater efficacy the grace of the Seven Sacraments, by a single operation, than either priest or Bishop could by conferring each separately? For I will baptize you in My precious Blood; I will confirm you in My victorious strength; I will espouse you in My faithful love; I will consecrate you in the perfection of My holy life; I will absolve you from all your sins by the charity of My heart; I will feed you Myself by My overflowing tenderness, and I will feed Myself also on you; I will purify you inwardly by so powerful an anointing of the sweetness

* " Renovatione."

of My spirit, that all your senses and your actions will breathe the most fervent piety, which, pouring down on you like holy oil, will sanctify you more and more unto life eternal."

Once when the Saint had risen to say Matins, although in a state of extreme weakness, and had already finished the first nocturn, another religious, who was also ill, came to her, and she immediately recommenced the Matins with her, with great charity and devotion.   Afterwards, being occupied with God during holy Mass, she perceived that her soul was magnificently adorned with precious stones, which emitted a most admirable brightness.   Our Lord then made known to her that she had received those gifts in recompense for her humble charity in having recommenced her Matins for the convenience of a younger sister ; and that she had received as many different ornaments as she had repeated words.   The Saint then remembered some negligence of which she had not been able to accuse herself in confession, on account of the absence of her confessor ; and as she mourned over this to our Lord, He said to her : " Why do you complain of your negligences,—you who are so richly clothed with the robe of charity, which covers a multitude of sins ? "   " How can I console myself," she replied, " when I still perceive that I am stained by them ? " But our Lord answered : " Charity not only covers sins, but, like a burning sun, consumes and annihilates the slightest imperfections, and overwhelms the soul with merit."

Gertrude once perceived that a person neglected some observances of the Rule, and feared that she would be guilty in the sight of God if she did not correct it, as she knew of it ; but she also apprehended that some who were less strict might think she interfered more than was necessary in trifling matters. This trouble, however, she offered, according to her custom, to our Lord; who, in order to show how agreeable her devotion was to Him, said to her: "Each time that, for love of Me, you suffer this reproach, or any similar to it, I will strengthen you mightily, and will encompass you, as a city is encompassed with trenches and walls, so that no occupation will be able to distract you, or to separate you from Me; and, further, I will add to your merit that which any one might have acquired if they had submitted themselves with humility to your admonitions."

CHAPTER LI.

Of the fidelity which we must only expect to find in God, and of the grace of patience.

As it usually happens that the injuries which we receive from a friend are more difficult to bear than those which we receive from an enemy, according to the words of Scripture, "If my enemy had reviled me, I would verily have borne with it" (Ps. liv.),—Gertrude, knowing that a certain person, for whose welfare she had laboured with extreme solicitude, did not respond with the same fidelity to her care, and even, through a kind of contempt, acted contrary to what she advised, had recourse to our Lord in her affliction, who consoled her thus: "Do not be grieved, My daughter, for I have permitted this to happen for your eternal welfare, that I may the oftener enjoy your company and conversation, in which I take so much pleasure. And even as a mother who has a little child whom she loves specially, and therefore desires to have always with her, places something that will alarm her, and oblige her to come back into her arms, when she has strayed from her, so also, desiring to have you always near Me, I permit your friends to contradict you in some things, that you may find no true fidelity in any creature, and therefore have recourse to Me with all the more eagerness, because you know that I possess the plenitude and stability of all contentment."

After this it seemed to her as if our Lord placed her in His bosom like a little child, and there caressed her in many ways ; and, approaching His adorable lips to her ears, He whispered to her : " As a tender mother soothes the troubles of her little one by her kisses and embraces, so do I desire to soothe all your pain and grief by the sweet murmur of My loving words." After the Saint had enjoyed these and many other consolations for some time, our Lord offered her His Heart, and said to her : " Contemplate now, My beloved, the hidden secrets of My Heart, and consider attentively with what fidelity I have ordered all that you have ever desired of Me for your benefit and the salvation of your soul ; and see if you can accuse Me of unfaithfulness to you, even by a single word." When she had done this, she beheld our Lord crowning her with a wreath of flowers, more radiant than gold, as a reward for the trial of which we have just spoken.

Then the Saint, remembering some persons who, she knew, were tried in other ways, said to God : " Surely these persons merit to receive from Thy liberality, Father of mercies, a richer recompense, and to be adorned with more splendid ornaments than I, since they are not assisted by the consolations which I receive, though so unworthy, and

* " Larvas.

since I do not bear what happens to me with the patience I ought?" Our Lord replied: " In these things, as in all others, I manifest the special charity and tenderness which I have for you; even as a mother who loves her only child wishes to adorn her with ornaments of gold and silver, but, knowing that she could not bear their weight, decks her with different flowers, which, without incommoding her, do not fail to add to her attractions. So, also, I moderate the rigour of your sufferings, lest you should fall under the burden, and thereby be deprived of the merit of patience."

Then, as the Saint reflected on the great care of the Divine mercy for her salvation, she began to praise Him with great gratitude; and she perceived that those flowers with which her sufferings had been mystically rewarded expanded more and more as she returned thanks. She understood also, that the grace that God had given her, of praising Him in adversity, was as much more excellent as an ornament of solid gold is to one which has merely been gilt.

CHAPTER LII.

The value of a good will.

A certain nobleman having sent to the monastery to ask the religious to found a convent, Gertrude—who was always anxious to accomplish the will of God, though she was unable to comply with this request—cast herself before a crucifix, and offered herself to God with her whole heart, praying that His holy will might be accomplished. It seemed to her that our Lord was so deeply touched by this offering, that He descended from the cross to embrace her with extreme affection and gladness, and received her with marks of ineffable joy—even as a sick person who had been given over by the physician would receive a remedy which he had long desired, and which he hoped might restore his health—and having then gently approached her to the adorable Wound of His Side, He said to her: "You are welcome, My beloved; * you are the balm of My wounds, and the sweetener of all My griefs." Gertrude knew by these words that when any one abandons his will without reserve to the good pleasure of God, whatever adversity may be impending, our Lord receives it as if he had anointed His Wounds, even at the very hour of His Passion, with the most precious and healing ointments.

After this, as Gertrude prayed, she began to think of many things by which she hoped to procure the glory of God and the advancement of religion. But after a time she reproached herself for these reflections, which perhaps could never bear any fruit, because she was so weak that she seemed more likely to die than to be able to undertake any laborious work. Then the Lord Jesus appeared to her in the midst of her soul, radiant with glory, and adorned with roses and fair lilies; and He said to her: "Behold how I am adorned by your good will, even as I was by the stars and the golden candlesticks, in the midst of which St. John, in the Apocalypse, declares that he saw the Son of Man standing, and having seven stars in His right hand; and know that I have received as much pleasure from the other thoughts of your heart as from this sweet and agreeable garland of lilies and roses."

"O God of my heart!" exclaimed the Saint, "why dost Thou embarrass my soul with so many different desires, which are all without effect, since it is so short a time

---

* "Bene venias mihi charissima."

since Thou didst give me the thought and desire of receiving extreme unction, and disposed my soul to receive it by filling me with such joy and consolation? And now, on the contrary, Thou dost make me desire the establishment of a new monastery, although I am still so weak that I am scarcely able to walk." "I do this," replied our Lord, "to accomplish what I have said at the commencement of this book, that 'I had given you to be the light of the Gentiles;' that is, to enlighten many people: therefore it is necessary that your book * should contain information on many subjects, for the consolation and instruction of others. And as two persons who love each other often find pleasure in conversing on subjects which do not specially concern them,— as a friend often proposes to his friend the most difficult and intricate questions,—so do I take pleasure in proposing many things to My elect which will never happen to them, in order to prove their love and fidelity for Me, and to reward them for many purposes which they cannot carry into effect, counting all their good intentions as if they had been carried into action. So I inclined your will to desire death; and, consequently, made you feel this wish to receive extreme unction. And I have preserved in the depth of My Heart, for your eternal salvation, all that you have done in thought or act to prepare yourself for this Sacrament. Thus you may understand these words: 'The just man, if he be prevented with death, shall be in rest.' † For if you were deprived of this Sacrament by sudden death, or if you receive it after you had lost consciousness,—which often happens to My elect,—you would not suffer any loss thereby, because all the preparation for death which you have made for so many years is preserved in the unfading

* " In libro tuo."   † Wisdom iv.

spring-time of My Divinity,* where, by My coöperation, it always remains green and flourishing, and fructifying for your eternal salvation."

CHAPTER LIII.

How we may profit by the merit of others.

GERTRUDE was requested by a person, when she offered to God all the gratuitous gifts with which He had favoured her, to ask that she might have a share in their merit.   As she prayed thus, she perceived this person standing before the Lord, who was seated on His throne of glory, and held in His hand a robe magnificently adorned, which He presented to her, but still without clothing her in it.   The Saint, being surprised at this, said to Him : " When I made a similar offering to Thee, a few days since, Thou didst at once take the soul of the poor woman for whom I prayed to the joys of paradise ; and why, most loving Lord, dost Thou not now clothe this person with the robe which Thou hast shown her, and which she so ardently desires, through the merits of the graces Thou hast bestowed on me, though so unworthy of them ?"   Our Lord answered : " When anything is offered to Me for the faithful departed, I immediately use it for them, according to My natural inclination to show mercy and pardon, either for the remission of their sins for their consolation, or for the increase of their eternal felicity, according to the condition of those for whom the offering is made.   But when a similar offering is made for the living, I keep it for their benefit, because they

---

* " In immarcessibili æternitatis meæ vernantiâ."

can still increase their merit by their good works, by their good desires, and by their good will; and it is only reasonable that they should endeavour to acquire by their labour what they desire to obtain through the intercession of others.

"Therefore, if she for whom you pray desires to be clothed with your merits, she must study these three things: First, she must receive this robe with humility and gratitude—that is to say, she must acknowledge humbly that she has need of the merits of others—and she must render Me fervent thanksgivings for having deigned to supply her poverty out of their abundance; secondly, she must take this robe with faith and hope—that is, hoping in My goodness, she must believe that she will receive thereby a great assistance to her eternal salvation; thirdly, let her clothe herself in charity, exercising herself in this and in other virtues. Let all those who desire a share in the merits and virtues of others act in like manner, if they would profit thereby."

CHAPTER LIV.

Prayer composed by the Saint.

GERTRUDE having been bled some time after the Fast,* she was frequently heard uttering these words: "O King, of all kings the most excellent! O illustrious Prince!" with others of a similar import; and as she recollected herself one morning in the place where she usually prayed, she said to God: "O most loving Lord! what wilt Thou that I should do with these words which so often present them-

---

* "Ante jejunium"—probably after Lent.

selves to my mind and my lips ? " Then our Lord showed
her a golden collar, composed of four parts, which He held
in His Hands. But as the Saint did not know what these
four parts signified, He made known to her in spirit that
the first part represented the Divinity of Christ; the second,
the Soul of Christ ; the third, every faithful soul whom He
had espoused in His own Blood ; and the fourth, the pure
and immaculate Body of Christ. She knew also that the
reason why the faithful soul was placed in this collar, between the Soul and the Body of Jesus Christ, was to show
with what indissoluble love the Saviour had united the
faithful soul to His own Body and Soul. And suddenly
she was inspired with these words, in a rapture, at the
sight of this collar :

Prayer.

" Thou art the life of my soul ! May all the desires of
my heart be united to Thee by Thy burning love ! may
they languish and die whenever they turn to any object
apart from Thee ; for Thou art the beauty of all colours,
the sweetness of all taste, the fragrance of all odours, the
harmony of all sounds, the charm of all embraces ! In
Thee is the voluptuousness of delight ; from Thee flows
forth a torrent of love ; to Thee are all drawn by Thy
powerful attractions ; and by Thee all receive the sweet
influences of love ! Thou art the overflowing Abyss of the
Divinity ! O King, greater than all kings ! supreme Emperor,
sovereign Prince, peaceful Ruler, faithful Protector! Thou
art the vivifying gem of human nobility with the noblest
sentiments ! * Thou art a Worker full of skill ; a Master
full of clemency ; a Counsellor full of wisdom ; a Defender

---

* " In vivificans gemma humanæ nobilitatis."

full of kindness; a Friend most faithful! Thou art the sweet savour of all delights! O gentle caresser, whose touch imparts healing! O ardent Lover, sweet and chaste Spouse! Thou art the Spring-flower of unchanging beauty! O loving Brother, beautiful Youth, joyful Companion, liberal Host, careful Administrator! I prefer Thee to every creature; for Thee I renounce all pleasures; for Thee I seek all adversity; and in all this I desire only Thy glory. My heart and lips testify that Thou art the quickener of all good. I unite, by the merit of Thy love, the fervour of my devotions to the virtue of Thy prayers, so that by the power of this Divine union I may be raised to the highest perfection, and all rebellious movements may be calmed within me."

All these sentences seemed like so many brilliant stones separately enchased in the gold of this collar. On the following Sunday, as Gertrude assisted at the Mass at which she was to communicate, and recited this prayer with much devotion, she perceived that our Lord was pleased with it, and she said to Him: "O most loving Lord! since I perceive that these words are so agreeable to Thee, I will advise as many persons as I can to offer it to Thee devoutly, as a precious collar of pearls." Our Lord replied: "No one can give Me what is Mine;* but whoever recites it devoutly shall feel his knowledge of Me increase, and shall receive light from My Divinity, which shall be showered down on him by the efficacy of these words; even as they who hold a plate of polished metal to the sun behold therein the reflection of its light." The Saint immediately felt the effect of these words, for as soon as she had recited this prayer

---

* "Nemo mihi dat, quod meum est."

she perceived that the surface of her soul * became radiant with Divine light, and she found an increase of sweetness and pleasure in Divine things.

CHAPTER LV.

Our Lord shows her His Heart.

JESUS CHRIST once appeared to the Saint, and, showing her His Heart, said to her : " My beloved, give Me your heart ; " and as she presented it to Him with profound respect, it seemed to her that He united it to His by a canal which reached to the ground, through which He poured forth abundantly the effusions of His infinite grace, saying to her : " Henceforth I shall use your heart as a canal through which I will pour forth the impetuous torrents of mercy and consolation which flow from My loving Heart on all those who shall dispose themselves to receive it, by having recourse to you with humility and confidence."

CHAPTER LVI.

Of charity towards an erring brother.

As the Saint prayed one day for some persons who had formerly injured the convent seriously by their thefts, and were again committing depredations, our Lord appeared to her as if suffering much pain in one of His arms, which was so drawn back that the nerves were seriously injured : and He said to her : " Consider what torment he would

---

* " Facies animæ suæ."

cause Me who should strike Me with his closed hand on this suffering arm : and reflect that I am outraged in like manner by all those who, without compassionating the danger to which the souls who persecute you are exposed, do nothing else but talk maliciously of their sins and what they have suffered in consequence, without reflecting that these unhappy people are members of My Body ; while all those who, touched by compassion, implore My mercy for them, that I may convert them, act towards Me as if they soothed the pain of My arm with healing ointments : and I consider those who, by their counsels and charitable warnings, try to induce them to amend their lives, as wise physicians, who endeavour to restore My arm to its proper position."

Then Gertrude, admiring the ineffable goodness of God, said to Him : " But how, Lord, can these unworthy persons be compared to Your arm ? " He replied : " Because they are members of the body of the Church, of which I glory in being the Head." " But, my God," exclaimed Gertrude, " they are cut off from the Church by excommunication, since they have been publicly anathematised for the violence they have done to this monastery." " Nevertheless," replied the Lord, " as they can be restored to the bosom of the Church by absolution, My natural goodness obliges Me to care for them, and I desire with incredible ardour that they should be converted and do penance."

The Saint then prayed that the monastery might be defended from their snares by His paternal protection, and she received this reply : " If you humble yourselves under My mighty Hand, and acknowledge before Me in the secret of your hearts that your sins have merited this chastisement, My paternal mercy will protect you from all the efforts of your enemies ; but if you rise up proudly against those who persecute you, wishing them evil for evil, then, by My just judgment, I will permit them to become stronger than you, and to afflict you still more."

CHAPTER LVII.

That the care of temporal affairs and exterior duties may be acceptable to God.

ONE year, when the convent was much burdened by a heavy debt, the Saint prayed to God with more devotion than usual that the convent procurators * might be able to pay their debts. He replied tenderly : " What advantage shall I gain if I assist them in this ? " The Saint replied : " They will then be able to occupy themselves with more fervour and recollection in their spiritual duties." " And what will this advantage Me," continued our Lord, " since I have no need of your goods, and it is equally the same to Me whether you employ yourselves in bodily or mental exercises, provided you refer your intention to Me ? For if I only took pleasure in spiritual exercises, I should have so reformed human nature after the Fall, that it would no longer have needed food, or clothing, or any of the other necessaries of life, which are now obtained with so much labour. And as a powerful emperor is pleased, not merely with bringing up noble ladies in the court of his empress, but also brings up in his own court nobles, captains, and soldiers, who are employed in different ways, that they may serve him when any occasion presents itself, so also I take pleasure, not only in the interior delights of contemplation, but also in the different exterior affairs and occupations of the children

* " Provisores claustri.

of men, with whom I love to dwell when they labour in them for My love and for My glory ; because in these occupations they are so much exercised in charity, patience, humility, and the other virtues."

After this the Saint beheld the person who had the principal charge of the temporal affairs of the monastery as if he were resting on the left Hand of the Lord ; and it appeared to her that he often rose with great pain, and offered Him a piece of gold enriched with a precious stone.   Our Lord then said to her : " Know, that if I lessened the troubles of him for whom you pray, I should be also deprived of these precious stones which are so acceptable to Me ; and he would lessen the recompense which he will receive ; for then he would only be able to offer Me with his right hand this piece of gold without any ornament.   He presents Me with a piece of gold who, without suffering any adversity, refers all his actions to God according to His adorable will.   But he who is constantly suffering, and still conforms himself to the decrees of Providence, offers Me gold enriched with very rare and precious stones."

Nevertheless, the Saint still continued to pray that the convent procurator might be relieved from his difficulties. But our Lord said to her: " Why does it seem hard to you that any one should suffer these inconveniences for love of Me, since I am the one true Friend whose faithfulness never changes ?   For when any one is deprived of all human help and consolation, and is driven to the last extremity, those who have formerly received kindness from them are sorry for their misfortunes, and yet their sorrow is often fruitless, and can afford no assistance to their friend.   But I am the only true Friend who, in such dire necessity, will console the afflicted with the merit and glory of all the good works they have practised during their whole life, whether by thoughts, words, or actions ; and these shall appear scattered over My vestments like roses and lilies ; while this delightful vision shall revive in the soul its hopes of eternal life, to which it beholds itself invited in recompense for its good works. Then the soul disposes itself in holy contentment to depart from its mortal body and to enter eternal felicity, so that amidst its joys it may say : ' Behold the smell of my beloved is as the smell of a fertile field ' (Gen. xxvii.) For even as the body is composed of many members united together, so also the soul consists of affections, such as fear, grief, joy, love, hope, anger, modesty ; in the exercise of each of which the more man acts for My glory the more he will find in Me that incomprehensible and ineffable joy, and that secure delight, which will prepare him for eternal happiness. For in the resurrection, when the body will be raised incorruptible, each of its members will receive a special recompense for the labours and actions which it has performed in My name and for My love. But the soul will receive an incomparably greater reward for all the holy affections it has entertained for My love, for its compunction, and even for having animated the body for My service."

Once again, as the Saint prayed that the faithful procurator might receive the full reward of his troublesome labours for the temporal good of the community, our Lord said to her : " His body, which is wearied by so many labours for Me, is like a treasure-house, in which I place as many drachms of silver as his limbs make movements to fulfil the duties with which he is charged : and his heart is like an ark, in which I place in reserve as many drachms of gold as he has had thoughts of providing carefully, for love of Me, for those persons who are under his care." Then the Saint exclaimed, in surprise : " It seems to me, O Lord, that this man is not so perfect as to undertake all that he does purely for Thy glory ; for I believe he also thinks of the temporal profit he obtains thereby, and consequently of his bodily convenience. How, then, canst Thou, my God, find such pleasure as Thou sayest in his heart and in his body ?" Our Lord condescended to reply thus : " It is because his will is so entirely submitted * to Mine, that I am always the principal cause of his actions ; and for this reason he will merit an inestimable recompense for all his thoughts, his words, and his works. If he applies himself to each action with a still greater purity of intention, he will increase his merit even as gold exceeds silver in value ; and if he endeavours to refer all his thoughts and anxieties to Me with a yet purer intention, they will become as much more excellent as refined gold is in comparison of that which is alloyed with a baser metal."

CHAPTER LVIII.

Of the merit of patience.

It happened one day that a person was injured from an accident which occurred during some employment, and Gertrude, compassionating her suffering, prayed that the limb, which had been injured in a holy occupation, might not be endangered. Our Lord replied : " It will not be endangered ; but, on the contrary, the pain will bring down on her soul a recompense of inestimable value. And further, all those who endeavour to soothe or cure her pain shall receive an eternal reward ; for even as a piece of cloth

---

* " Adaptata."

which has been dipped in saffron imparts the same colour to whatever it touches, so, when one member suffers, all the members who serve her shall be crowned with her in glory." "But, my God," inquired the Saint, "how can those who thus assist each other render themselves worthy of so great a recompense when they labour thus, not that she who is wounded may suffer longer or more patiently for love of Thee, but merely to lessen her pain?" To this our Lord vouchsafed a reply full of ineffable consolation : "The patience with which any one endures an evil for My love and for My glory, which cannot be remedied by any human means, is not a patience which I condemn ; on the contrary, having sanctified it by these words which I addressed in My agony to My eternal Father, 'My Father, if it be possible, let this chalice pass from Me' (Matt. xxvi.), it becomes of incomparable merit and value." "But," inquired Gertrude, "is it not better to endure patiently every evil which happens, than merely to bear it because we cannot prevent it?" Our Lord answered : "This is a secret hidden in the abyss of My Divine perfection, and which surpasses human understanding ; but, to speak according to the manner of men, there is the same difference between these two kinds of sufferings as between two beautiful colours, which are both so brilliant and attractive, that it is difficult to give the preference to either." Then Gertrude prayed that our Lord would make this known to this person Himself, and thus give her effectual and true consolation ; but He answered : "This must not be ; but know that I refuse her this by a secret dispensation of My Divine wisdom, in order to prove her further, and to give her the merit of three virtues—patience, faith, and humility : patience, because if she found such consolation in these words as you now experience, all her pains would be so sweetened that the merit of her patience would be thereby much diminished; faith, in order that she may believe on the word of another what she has not experienced herself, since faith remains without merit and unfruitful when human reason has perceived what it believes; humility, that she may believe that others excel her, because they know by Divine inspiration what she does not merit to know."

CHAPTER LIX.

Of the aversion which God has for impatience—And how agreeable it is to Him that we should return thanks for His benefits.

As the Saint prayed for a person for whom she had great compassion, because she knew that in a moment of impatience she had asked why God had permitted her to be tried in a way which she thought she had not deserved, our Lord said to her: " Ask this person why these trials are not proportioned to her; and tell her, that since the kingdom of heaven cannot be obtained without suffering, that she shall choose herself whatever suffering she thinks most suitable for her; and when it happens to her, let her bear it with patience." She understood by these words, that the most dangerous kind of impatience is that in which persons imagine that they would be patient under other trials, but that they cannot be patient under what God sends them; whereas, on the contrary, they ought to be firmly persuaded that all which comes from God is most advantageous to them, and that when they do not receive it with patience, they ought at least to make it an occasion of humiliation.

Our Lord then addressed His faithful spouse thus:

" And what do you think of My conduct in your regard ?
Do you think that I have sent you suffering which is beyond your strength ? " " Assuredly not, my God," she replied ; " but I sincerely confess, and will acknowledge to
my last breath, that Thy providence has governed me, both
spiritually and temporally, in prosperity and adversity, in
so prudent a manner, that all the wisdom of the world from
its commencement even until now could not have acted
thus, and that Thou only, my sweetest Lord, who art the
Uncreated Wisdom, wert capable of it : ' Who reachest
from end to end mightily, and orderest all things sweetly' "
(Wis. viii.)

Then the Son of God led her to His Father, and asked
her what she would say to Him. " I render Thee thanks,
Holy Father," she exclaimed, " with all my power, through
Him who sittest at Thy right hand, for all the magnificent
gifts which I have received from Thy bounty, knowing that
this could not be effected by any creature, and could only
be accomplished by Thy Divine omnipotence, who causest
all things to exist." Then He led her to the Holy Spirit,
that she might offer her thanksgivings to Him for all His
benefits ; and she said : " I give Thee thanks, O Holy Ghost
the Comforter, through the merit of Him who, by Thy co-
operation, was made Man in the womb of a Virgin, that
Thou hast charitably prevented me in all things with the
gratuitous benediction of Thy sweetness, though I am so
unworthy ; and I am convinced that Thine ineffable charity
alone could have bestowed such benefits on me, in which
resides, from which proceeds, and through which we receive,
every good."

Then the Son of God, addressing her with the greatest
possible tenderness, said to her : " I take you under My
protection more especially than any other creature ; and I

shall have a greater care of you than I owe to them by right of creation, redemption, or even of My own free choice." From this the Saint knew that when any one renders similar thanksgiving to the Divine Goodness, and abandons himself with confidence and gratitude to His holy providence, that the Lord takes a particular care of him even as a Superior is obliged to watch specially over one whose vows he has received.

CHAPTER LX.

That God is pleased with us when we are displeased with ourselves.

As Gertrude prayed for a person with special affection, and said to our Lord, " Hear me, O loving Lord, according to the sweetness of Thy paternal love, for her for whom I pray,"—our Lord answered : " I usually hear when you pray for her." " Why, then," replied Gertrude, " does she so often entreat me to pray for her, alleging always her unworthiness and nothingness, as if she never received any consolation from Thee ?" " This," answered the Saviour, ' is the sweetest way in which My spouse could gain My affection ; this ornament becomes her best, and in this she pleases Me most, because thus she is displeasing to herself, and this grace increases in her in proportion as you pray for her." On another occasion, when she prayed at the same time for this person and also for another, our Lord said to her : " I have brought her nearer to Me, and therefore it is necessary she should be purified by some little trial ; even as a young girl who, on account of her love and tenderness for her mother, wishes to seat herself beside her, although she may be more inconvenienced thereby than her sisters, who take their proper seats round their mother,—the mother also cannot look so easily and lovingly on the child beside her as on those who sit opposite to her."

CHAPTER LXI.

Of the effect of prayers for others.

§ 1. *That we must pray with faith.*

As Gertrude once prostrated at the feet of our Lord Jesus, and kissed His Wounds with all possible respect and devotion, before praying for several persons and several affairs which had been recommended to her, she saw a stream breaking forth from the Heart of Jesus, which appeared to water all the place where she was. She understood that this stream was the efficacy of the prayers which she had offered at His feet, and said to Him : " My Lord, what advantage will those persons receive for whom I have prayed, since they cannot feel the effect of my prayers, and consequently cannot expect any consolation therefrom ? " Our Lord answered by the following similitude : " When a king makes peace after a long war, those who live at a distance cannot be made aware of it until a favourable opportunity occurs ; thus they who separate themselves from Me by their diffidence or other defects cannot perceive when others pray for them." " But, Lord," she replied, " Thou hast Thyself made known to me that some of those for whom I have prayed are not separated far from Thee." " It is true," answered our Lord ; " but he to whom the king gives his orders personally, and not through his officers, must wait for the convenience of his prince. And thus I will Myself make known to them the effect of your prayers, when I find it will be most advantageous to them to do so."

Gertrude then prayed specially for a person who had persecuted her formerly, and received this reply: "As it would be impossible for any one to have his foot pierced through without his heart sympathising in its sufferings, so My paternal goodness cannot fail to look with eyes of mercy on those who, while they groan under their own infirmities and feel their need of pardon, are nevertheless moved by a holy charity to pray for the welfare of their neighbour."

§ 2. *What we should ask for the sick.*

As it is a duty of humanity to pray often for the sick, the Saint inquired of God what would be most for the advantage of an invalid for whom she prayed. Our Lord replied: "Say two words for her with devotion—first, pray that she may preserve her patience; and secondly, pray that I may make every moment of suffering serve for her spiritual advancement and for My glory, according as the charity of My paternal Heart has ordained from all eternity for her salvation. And know that each time you pray thus, you will increase your merit and that of the sick person, even as an artist makes the colours brighter by retouching his painting."

§ 3. *How we should pray for those who occupy elevated positions in the Church.*

As Gertrude prayed for persons in office, she understood that what God desired most from them, and especially from prelates, was, that they should possess these dignities as if they possessed them not—that is to say, that they should use their authority as if it had only been granted to them for a day or an hour, and that they should be ready at any moment to resign their charge, yet without ceasing to do all in their power for the glory of God, saying to themselves continually in their hearts : " Courage ! let us neglect nothing which may procure the honour of our Lord in these matters, that we may at last lay down our burden without fear, when we have promoted His glory and the advantage of our neighbour."

§ 4. *Of the value and importance of recommending ourselves to the prayers of others.*

As the Saint prayed for a person who had requested her prayers with great humility, both personally and through others, she saw our Lord approach this person, encompassing her with celestial light, and pouring forth on her in the midst of this splendour all the graces which she had hoped to receive through the merits of the prayers of Gertrude. Our Lord taught her by this, that when any one confides in the prayers of another, with a firm confidence that through their intercession they will receive grace from God, the Lord in His goodness pours forth His benedictions on them according to the measure of their desires and their faith, even when he to whose prayers they have recommended themselves neglects to pray for them.

CHAPTER LXII.

Instructions for different persons in different states of life.

§ 1. *For one who has an ardent desire to advance in perfection.*

As Gertrude prayed for a person who had an ardent desire to advance in perfection, she received this instruc tion : "Tell her from Me, that if she desires to unite herself to Me by the tie of special love, she must, like a noble bird,* make a nest at My feet of the branches of her own nothingness and the palms of My greatness, where she may repose by a continual remembrance of her unworthiness, because man is aways inclined to evil of himself, and not to good, unless he is prevented by My grace. Let her often reflect on My mercy, and on the paternal goodness with which I am ready to receive men when they have fallen, if they return to Me by penance. When she desires to leave this nest in order to seek for food, she must fly into My bosom, wherein, with affectionate gratitude, she must reflect on the different blessings with which I have enriched her by My superabundant kindness. If she desires to fly further, and to ascend higher on the wings of her desires, she must rise with the swiftness of an eagle to the contemplation of heavenly things, which are above her ; she must fly around My face, supported like a seraph on the wings of charity, and gaze with the piercing eyes of her spirit upon the glory of the King of kings.

"But since it is impossible for her during this life to

---

* "Nobilis avis ; " probably the eagle is intended.

continue long in this high contemplation, even for an hour, she must depress her wings, by thinking frequently of her own nothingness, and return to her nest, remaining there in repose until she is able again to renew her flight by acts of thanksgiving and gratitude ; then let her seek once more her pasture, and elevate herself again in ecstasy to the highest contemplation of the Divine Majesty. Thus, by repeating frequently these difficult movements, entering into her nest by considerations of her unworthiness, and coming forth from it by meditating on My benefits, she will elevate herself to heavenly contemplation, and she will always taste celestial joys."

§ 2. Instruction for one who had entered religion at an advanced period.

Gertrude now prayed for another person who had been particularly recommended to her, and who, having renounced the world after passing the flower of her youth in it, had consecrated herself to God in religion. She besought Him, by the same love with which He had promised her that He would use her heart as a canal through which to pour forth His grace on others, that He would now accomplish this promise for His own glory, and for the satisfaction and advantage of this person ; and as she prayed thus, she saw her heart united, under the form of a little canal, to the loving Heart of Jesus, the Son of God, who appeared seated on His royal throne.

Then Gertrude also saw the person for whom she prayed prostrating humbly before God ; she beheld our Lord offering her His left hand, and saying to her : " I will place you under the protection of My incomprehensible omnipotence, My inscrutable wisdom, and My ineffable goodness," —at the same time presenting to her three fingers of His left hand, with which He touched hers; thus indicating three different manners in which she should endeavour to regulate her life. First, that when she commenced any duty, she should always submit herself humbly to the Divine omnipotence, acknowledging herself a useless servant, since she had passed her best years unfruitfully, without thinking of God her Creator; praying fervently that the Almighty would give her grace to act as she ought therein. Secondly, that she should protest, before the impenetrable wisdom of God, that she was unworthy to receive any effusion of Divine knowledge, because she had not accustomed her senses from her infancy to occupy themselves with Divine things, but rather had used them for human pride and vainglory. Thus abasing herself in profound humility, she should detach herself from everything earthly, and apply herself solely to the contemplation of God ; and that she should, according to the circumstances of time and place, endeavour to impart to others the effusions of Divine grace which were poured forth on her. Thirdly, that she should receive with great thanksgiving the good will which the Lord had freely bestowed on her, and by means of which she would be enabled to observe the two preceding counsels.

It appeared to the Saint, also, that our Lord wore a ring on the ring-finger of His left hand, the material of which was of little value, though it contained a very rare and precious stone of the colour of fire ; and it was revealed to her that this ring symbolised the imperfect life of this person, which she had offered to God by forsaking the world, and enrolling herself under the Divine standard ; and that the precious stone signified the mercy and ineffable liberality whereby our Saviour had inspired her with a good will, so that all her works might become perfect be-

fore God. Therefore the voice *—that is to say, the intention—of this person ought to be a continual thanksgiving
and praise to God for this immense grace. She knew, also,
whenever this person performed any good work by Divine
assistance, that our Lord placed it on His right hand as a
ring of great value, displaying it before all the heavenly
court, and appearing to take satisfaction in having received
the gift from His spouse,—that is, from the soul of this
person. This gave all the blessed souls a love for her, as
princes have for the spouse of their king; and they rendered their services to this person, whenever God desired
it, with all the fervour and devotedness which the Church
triumphant in heaven renders to the Church militant on
earth.

§ 3. *Instruction for a person who was desired to make her
nest in the hole of the rock—that is, in the wounded
Side of Jesus.*

As the Saint prayed with much devotion for another
person, she received this instruction for her : that she was
to make her nest in the hole of the rock,—that is, in the
adorable Side of Jesus Christ,—so that, reposing there, she
should suck honey from the rock,—that is, the sweetness
of the intention of the Deified Heart of Jesus,—and thus
she might learn to imitate His example, according to the
instruction of Holy Scripture; but especially in three
things. First : as our Lord frequently passed whole nights
in prayer, she should imitate Him by having recourse to
prayer in every trial and adversity. Secondly : that as
Jesus Christ preached in the towns and villages, she should
endeavour to edify her neighbour, not only by word, but

---

* " Vox."

by works; by her conduct, and even by the least movement of her body.   Thirdly : that as our Saviour was always
ready to assist the needy, she should also render service to
her neighbour by word and act; that whenever she was
about to perform any action, she should always recommend
it to God, uniting it to His most perfect works, that it
might be accomplished according to His adorable will, for
the salvation of the world ; and at its conclusion she should
again offer it to the Son of God, that He might amend its
defects, and present it to God His Father for His eternal
glory.

Whenever this person came forth from her nest, she
was to use three supports ; one to assist her in walking,
and the other two to support her on either side.   The first
support was to be a fervent charity, by which she was to
endeavour with all her might to draw all kinds of persons
to God, and to be useful to them for the glory of God, in
consideration of that Divine love by which He had laboured
for the common salvation of the whole human race.   The
second support, which she was to use on the right side, was
a humble subjection, by which she was to submit herself
to all for the love of God, and to take the utmost care that
neither her superiors nor her inferiors should be scandalised
by her words or actions.   The third support, which she was
to use on the left side, was an exact vigilance over herself,
by means of which she should endeavour to preserve herself
from all sin, and to avoid the stains which she might contract by thought, word, or action.

§ 4. *Instruction for another person who was to erect a*
mystical throne.

As Gertrude prayed for another person, her spiritual
life was thus represented to her : She appeared before the

throne of God as if engaged in building a magnificent throne
of precious stones, the cement of which was pure gold.
Sometimes she rested on this throne, and then rose up
again to resume her labour with greater fervour. The
Saint understood that these precious stones represented the
different afflictions by which the grace of God was preserved
and strengthened in the soul of this person ; for the Lord
leads His elect through this life by rough and difficult
paths, lest pleasures here should make them forget the
pleasures of their fatherland.*   The gold which cemented
these precious stones together represented the habitual
grace which this soul possessed, and by means of which,
with a lively faith, she made such profit of all the trials
she suffered, whether exterior or interior.   The repose
which she took when sitting on this throne signified the
sweetness of Divine consolation which she enjoyed ; and
the rising again, the good works in which she persevered
continually, and by which she profited so much that she
daily rose to a higher degree of perfection.

§ 5. *The life of another person represented under the figure*
of a tree.

As the Saint prayed for another person, her life was
thus represented to her: She beheld before the throne of
the Divine Majesty a very beautiful tree, the trunk and
branches of which were green and flourishing, the leaves
shining like gold.   The person for whom she prayed appeared to ascend into this tree, and to cut off some little
branches which had commenced to wither ; and she had
no sooner effected this, than Gertrude beheld the same

---

* " Ne dum delectantur in via, obliviscantur eorum quæ sunt in
patria "

number of branches coming forth from different parts of the throne of God, which were presented to this person to take the place of those which she had cut off ; and when these were grafted on the tree, they appeared to bring forth fruit of a red colour, which she gathered and presented to God, who received the offering with much pleasure.

The tree represented the religious life into which this person had entered to serve God ; the gold-coloured leaves the good works which she practised in her monastery—and these were rendered of still more value by the prayers of one of her relatives, who had induced her to become a religious, and had recommended her to God with much fervent prayer.   The instrument with which she cut off the withered branches represented the consideration of her own defects, in order to extirpate them by penance.   The branches which came forth from the throne of God to replace those which she had cut off, signified the perfect and holy life of Jesus Christ, who, through the merits and prayers of her relation, was always ready to supply her defects.   Lastly, the fruit which she gathered and presented to God signified the good-will she had to correct her faults, which was most acceptable to the Lord, who thinks more of the good-will of a sincere heart than of great actions without a pure intention.

§ 6. *Instruction for a learned and for an ignorant person, figured by the three Apostles on Mount Thabor.*

As the Saint prayed fervently for two persons who had been recommended to her prayers, but of whom she knew nothing, she besought our Lord to reveal their spiritual state to her.   Our Lord then desired her to inform them of two revelations which had been made to her for two other persons for whom she had been praying previously, one of whom was learned and the other illiterate ; and He added, that all persons, whatever might be their state or condition, would find instruction in the preceding reve-lations, as well as in those which follow. Of the learned person, our Lord said : " I have taken her up, with My Apostles, on the mountain of new light ;* therefore, in regulating her conduct, let her be instructed by the mean-ing of the names of the Apostles who were led to that mountain. Now, Peter, according to the interpreters, sig-nifies 'knowledge ;'† let her then endeavour, in all her reading, to attain to self-knowledge. For example : when she reads of vices or virtues, let her examine if she has any vices, and see what progress she has made in virtue. Then, when she has obtained a more perfect knowledge of herself, let her follow the signification of the name James, which is interpreted 'supplanter, and endeavour to fight cou-rageously against her vices, and to advance in virtues. And since the name John signifies ' grace,' let her endea-vour, at least for one hour each day, in the morning or evening, or whenever she finds it most suitable, to separate

---

* " In montem novi luminis."

† This passage is a difficult one. We are happy, however, in being able to append a note with which we have been favoured by one of the Benedictine Fathers of Solesmes, to whom we are deeply indebted for valuable assistance. In reply to our query, he writes thus : " As regards the names, ' Petrus,' &c. : Simon, in the Hebrew, is the same as hearing, obeying ; for *scama* means, ' to hear, to obey ;' but this hardly agrees with the interpretation given,—*i.e.*, ' Petrus itaque interpretatur agnoscens.' James, from the Latin ' Jacobus,' which means ' supplanter' (Gen. xxvii. 26), because he took hold of his brother's foot (*plantam*) : Jacob, in Hebrew, meaning 'a supplanter.' John, in Latin ' Johannes,'—*i.e.*, ' Deus donavit, vel, Deus misertus est, aut, Dei donum gratia et misericordia,'—from *ia* (Hebrew), a contraction for *Jehovah* (Deus) and *chanan,—i.e.*, ' Misertus est,' or ' donavit.'"

herself from all exterior things, and to recollect herself interiorly, to think of Me and know My will; and let her
thus exercise herself devoutly, as far as she can during the
time which she has chosen, in all that I inspire her with ;
whether it be praise, thanksgiving for the special favours
I have bestowed on her, or for those which I have granted
to others, or prayer for sinners, or for the souls in purgatory."

The following instruction was given for the unlearned
person because she was much troubled that she could not
apply to prayer as she desired, being hindered by the duties
of her office : "I have not merely chosen her to serve Me
for an hour in the day, but that she may be continually
with Me,—that is, that she may perform all her actions for
My glory, and with the same intention with which she
would desire to pray.   Let her also practise this devotion
in all the trouble which she finds in her employment,—
namely, to have a constant desire that all those who benefit
by her labour may not only find bodily refreshment, but that
they may be incited to love Me interiorly, and be strengthened in all good ; and each time that she acts thus, her
labours and works will be to Me as if she presented Me
with so many different and delicious viands."

CHAPTER LXIII.

That the Church is figured by the members of Jesus Christ—How
we must act towards those members which are diseased, and
in regard to our Superior.

As the Saint prayed for another person, the Lord Jesus,
the King of Glory, appeared to her, showing her, under the

figure of His natural Body the mystical Body of His Church, of which He is the Head and the Spouse. He appeared to have the right side of His Body magnificently clothed with a royal and Divine habit ; but the left was uncovered, and seemed all over ulcers. The Saint was instructed by this, that the right side of our Lord signified the elect who are in His Church, and who have been prevented by special gifts of grace ; the left side represented the imperfect, who are still full of vices and imperfections. The ornaments with which the right side of our Lord was adorned represented the benefits and services which some had rendered by a singular zeal to those whom they knew to be more advanced in virtue than others, and to enjoy more familiarity with God ; because, whenever they acted thus, they bestowed, as it were, a new ornament on the Lord. But there are also those who, while they willingly do service to virtuous persons for the love of God, reprehend the faults of the wicked and imperfect with such severity that they increase these wounds instead of healing them.

Our Lord then spoke thus to Gertrude : " Let all learn from My example in this matter how they should heal the wounds of the Church, which is My mystical Body,—that is, how they should correct the faults of their neighbours. First, they must touch them gently, and endeavour, by their kind and charitable advice, to withdraw them from their imperfections. When they see that these means are ineffectual, then, in the course of time, they may use stronger remedies to effect their cure. Those who care nothing for My words are they who, while they know of the faults of others, concern themselves so little about them, that they would not correct them, even by a word, for fear of giving themselves the least trouble, saying, with Cain, 'Am I my brother's keeper ?' They plaster over My wounds who, instead of trying to heal them, draw them out, and cause them to become corrupt, by allowing the imperfections of their neighbours to continue by their silence, when they might cure them by their words.

"There are others who discover the faults of their neighbours, but give way to anger if they are not corrected and chastised for them at the moment, according to their fancy ; and such persons resolve in their hearts never again to advise or reprehend another, imagining that their advice has been disregarded ; and yet they will condemn others harshly themselves, even injuring them, by untruths, without giving them one word of advice for their amendment. And they who act thus seem as if they placed a plaster on My wounds exteriorly, while interiorly they tear them with burning irons.

"They who neglect to correct the faults of others more from negligence than from malice act as if they trod on My feet.   And those who follow the impulses of their own will, without caring how they scandalise My elect, so that they gratify their inclinations, seem to pierce My hands with red-hot needles.

"There are others, also, who sincerely love, as they ought, good and holy Superiors, and who show them every respect by their words and actions, and yet despise those who appear less perfect, and condemn their actions in their own minds too rigorously ; and these act as if they adorned the right side of My head with pearls and precious stones, and, at the same time, struck the other side violently and without mercy when I desire to lay it down upon them to rest.   There are some also who applaud the ill-regulated actions of their Superiors, in order to insinuate themselves into their friendship, and thus to be permitted more easily to follow their own will ; and these act as if they dragged

My head back rudely, insulting Me in My suffering, and finding pleasure in My wounds."

CHAPTER LXIV.

On the spiritual participation of merits.

As the Saint prayed for another person who had been devoutly recommended to her prayers, she commenced by asking God to allow her to participate in all the good which she might effect, however unworthy, by her vigils, her fasts, her prayers, and other good works. Our Lord replied : " I will communicate to her all the favours which the gratuitous goodness of My Divinity has operated or will operate in you even to the end." The Saint then asked : " Since Thy holy and universal Church participates in all the good which Thou dost operate in me, by me, and by all Thine elect, what particular advantage will this person receive from Thy bounty, in consequence of my ardent desire that she should share in all the graces which Thou conferrest on me ? " Our Lord answered by this comparison : " Even as a lady of rank, who understands the art of skilfully arranging pearls and precious stones to adorn herself and her sister, does honour to her house and her parents, and though she who is thus skilled obtains the greatest applause, still those whom she adorns are more admired than those who are altogether deprived of such jewels ; so also the Church shares in what is granted to each individual ; but they who have received them, and those whom they desire to participate in them, receive the greatest profit from them."

Then the Saint told our Lord that a person who had

attended Dame Mechtilde in her illness complained that she had not attended her as she wished ; above all, she grieved that she had not spoken to her about her soul as she had desired, fearing, if she did so, that she might incommode her.   Our Lord replied : " She serves Me daily at My table, as a prince would his emperor, by the good-will with which she so often served My spouse with such alacrity and liberality ; for I take pleasure in all the services which she has rendered to her, whether by serving her with food and drink, or by soothing her sufferings by her words or actions. And as for the complaint which she makes of not having spoken to her often enough of spiritual things, I will supply for this Myself, as a charitable bridegroom, who, seeing that his bride from respect refrains from asking him for something that she ardently desires, grants double to her modesty.   Furthermore, on account of the joy which she feels for all the favours which I have granted to My spouse, her soul will receive in heaven an inestimable delight for all the graces which have been poured forth on her from the incomprehensible source of light.   For as the rays of the sun, when they fall on the surface of the water, reflect themselves again on some other surface, so the brightness of My grace, which shines into the souls of those whom I have presented on earth with the sweetness of My benediction, will cast their light through eternity upon the souls of those who have rejoiced in their happiness, and form an image brighter than that of the most highly-polished mirror."

CHAPTER LXV.

Of the utility of temptation.

As Gertrude prayed for a person who was greatly tried by
temptation, she received this reply : " It is I who have sent
this temptation, and who permit it, that she may thus perceive and repent of her defects, and efface those defects
which she does not see ; as it usually happens that, when
men perceive any stain on their hands, they wash them,
and thus thoroughly cleanse away lesser stains, which they
would not have perceived or removed if they had not seen
a greater one.

CHAPTER LXVI.

That frequent Communion is agreeable to God.

A CERTAIN person, moved by a zeal for justice, sometimes
exclaimed against those whom she thought approached the
Holy Communion with too little preparation and fervour,
and rendered them so fearful, that they dared not communicate.   On this account, as Gertrude prayed for this
person, and inquired how our Lord received her zeal, He
replied : " Since I find My delight in dwelling with the
children of men, and have left them this Sacrament by an
excess of love, for a remembrance of Me, that by this
they may remember Me frequently ; and, finally, have
obliged Myself to remain in this mystery until the consummation of ages,—all who, by their words or persuasions,
drive away those who are not in mortal sin, and thus hinder and interrupt the delight which I find in them, act like
a severe master, who forbids the children of the king to
speak to those of their own age who may be poor or be-

neath them in rank, because he considers it more correct
that his pupils should receive the honour due to their dignity than to permit them this enjoyment." "But, Lord,"
inquired the Saint, "if this person formed a firm resolution not to commit this fault any more, wouldst Thou not
pardon her for the past?" "I would not only pardon her,"
our Lord replied; "but her action would be as agreeable
to Me as it would be to the king's son if his master allowed
him to play with those children from whom he had previously driven him away with such severity."

CHAPTER LXVII.

Of the right manner of exercising zeal.

As Gertrude prayed for a person whose conscience was
troubled, fearing that she was guilty before God for not
having borne with sufficient patience the negligence of some
persons by whose bad example she feared religious discipline would become relaxed, our Lord, who is the best of
all masters, instructed her thus: "If any one desires that
her zeal should be an acceptable sacrifice to Me, and useful to her own soul, she should have a special care of three
things; first, she should show a gentle and serene countenance towards those whom she desires to correct for their
faults, and even, when opportunity offers, she should manifest her charity towards them by her actions as well as by her
words; secondly, she should be careful not to publish these
negligences in places where she neither expects amendment
in the person corrected nor caution in the listeners; thirdly,
when her conscience urges her to reprehend any fault, no
human consideration should induce her to be silent, but, from

a pure motive of giving glory to God and benefiting souls, let her seek an opportunity of correcting these imperfections with profit and charity. Then she will be rewarded according to her labour, not according to her success ; for if her care entirely fails of effect, it will not be her fault, but the fault of those who refuse to hear her."

As the Saint prayed again for two persons who had a verbal disagreement, one anxious for the maintenance of justice, and the other for charity, our Lord said to her : " When a father who loves his little children sees them playing together and disporting merely for amusement, he appears not to notice it ; but if he perceives that one rises up against the other too harshly, then he immediately reprehends severely the one who is in fault. Thus also I, who am the Father of mercies, when I see two persons arguing together with a good intention, appear not to perceive it, though I would much prefer to see them enjoy an entire peace of heart ; but if one becomes angry with the other, she shall not escape the rod of My paternal justice.'

CHAPTER LXVIII.

That we do not always receive the fruit of our prayers immediately

As another person complained that she did not receive the fruit of the prayers which were offered for her, the Saint laid the matter before God, and received this reply : " Ask this person what she would think most advantageous to a cousin or any other relative for whom she ardently desired a benefice,—whether the right to it should be conferred on him as a child, or whether he should be allowed the revenues also, and permitted to use them as he pleased? According to human prudence, she could only reply that it would be more advantageous to confer on him the right to the benefice, and the revenue when he could use it properly, than when he might squander it wastefully. Let her, then, confide in My wisdom and My Divine mercy, since I am her Father, her Brother, and her Spouse, and I will obtain what will be advantageous for her body and soul with far more care and fidelity than she would for any relative; and let her believe that I preserve carefully the fruit of all the prayers and desires which are addressed to Me for her, until a suitable time comes to permit her the enjoyment of them; then I will commit them to her entirely, when no one will be able to corrupt them, or to deprive her of them by their importunities. And let her be persuaded that this is far more useful to her than to pour into her soul some sweetness which might, perhaps, be an occasion of vainglory to her, or become tarnished by her pride; or than to grant her some temporal prosperity, which might prove an occasion of sin."

CHAPTER LXIX.

The value of exact obedience.

As the Hebdomadaria recited the chapter at Matins by heart, it was revealed to Gertrude that she acted thus to satisfy a precept of the Rule * which requires that it should be recited thus, and that she acquired as much merit by

---

* Chapter xii., the manner of singing Lauds: " To these (the Psalms) shall be subjoined a lesson of the Apocalypse, which shall be recited from memory," &c. The Hebdomadaria—the person who officiates for the week.

this as if as many persons as there were words in what she chanted interceded for her with God. She remembered what St. Bernard has said will happen at the hour of death, when our actions will address us thus : "You have produced us ; we are your work ; we will never leave you, but will abide continually with you, and appear with you at the judgment." Then God will permit all the actions of the obedient to appear as so many persons of distinction, who will console him, and intercede for him with God ; so that each good action performed through obedience, with a pure intention, will obtain the pardon of some negligence, and thereby afford extreme consolation to persons in their agony.

CHAPTER LXX.

Instructions on different subjects.

§ 1. *For the Hebdomadaria.*

ANOTHER Hebdomadaria, who was appointed to read the Psalter, having recommended herself to the prayers of the Saint, she began to intercede for her, and saw in spirit the Son of God elevating this person before the throne of His Eternal Father, praying Him to grant her a share in the zeal and fidelity with which He had desired the glory of God His Father and the salvation of the human race. After He had prayed thus for this person, she appeared clothed with ornaments like His. Therefore, as the Son of God is said to stand before His Father to render Him favourable to His Church, so this person, like another Esther, stood with the Son of God before the Eternal Father praying for her people, that is to say, for her community. And as she thus acquitted herself of the obligation of reciting the Psalter, the heavenly Father received her words in two different manners, like a lord who receives a debt by the person who has entered bail for his debtors, and like a sum of money given by his steward to distribute amongst his friends. It appeared, also, that our Lord gave this person all she desired to obtain by her prayers for the community, and that He had granted them all they asked.

§ 2. *Why God permits faults in superiors.*

As St. Gertrude prayed to God to correct a fault in one of her superiors, she received this reply : " Do you not know that not only this person, but also all those who have charge of this My beloved community, have some defects, since no one can be entirely free from them in this life ? And this happens by an excess of the mercy, tenderness, and love with which I have chosen this congregation, that by this means their merit may be greatly increased. For it is far more virtuous to submit to a person whose faults are apparent, than to one who always appears perfect." To this the Saint replied : " Although I am ful of joy in perceiving great merit in inferiors, I ardently desire that superiors should be free from faults, and I fear they contract them by their imperfections." Our Lord answered : " I, who know all their weaknesses, sometimes permit them, in the diversity of their employments, to be sullied by some stain, because· otherwise they might never attain so high a degree of humility. Therefore, as the merit of inferiors is increased both by the perfections and imperfections of their superiors, so the merit of superiors increases by the perfections and imperfections of inferiors, even as the different members of the same body contribute to mutual increase."

From these words Gertrude learned to admire the infinite wisdom of God, who arranges all things for the perfection of His elect with such care, that He even uses their defects for their increase in perfection ; so that, were there no other subject than this wherein the mercy of God shone forth, the united thanksgivings of all His creatures would not suffice to praise Him for it.

§ 3. *Of the fruits of adversity, and how we should correct our faults.*

As the Saint prayed for a person who was in trouble, she received this reply : " Do not defide in Me, for I will never permit My elect to be tried beyond their strength ; and I am always with them to moderate the burden of their adversity, even as a mother who wishes to warm her little child at the fire always holds her hand between the fire and her child ; so, when I know that it is necessary to purify My elect by sufferings, I send them not for their destruction, but to prove them and to contribute to their salvation." As she prayed afterwards for a person whom she had seen commit a fault, she said, in the fervour of her desires : " Lord, although I am the least of Thy creatures, since what I ask for this man is for Thy glory, why dost Thou not hear me, Thou who art almighty, and canst do all things ? " The Lord answered : " As My omnipotence can do all things, so does My wisdom discern all things ; therefore I do nothing that is not suitable. And as an earthly monarch who had the power and will to cleanse his stables would not do so himself, because it would be unsuitable, so I do not withdraw persons from the evil into which they have fallen of their own will, if they do not change their will, and render themselves agreeable in My sight, and worthy of My love."

§ 4. *Of avoiding negligence and confusion in the Divine Office.*

As the Saint watched a person who went round the choir during Matins to remind the sisters of some observance which had been forgotten, and thereby caused some confusion, she inquired of God if this action was agreeable to Him. He answered : "Whosoever endeavours to prevent any neglect in the Divine Office for My glory, and admonishes others for the same purpose, I will supply what he has omitted in this duty of piety and devotion which he is obliged to practise."

CHAPTER LXXI.

Of the loss of friends ; and how we should offer our trials to God.

As the Saint prayed for a person who was grieved at the illness of a friend whose death she expected, she received this instruction from God : "When any one has lost, or fears to lose, a faithful friend in whom they find not only the consolation of friendship, but also great assistance for their advancement in virtue, if they offer Me this affliction, and would rather My will should be accomplished than that their friend should live, they may be assured, if they form this desire in their hearts even for a single hour, that I will preserve their offering in the same beauty and freshness as it was presented to Me ; and all the afflictions which may happen to them afterwards through human weakness will contribute to the advancement of their salvation in such a manner, that all thoughts which may grieve them—as, for example, when they remember such or such a consolation which they might have found in this person, and of which they are now deprived—all those griefs and inquietudes which overwhelm man through the weakness of his human nature—will only serve to make place in their souls for Divine consolations, after the offering of which I have spoken ; for I will bestow on them as many consolations as they have suffered afflictions. And I will act towards them even as a lapidary who is obliged to place in his work of gold or silver as many precious stones as he has made niches to receive them. Now, My Divine consolation is like a precious stone, because precious stones are said to have strength ; * so the Divine consolation which man obtains by enduring a passing affliction has such efficacy, that there is nothing which can be renounced in this life, however great, which will not be restored a hundredfold in this life, and a thousandfold in eternity."

CHAPTER LXXII.

Instructions on various subjects.

§ 1. *Of the stains which might tarnish the purity of virginity.*

As Gertrude prayed once for a person who ardently desired to have the merit of virginity before God, but who feared to have tarnished its brightness by some human weakness, she appeared in the arms of the Lord, clothed modestly in a snow-white robe ; and He gave this instruction : " When virginity receives some slight stain through human weakness, and this becomes the occasion of exercising a true and solid penance, I cause these stains to appear as ornaments on the soul, and they adorn it as folds adorn a robe.† Nevertheless, as Scripture, which cannot be in

---

* " Dicuntur habere vires."   † " Sicut plicæ in vestimento."

error, assures us ' that incorruption bringeth near to God'
(Wis. vi.), it must be observed, that if these stains were
caused by great sins, they would impede the effusions of
Divine love."

§ 2. *Of renouncing our own judgment.*

As she prayed for another person who desired Divine
consolation, she received this reply : " She is herself the
obstacle which prevents her from receiving the sweetness
of My grace ; for when I draw My elect to Me by the interior attractions of My love, they who remain obstinate in
the exercise of their own judgment place the same impediment to it as one would who closed his nostrils with his
robe to prevent himself from smelling a delicious perfume.
But he who, for love of Me, renounces his own judgment to
follow that of another, acquires a merit all the greater for
acting contrary to his inclination, because he is not merely
humble, but perfectly victorious ; for the apostle says none
will be crowned ' except he strives lawfully ' " (2 Tim. ii.)

§ 3. *That the will is reputed before God as an act.*

As the Saint prayed for a person who found great difficulty in a work which had been commanded her, our Lord
instructed her thus : "If any one desires, for love of Me,
to undertake any painful work, by which he fears to be
hindered from his devotions, if he prefers the accomplishment
of My will to his soul's good, I will so esteem the purity
his intention, as to consider it as if it had really been of
carried into action ; and even if he never commences what
he has undertaken, he will not fail to obtain the same reward from Me as if he had accomplished it, and had never
committed the least negligence in the matter.

§ 4. *That we ought not to prefer exterior things to interior.*

On another occasion, when the Saint prayed for a person who was troubled about some subject of which she was herself the cause, she received this reply : " By these pains I purify the negligence which she has contracted by preferring, from human motives, an exterior utility to her interior advancement." " But since she cannot live without the exterior goods," replied the Saint, " what fault can she have committed by this foresight, which is a necessity of her office ? " Our Lord answered : " It is an honour and an ornament to a lady of rank to wear a mantle lined with furs ; but if she turned it inside out, what was suitable for her rank would become a subject of confusion, so that her mother, to prevent such an exposure, would cover her with another mantle, lest she should be considered to have lost her senses. Thus I, who tenderly love this person as My own child, cover her defects with different kinds of afflictions, and I permit them to happen to her for this reason, without any fault of hers. Further, I have adorned her with patience as a special ornament ; for I have recommended in the Gospel that men should seek first the kingdom of God and His justice—that is, the perfection of the interior man—and then, not that they should seek exterior things, for I have promised that they shall be added to them." These words should be carefully considered by all religious who desire to be friends of God.

PART IV.

THE REVELATIONS OF ST. GERTRUDE.

COMPILED BY THE RELIGIOUS OF HER MONASTERY.

———◆———

CHAPTER I.

With what devotion we ought to prepare ourselves for festivals—
Advantages of recommending ourselves to the prayers of others
—Our enjoyment of God corresponds to our desires and our
capacity to receive it.

AS the Saint was watching during the greater part of
the night which preceded the Vigil of Christmas,
before Matins, and had occupied herself entirely in meditating on the Response *De illa occulta*,* in which she took
great pleasure, she was suddenly ravished in spirit, and in
her rapture she beheld Jesus Christ reposing sweetly and
peacefully in the bosom of His Father; and the desires
which were addressed to Him by those who wished to
spend this feast with great devotion appeared under the
figure of a certain vapour. Then this beautiful and gentle
Jesus sent forth from His Divine Heart a light which
spread itself over this vapour, which showed them the way
in which they should come to Him. As each approached

———

* We have not been able to ascertain where this Response occurs;
it is not in the present Benedictine Breviary.

to God, she perceived that those who had recommended themselves humbly to the prayers of others were led by the hand by persons who surrounded them, and thus they went direct to God in the splendour of this light, which came forth from His Heart : whereas those who had confided merely in their own efforts and prayers wandered from this path, but arrived at last at the term by a light which came to them from God.

As the Saint desired to know with what special grace it had pleased God to communicate Himself to each of her sisters, she immediately beheld them all reposing in the bosom of the Son of God, where each was filled with joy according to her capacity and desires. She observed that none hindered the other, but that each enjoyed God as fully as if He had given Himself to each individually; that some embraced Him lovingly, as a Child about to be born for us : that others regarded Him as a faithful Friend, to whom they could therefore disclose every secret of their hearts ; while others, pouring forth the whole joy of their souls, caressed Him as a Spouse chosen amongst a thousand, and more beloved than all,—so that each found in Him, in a most pure and holy manner, the accomplishment of her individual desires.

Then the Saint came forward, according to her usual custom, and cast herself at the feet of her Lord, saying to Him : " O most loving Lord ! what should my dispositions be, and what devotion can I offer to Thy most blessed Mother at this Divine birth, since my bodily infirmity prevents Me even from reciting the Hours to which my profession obliges me ? " It appeared to her then that our Lord, moved by compassion for her poverty, gathered together all that she had said for the glory of God or the good of souls during the Advent, and offered it lovingly to His sweetest Mother, who was seated in glory at His side ; and to this He joined all the fruits which her words might have produced, even to the end of ages, to supply for any negligence which she might have committed in her service. The Mother of God, having received this offering, appeared as if adorned by it ; and Gertrude approached her, beseeching her to intercede for her with her Son. Then the Blessed Virgin turned towards Him with a loving countenance, and, after embracing Him, addressed Him thus : " My beloved Son, I beseech Thee to join Thy affection to mine, and to grant to the prayers of this soul, who loves Thee with so much fervour, all she asks of Thee." Then the Saint addressed our Lord thus : " O Sweetness of my soul ! O Jesus, most loving and most desirable ! O dearest of all who are dear ! " After having said these and many similar words, she exclaimed : " What fruit can there be in these words, uttered by one so vile ? " Our Lord replied : " What does it matter what kind of wood is used to stir up perfumes and vases of incense, since, whatever they are stirred with, they always emit the same odour ? Thus, when any one says to Me, ' My sweetest Lord,' &c., what does it matter if they think themselves utterly vile, since My goodness, like a perfume stirred up, exhales an odour in which I take extreme pleasure, and which gives to those who move it by their words a sweetness which is to them a foretaste of eternal life ? "

CHAPTER II.

Instructions for celebrating the Feast of the Nativity.

THE next day, the Saint watched for some time before Matins, and occupied herself with reflecting, in the bitterness of her heart, on some impatience to which she had given way on the preceding evening, in consequence of a negligence of those who attended her. As she heard the first signal for Matins, she was filled with joy, praising God for the announcement that the Feast of the most sweet Nativity of her Lord was so near at hand. Then the Eternal Father addressed Himself lovingly to her, saying : "Behold, I am going to send into your soul the affection which I sent before the face of My only Son to purify the world from its sins, and I will enkindle it in your soul, that you also may be purified from all the sinful stains of your past negligences, and thus you may be prepared to celebrate the approaching feast worthily." After this favour, she reflected bitterly on the faults which she had committed, and considered herself as a creature altogether unworthy of the graces of God, since a trifling negligence in one of His servants had caused her to give way to such great impatience.

But the Divine mercy instructed her that all the reflections which men make with sorrow for their faults, after they have done penance for them, will serve to prepare them for receiving the grace of God, as Scripture teaches : "If the wicked do penance for all his sins, he shall live, and not die" (Ez. xviii.)

At the second bell for Matins, the Saint again began to praise God ; and God the Father spoke thus to her : "Behold, I will again place in your soul that which I sent before My Son to correct the defects and weaknesses of man, that those defects may be amended which are not for your perfection ; for there are certain faults in men, the knowledge of which serves to humble them, and causes a holy compunction, and these faults further their salvation ; and I permit these defects even in those whom I love most, in order to exercise their virtue. But there are other faults of which they think little, and, what is still worse, they defend them as if they were virtues, and will not be corrected for them. These faults place the soul in great peril of eternal damnation ; but from these your soul is now purified."

At the third toll of the bell, as she continued to praise God, the Eternal Father filled her soul with all the virtues which had been found in the souls of the Patriarchs, Prophets, and the Faithful before the advent of His Son—such as humility, desire, knowledge, love, hope, &c.—that she might celebrate so great a feast worthily. The Lord then adorned her with these virtues as so many brilliant stars, and stood before her, saying : " My daughter, which would you prefer—that I should serve you, or that you should serve Me ? " For she enjoyed God in two ways—first, by a rapture which absorbed her entirely in God, so that she could not explain much of what she learned therein for the edification of others ; and secondly, by a grace which God conferred on her of instructing her in Holy Scripture, of which He imparted to her the spirit and meaning, so that it seemed to her as if she conversed with God familiarly, as a friend would with his friend ; and this enabled her to be extremely useful to others. God then asked her which she preferred—that He should serve her in the first manner, or that she should serve Him in the second ? But as she sought not her own things, but those of the Lord Jesus, she preferred having the labour of instructing her neighbour for the glory of God, to seeking her own satisfaction by tasting His sweetness ; and God appeared well pleased with her choice.

As matins commenced, she implored the Divine assistance by the words *Deus in adjutorium ;* by the *Do-*

mine labia mea aperiis, which is repeated three times, she
saluted and adored, with her whole heart, her whole soul,
and all her strength, the infinite power of the Father, the
impenetrable wisdom of the Son, and the ineffable goodness of the Holy Ghost—adoring the Trinity in Unity, and
the Unity in Trinity ; then, at the first five verses of the
Psalm *Domine quid multiplicati sunt*,* she approached in
spirit to the holy Wounds of Jesus Christ, and embraced
them lovingly ; at the sixth verse of this Psalm, she prostrated at the Feet of our Lord, to adore and thank Him for
the remission of all her sins ; at the seventh, she approached
His sacred Hands, and thanked Him for all the favours
which she had received during her whole life from His
goodness ; at the eighth, she inclined profoundly before the
loving Wound of His sacred Side ; at the ninth (the *Gloria
Patri*), she united with all creatures in adoring the effulgent
and ever-peaceful Trinity, and, approaching the Heart of
Jesus, she saluted it with the deepest affection, extolling it
for having hidden within it all the incomprehensible riches
of the Divinity.

At the first verse of the Psalm *Venite*,† having prostrated once more to adore the Wound of the Lord's Left
Foot, she obtained through it a full remission of all the

---

* Psalm. iii., proper to Benedictines, who say it at the commencement of Matins. See Rule of St. Benedict, ch. ix. It will
be remembered that the *Domine labia* is repeated three times by
Benedictines.

† Psalm. xciv., said at the commencement of Matins. It is divided into five parts. An Antiphon called the Invitatory is said
after each, and before and after the *Gloria Patri*, with which it
concludes. The Invitatory varies with the festival or feria, but
is always an invitation to sing the Divine praises. The *Hodie
scietis*—" To-day ye shall know that the Lord will come, and to-
morrow ye shall see His glory "—is the Invitatory for the Vigil of
Christmas, as above.

sins which she had committed by thoughts or words.
Then she adored the Right Foot at the second verse, and
obtained pardon of all the sins of omission by which she
had failed in the perfection of her thoughts and words ; at
the third verse, she turned to the Blessed Wound of the
Left Hand, and received the remission of all the sins she
had committed by act ; at the fourth, she received from the
Right Hand of the Lord what supplied for all the omissions
in her good works ; lastly, at the fifth verse she approached
the most holy Wound of the Side of her Beloved (which
abounds and superabounds in all good), and, having kissed
it very devoutly in the place from whence the precious
water sprang forth at the touch of the soldier's lance, she
was purged from every stain, made whiter than snow, and
adorned with every virtue by the precious Blood ; then,
chanting the *Gloria Patri*, and honouring the adorable
Trinity as at the preceding Psalm, when singing the *Sicut
erat*, she concluded all in the heart of Jesus, which contains
all that is Divine and satisfying. During the Invitatory
Hodie scietis, which is repeated five times in the *Venite*
and twice after it, God purified seven affections in her,
which became marvellously ennobled by being united with
the affections of Jesus Christ.

While they sang the other Psalms, she remained in the
presence of the Lord clothed with virtues, as with so many
brilliant stars. At this moment, as all her desires tended
towards God, she prayed that all which she might do,
whether exteriorly or spiritually, on the day of the Nativity
of her sweet Jesus, might be done to the honour and glory
of the most holy and adorable Trinity. When the bell rang
for Lauds, our Lord said to her : " As the sound of these
bells announce the Feast of My Nativity, I will grant
that all which you do on this festival—whether by chant-

ing, reading, praying, meditating, or even by exterior exercises, such as eating and sleeping—shall resound to the praises of the Most Holy Trinity, by union with My desires and love, which were ever in harmony with the will of God the Father."

When they lit the seven candles,* she received from God the seven gifts of the Holy Spirit, as far as she was capable, and in proportion even as Jesus Christ was filled with them Himself. As she besought our Lord, by the condescension with which He willed to be born in a stable,† to prepare her heart for His birth, this most clement Lord complied with her desire, and made a stable in her heart, giving her His omnipotence, wisdom, and benignity for a roof and walls.

She now beheld with great joy and admiration all the good works which God enables men to perform by His goodness and power, and in which He allowed her to share as a preparation for this feast, attached to these walls like little bells. Then she beheld the Lord Jesus, who imparted new joys and gifts to her, while he was attended by the princes of heaven.

After this, as the Saint repeated, two hundred and twenty times, " I adore Thee, I love Thee," &c., it seemed to her that at each prayer His members were presented to her to use as instruments of Divine praise ; and that afterwards Jesus Christ purified, in a marvellous manner, all her senses, exterior and interior, and renewed them in purifying them, so that they became sanctified by union with

---

* "Septem candalæ accenderunt." In monastic churches, there were formerly seven candles before the altar. See Dom Martene, *De Ant. Mon.* lib. v. c. i.

† "Diversorio."

His. As the bell rang for Chapter, she again praised God for His goodness in assisting thereat in person, as had been revealed to Mechtilde, her sister ; and she knew that He was present by the devotion which she observed in the sisters who assisted at Chapter, and who burned with ardour to see this revelation accomplished, because it seemed as if our Lord waited with extreme joy until all the community were assembled, being seated in the place of the Lady Abbess, in whose person He appeared to preside, but with a marvellous glory, and accompanied by a great number of blessed spirits, who surrounded the throne of His Majesty.

When the religious were seated, our Lord said, as if in a transport of joy : "Behold My friends who have assembled here ! " One of the religious then having said the *Jube, Domne*,* and another replying, *In viam mandatorum suorum*, our Lord extended His venerable Hand, and blessed the convent, saying : " I consent to all which shall be done or enacted, reposing on the omnipotence of My Father." Then, as the religious commenced the words, " JESUS CHRISTUS, FILIUS DEI VIVI, IN BETHELEHEM JUDA NASCITUR," all the choirs of angels, hearing the announcement of the birth of their Lord and King, were filled with ineffable joy, and fell prostrate on the ground to adore Him. The sisters then commenced the *Miserere*, according to custom. The angel

---

* The reading of the "Christmas Martyrology" is a ceremony of great state and magnificence in monastic houses. What honours could be sufficiently great for the announcement of the Divine Birth ? The Community generally proceed from the choir to the chapter-house, or room, after Prime, and there, when the blessing has been asked in the usual form, the Martyrology is solemnly chanted, all falling prostrate in adoration when the words *Jesus Christus Filius Dei vivi, in Bethelehem Juda nascitur*, are chanted.

guardian of each religious presented her heart with joy to
God; and it seemed as if our Lord received from each a
certain knot * or twisted cord, which He placed in His
bosom.   When those who loved God with the greatest
fervour offered Him their hearts, the angels of the choir
of Seraphim, who attended our Lord and supported Him,
disposed those religious for their offering.   When the
hearts of those who were most enlightened in the knowledge of God were offered, the angels of the choir of Cherubim came to present their homage.   When the hearts of
those who exercised themselves most in virtue were offered,
the angels of the choir of Virtues came to their assistance;
and thus also the other angels exercised their ministry,
according as those whose virtues corresponded to their
nature came to offer their hearts to our Lord.   But as for
those in whom this revelation excited no more devotion
than usual, they were offered to God by the angels; but
their bodies appeared at the same time as if prostrate on
the ground.

Then Gertrude approached her Spouse, and offered
Him the first *Miserere*, which was said for her, exclaiming:
" O my loving Spouse, I renounce my own interest in this,
and I offer it to Thee for Thy eternal praise, that it may
please Thee to grant some grace to Thy special friends or
mine, as it shall please Thy mercy."   Our Lord then received this *Miserere* as a brilliant and beautiful pearl,
placing it in a ring which He had before Him, which was
marvellously embellished with precious stones and flowers
of gold, saying: " Behold, I have placed this pearl which
you have offered Me in the centre of this ring, that all
those who recommend themselves to your prayers, or who

* " Nexum."

merely implore your assistance by a look, may derive the same advantage from it as the Jews drew from looking at the brazen serpent, which I caused to be lifted up in the wilderness by Moses."

When the Psalms were finished, and the sisters had accused themselves of their faults, two princes appeared, who bore a tablet of gold, which they held before our Lord. He then opened the knots, which had been hidden in His bosom ; and all the words of the Psalms and prayers which had been said were seen under the form of brilliant and beautiful pearls, each of which shone marvellously, and gave forth a sweet and melodious sound. This brilliancy was an indication of the zeal and love with which these souls endeavoured to please our Lord, and the melodious sound a prediction that the fruit which the whole Church would gather from their prayers would be rendered to them twofold.

Gertrude perceived that the Lord effected all these marvels in consequence of the particular devotion which the community had, expecting that He would preside that day at the Chapter. While the names were read from the tablet * of those who were to chant or read at Matins, our Lord looked at them with pleasure, and inclined His Head to those who listened attentively to what was prescribed them with such sensible marks of tenderness, that the tongue of man would fail to describe it ; and He consoled those who were grieved that nothing was given them to chant in

---

* In most religious houses, the name of the sister who is to officiate for the week, and of those who are to read the Lessons, to serve, to read in the refectory, &c., are read out at Chapter. This passage alludes to the custom, which was evidently in use in St. Gertrude's time, and shows how dear is a ready acceptance of the will of superiors, even in trifling matters, to our blessed Lord.

an ineffable manner.   Gertrude, who beheld all this in spirit, said to our Lord : " O Lord, if this community only knew what extreme tenderness Thou hast for them, how those sisters would be grieved whose names were not read out."   Our Lord replied : " All those who have the desire of singing or reading, although they do not do so, will be treated by Me with the same goodness as if they did ; for their will pleases Me as much as their action, and it will be equally rewarded.   And all those who listened to what was prescribed them, and received it with an inclination of the head, desiring to accomplish it for My glory, and beseech- ing Me to aid them to perform it worthily, will so draw down the sweetness-of My love upon them, that I will not defer bestowing new graces on them as a mark of My approbation."

When the Prioress, according to the rules of the Order,* accused herself of negligence, in the name of the Community, before the Lady Abbess, our Lord spoke thus : " I absolve you, by the power of My Divinity, from all the negligences of which you have accused yourself before Me ; and when-

---

* The superioresses of some Benedictine monasteries are termed abbesses; of others prioresses.   When there is an abbess, the second superioress is called prioress ; and when the superioress is a prioress, her assistant is termed sub-prioress.   Convents founded by royal charter are abbeys ; but if the right of nomination is in royal hands, the appointments are not always such as could be desired.   As far as we have been able to ascertain, the *Miserere* is not said now at Chapter ; but the beautiful custom of the prioress asking pardon of the community for her faults towards them is still continued on the eves of great festivals.   The community then ask her pardon for their faults towards her ; and finally ask pardon of each other for any mutual disedification.   When superiors humble themselves thus for their faults, they can scarcely fail to receive the love and respect due to such true Christian humility.

ever you fall again through human frailty, I will pardon you and show you mercy."

As they read the seven Penitential Psalms as a penance for their sins of negligence and inattention, each word appeared on the same tablet in the form of pearls ; but they were of a dark colour, and arranged near the brilliant ones of which we have already spoken ; because these Psalms were repeated through custom, not from special devotion : from whence we may learn, that what is done through custom contributes in some degree to our merit, though God regards as infinitely more excellent and agreeable what is done through devotion.

As the verse *Gloria tibi, Domine*,* was chanted at Vespers, the Saint beheld a multitude of angels flying round the convent, and singing the same words in loud and joyful accents. She then inquired of our Lord what advantage men gained when the angels joined thus in their Psalmody. As He did not reply, and she continued to desire this information, she was interiorly told, by Divine inspiration, that when angels are present at our solemnities, they pray to God that those who imitate them in their devotion may imitate them in purity of body and soul.

Then she began to be doubtful, as often happens, whether this thought had come from God, or whether it proceeded merely from her own imagination. But our Lord consoled her by this reply : " Do not fear ; for your will is so perfectly united to Mine, that you can only will what I do, and consequently you desire only My glory. Be assured the holy angels are so submissive to your good desires, that if until now they have not prayed for you as you

---

* Last verse of the hymn for Vespers at Christmas ; the same termination is used until the Epiphany to all hymns.

wish, they will henceforth do so with the greatest fervour. And because I, as their King, have made you in some sort a queen, they are so disposed to obey you, that if you require anything from them, they will endeavour to accomplish it the moment you desire it."

After Vespers, as the relics of the convent and the image of the Blessed Virgin were carried in procession as usual, the Saint felt grieved that her illness had prevented her from reciting a number of prayers, and performing some acts of devotion which she wished to offer to the Mother of God on this solemn Feast; but she found herself at the same time filled with an unction of the Holy Spirit, so that she offered her the sweetest and most noble Heart of Jesus Christ to supply for all her negligences. The Blessed Virgin received this offering with great satisfaction and pleasure, because she considered this Heart as the most honourable gift which could be offered her, as it contained every good.

CHAPTER III.

For the Feast of the Nativity—Apparition of the Infant Jesus and His Blessed Mother.

On the night of the Nativity, at Matins, as the Saint continued these exercises, our Lord, to correspond with her movements of fidelity and devotion, drew her entirely to Himself, so that, by a sweet influence of His Divinity in her soul, and by a reflux of knowledge which passed from her soul to God, she knew all that was chanted at Matins, whether Responsories or Psalms; and this knowledge gave her ineffable and incomprehensible joy. While this continued, she beheld all the saints standing before the throne of the King of kings, reciting Matins with great devotion, for His Divine honour and glory.

Remembering several persons who had been recommended to her prayers, she said, with great humility : " How can I, who am so unworthy, pray for persons who stand praising Thee with such labour and devotion, since my infirmity prevents me from following their example ? " Our Lord replied : " You can very well pray for these persons, for I have hidden you in the bosom of My paternal goodness, that you may ask and obtain from Me whatever you will." "But, Lord," replied the Saint, "since it pleases Thee that I should pray for them, I beseech Thee to appoint a time in which I may do so with fidelity, in manner worthy of Thee, and with utility to them without losing the happiness with which Thou dost honour me in partaking of Thy celestial joys." To this our Lord replied : " Recommend each to My Divine kindness and love, since it is this love that has made Me descend from the bosom of My Father to serve men." When she had named each individually, our Lord, won by His tender love, supplied the needs of each by a most loving compassion.

After this, the Blessed Virgin appeared to her, seated honourably near her Divine Son ; and while the *Descendit de cœlis* * was chanted, our Lord appeared to recall the

---

* The Responsory, iv. Lesson, i. Nocturn, Matins for Christmas ; "Descendit de cœlis Deus verus, a Pater genitus, introivit in uterum Virginis, nobis ut appareret visibilis, indutus carne humana protoparente edita : Et exivit per clausam portam, Deus et homo, lux et vita, conditor munda "—The true God. born of the Father, descended from heaven, and entered into the Virgin's womb, that He might appear visibly to us, clothed with the flesh given to our first

extreme goodness which had made Him descend from the bosom of His Father into that of the Virgin, and He looked so lovingly upon His mother, as to move her very heart; and by His embrace He renewed all the joys which she had when in the world in His holy Humanity.

She also beheld the sacred and virginal womb of the Mother of God, which was clear as crystal, and in which our Lord appeared in the form of an infant, and flew promptly and lovingly to her heart : by this she understood that, as the Humanity of Christ fed upon her virginal milk, so did His Divinity feed on the purity and love of her heart.   At the response, *Verbum caro factum est,** when all the sisters made a profound inclination to honour the Incarnation of Jesus Christ, she heard Him saying : " Whenever any one inclines at these words, from gratitude and devotion, giving Me thanks for having become Man for his sake, I also incline to him, by a pure movement of My goodness ; and I offer, from My inmost Heart, all the fruit and merit of My Humanity to God the Father, that the eternal beautitude of this person may be doubled."

At the words *et veritatis,* the Blessed Virgin came forth

---

parents, and came forth through the closed gate God and man, Light and Life, the maker of the world."   This *clausam portam* of Ezechiel is constantly referred by the Fathers to the Blessed Virgin.   St. Bernard, in his sermon on the Twelve Privileges B.V.M. says, Mary is the eastern gate, which none could pass but one.   St. Jerome writes : " She (Mary) is the eastern gate of which Ezechiel speaks as always closed."   St. Augustine, in his sermon on the Nativity : " The closed gate is the emblem of the integrity of her immaculate flesh. She remained inviolate after childbirth, and became more holy by conception.

* Responsory, xii. Lesson, iii. Nocturn ; the *Te Deum* follows, and on Christmas night the Midnight Mass is said, after which Lauds are commenced.

with the double ornament of her virginity and her mater-
nity, and, accosting the first sister on the right side of the
choir, she embraced her closely, presenting her Divine Son,
whom she held in her arms; and in this manner she
proceeded to each sister, allowing each to embrace this incomparably amiable Child. Amongst those who were thus
favoured, some held Him in their arms most carefully,
appearing very anxious that He should suffer no inconvenience; others, on the contrary, neglected these pre-
cautions, and permitted His Head to hang down in a very
painful manner. By this she understood, that those who
had no will but that of God rested the Head of the loving
Jesus on a soft pillow, that supported Him, by their good
will; while those whose wills were inflexible and imperfect
allowed the Head of the Infant Jesus to hang down incon-
veniently. Therefore, my beloved, let us empty our hearts
and consciences of all self-will, and offer our hearts to our
Lord with full and entire obedience to His good pleasure,
since He only seeks our spiritual advancement; why should
we disturb, even by the merest trifle, the repose and consolation of so delicate and tender an Infant, who comes to
us with such goodness and love?

At the Mass *Dominus dixit*,* our Lord again imparted
to her a knowledge of all that was said, which gave her
ineffable joy.

Then, from the *Gloria in excelsis* to the words *Primogenitus Mariæ virginis matris*, she began to think that the
title of only Son was more suitable than that of first-born,
because the Immaculate had only brought forth this Son,
whom she merited to conceive by the power of the Holy

---

* The Introit of the first or Midnight Mass. *Primogenitus*—probably a reference to the Gospel for that Mass.

Ghost; but the Blessed Virgin said to her sweetly : " Call my beloved Jesus my first-born, rather than my only begotten, for I brought Him forth first ; but after Him, or rather by Him, I have made you His brethren and my children, when I adopted you as such by the maternal affection which I have for you."

At the offertory, the Saint, in spirit, beheld the sisters offering to our Lord all the devotions which they had performed during Advent.   Some placed them in the bosom of the Divine Infant, whose image had been impressed on their souls ; and the Blessed Virgin inclined towards each with unparalleled condescension, placing her Divine Son so that He could receive in His Hands what they offered : others appeared to advance towards the altar, and remained in the centre of the choir, where they offered their prayers to the Blessed Virgin and to her Son ; but He was not placed so that He could receive them, and made signs to that effect. She understood from this, that those who placed their offerings in the bosom of the Child Jesus were they who were united to the Lord with their whole hearts, wherein He was spiritually born, and that the Blessed Virgin assisted them in this with all her power, rejoicing with them in their devotion and spiritual advancement ; but those persons who had offered their gifts in the centre of the choir were they who only thought of the Birth of our Lord on the Festival, and because they were reminded of it by the special devotion of the Church.

Then this blessed soul approached the King of Glory, to present Him the good-will of those who would have accomplished many things, had they not been hindered by a lawful cause.   And she was instructed in spirit that all the prayers which had been made with devotion were placed as pearls in the tablet, and that the good-will of those who would have performed the same devotions, had they not been occupied, and who grieved and consequently humbled themselves for this omission, should be placed in the chain with which our Lord's bosom was adorned, and that they would obtain such advantage from this nearness to the Heart of Jesus, that they would be as if they had the key of a treasure which contained all they could desire.

CHAPTER IV.

For the Feast of St. John the Evangelist.

His virtues, and the manner of imitating His purity.

THE Apostles and Evangelist St. John appeared to this virgin as she prayed one day during Advent. He was clothed in a gold-coloured habit, covered with golden eagles ; which signified that, though this Saint was elevated to the highest contemplation, even while in the body, he always sought to humble himself by the consideration of his own unworthiness. As Gertrude began to consider these ornaments, she perceived a red light shining from under the golden eagles ; from which she learned that St. John always commenced his contemplation by the remembrance of the Passion of the Lord, which he had beheld with his own eyes, and which he had never ceased to mourn in his inmost heart ; and thus by degrees he flew to the sublimity of the Divine Majesty, which he contemplated without pain by the eyes of his soul, as far as it is possible for man to do. He had also two golden lilies on his two shoulders—on the right was written, in marvellous characters, the words of the

Gospel *Discipulus quem diligebat Jesus ;* and on the left,
Iste custos Virginis ; * to mark the singular advantage which
he enjoyed of being called, and of being the disciple whom
Jesus loved above the rest of His Apostles, and of having
been found worthy by Christ Himself to receive from Him
the charge of His Mother before He expired, on account of
his surpassing purity.

The Apostle had a magnificent rational † on his breast,
to indicate his prerogative of having reposed on the bosom
of Jesus during the last Supper.   The words, *In principio
erat verbum,* were written on it in letters of living gold, to
show the marvellous virtue of the words contained in his
Gospel.   Then St. Gertrude said to our Lord : " O most loving
Lord, why is Thy beloved one manifested to a creature so
unworthy as I am ?"   Our Lord answered : "I have done
this that he may be united to you by a special friendship ;
and as you have no apostle, ‡ I have appointed him to be
ever your faithful advocate with Me in heaven."   " Teach
me, then, my sweetest Lord," she replied, " how I can
show my gratitude to him."   Our Lord answered : " If any
person says a *Pater noster* daily in honour of this Apostle,
reminding him of the sweet fidelity with which his heart

---

* " The disciple whom Jesus loved." " This is the guardian of the
Virgin."

† The rational was the high-priest's breast-plate (Ex. xxv. 7).
Calmet speaks thus of it : " This appellation was given to an embroidery
about ten inches square, which the high-priest wore on his breast.
On it were placed four rows of precious stones, on each of which the
name of one of the tribes of Israel was engraven.   The rational was
doubled, and contained within it the mystic Urim and Thummim.
The name 'rational,' or 'rational of judgment,' was given to it either
because the judgment and will of God were made known thereby, or
because the high-priest wore it when he pronounced judgment on
grave affairs."

‡ " Et cum nullum habeas Apostolum."

was filled when I taught this prayer, he will not fail to obtain for whoever prays thus the grace of persevering faithfully in virtue, even to the end of his life."

This Apostle also appeared to the Saint as she assisted at Matins, on his Feast, when she applied with special fervour to her usual exercises. Gertrude then recommended some of the religious of whom she had charge very fervently to him ; he received her prayer very lovingly, and said : "I am like my Master in this—that I love those who love me." The Saint inquired : "What grace, then, and what benefit, can I hope for, who am so unworthy, on your dear Feast ?" " Come," he replied ; " come with me, thou elect one of my Lord, and let us repose together on the sweetest bosom of the Lord, in which all the treasures of beatitude lie hidden." Then, taking her up in spirit, he presented her to our loving Saviour; and having placed her on His right, he placed himself on the left, and reposed there. Then he exclaimed, pointing reverently to the bosom of Jesus : " Behold, this is the Saint of saints, who draws to Himself all that is good in heaven and on earth ! "

She then inquired of St. John why he placed himself on the left hand, and had given the right to her. He replied : " It is because I have become one spirit with God, and am able to penetrate where flesh cannot enter; but you are not yet able to penetrate into such high things, because you are still in the flesh. I have therefore placed you at the opening of the Divine Heart, from whence you may drink in all the sweet consolations which flow from it with such impetuous abundance, that it is capable of satisfying all who desire to taste thereof." Then, as she felt the constant pulsations of the Divine Heart, and rejoiced exceedingly thereat, she said to St. John : " Beloved of God, didst not thou feel those pulsations when thou wert lying on the Lord's breast at the Last Supper ? "   " Yes," he replied ; " and this with such plenitude, that liquid does not enter more rapidly into bread than the sweetness of those pleasures penetrated my soul, so that my spirit became more ardent than water under the action of a glowing fire."

" And why," she inquired, " have you neither said nor written anything of this for our edification ? "   He replied : " Because I was charged with instructing the newly formed Church concerning the mysteries of the uncreated Word, that those truths might be transmitted to future ages, as far as they would be capable of comprehending them, for no one can comprehend them entirely ; and I deferred speaking of these Divine pulsations until later ages, that the world might be aroused from its torpor, and animated, when it had grown cold, by hearing of these things."   Then, as she contemplated St. John reposing upon the bosom of the Lord, he said to her : " I now appear to you in the same form as when I lay on the bosom of my beloved Lord and only Friend at the Last Supper ; but if you wish it, I will obtain for you the favour of beholding me in the form in which I now enjoy the delights of heaven."   And as she desired this favour very ardently, she beheld an immense ocean within the Heart of Jesus, in which St. John appeared to float with ineffable joy and perfect freedom ; and she learned that the Saint became so filled and inebriated with the torrent of pleasure which he tasted in God, that a vein came from his heart, whereby he poured forth the sweet waters of the Divinity—that is to say, his instructions, and above all, his Gospel—over the face of the earth.

On another occasion during the same feast, as the Saint took great satisfaction in the frequent praises which were given to the Apostle for his perfect virginity, she asked this special friend of God to obtain by his prayers that we might preserve our chastity with such care as to merit a share in his praises.

St. John replied : " He who would participate in the beatitude which my victories have won, must run as I ran when on earth." Then he added ; " I frequently reflected on the sweet familiarity and friendship with which I was favoured by Jesus, my most loving Lord and Master, in reward for my chastity, and for having watched so carefully over my words and actions that I never tarnished this virtue in the slightest degree. The Apostles separated themselves from such company as they considered doubtful, but mixed freely with what was not (as it is remarked in the Acts, that they were with the women, and Mary the Mother of Jesus) ; I never avoided women when there was an opportunity of rendering them any service, either of body or soul ; but I still watched over myself with extreme vigilance, and always implored the assistance of God when charity obliged me to assist them in any way.   Therefore these words are chanted of me : *In tribulatione invocasti me, et exaudivi te* (Ps. lxxx.) *   For God never permitted my affection to render any one less pure ; wherefore I received this recompense from my beloved Master, that my chastity is more praised than that of any other saint ; and I have obtained a more eminent rank in heaven, where, by a special privilege, I receive with extreme pleasure the rays of this love, which is as a mirror without spot and the brightness of eternal light. †   So that, being placed before

* This is not in the Office of the Saint in the present Benedictine Breviary.

† " She is the brightness of eternal light, and the unspotted mirror of God's majesty " (Wis. vii.)

this Divine love, whose brightness I receive each time **that** my chastity is commemorated in the Church, my loving Master salutes me in a most sweet and affable manner, filling my inmost soul with such joy, that it penetrates into all its powers and sentiments like a delicious beverage.   And thus the words, *Ponam te sicut signaculum in conspectu meo,* * are sung of me ; that is, I am placed as a receptacle for the effusions of the sweetest and most ardent charity."

Then St. Gertrude, being raised to a higher degree of knowledge, understood by these words of our Lord in the Gospel, " In My Father's house there are many mansions " (John xiv.), that there are three mansions in the heavenly kingdom, which correspond with three classes of persons who have preserved their virginity.

The first mansion is for those who, like the Apostles, fly from what is doubtful, but associate freely with others ; who vigorously resist all temptations, and if they fall perform worthy fruits of penance.

The second mansion is for those who avoid alike the doubtful and that which appears safe ; carefully shunning what might prove an occasion even of temptation ; and chastise their flesh, subduing it so that it can no longer rebel against the spirit : to this rank belong St. John the Baptist and other spiritual persons, who also are placed in the second mansion after they have been prevented gratuitously by the mercy of God, and have coöperated faithfully with His graces, so as to avoid evil and to exercise themselves in the practice of good.

---

* " In that day I will uphold **My** servant, and I will place thee as a seal before Me " (Responsory, ix. Lesson, iii. Nocturn, Matins for the Feast of St. John).

The third mansion is for those who, prevented by the sweetness of the benedictions and grace of God, have a natural horror of all evil; * but who, nevertheless, in the different accidents of life, find themselves sometimes with the good and sometimes with the wicked, but always detest evil and adhere to good, endeavouring to render both their own conduct and that of others perfectly irreproachable. Such persons draw marvellous fruit from the human affections, which they have in common with others; since they fear because of their affections, and humble themselves, watching over their hearts with greater diligence; as St. Gregory says: " It shows a good conscience to fear a fault where there is none." In this class St. John obtained the first rank.

Hence these words are chanted on his Feast: *Qui vicerit, faciam illum columnam in templo meo;* † for whoever conquers nature—that is, his affections—becomes as a pillar whereon God can repose while pouring forth the abundance of His sweetness. *Et scribam super eum nomen meum;* that is, to imprint upon him the visible marks of His Divine friendship. *Et nomen civitatis novæ Jerusalem;* that is, he shall receive, both exteriorly and interiorly, a particular recompense for each person whose spiritual welfare he has procured on earth.

St. Gertrude was favoured also with another vision, referring to the same subject; for as she began to consider why the Church extolled the virginity of St. John the Evangelist more than that of St. John the Baptist, God,

---

" Omne malum quasi naturaliter abhorent."

† Responsory after the v. Lesson, ii. Nocturn: " He that shall overcome, I will make him a pillar in the temple of my God, and I will write upon him the name of my God, and the name of the city of my God the new Jerusalem" (Apo. iii. 12).

who knows the thoughts of men, caused her to see the two
Saints in a vision.   St. John the Baptist was seated on an
elevated throne, in the middle of the sea, separated from
all the world; St. John the Evangelist stood in the
midst of a furnace, surrounded on all sides by flames.   As
the Saint beheld this, and marvelled thereat, our Lord said
to her, for her instruction : " Which do you consider most
wonderful,—to see the Evangelist not burning, or the
Baptist not consumed ? " From this she learned that
there will be a great difference between the reward of those
whose virtue has been assaulted and of those who have
preserved it in peace.

One night, also, when the Saint was engaged in prayer
with great devotion, she beheld St. John approaching our
Lord, resting himself upon Him, and embracing Him
very lovingly and ardently.   Then, as she cast herself
humbly at the feet of our Lord, to implore pardon for her
sins, St. John said to her, with great condescension : " Do
not let my presence trouble you ; behold one whose love
will suffice for thousands ; behold a mouth in which each
will find a special sweetness ; behold an ear which will
guard inviolably all the secrets confided to it."

As they chanted the words, *Mulier, ecce filius tuus*, *
Gertrude beheld a marvellous light, which came forth from
the Heart of God, and shone upon St. John, obtaining for
him the respect and veneration of all the saints.   She also
saw the Blessed Virgin manifesting a special joy towards
him when she was called his mother ; and the beloved disciple saluted her also with the deepest respect and affection.
Also, when the words were chanted which referred to the

---

* " Woman, behold thy son."   These words are not in the present
Office.

particular privileges of friendship which the saint had received from his Divine Master, such as these: *Iste est Jo-
annes, qui supra pectus Domini in cœna recubuit;* and, *Iste
est discipulus quem diligebat Jesus,** he appeared sur
rounded with a new light of glory, which distinguished
him from the other saints; and for this they praised God
with their whole souls, which caused the blessed John to
rejoice greatly.

At the words *Apparuit caro suo,* she understood that by
the form under which our Lord visited St. John He renewed in him all the sweetness of that mutual friendship
which he had enjoyed during his mortal life. Therefore
the Apostle, changed as it were into a new man, tasted in
some degree the joys of eternity; and this principally in
three things, for which he thanked God when he was
dying. For he said, first: "I have seen Thy face, and I
am renewed thereby." Secondly: "The sweetness of Thy
perfumes, Lord Jesus, has kindled eternal desires within
me." And thirdly: "Thy voice is full of sweetness." For
the virtue of His presence had imparted the vigour of
immortality; the strength of His Divine vocation had
replenished him with the sweetest hope; and His gentle
words had filled his soul with surpassing gladness. Again,
as they read that he rose up to follow Jesus,† he appeared
to dispose himself to follow Him in heaven; and she
knew that St. John had such a full and entire confidence
in the goodness of his beloved Lord and Master, that he
hoped he would die without feeling the pains of death; and

---

* "This is John, who leaned on the Lord's breast at supper;"
"This is the disciple whom Jesus loved." Response after the iii.
Lesson, i. Nocturn, and Antiphon at Benedictus.

† St. John xxi. 20.

he merited to obtain this favour, because it was the greatness of his love, and not the fear of death, which had caused him to desire it.

Then the Saint began to marvel how it could be, when it was inferred from Scripture, St. John had not tasted the pains of death, because he had suffered so deeply in spirit at the foot of the cross, that it should be said now, this privilege had been granted to him for his confidence. But our Lord replied : " I have rewarded My elect in heaven with a special glory for his virginity, and for the compassion which he had at My death ; but I have also recompensed his lively hope, which made him believe that I would refuse him nothing, by withdrawing him from the world without permitting him to experience the pains of death, and by having preserved his body from corruption."

CHAPTER V.

For the Feast of the Circumcision.

Of the holy name of Jesus ; and the renewal of our good intentions at the commencement of the new year.

ON the Feast of the Circumcision, St. Gertrude offered certain salutations of the sweet name of Jesus, which had been compiled by devout persons ; and these salutations appeared before God with the brilliancy of stars, and in the form of white roses ; from each of which hung a little golden bell, which gave forth the sweetest melody, and caused ineffable pleasure to the Divine Heart of Jesus. As she uttered the words, " Hail, Jesus ! most loving, most benign, most desirable ! " &c., she desired very ardently to find other expressions to add to the name of Jesus, that His Heart might be still more touched thereby ; but the earnest love with which she sought to accomplish this exhausted her strength, and our Lord, moved with pity, and as it were vanquished by her love, inclined towards her, and embraced her with exceeding love, saying : " Behold, I have imprinted My name upon your lips, that you may bear it before the whole world ; and whenever your lips move to utter it, it will resound before me as a most harmonious melody."

After this she found the name of JESUS written on the upper part of her soul* in characters of living gold, which appeared like shining stars emitting a soft light.   The word JUSTICE was written in the same manner on the lower part. By the inscription " Jesus," which signifies Saviour, she understood that she was to manifest Him to all as the Source of life and salvation ; by the inscription " Justice," she understood that she was to represent all the rigours of Divine justice to those whose minds were hardened, that the fear of God's judgments might serve to deter them from evil, if they would not be won by His mercies.

Then she said to our Lord : " O sweetest love ! I beseech Thee to give our congregation, which always belongs entirely to Thee, a new-year's gift, even as a bridegroom does to his bride."   Our Lord replied : " ' Be renewed in the spirit of your mind ' " (Eph. iv. 23). She answered : " O Father of Mercies ! do not forget to circumcise all our imperfections on this blessed festival of Thy holy Circumcision."   To this our Lord answered : " Circumcise yourself by meditating on your Rule."   " O loving Lord ! " she replied, " why dost Thou reply to me so seriously, since Thou knowest that if Thou dost not assist us with Thy grace, we shall fail in our endeavours ; for Thou hast

---

* " In superiori labio animæ suæ "

Thyself said, that it is not possible for us to do any good without Thee." Then our Lord, as if won and carried away by the words of the Saint, placed her soul in His bosom, and said to her with great sweetness : " Yes, I desire that you should coöperate with Me in this ; and all those amongst you who, at the commencement of this year, repent with all their hearts, for My love, of the faults which they have committed against their Rule, and resolve to avoid them for the future, shall obtain this favour—that I will be to them as a kind master, who holds the child whom he teaches in his arms, to point out his letters to him, to efface his imperfections, or to supply his defects ; and thus My mercy will amend their defects, and My paternal love will supply their negligences. And if they forget any duty through dissipation of mind, I will supply it to them by the reflections which I will cause them to make on it." He added : " Those who endeavour to turn their minds from all which they know to be displeasing to Me, and who endeavour to please me in all things, shall receive the light of My Divine heart to direct their thoughts ; and I will so dispose their works, that they shall be able each year to offer Me a new gift,* which will not be unworthy of My acceptance, and which will be salutary for them.

As the Saint prayed for a person who had asked that she would obtain from God for her, as a new-year's gift, that her heart might always remain faithful to him in prosperity and in adversity, our Lord replied sweetly : " I accept the desire of this person for whom you pray as a most acceptable new-year's gift ; but as it is right that I should give her what she asks in return, I wish that this gift should be shared between us ; that it should be advan-

---

* " Xenium.

tageous to her, and agreeable to Me ; that it should redound
to My glory on the one hand, and that it should continually
impart new ornaments of virtue to her on the other. For,
as a mother, when she is teaching her child to work, guides
her hand by her own knowledge, so also I use My eternal
wisdom in teaching this person to prepare these gifts.

Then the Saint understood that the pearls with which
these gifts were to be embellished were the holy desires
and good sentiments which drew the soul to God ; such as
fear, love, hope, joy, and such-like, the least of which is
not overlooked by God when He labours for the salvation
of our souls.

As she prayed then for many other persons, and especially
for one whose soul had lately become troubled, and, as
Gertrude believed, through her, our Lord said to her : " I
am using her very affliction and trouble to expand her
heart and to open her hands, that she may receive more
abundantly and suitably the gifts which I have prepared
for her." "Alas, Lord!" exclaimed the Saint, "was it
necessary that I should be the scourge with which Thou
didst purify this soul ?" Our Lord answered : "Why say
' Alas !' when those who thus purify My elect, without any
intention of afflicting them, but, on the contrary, compassionating their sufferings with all their hearts, are as a
gentle rod in My hands, and their merit increases in proportion as the souls are purified ?"

CHAPTER VI.

For the Feast of the Epiphany.

Of the oblations which are acceptable to God.

On the Feast of the Epiphany this holy soul offered to God, in imitation of the three kings—for myrrh, the Body of Jesus Christ, with all the merits of His Passion, for the remission of all the sins of men, from the first to the last of the human race ; for incense, the Soul of Jesus Christ, with all His holy actions, for the negligences of the whole world ; for gold, His Divinity, with all its perfections and joys, in satisfaction for the defects of all creatures. Then our Lord appeared, and presented her offering, as a most worthy new-year's gift, to the Most Holy and august Trinity.   As He passed through the midst of heaven, all the celestial court inclined profoundly before Him to honour this gift, as men prostrate before the Holy Sacrament when it is present.

As she prayed devoutly for a certain person who had asked her to offer the oblation which she had made before the Epiphany for her, our Lord appeared to her, bearing this offering through the midst of heaven, to present it to God the Father ; and she saw that all the celestial court considered the offering of great value.   From this she learned that when we offer our prayers, or any other gift, to God, the celestial court praises and extols Him for our devotion ; and when a soul, not satisfied with its own actions and prayers, offers with them those of Jesus Christ —which are infinitely more perfect—the value of his offering cannot be increased, and is worthy to be presented to the Most Holy Trinity.

On another occasion, on the same feast, as the words of

the Gospel were read, " And, falling down, they adored Him ; and opening their treasures, they offered Him gifts " (Matt. ii. 11), the Saint, animated by the example of the magi, and transported with zeal, rose to prostrate herself devoutly and humbly at the feet of our Lord Jesus Christ ; adoring Him for all in heaven, on earth, and under the earth ; and, finding nothing worthy to offer Him, she sought anxiously and eagerly amongst all creatures to find something which she could present to her only Love. And as she thus searched, she beheld some vile and miserable creatures, who contributed nothing to the glory of the Saviour, and these she endeavoured to bring back to Him whom all creatures are bound to serve. Then, in the fervour of her desires, she gathered up in her heart all the fears, griefs, pains, and inquietudes which had been suffered by creatures, not for the Divine glory, but because of human infirmity ; and these she offered to the Lord as myrrh. Then she charged herself with all the pretended sanctity of hypocrites, Pharisees, heretics, and other such persons, and offered this to God as incense. Then she took on herself all the falsehood and impurity which had been in the hearts of men, and offered it to God as gold ; while her heart burned with desire to reduce all the insubordination of creatures into a profound subjection to their Creator. And as she offered these things to God, they appeared like shining gold purified in the furnace.

As our Lord accepted all this with great satisfaction, and collected these new year's gifts as if they were precious gems for His diadem, He said to the Saint : " Behold the gems which you have offered Me ; I consider them of great value, and I will always bear them on the diadem which adorns My Head, in memory of your singular affection for Me, that they may increase My glory in My celestial court even as an earthly monarch adorns himself with the rarest and most precious jewel * in his kingdom."

Then the Saint remembered a person who had often asked her to make some offering for her on that day ; and she asked the Lord what He would wish her to offer.   He replied : " Offer Me her feet, her hands, and her heart.   The feet indicate the desires ; and as this person desires to make a return to Me for My Passion, let her endeavour to suffer patiently all pains of body or mind, in union with My Passion, for the glory of My Name, and the benefit of My Spouse, the Church ; and I will accept this as myrrh.   As the hands indicate action, let her endeavour to unite all her actions, whether corporal or spiritual, to the perfect actions of My most holy Humanity, and all her actions will obtain thereby a most marvellous excellence ; and I will receive them as an incense of the most fragrant odour.   As the heart indicates the will, let her always humble herself to all, and be guided by a prudent counsellor, that she may know My will, and then let her accomplish it freely and cheerfully : I will accept this union of her will with My Divine will as an amalgam † of pure gold, which can never be separated."

Then, as the Saint prayed for certain persons who had been specially recommended to her, she beheld our Divine

---

* " Qui vulgari lingua vocatur, *cin Besant* " (the B for P). The etymology of this word is not clear. Amort, in his commentary on this passage, observes, that it is not the name of a gem or precious stone, but more probably the epithet of some precious stone. He adds, that after seeking in all dictionaries and catalogues of precious stones, he could not find any called by the name of *Pesant* (heavy). Perhaps some precious stone of great weight went by this popular name.

† " Electrum."

Lord, with a kind of bag * under His left arm, so arranged that He could easily put His right hand therein ; and here He placed the prayers which she had offered, to reserve them for the benefit of His special friends. And as she offered for each what they had requested, she beheld these petitions arranged before our Lord as so many beautiful new-year's gifts, with which He adorned the souls of those who approached Him with less perfect dispositions. She knew that the fidelity, or rather the confidence, of these persons, in recommending themselves to her prayers, had merited this special favour from God, inasmuch as they were not concerned whether she offered these prayers from herself or from them, provided that they were acceptable to God.

CHAPTER VII.

For the Second Sunday after Epiphany.

St. Gertrude receives absolution from our Divine Lord—Instruction for Holy Communion.

On the Sunday *Omnis terra*,† St. Gertrude prepared herself, by a spiritual confession, to behold the Sacred Face of

---

* "Marsupium."

† *Omnis terra*—the Introit for Mass, Second Sunday after Epiphany, in the Roman Missal. The Mass of the Holy Name is now, however, generally substituted for it. The devotion to the Holy Face, like all Catholic devotions, has only deepened with the lapse of ages, and the faithful still venerate it as lovingly and ardently as when the great St. Gertrude wrote of it. It is still shown at Rome, on the very same day mentioned by the Saint. M. le Chanoine de Montault, in his *Année liturgique à Rome*, p. 25,

the Lord, as the faithful do on this day at Rome ; and she represented this Face to herself as all disfigured by her sins, and cast herself at the feet of the Lord, to ask pardon for all her transgressions.   Then He lifted up His venerable Hand, and blessed her thus : " I grant you, by the bowels of My mercy, the pardon and remission of all your sins ; and that you may truly amend your life, I enjoin you this satisfaction—that each day during this year you will perform some action in union with, and in memory of, the mercy by which I grant you this indulgence."   The Saint accepted the satisfaction with great thanksgiving : but fearing her frailty, she said : " But what shall I do, O Lord, if I should fail in this, through my negligence ? "   " Why should you fail in so easy a matter ? " he replied ; " for I will accept the least thing which you do with this intention, if it be only to lift a pebble or a straw* from the ground, to utter a single word, to show kindness to any one, to say the *Requiem æternam* for the faithful departed, or to pray for sinners or the just."

The Saint was exceedingly consoled by this, and began

---

says : " Second Sunday after Epiphany, at the Basilica of the Vatican, at half-past three, procession of the Confraternity of the Holy Ghost, and exposition of the great relics of the Passion ; the Holy Lance, the Wood of the Cross, and the Veil of St. Veronica."

Dom Gueranger, in his *Année liturgique*, also mentions a solemn exhibition of this holy relic, at which the Pope assists, on Easter Sunday, after the Post-Communion.   The devotion to the Sacred Face has been much propagated in France during the last few years, and has been the means of procuring many miraculous graces and cures.   It is, indeed, a consoling devotion ; for we shall be judged standing before the Face of Christ, but no longer the suffering Face. If, then, we have been devout to it during life, surely we may hope that it will look mercifully and lovingly upon us when we stand before the judgment-seat.

* " Calcaveris, seu calamum."

to pray for her particular friends, beseeching our Lord to grant them the same favour. He granted her petition, and said : " All who wish to share with you in the satisfaction which I have imposed on you, will also receive a similar indulgence and remission of their sins." And then extending His sacred Hand, He gave her His benediction a second time. After this He said : " Oh, what abundant benedictions I will pour forth on him who returns to Me at the end of this year with works of charity exceeding the number of his sins !" But the Saint exclaimed distrustfully : " How can this be, since the heart of man is so prone to evil, that scarcely an hour passes in which he does not sin in many ways ?" Our Lord replied : " Why should you think this so difficult, when there are many things that please Me, and there is nothing, however difficult, which My grace cannot accomplish." " Lord," inquired Gertrude, " what will you give to him who accomplishes this in Thy strength ?" " I can give you no better answer than this," He replied, " That I will give ' What eye hath not seen, nor ear heard, neither hath it entered into the heart of man to conceive'" (1 Cor. ii. 9). How happy will he be who has practised this devotion for a year, or even for a single month, since he may expect the same reward from the liberality of His God !

On the following day, as she prayed for those who communicated according to her advice, but could not approach the Sacrament of Penance, on account of the absence of their confessor, it appeared that our Lord clothed them with a white robe, as a sign of innocence, adorned with precious stones, which had the form and the scent of violets, as a type of the humility with which they had followed her advice. A rose-coloured mantle was also given to them, covered with flowers of gold, which signified the loving

Passion of our Lord, in virtue of which they obtained a worthy preparation for Communion. "Let them be seated near me," said our Lord, "that it may be known that it is not by accident, but on purpose, that the first place is kept for them ; because from all eternity it has been ordained that those who have followed your advice shall receive extraordinary favours from Me to-day ; and those who have communicated without confessing and without asking your advice, resting on the goodness and grace of God, shall receive a rose-coloured mantle with gold flowers, and shall also be seated at the table of the Lord."

Those who, through humility and compunction, had abstained from Communion, appeared as if standing before the table, and rejoicing in its delights. Then the Lord, moved by His own mercy, blessed them with His Hand, saying these words : "All those who meditate frequently on the vision of My Divine Face, attracted by the desires of love, shall receive within them, by the virtue of My Humanity, a bright ray of My Divinity, which shall enlighten their inmost souls, so that they shall reflect the light of My countenance in a special manner in eternity."

CHAPTER VIII.

For the Feast of St. Agnes, Virgin and Martyr.

Apparition of St. Agnes —Virtue of the words which she uttered at her death.

On the night of the Feast of St. Agnes, the beloved of God,* as Gertrude rejoiced greatly for the glory which the love of

---

* January 21.

this Saint had given to our Lord, and for the words she
had uttered which gave such joy to the heavenly court,
she exclaimed : " Alas, Lord ! what joy and consolation
would I not have experienced at hearing these words
chanted, if my infirmity had not prevented me ! " Our
Lord replied : " I reserve this for you in myself ; and,
either in this life, or in the next, you shall taste other consolations, which will be all the sweeter to you because they
will have less of the insipidity of your own will."

From this she understood that nothing can diminish
the spiritual welfare of the elect, unless through their own
fault.   As they read the sixth Lesson (which related that
St. Agnes was accused of being a Christian from her childhood, and so bewitched by magic that she called Jesus
Christ her Spouse), St. Gertrude exclaimed sorrowfully :
" Alas, my Lord and my God, what does not Thy Divine
Majesty suffer from men ! " Our Lord replied : " The
perfect love which united Me and Agnes satisfies Me for
all these indignities."   "O Lord," replied the Saint, "grant
to all thy elect the grace to attach themselves so inviolably
to Thee, that Thou mayest no longer think of the injuries
by which men outrage Thee."

On the Feast of St. Augustine,* as God showed Gertrude
the merits of many saints, she desired to know something
of the merits of St. Agnes, whom she had loved from her
very infancy with the greatest tenderness and devotion.
Our Lord yielded to her desire and prayer, and showed
her that great Saint, so united to His Heart as to indicate
her extraordinary innocence, and to manifest the truth of
what has been said by the Wise Man, that " Incorruption
bringeth near to God " (Wis. vi. 20.) ; for she seemed so

* May 26.

near God, that it appeared as if no one in heaven could equal her innocence and love,

From this she learned that there is not an instant in which God does not place before Him the devotion and joy which holy souls either have felt or will yet feel from the sweet words of St. Agnes which are recited by the Church,* and that He causes the pleasure which He finds therein to pour forth from His Heart into that of this holy virgin, which is so intimately united to His, while she becomes marvellously adorned thereby with new jewels, casting rays of light every moment into those souls who rejoice in her devotion.

CHAPTER IX.

For the Feast of the Purification.

ON the Feast of the Purification of the Blessed Virgin, as the Saint rejoiced in spirit at the first sound of the bell for Matins, and said to our Lord, " My heart and my soul salute Thee, O loving Saviour, at the sound of the bell which announces the Feast of the Purification of Thy most holy Mother," He replied condescendingly : " And the bowels of My pity knock at the gates of Divine Mercy for you, to obtain the full remission of all your sins." As the bell for Matins ceased to ring, our Lord wished to recompense her salutation a thousandfold, and said to her : " O joy of My Heart, My Divinity salutes thee ; and I

---

* The Lessons and Responses for the Office of St. Agnes are full of singular beauty, and enriched with the utterances of burning love which she poured forth at the moment of trial and death.

send you all the merits of My holy Humanity, to enable
you to pass this festival in a manner pleasing to Me."

Some months after, as she desired to hear what was
chanted in choir, and grieved for the infirmity which detained her in bed, she said complainingly : " O Lord, if
distance did not prevent me from hearing, how my heart
would rejoice for each word chanted at Matins ! " But our
Lord answered : " My spouse, if you know not what is
chanted in choir, turn to Me, and contemplate attentively
what passes within Me, and you will not fail to find what
will satisfy you." Then she knew in spirit that the
Lord took unto Himself all the good that holy souls were
doing in the Church, and that, having purified and perfected
it in Himself, He offered it in eternal praise to the Most
Holy Trinity ; and that, drawing into His Divine Heart the
good works which were done for the glory of God, He ennobled and perfected them ; and she perceived that, while
the works united to the members of Jesus Christ operated
in the soul a good of inestimable value, those which He
drew into His Heart surpassed the others in perfection and
excellence, even as a living man exceeds in dignity one who
is dead.

After this, as she heard the second Response, and
grieved that she had not heard the first, which was *Adorna
thalamum*, she said to our Lord : " Teach me, I implore
Thee, my Beloved, how I can adorn the couch of my heart,
so that it may please Thee." Our Lord replied : " Open
your heart to Me, and let Me see therein the images which
you know to be most pleasing to Me." From this the
Saint understood that our Lord is exceedingly pleased when
we open our hearts by remembering His sufferings, and
thanking Him for His benefits. As they sang *Post par-
tum virgo*, at the second Nocturn, at the words *Intercede*

*pro nobis,** St. Gertrude saw the Blessed Virgin wiping away all stains from the religious of the convent ; and hiding them in a corner, she placed herself before them, so as to conceal them from the eyes of Divine justice. During the Antiphon *Beata mater*, at the word *Intercede* she saw the Blessed Virgin, elevated and radiant with glory, offering to her Son, who is the King of kings, after a gentle embrace, all the devotions of the sisters, in union with her own.

But as Gertrude still complained of the obstacles which were caused by her infirmities, our Lord said to her : " If Simeon and Anna—I mean the effects of your infirmity— still hinder you from attending the Divine Office, come forth with Me on Mount Calvary, where you will find a young man full of beauty and affection to place you upon a cross."

She therefore followed Him there in spirit, and the memory of the Passion caused a marvellous delight in her soul. Then she went forth by a gate on the northern side, and entered into a magnificent temple, where she beheld the blessed old man Simeon standing near the altar, and uttering these words as he prayed : " When will He come ? when shall I behold Him ? shall I live until He comes ? " And as he repeated the same and similar words, he felt his soul thrill within him, and turning round suddenly, he beheld the Blessed Virgin before the altar, holding in her arms the Infant Jesus, the most beautiful of the children of men. As soon as he beheld Him, he was enlightened by the Holy Ghost, and recognised the Redeemer of the world ;

* " After childbirth thou didst remain a virgin. Intercede for us, O Mother of God ; " v. Ant. ii. Nocturn. *Beata mater* is the Antiphon at *Magnificat* in the Little Office B. V. M.

and then taking Him into his arms with great joy, he exclaimed : *Nunc dimittis servum tuum, Domine ;* at the words *quia viderunt oculi mei,* he kissed Him lovingly ; and at the words *quod parasti,* he lifted Him before the Ark, to offer Him to God the Father as the salvation of His people. The Ark then became brilliant with light, and the image of the Infant Jesus appeared therein resplendent with beauty, which signified that He was the consummation of all the sacrifices of the old and new covenants. Then Simeon exclaimed, in the fervour of his love : *Lumen ad revelationem gentium,* and returned the Child to His Mother, saying : *Et tuum ipsius animam pertransibit gladius.* Then the Blessed Virgin offered two young doves for her Divine Son, which indicated the innocent lives of the faithful, who, like doves, reply in sweet murmurs to all evil, and collect pure grain—that is, endeavour to follow the example of the Saints ; and those who act thus redeem the Lord Jesus, when they fill up and accomplish what our Lord has left for them to do.

At the eighth Response, *Ora pro nobis,* &c., the Queen of Virgins knelt before God as the mediatrix between Him and the religious, praying for each individually ; but her Divine Son raised her up respectfully, and placed her near Him on the throne of His glory, granting her full authority to command what she would. Then she desired the choir of Powers to surround the convent, and to defend it mightily against the wiles of the ancient enemy. The angels immediately obeyed the orders of the Queen of Heaven, and, joining their shields together, encompassed the convent on all sides.

Then St. Gertrude said to the Blessed Virgin : "O Mother of Mercy, will not those who have not assisted in choir have a share in this mighty defence ?" The holy

Virgin replied : "They will share in it, and so will all those who, here or elsewhere, preserve the true spirit of religion ; but if any fail in religious observance, and are not earnestly seeking to attain perfection, they will not merit to be under the protection of the angels." To this our Lord added : "Let those who desire to live under so powerful a protection make shields for themselves in this manner : narrow below—that is, towards themselves—by humility, and large above—that is, towards Me—by a full and perfect confidence in My goodness."

When the Versicle *Ora pro nobis* was sung at the procession, the Blessed Virgin appeared to place her Son gently upon the altar, and then, prostrating devoutly before Him, she interceded for all the congregation ; and this royal Child inclined towards her, to signify that He not only heard her prayers, but that He would also accomplish all that His beloved Mother desired.

CHAPTER X.

For Septuagesima Sunday.

Instruction concerning receiving and abstaining from the Holy Communion.

ON the Sunday *Circumdederunt*,* St. Gertrude, though still very weak, desired ardently to receive the Sacrament ; but although she had prepared herself with great fervour, she abstained, by the advice of her spiritual mother, through discretion. As she offered this privation to God, she found

---

* *Dominica circumdederunt.* "The groans of death surrounded me," &c.—Introit for Septuagesima Sunday.

herself standing before the Lord ; and He inclined sweetly towards her, placing her in the bosom of His paternal goodness, saying to her, with the caresses and affability of a mother to her child : " Since you abstain from receiving Me purely for Me, I will keep you in My bosom, so that no exterior labour may trouble you." The Saint, being overwhelmed with delight on the bosom of our Lord, said to Him : " O most loving Spouse, since the whole world is seated in wickedness (1 John v. 19), and opposes Thy glory at this time more than at any other by the excesses into which it plunges, I desire with all my heart that my congregation should be employed in making reparation to Thee. Therefore, if Thou wilt deign to acknowledge me as Thy servant, though, alas ! so unworthy, and accept me as Thine ambassador, I will gladly announce some special exercise for Thy love to all who are devoutly disposed, in order to honour Thee in reparation for the sins now committed." Our Lord replied : " Whoever will be My ambassador on this occasion will have this reward—that all which he gains for Me will be acquired and gained for himself."

From this she learned that all who labour to instruct others, either by their words or their writings, for the honour of God and the advancement of their neighbours' salvation, will receive a reward even to endless ages for the fruit which has been drawn from their books or their instructions. Then He added : " Whoever offers Me the satisfaction of his corporal necessities, such as eating, drinking, sleeping, &c , saying in his heart or with his lips : ' Lord, I take this food ' (or whatever it may be) ' in union with the love with which Thou didst perform the like action when on earth, for the glory of Thy Father and the salvation of men,' praying that, in union with My Divine love, it may serve for the salvation of all in heaven, on earth, or in purgatory—each time he makes this offering, he presents Me with a strong shield to protect Me against the insults and outrages of sinners."

Then, as the sisters communicated at the Mass, our Lord placed Gertrude tenderly at the loving Wound of His Side, and said to her: "Since discretion obliges you to abstain from receiving Me corporally in the Sacrament, drink now from My Heart the sweet influences of My Divinity." Having drunk of this torrent of sweetness and delight, as she thanked our Lord devoutly for it, she saw all those who had communicated that day standing in the presence of the Lord, who gave to each a marvellously beautiful habit, and a special gift, which enabled them to prepare themselves worthily for Communion. As they obtained these great favours through the merits of Gertrude, they also offered to our Lord in their turn the advantages which they had received through her, for the increase of her glory and merit. From this she understood that those who dispose themselves for Holy Communion by particular prayers and devotions, and who nevertheless abstain for good reasons, as through obedience or humility, are replenished by God with the torrent of Divine delights; while their preparation for Communion contributes to prepare others, and the fruit which others derive thereby returns to their advantage. Then St. Gertrude exclaimed: "O Lord, if it is true that those who abstain thus from communicating receive such great fruit, is it, then, more advantageous to abstain?" Our Lord replied: "By no means; for those who approach the Sacrament for love of My glory receive the food of My Divine Body as the delicious nectar of the Divinity, and are adorned with the incomparable splendour of My Divine virtues." "Lord," inquired the Saint, "what will happen to those who abstain from Communion on account of their negligences, and yet pass the day in the same negligences?" He replied: "They render themselves still more unworthy of Communion, and they deprive themselves of the fruit of the Communions made on that day throughout the Church." Then the Saint continued: "Tell me, I beseech Thee, O Lord, why it happens that certain souls, who judge themselves unworthy of Communion, and apply themselves less earnestly to prepare for it, are nevertheless pressed by so ardent a desire to receive Thy sacred Body, that it grieves them exceedingly to abstain on the days appointed for receiving it?" Our Lord replied: "This happens to them by a special grace of My sweet Spirit; as a king, who is always accustomed to the court, naturally prefers the pleasure which he always enjoys there, to the satisfaction which others find in roaming through the streets and squares."

CHAPTER XL.

For Sexagesima.

Instruction on Noah's ark; a mystical day therein.

ON the Sunday *Exurge*, as she was still confined to bed, she heard the words *Benedicens ergo* * chanted at Matins: and reflecting on the sentiments of joy and devotion which she had so often experienced in listening to this Response,

---

* This Response is not in the present Benedictine Breviary. The Book of Genesis is commenced at Matins for Septuagesima Sunday. On Sexagesima Sunday the Lessons refer to the Flood, &c.; hence the peculiar applicability of the following revelations to the time and the train of thought suggested by the Office. *Exurge* —"Arise! why sleepest Thou, O Lord?"—Introit for Sexagesima Sunday.

she exclaimed : "O Lord, thou knowest with what fervent
love I have often chanted this Response and many others
when I was carried up before Thy throne of glory, and
there intoned each note and word in Thy Heart, as on a
most sweet organ. But, alas ! now that I am infirm, I
neglect many things." "My beloved one," replied our
Lord, "I can testify to the truth of what you say, and I
know that you have often chanted these words most sweetly
on the organ of my Divine Heart ; therefore I am now
going to chant for you in return." Then He added: "Even
as I swore to My servant Noe that I would no more destroy
the earth with a flood, so do I swear to you also, by My
Divinity, that all those who listen to your advice with
humility, and avail themselves of it to regulate their lives,
shall never perish, but shall assuredly attain to Me safely
and without wandering, who am the Way, the Truth, and
the Life; and I confirm this oath to you by the seal of My
most holy Humanity." "O Eternal Wisdom," replied Gertrude, "since thou foreseest all the excesses and crimes
into which men will again precipitate themselves, why didst
Thou make so solemn a promise in their favour that Thou
wouldst not again destroy the world by a deluge ?" Our
Lord replied : "I made it to strengthen them in their good
resolutions during the calm of prosperity, so that in the
storm of affliction they may be bound in honour to keep
their promise." Then she said : "O Lord God, wilt Thou
teach Thy handmaid how to build an ark for Thee during
this week ?" Our Lord replied : "You can build an ark
in your heart, which will be very pleasing to me ; but observe carefully that there were three chambers in Noe's
ark : the birds were in the highest, men in the middle,
and beasts in the lowest. Thus you should divide the day
into three parts : from early morning until None return

Me thanks, on the part of the whole Church, and from the very bottom of your heart, for all the benefits which I have bestowed on men from the creation of the world to the present time, and especially for the signal benefit which I confer on them by immolating Myself to God the Father daily, from daybreak until None, on the Altar for their salvation, while men employ themselves in feasting and debaucheries, without a thought of gratitude. If you therefore study to repair their faults, and supply for their lack of thanksgivings, you will gather birds into the first stage of your ark. From None until Vespers, by attaching yourself firmly to the exercise of good works, and by uniting them to those performed by My sacred Humanity, in satisfaction for the negligence and ingratitude of men, who refuse to correspond with My benefits, you will enclose men in the centre of the ark. From Vespers you may reflect and consider in the bitterness of your heart how men have the impiety to add to their ingratitude an infinity of crimes which excite My anger, and by offering in atonement all the bitterness and pains which I suffered in My Passion and Death, though I was innocent; and thus you may enclose beasts in the lowest part of the ark."

Then she said to the Lord : " As I have asked this instruction of Thee so earnestly, I cannot feel certain that Thou, O best of teachers, hast taught it to me." He replied : " You ought not to esteem it less because I have given it to you on account of the earnest desire you expressed ; for I have created your senses for My service. Was it not a more wonderful thing to say, ' Let us make man to Our image and likeness,' when I created him with deliberation and counsel, than to say, when I created other things : ' Let there be a firmament,' or ' Let there be light ? ' " She replied : " If I availed myself of this authority to introduce this exercise for the benefit of others, some one else might introduce other things, which might not be an effect of Thy Divine grace." Our Lord replied: "Add this caution: whoever knows in his heart that his will is so united to Mine as never to dissent from it, either in prosperity or adversity, and who acts and suffers in all things purely for My glory, may certainly affirm that whatever he learns interiorly is from Me, if it is useful to others, and not contradictory to Scripture."

Then the Lord stood before this soul, and said: "Now, queen and lady,* console Me, as I have consoled thee;" and having said this, He inclined lovingly towards her. But this soul, being overwhelmed with amazement at such unheard-of condescension, exclaimed, with the deepest humility, from her inmost heart: "Ah, Lord! Thou art the Creator, and I am but a creature." As she uttered these words, her soul was drawn and united to God in a marvellous manner, and enjoyed with Him the sublimest beatitude. Then she said to the Lord: "Vouchsafe, O Father of mercy, to give a little rest to Thy servant, who is weakened by the remedies she has used, that I may communicate worthily to-day." He replied: "The union with Me, which you now enjoy, will render you stronger than any bodily repose which you could take." While Mass was being celebrated, as she complained in the presence of God that her infirmity prevented her from hearing it, our Lord said to her: "Repeat the *Confiteor*." When she had concluded, He pronounced these words: "May My Divinity have mercy on you, and pardon you all your sins!" and extending His venerable Hand, He gave her His benediction. Then the Lord took her into His arms, and said;

---

* "Eia, domina regina."

" And God created man to His own image." Then He signed* her eyes and her ears, her mouth and her heart, her hands and her feet; and sweetly repeating these words each time, he renewed His image and resemblance in her soul.

On the Tuesday before Ash Wednesday, a day on which people in the world commit the greatest excesses in eating and drinking, St. Gertrude heard the bell ringing for the workmen's breakfast, and exclaimed, with a sigh: "Alas, my Lord, how early in the day men begin to offend Thee by their gourmandising!" But our Lord replied: " Do not grieve, My beloved ; those who are now summoned to their meal are not of the number of those who offend Me by greediness, since this refection is a warning to them to apply to work ; and I take as much satisfaction in seeing them eat, as a man would in seeing his horse refreshed when he needed its labour."

CHAPTER XII.

For the Saturday before Quinquagesima.

Devotions for the time of the Carnival—Of the value and efficacy of suffering.

ON the Saturday before Quinquagesima Sunday, as St. Gertrude disengaged herself from all exterior cares, and recollected herself in prayer, she was received into the bosom of the Divine goodness, where she enjoyed the sweet influences of His delights with such perfect power, that it appeared to her as if she disposed of the kingdoms of hea-

---

* "Consignans."

ven and earth with her Spouse. The day passed in these spiritual delights ; but towards evening she began to be troubled about a trifling matter, so that she no longer enjoyed them. At last, before Matins, as she had passed the greater part of the night in this disquiet, which prevented her from sleeping, she besought our Lord that He would remove this obstacle to her enjoyment of His Divine delights, if it was for His glory. The Lord replied : " If you desire to soothe My pains, you must bear your own, and stand at My left, so that I may recline upon you, and look into your heart, where the sweet concert of your holy desires, your perfect confidence in Me, and the ardour of your zeal for the eternal salvation of all mankind, may move me powerfully, appeasing My justice. Further : as the rich treasures of your heart will be open to Me, I may impart them to those who are in need, and whose wants and necessities you would desire to relieve as far as you could. For if you stood on My right hand, that is in prosperity, you would deprive Me of these delights."

Then the Saint asked our Lord to prescribe some exercise by which she might serve Him lovingly during these three days, on which men commit so many crimes and excesses. Our Lord replied : " You could not please Me better than by suffering patiently all that grieves or tires you, whether interior or exterior, in memory of My Passion, and by doing whatever you find most difficult ; and you will do this most effectually by controlling and restraining your senses. Whoever acts thus in memory of My Passion may hope for a great reward from Me." " But," continued the Saint, " I desire ardently to know from Thee, O most loving Teacher,* what sufferings are most capable

---

* " Doctor amantissime."

of appeasing the just anger which Thou feelest during these three days of excess." Our Lord replied : " You can do nothing more acceptable to Me than to say the *Pater noster* three times, or the Psalm *Laudate Dominum, omnes gentes;* and at the first repetition, offer to God all the wearinesses and labours of My Heart for the salvation of men ; and suffer or labour, praise or give thanks, in reparation for all the unlawful pleasures in which the human heart indulges at this time. At the second repetition, offer to God My Father all the abstinences and mortifications of My lips, whether in eating, speaking, preaching, or praying, in satisfaction for all the sins of the tongue now committed. At the third repetition, offer to God my Father all the actions and movements of My most holy Body, and of each member thereof, with all the bitterness of My Passion and Death, in satisfaction for all the sins which men commit now against their own salvation."

At the hour of Terce, our Lord appeared to St. Gertrude in the position in which He was when tied to the pillar between two executioners, one of whom tore Him with thorns, and the other bruised Him with a whip full of large knots ; both striking His Face, which seemed so disfigured, that her very heart melted away with compassion ; nor could she restrain her tears whenever she recalled that mournful spectacle during the day, since it appeared to her that none upon earth had ever been so cruelly used as her sweet Lord Jesus. Even the very pupil of the eye was torn and inflamed, both by the thorns and the blows of the scourge. It appeared also to her that her Lord turned His blessed Face from side to side ; but when He turned it from one executioner, the other struck it still more furiously; then He turned to her, and exclaimed : " Have you not read what is written of Me : *Vidimus eum tanquam leprosum ?* "—" We have thought Him as it were a leper" (Is. liii. 4). The Saint replied : " Alas, Lord ! what remedy can we find to soothe the agonising pains of Thy Divine Face ! " Our Lord replied : " The most efficacious and the tenderest remedy which you can prepare for Me is to meditate lovingly on My Passion, and to pray charitably for the conversion of sinners. These two executioners represent the laity, who offend God openly, striking Him with thorns, and the religious, who strike Him still more unpitiably with the knotted cords of secret sins. But both offend Him to the face, and outrage the very God of heaven."

She then understood that the Passion of our Lord is read in the Gospel* that it may be recalled to mind by His special friends, for His glory and for the good of the Church ; that the scourging is mentioned therein twice according to the vision which she beheld ; and that charity is recommended in the Epistle to exercise us in the love of God and our neighbour ; suffering with God all the opprobriums which men made Him suffer, and pitying the neighbours for the misery to which they reduce themselves by offending God in this manner.

At Mass the Saint began to invoke the Divine assist-

---

* This probably refers to the Gospel for Quinquagesima Sunday (Luke xviii. 31), in which it is remarkable that our Lord mentions the scourging *twice :* " He shall be mocked and scourged and spat upon ; and after they have scourged Him," &c. The Epistle is 1 Cor. xiii. 1-13, which, it will be remembered, is the Apostle's great lesson of charity. The reference may be, however, to the Matins ; and this seems most probable, as the Mass is mentioned after. The Gospel read at the end of Matins is the same : *In illo tempore : Assumpsit Jesus duodecim;* and the Little Chapter at Lauds is from the Epistle : *Fratres : Si linguis hominum loquor,* &c.

ance in the words of the Introit ; * but our Lord appeared to use the same words in addressing her as if He needed her assistance against the evils and cruelties then exercised against Him, saying to her : " You are my beloved one ; be My protector, by your resolution of being My defence against all those who injure Me and treat Me with contempt ; for I come to you to hide Me." Then the Saint embraced her Lord, striving with all her power to draw Him into her very soul ; but she became so ravished in God, that she did not know whether the sisters stood or sat in the choir. When she was told that she was not conforming to the accustomed usage, she besought our Lord that nothing might be observed of what was passing within her. He replied : " Let your love keep your place near Me ; and as for yourself, you can attend to your exterior deportment." " O most loving Lord," she replied, " if it is true that my love can keep my place near Thee, I hope that reason will suffice to guide my exterior conduct, that I may love Thee more freely." And she obtained this gift from God ; for while she continued absorbed in God, she still followed exactly the common exercises of the other religious.

* Introit for Quinquagesima Sunday : *Esto mihi in Deum protectorem, et in locum refugii*, &c. — " Be thou unto me a God, a protector, and a place of refuge to save me," &c.

CHAPTER XIII.

For Quinquagesima (continued).

How acceptable good works are to our Lord during the three days of
the Carnival; and how such works obtain merit by union with
the Passion of Christ.

ON the night of Quinquagesima Sunday the Lord Jesus
appeared to Gertrude, seated on a throne, and attended by
St. John the Evangelist, who sat at His feet writing. As
she inquired what he wrote, our Lord replied: "I have
desired him to note carefully on this paper the services
which the community rendered Me yesterday, and I will
also have those noted down which they will render Me on
the two following days; so that when I am enthroned as
Judge by My Father, I may render to each, after her death,
good measure for what she has done; that the fruit of My
Passion, which is the source of all the merit and excellence the actions of men can have, may render this measure pressed down; and that this parchment * which I will
bring to My Father may render the measure so heaped up,
that it will pour forth abundantly: and this is for the services which they render Me at a time when men overwhelm
Me with injuries by their debaucheries; for as I never fail
in fidelity, I cannot be wanting in justice to those who serve
Me. Furthermore, although King David acknowledged
during his life the services which his friends had rendered
to him, still he recommended Solomon to show favour after
his death to the children of Berzellai the Galaadite, and to
admit them to his table, because they came to meet him when
he fled from Absolom. For as the services which we ren-

---

* "Cartha" in two editions; evidently a misprint for "Charta."

der in adversity are far more esteemed than those which are rendered in prosperity, so I esteem far more the services which are offered to me now, when the world offends Me so much more than at any other time.

As St. John sat and wrote, she saw him dipping his reed into the horn which he held in his hand, and then the writing appeared black ; but when he dipped his reed into the loving Wound of the Side of Jesus, the writing appeared rose-coloured ; in some places it was diversified with black and gold. She understood by this, that the black writing signified the works which were done by the religious through custom, such as fasting, &c., which all religious communities commence now ; that the red letters, diversified with black and gold, indicated the works which were done in memory of our Lord's Passion, to obtain grace or other similar intentions. But those works which were done purely for the glory of God, and in union with the Passion of Christ, for the salvation of all mankind, without any view of self-interest, of grace, or merit, were written in letters of pure gold ; and these works would obtain the greatest reward from God, since what is done purely for the love and glory of God is of the highest merit and value, and increases beyond all measure the recompenses of eternal life.

The Saint also perceived spaces between the writing ; and as she inquired what this signified, our Lord replied "As your community is accustomed to remain with Me at this time, and to offer your petitions in honour of My Passion, I have caused each thought and word to be inscribed here ; in the vacant places all that you have done in memory of My Passion, and not from mere custom, is inscribed." "But how could all our actions be thus acceptable ?" inquired Gertrude. "They would be so," replied our Lord, "if your fasts, vigils, and regular discipline were performed in memory of My Passion, and were offered to Me in union with the mortification of My senses which I practised during My Passion. For although I could have silenced My accusers by a single word, I was as a sheep led to the slaughter; I inclined My head humbly, and cast My eyes to the ground, never opening My lips before My Judge, or replying even to one of the false accusations which were brought against Me."

"Ah!" exclaimed Gertrude, "teach me, O best of teachers, how to perform even one action perfectly in memory of Thy Passion." Our Lord replied: " When you are praying, extend your arms to represent the manner in which I extended Mine to God My Father in My Passion; and do this for the salvation of every member of the Church, in union with the love with which I stretched out My arms upon the cross." " If I do this," she replied, " I must hide myself in a corner, for it is far from being customary." Our Lord replied: " If any one prays thus with his hands extended, without fear of contradiction, he pays Me the same honour as one would do who solemnly enthroned a king."

St. Gertrude also observed in these writings, that the actions of those who, for the love of God, gave good advice to others, were noted down; from which we perceive the exceeding goodness of God, who not only delights in procuring our salvation, but even seeks to recompense doubly the least good that we do. Then the Saint said: "O Lord! why is it that St. John has been chosen to write these things rather than our holy Father St. Benedict, who belongs to our own Order?" Our Lord replied: "I have chosen My beloved disciple because he has written of the love of God and the neighbour, therefore is most fit for this office ; for I have confidence in him that he will record what is most suitable to My power and My Divinity, as well as what will be most for your advantage."

On Ash Wednesday St. Gertrude came to our Lord, in the person of the Church, and with the Church, offering to him the penance of the fast for the Church ; and she was received by Him with so many tokens of love, and in so favourable a manner, that she learned indubitably, and by experience, the strength and tenderness of the affection which Christ has for the Church His Spouse, in whose person she approached Him.

CHAPTER XIV.

Instruction for the First Sunday of Lent.

How the soul is purified and embellished by the merits of Jesus Christ.

ON the Sunday *Invocabit*,* as Gertrude felt unable to receive the Body of our Lord, she besought Him with her whole heart to supply, by His forty days' fast, for the dispensations which her infirmity obliged her to accept. Then the Son of God rose up and knelt before His Father, with a joyful countenance, saying : " I, who am Thy only Son, co-eternal and consubstantial with Thee, know, by My inscrutable wisdom, the defects of human weakness as man could not know ; therefore do I abundantly compassionate this weakness, and, desiring to supply for it perfectly, I offer Thee, O holy Father, the restraints of My

---

* *Invocabit :* " He shall call upon Me, and I will hear him," &c. --Introit for the First Sunday in Lent.

blessed Mouth, in atonement for all sins of omission and
commission of which the tongues of men are guilty ; I offer
Thee, O just Father, the restraints of My Ears for all their
sins of hearing ; I offer Thee the restraints of My Eyes for
all their sins committed by seeing ; I offer Thee the restraints of My Hands and Feet for all the sins of those
members.   Lastly, I offer to Thy Majesty, O most loving
Father, My Divine Heart for all their sins of thought,
desire, or will."

Then the Saint stood before God the Father, clothed in
a red and white garment, and adorned with many ornaments.   The white robe indicated the innocence conferred
on her soul by the mortifications of Christ ; the red signified
the merits of His fasts ; and the diversity of ornaments, the
many ways and exercises by which our Lord laboured for
our eternal salvation.   Then the Eternal Father took this
soul thus adorned, and placed it at a banquet between Himself and His only Son.   On the one side, the splendour of
the Divine omnipotence overshadowed her, to enhance her
apparel and her dignity; on the other side, she was illuminated by the light of the inscrutable wisdom of God the Son,
which had adorned and embellished her with the treasures
and perfections of His life.   Between these two lights there
was an opening,* through which might be seen the humble
sentiments which this soul had of her baseness and defects ;
and her humility pleased God so much, that it won for her
the tenderest affection of this Almighty King.

Then our Lord placed before St. Gertrude the three
victories,† which are mentioned in the Gospel of the day,

* "Rima."
† Our Lord's three victories over His threefold temptations in
the wilderness, related in the Gospel for the First Sunday of Lent,
Matt. iv. 1-11 ; the Epistle is 2 Cor. vi. 1-10.

under the form of different kinds of food,* that they might serve her as an antidote against the three vices to which men are most subject—namely, delectation, consent, and concupiscence.† First, He manifested to her the signal victory which He had gained over the devil, who tempted Him to the pleasure of eating, when he asked Him to change the stones into bread, and our Lord wisely answered him, that man doth not live by bread alone ; and He desired her to offer it to God, in satisfaction for all the sins which she might have committed through love of pleasure, and to obtain strength to resist such temptations for the time to come. For the more we yield to temptations, the less capable we are of resisting them ; and each may thus offer our Lord's victory for their own needs. Our Lord then gave her His second victory for the remission of all the sins which she might have committed by consent, and to obtain grace for the future to resist these temptations efficaciously ; and each may also offer this victory, for the same end, and with the same advantage, to obtain from God the pardon of all sins of thought, word, or act, and grace to avoid falling for the time to come. Lastly, our Lord gave her His third victory as a remedy against avarice, which desires the goods and advantages of earth, and to obtain strength to resist this temptation.

During the Epistle at Mass, the Saint applied herself to noting the virtues mentioned therein, which she thought might be most useful to practise or to teach others ; and as she felt she needed the gift of understanding, she said to the Lord : "Teach me, O Beloved, which of these virtues will please Thee best ; for, alas ! I am not specially earnest

---

* " Ferculorum."
† " Delectatione, consensu, et concupiscentia."

in any." Our Lord replied : " Observe that the words *In Spiritu Sancto* ('in the Holy Ghost') occur in the middle of these victories. As, therefore, the Holy Spirit is a good-will,* study above all things to have this good-will, for you will gain more by it than by any other virtue, and it will obtain for you the perfection of all virtue. For whoever has a perfect will to praise Me, if he could, more than all the world, or to love Me, thank Me, suffer with Me, or exercise himself in the most perfect manner in all kinds of virtue, will certainly be recompensed by My Divine libe-rality more advantageously than one who has actually performed many other things." Then the Holy Spirit appeared before Gertrude, enlightening in a marvellous manner that place where the depravity and imperfection of her soul could be seen ; so that, the virtue of this Divine light having entirely removed her defects, she found herself happily immersed in the Source of eternal light.

CHAPTER XV.

For the Monday after the First Sunday of Lent.

Of the true manner of spiritually performing the corporal works of mercy.

THE second *feria* after the Sunday *Invocabit*, as these words were read in the Gospel, † "Come, ye blessed of My Father ; for I was hungry," &c., St. Gertrude said to our Lord : " O my Lord, since we cannot feed the hungry and give drink to the thirsty, because our Rule forbids us to possess any-

---

* " Spiritus Sanctus est bona voluntas."

† Gospel for the Monday after the First Sunday in Lent, Matt. xxv. 31-46.

thing of our own, teach me how we may participate in the sweet blessings with which Thou hast promised in this Gospel to reward works of mercy." Our Lord replied : " As I am the Salvation and Life of the soul, and as I continually hunger and thirst for the salvation of men, if you endeavour to study some words of Scripture every day for the benefit of others, you will bestow on Me a most sweet refection. If you read with the intention of obtaining the grace of compunction or devotion, you appease My thirst by giving Me an agreeable beverage to drink. If you employ yourself in recollection for an hour each day, you give Me hospitality ; and if you apply yourself daily to acquire some new virtue, you clothe Me. You visit Me when sick, by striving to overcome temptation, and to conquer your evil inclinations ; and you visit Me in prison, and solace My afflictions with the sweetest consolations, when you pray for sinners and for the souls in purgatory." He added : "Those who perform these devotions daily for My love, especially during the holy season of Lent, will most certainly receive the tenderest and most bountiful recompense which My incomprehensible omnipotence, My inscrutable wisdom, and My most loving benevolence, can bestow."

CHAPTER XVI.

For the Second Sunday in Lent.

Of the oblation of the merits of Jesus Christ for the sins of the Church.

On the Sunday *Reminiscere*,* St Gertrude, being favoured

---

* " Remember, O Lord, Thy compassions and Thy mercies," &c. —Introit, Second Sunday in Lent.

with singular marks of the love and tenderness of her
Spouse, such as no human being could describe, besought
our Lord to indicate some practice which might be profit-
able during this week.   Our Lord replied: "Bring Me
two good kids *—I mean the souls and the bodies of all
mankind."

The Saint understood from this that she was required
to make satisfaction for all mankind; and then, impelled
by the Holy Ghost, she said the *Pater noster* five times, in
honour of the Five Wounds of our Lord, in satisfaction for
all the sins which men had committed by the five senses;
and three times for the sins committed by the three powers
of the soul—namely, by reason, temper, and concupiscence;†
and for all omissions or commissions : offering this prayer
with the same intention, and for the same end, as our
Lord had formed it in His sweetest Heart ; that is to say,
in satisfaction for all the sins of frailty, ignorance, or
malice which man had opposed to His omnipotent power,
His inscrutable wisdom, and His overflowing and gratuitous goodness.

When Gertrude offered this prayer, our Lord appeared
to take an incredible pleasure therein, and made the sign
of the cross on her from her head to her feet ; blessing her,
and then embracing her, He led her to His Father to receive His benediction also.   God the Father also received
her with great condescension and magnificence, and blessed
her in so ineffable a manner, that He gave her as many
benedictions as He would have given to the whole world
if it had been prepared to receive this favour and grace.

This prayer may be offered to God during this week to

---

* " Duos hædos optimos."
† " Rationali, irrascibili, et concupiscibili."

obtain the pardon of our sins and omissions, and in satisfaction for the sins of the Church, that we may obtain the
effect of so salutary a benediction through the merits of
Jesus Christ, who with such condescension and goodness
has deigned to be the Spouse and Head of His Church.

CHAPTER XVII.

For the Third Sunday of Lent.

How we may obtain a share in the merits of the Life of Jesus Christ.

ON the Sunday *Oculi*,* as the Saint desired, as usual, to
conform her devotions to the Church's offices, she asked
our Lord to teach her how she should occupy herself
during this week.   He replied : " As in chanting your
Office during this week you record how Joseph was sold
by his brethren for twenty pieces of silver,† recite the *Pater
noster* thirty-three times, and thus purchase the merit of
My most holy Life, which lasted for three-and thirty years,
during which I laboured for the salvation of men ; and
communicate the fruit of what you thus acquire to the
whole Church, for the salvation of men and My eternal
glory."   As the Saint complied with this direction, she per-

* *Oculi*—Introit for Third Sunday in Lent.
† The Lessons of the i. Nocturn for the Third Sunday in Lent are
taken from the 37th chapter of Genesis, which details the history of
Joseph sold into Egypt. In an Italian translation of 1606 it is
" trenta dinari ; " and in the French, " trente deniers ; " two Latin
editions have " xxx. denariis " also—probably a mistake of a tran-
scriber, which has been thoughtlessly perpetuated.

ceived in spirit that the whole Church was like a spouse adorned and embellished in a marvellous manner with the fruit of the perfect life of Jesus Christ.

CHAPTER XVIII.

For the Fourth Sunday of Lent.

The Saint is instructed how to atone for the sins of the Church.

ON *Lætare* Sunday, as the Saint sought for some instruction from our Lord how to spend this week, He replied to her : " Bring those persons to Me whose souls you prepared seven days since, through the virtue of My Life ; for they must eat at My table." She replied : " How can I do this ? For myself, however unworthy I am, I will venture to say, that if I could bring to Thee all the children of men, in whom Thou dost take delight, I would willingly traverse the whole earth with bare feet from this moment until the day of judgment, and carry them in my arms to Thee, to correspond, in some manner, with Thy infinite love. And were it possible for me to do so, I would divide my heart into as many portions as there are men living in the world, to impart to each a share in the good-will which is most pleasing to Thy Divine Heart." Our Lord replied : " Your good-will suffices and satisfies Me perfectly." Then she beheld the whole Church marvellously adorned and presented to the Lord, who said to her : " You shall serve all this multitude to-day."

Then St. Gertrude cast herself at the feet of her Spouse, being divinely inspired, and kissed the Wound of His Left Foot, in satisfaction for all the sins which had ever been committed in the Church, by thought, will, or desire ; beseeching our Lord to give her for this purpose the perfect satisfaction which He had made by washing away the sins of all men. Our Lord then imparted this grace to her under the form of bread, which she immediately offered Him with thanksgiving, and which He received with great condescension, and, raising His eyes to His Eternal Father, blessed it, and gave it to her to distribute to His Church. Then she kissed the Right Foot of our Lord, in satisfaction for the omissions of the faithful in good thoughts and desires, and in good-will; beseeching our Lord to impart to them a share in that perfect satisfaction which He had made for the debts of all men. Then she kissed the Wound of the Left Hand, in satisfaction for the sins of the whole world, whether committed by word or deed; beseeching our Lord to grant the merits of His words and actions for this intention. She then kissed the Wound of the Right Hand, in satisfaction for the omissions of good words and works; beseeching our Lord to impart the plenitude and perfection of His action to supply what was deficient in His Church.

At each of these offerings she received bread, and returned each portion to our Lord, who blessed it, and gave it to her to distribute to the Church. Then she approached the loving Wound of the Side of Jesus, and embracing it with her whole heart, besought Him to supply to His Spouse the Church what was wanting to her perfection and merits, even after He had so perfectly expiated her sins, and so fully supplied for her defects; so that His Divine Life—which is agreeable in the sight of God the Father, and shines with such surpassing brightness—might become her crown and everlasting beatitude. Then the Saint rejoiced for the grace which God had given her, and distributed these loaves as one would a dessert after a meal, and said to our Lord : " Ah, Lord! what wilt Thou give me for Thy

Spouse the Church, instead of the fish which are mentioned in to-day's Gospel ? " * Our Lord replied : " I will give you all My most perfect actions to distribute to those who have neglected to serve Me as much as they ought to have done, and all the most noble actions of My soul to atone for their coldness and want of fervour in praising Me for the benefits which they have received from Me."

By the loaves which our Lord presented to the Saint she understood that whenever any one performs a good action for God—even should it be only to say a *Pater noster* or *Ave Maria*, or any other prayer for the Church—that the Son of God receives it as if it were the fruit of His holy Humanity, and offers it to God His Father, blessing it and multiplying it by this benediction, so that it may be distributed for the good and advancement of the whole Church.

This devotion may be performed by any one who says five *Pater nosters* in honour of our Lord's Five Wounds, kissing them in spirit, and praying for all sinners who are in the bosom of the Church, to obtain the remission of their sins and negligences, if they hope firmly to receive this grace from the Divine goodness.

* Gospel for Fourth Sunday in Lent, John vi. 1-15, which relates the miraculous multiplication of the five loaves and the two fishes, and so renders the mystical offering of the five loaves given to the Saint in peculiar harmony with the offices of the day.

CHAPTER XIX.

For the Feast of St. Gregory, Pope.

Of the glory and prerogatives of St. Gregory, and the recompense
reserved for this Doctor of the Church.

As St. Gertrude heard Mass on the Feast of St. Gregory,[*]
and offered him singular testimonies of veneration and devotion, he appeared to her full of majesty and glory ; and
she thought that he equalled all the saints in merit. He
was a Patriarch, by the careful and paternal diligence with
which he watched, night and day, over the Church which
had been confided to him ; a Prophet, since in his admirable writings he had discovered the snares and deceits of
the ancient enemy, and had given advice and remedies
against his wiles, so that he was more glorified than any of
the Prophets. He equalled the Apostles from his inviolable
and faithful attachment to God in prosperity and adversity,
and by his zeal in the promotion of the Gospel. He resembled the martyrs and confessors by his great bodily
austerities, and the ardent love which he had for religion
and holiness. Above all, he excelled in chastity ; and as a
recompense for his virginal purity, he enjoyed an incomparable glory for every thought, word, or work which had
been accomplished to preserve the purity of his body and
soul, or to teach others to preserve the same treasure.

[*] St Gregory was born at Rome about the year 540. The English nation owes him a singular debt of gratitude for his zeal for
their conversion. He would himself have undertaken the mission
which he so ardently desired ; but at the request, or rather the
clamorous demand, of the whole city of Rome, he was recalled by
the Pope, then Benedict I., when on his road to England. His Feast
occurs on the 12th March.

Our Lord then said to St. Gertrude : " Consider, now, how suitable this Psalm is to this elect soul—' According to the multitude of my sorrows in my heart, Thy comforts have given joy to my soul ' (Ps. xciii. 19)—since he has been recompensed by these inestimable delights for all the pain he suffered in word or works, or even in thought At his death, which is commemorated to-day, his body did not rejoice because it had to pass through the torrent of death ; and the whole Church, as well as those who stood round him on that day, were exceedingly afflicted at being deprived of so affectionate and thoughtful a father. But now, on the same day, there is the greatest joy when his solemn feast is observed."

Then Gertrude said to her Lord : " What glory hast Thou gained by the writings of this Saint, which have so enriched and enlightened the Church ? " He replied : " My Divinity and My Humanity find extreme delight therein, and he himself enjoys the same delight with Me whenever the Church recites any of his writings, and whenever any one is moved by them to compunction, excited to devotion, or influenced by love. And for this he receives the same honour from the celestial court as a soldier or a prince whom the king clothed in his own garments and fed at his own table." He added : " St. Augustine and St. Bernard, whom you love so much, and the other Doctors of the Church, enjoy the same honour and the same prerogative, each according to the merit and the utility of his labours."

While the twelfth Response was chanted, which commences with the words, *O Pastor,** St. Gregory knelt before God, and lifted up his hands interceding for the

* Not in present Office.

Church. Then the Lord opened His Divine Heart, that he might take what he would ; and the Saint, placing both hands therein, took from thence the grace of Divine consolation, and poured it forth for the necessities of the Church. Then she beheld the Lord encircling him with a magnificent cincture of the purest gold. This cincture indicated the justice of God, which withheld him from descending on the earth—suspending him in the air, to prevent him from bestowing these graces on the ungrateful and unworthy ; but permitting him to give them freely to those who desired and merited them.

CHAPTER XX.

For the Feast of the glorious St. Benedict.

The beatitude and glory of this Saint shown to St. Gertrude— The particular recompense reserved for those who observe regular discipline faithfully.

ON the Feast of the glorious father St. Benedict,[*] St. Gertrude assisted at Matins with special devotion to honour so excellent a father ; and she beheld him in spirit, standing in the presence of the effulgent and ever-peaceful Trinity,

---

[*] The life of the great St. Benedict is too well known to require comment here. He founded twelve monasteries during his life ; and since his happy death, thousands of saintly souls have lived and died under his holy Rule, distinguished for that which alone could constitute them his true children—the faithful observance of his Rule, and communion with the Holy Catholic Church, by which it has been sanctioned, and which alone could authorise its use or the profession of its observances. His feast is kept on the 21st of March.

radiant with glory. His countenance was full of majesty and beauty ; his habit shone surpassingly ; while bright and living roses seemed to spring forth from his limbs, each rose producing another, and these others, the last surpassing the first in fragrance and beauty, so that our holy father, blessed both by grace and by name,* being thus adorned, gave the greatest pleasure to the adorable Trinity and the heavenly court, who rejoiced with him because of his beatitude. The roses which thus sprang forth from him signified the exercises which he had used to subjugate his flesh to his spirit, and all the holy actions which he had performed, and also those of all whom he had drawn by his persuasions or induced by his example to leave the world and live under regular discipline, who, following him in this royal road, had attained, or will yet attain, to the port of the celestial country and to life eternal, each of whom is a subject of particular glory to this great patriarch ; and for which all the saints praise God, and congratulate him continually.

St. Benedict also carried a sceptre, which was marvellously embellished on each side with precious stones of great brilliancy. As he held it in his hand, the side which was turned towards him emitted a glorious light, which indicated the happiness of those who had embraced his Rule and amended their lives, and on their account God overwhelmed him with inconceivable joy. On the side which was turned towards God, the Divine justice shone forth which had been magnified in the condemnation of those who had been called to this holy Order, but who had rendered themselves unworthy of it, and therefore had been condemned to eternal flames ; for it is just that he whom God has called to the

---

* "Sanctissimus Pater, gratia et nomine Benedictus."

holiest of Orders should be most severely punished if he lives an evil life.

Now, as St. Gertrude offered the blessed father the recital of the entire Psalter in his honour, on the part of the community, he appeared exceedingly rejoiced, and he offered the verdure with which he was adorned for the welfare of those who sought his protection with pure hearts, and walked in his footsteps by faithful observance of his Rule.

While the Response, *Grandi Pater fiducia morte stetit preciosa*,* was chanted, St. Gertrude said to him : " Holy father, what special reward have you received for your glorious death ?" He replied : " Because I gave up my last breath while I was in prayer, I now emit a breath of such surpassing sweetness, that the saints delight to be near me." Then she besought him, by his glorious death, to assist each religious of that monastery in their last hour. The venerable father replied : " All who invoke me, remembering the glorious end with which God honoured me, shall be assisted by me at their death with such fidelity, that I will place myself where I see the enemy most dis posed to attack them; thus, being fortified by my presence, they will escape the snares which he lays for them, and depart happily and peacefully to the enjoyment of eternal beatitude."

---

* This Responsory is not in the present Office.

CHAPTER XXI.

For the Vigil and Feast of the Annunciation.

Exercises of devotion to the Blessed Virgin.

As St. Gertrude heard the bell for Chapter on the Vigil of the Annunciation, and endeavoured to recollect herself in God, she beheld the Lord Jesus and His Virgin Mother seated in the place of the Superior,* and waiting with great tranquillity until the sisters had assembled, receiving each as she entered with the tenderest marks of friendship and affection.   When the Feast of the Annunciation was read in the Martyrology,† Jesus turned to His Mother and saluted her with such goodness and condescension, as to renew in her that sweet and inestimable joy which she had felt when His Divinity took flesh in her womb, and united itself to our nature.   When the community began to recite the *Miserere*, our Lord placed each word in the hand of His Virgin Mother under the form of pearls of different colours.   She saw that the Blessed Virgin had a quantity of sweet perfumes ‡ in her bosom, which she mixed with the pearls—that is, with the prayers of the religious— which her Son had presented to her.

---

* In the Life of the venerable Mother Ann of St. Bartholomew, the special friend and confidante of St. Teresa, she says : "When the Saint (Teresa) held Chapter at Avila, I beheld Jesus Christ at her side, clothed in such splendour, that the religious appeared to me quite deified ('toutes divinisées '); and, in truth, they left the Chapter with overflowing hearts, and filled with ineffable con- solation."

† " Kalendario."   ‡ " Olfactoriola."

The Saint understood that these perfumes signified the crosses which the religious had suffered on the preceding day, without having given any occasion for them; and when she marvelled why these crosses were represented as perfumes, our Lord told her: " As a delicate person is more pleased with perfumes than with any other present, so do I delight in the hearts of those who suffer their trials with humility, patience, and thanksgiving, abandoning themselves entirely to My paternal goodness, which converts both prosperity and adversity to their good."

As Gertrude began to reflect why our Lord had instructed her now and on many other occasions by corporal visions, he recalled to her mind the words which had been chanted that day of the closed gate which the Prophet Ezechiel had seen,[*] and said to her: " As I have explained the manner and order of My Incarnation, Passion, and Resurrection to the prophets by mystical figures and similitudes, so I use sensible things to make men comprehend what surpasses the apprehension of their senses. For this reason, no one should esteem spiritual things less because they are represented under corporal images; but rather

---

[*] Ez. xliv. 2 : " The eastern gate, through which the prince alone could pass." This passage is not referred to in the present Office for the Annunciation ; but it is mentioned in i. Ant. ii. Vespers in *Responsorialia et Antiphonaria S. Gregorii Papæ*. The Fathers frequently refer this passage to the Blessed Virgin, as the true eastern gate, which opened only to the King, and never admitted any other. St. Augustine, in his sermon on the Nativity, says : " The closed gate indicates purity, and the integrity of the immaculate flesh ; it is not defiled by childbirth ; it becomes more holy by conception." St. Bernard says : " She is prefigured by the eastern gate in Ezechiel's vision, through which only one could pass."

should endeavour to render themselves capable thereby of tasting the sweetness contained therein."

While the *Ave Maria* * was chanted at Matins, St. Gertrude beheld three streams, which flowed with a gentle impetuosity from the Father, the Son, and the Holy Ghost into the heart of the Blessed Virgin, and flowed back again from her heart with the same impetuosity to its original source. The Saint understood by this that the Blessed Virgin is most powerful after the Father, most wise after the Son, and most benign after the Holy Ghost.† She knew also, when any one recited the *Ave Maria* with devotion, that these three streams sweetly encompassed the Blessed Virgin, and then returned to their source in the Heart of Jesus Christ, and from them little streams of joy and salvation flow forth on the saints and angels, and especially on those who recite the Angelic Salutation with devotion, which renews in them all the benefits which they acquire by the Incarnation of the Son of God.

Each time also that they recited any words referring to the chastity of the Blessed Virgin, such as these : " Domus pudici pectoris ; clausa parentis viscera," &c.,‡ all the saints rose up, and reverenced her as their queen and mistress, returning most fervent thanks to God for all the favours which He had granted to men through her. The Archangel Gabriel appeared also as if arrayed in a new brilliancy each time that the Annunciation was mentioned, which was effected by his ministry ; and at the name of St. Joseph,

* Response after ii. Lesson, i. Nocturn.

† " Potentissima post Patrem ; sapientissima post Filium; et benignissima post Spiritum Sanctum."

‡ From the hymn at Lauds on Christmas-day, *A solis ortus cardine*, which may have been then sung on the Nativity of the Blessed Virgin also.

the spouse of the Virgin Mother, all the saints made a profound inclination to him, testifying, by the serenity and
sweetness of their looks, that they rejoiced with him for
his exalted dignity.

During Mass, at which St. Gertrude communicated, she
beheld the Mother of God, gloriously adorned with every
virtue; and she prostrated humbly at her feet, beseeching
her to dispose her to receive worthily the august Sacrament of the Body and Blood of her Divine Son. The
Blessed Virgin then gave her a magnificent necklace, which
had seven rays or points, to each of which a precious stone
was attached, and these stones indicated the signal virtues
which had pleased our Lord most in His Blessed Mother.
The first was her exquisite purity; the second, her faithful humility; the third, her ardent desires; the fourth,
her clear knowledge; the fifth, her unquenchable love;
the sixth, the sovereign pleasure which she took in God;
the seventh, her peaceful tranquillity. When St. Gertrude
appeared before our Lord with this collar, He was so won
by the brilliancy of her virtues, that He inclined lovingly
towards her; drawing her to Himself, and enclosing her
as it were in His bosom, He honoured her with His pure
and holy caresses.

At the Antiphon for the *Magnificat—Arte mirabili* *—
the Holy Spirit appeared to come forth from the Heart of
our Lord like a soft wind, which gently moved the collar
with which the Saint was adorned, chanting this Antiphon
as on a musical instrument in honour of the Most Holy
Trinity. Then, at the words of the Gospel *Ecce ancilla*, St.
Gertrude saluted the Mother of God with great devotion

* This Antiphon is not in the present Benedictine Breviary. The
one now used commences, "Gabriel angelus locutus est Mariæ."

recalling to her the ineffable joy which she had experienced when she abandoned herself and all that concerned her, with perfect confidence, to the Divine will. The Blessed Virgin replied to her, with a look of exceeding serenity: " When any one reminds me devoutly of this, I will truly be to them what they ask in the hymn *Monstra te esse matrem,** which is used on this Feast, showing myself in truth the Mother of the King of Glory and the advocate of men, using my power with the King to succour them, and assisting them with the tenderest compassion."

When the Antiphon *Hæc est dies*† was chanted, at the words, "Hodie Deus homo factus est," the community prostrated, to honour the glorious Incarnation of our Lord, and the Son of God, remembering the love which had made Him become man, rose from His regal throne, and, standing before His Father, said to Him : " Eternal Father, My brethren are come to Me " (Gen. xlvi. 31). And the Eternal Father was moved to compassionate and show grace to these brethren for whom His only and beloved Son interceded thus lovingly and tenderly, with infinitely more affection than Pharao felt for Joseph when he rejoiced with him at the arrival of his brothers.

As St. Gertrude inquired what devotion would be most acceptable to the Blessed Virgin at this time, she taught her that any one who recited the *Ave Maria* devoutly forty-five times each day during the Octave, in memory of the

---

* " Show thyself a mother ;
    Offer Him our sighs,
    Who for us incarnate
    Did not thee despise."

From the hymn *Ave maris stella,* at Vespers, Feasts of the Blessed Virgin.

† This was formerly sung at procession after Vespers. Gerbert. *Mon. Vet. Lit. Allmannicæ,* p. ii. p. 231.

time our Lord had remained in her holy womb, they would render her the same service as if they had attended her with the greatest care from the moment of the conception to the time of the birth ; and as she could have refused them nothing under such circumstances, so now she would be equally willing to give all they asked.

The Saint was then instructed to say the *Ave Maria* in this manner: at the words " Ave Maria," to desire the consolation of the afflicted ; at the words " gratia plena," to ask grace for those who had it not ; at " Dominus tecum," to pray for sinners ; at " benedicta tu in mulieribus," to ask grace for those who had begun to live well ; at " benedictus fructus ventris," to pray for the perfection of the elect ; to repeat the words " Jesus, splendor-paternæ charitatis," that all may know Him ; and " figura substantiæ ejus," to obtain Divine love : for these words—" Jesus, splendour of the Father's glory, and image of His substance" —should be repeated at the end of each *Ave Maria.*

CHAPTER XXII.

For Passion Sunday.

Exercises of devotion for that day.

ON the Sunday *Judica,* St. Gertrude having offered her body and soul to our Lord, that she might suffer therein, in honour of His Passion, whatever afflictions He might please to send her, her offering was accepted graciously ; and the Saint, impelled by Divine inspiration, commenced to salute and adore the different members of our Lord's Body which had suffered for us during His Passion. As she saluted each member, a Divine splendour shone forth from each, which enlightened her soul, by means of which the innocence which our Lord acquired for His Church was communicated to her. When she was thus enriched and adorned with the innocence of Jesus Christ, she said to our Lord : "Teach me, O Lord, I beseech Thee, how I can worthily honour Thy Divine Passion with the innocence with which Thy goodness has endowed me." Our Lord replied : " Reflect frequently with gratitude and compassion on what I, your Lord and Creator, suffered in My long agony and prayer, when the vehemence of My desires and My love caused Me to bedew the ground with a sweat of blood ; offer Me all your actions and all that concerns you, in union with the entire submission with which I said these words : ' My Father, Thy will be done ; ' and so receive all that happens to you, whether painful or agreeable, with the same love with which I send it to you for your salvation. Be grateful in prosperity, uniting yourself with the love which made Me send it to you, condescending to your weakness, that temporal prosperity may lead you to think of spiritual joys, and to hope for them; receive adversity also in union with the charity with which My paternal love sends it to you, to prepare you for eternal good."

Then St. Gertrude resolved to say the following prayer during the remainder of the week, saluting the sacred Limbs of the Son of God with these words : " I salute you, O precious Limbs." And she perceived that this pleased our Lord ; and if we desire the same grace, let us use the same prayer.

During the Mass which followed, as the words of the Gospel *Dæmonium habes* * were read, she was grieved in her inmost soul for the contempt offered to our Lord ; and

---

* " Thou hast a devil," St. John viii. 46–59.

as she could not endure to hear these words, she exclaimed in the depth of her heart, in the sweetest and most loving manner: " Hail, vivifying Gem of Divine nobility ! Hail, most loving Jesus! unfading flower of human dignity! Thou art my Sovereign and only Good." And this benign Lord, to reward these testimonies of affection, inclined tenderly towards her, and whispered to her: " I am thy Creator, Redeemer, and Lover. I left My beatitude to redeem thee by a bitter death." Then all the saints, being rapt in admiration of the marvellous friendship which He manifested to her, praised God for it with the greatest joy.

Our Lord then said to her : " Whoever salutes Me, as you have done, in reparation for the blasphemies and outrages which are poured forth on Me throughout the world, when he is tempted at the hour of his death and accused by the demon, will be consoled by Me with the same words with which I have consoled you, and I will testify the same affection towards him ; and if the saints were thus amazed at the words I whispered into your ear, how astonished and amazed will be the enemies of his soul when they shall see him so marvellously consoled by My goodness !"

CHAPTER XXIII.

For Palm Sunday.

Of Spiritual Communion, and other exercises for this holy day.

ON the Feast of Palms, as Gertrude was filled with the delights of Divine consolation, she said to our Lord: " Teach me, I beseech Thee, O Beloved, how I can go forth to meet Thee to-day, who art approaching Thy

Passion for my salvation." Our Lord replied : " Give Me an ass * to ride ; a troop of people to precede Me with acclamations ; another troop to follow Me with praises ; and another to minister to Me.

" You will give Me an ass to ride, if you acknowledge with a contrite heart that you have failed to be guided by reason, and have had no more understanding than a beast of all that I have done for your salvation. This negligence has caused you to lose My sweet tranquillity ; so that when I thought to find some consolation in you, it was necessary for Me to purify you by some exterior or interior suffering. And thus I was obliged to suffer in you ; for My love, which could not restrain itself, obliged My goodness to compassionate you in all your adversities. But when you give Me the conveyance which I desire, I shall be satisfied.

" You will give Me a troop of people who will make acclamations before Me, when you receive Me with full affection in the name of all men, in union with the love which made Me, your Lord and Creator, enter Jerusalem for the salvation of the world, and in satisfaction for all those who have failed to thank Me worthily, and with perfect affection, for this great grace.

" You will give Me another troop to follow Me with praises, when you avow sincerely that you have never imitated the example of My perfect life as you should ; and if you offer Me such a fervent will, that if you could you would urge all men to imitate what is most perfect in My Life and Passion, and this for My honour and glory ; and pray that you may obtain the grace to imitate Me in true humility, patience, and charity (the virtues which I exer-

* " Jumentum."

cised most during My Passion), desiring with the utmost ardour to follow My example.

"You will give me those who will attend Me, if you confess that you have never defended My truth and justice as you ought, resolving firmly to defend them for the future, both by your words and actions." He added: "Whoever presents himself to me in these four ways will not fail to obtain life eternal as the reward of his piety."

Then, as she was about to communicate, and offered her whole heart to God with great fervour, she beheld it opening in its charity, as Jerusalem opened to receive our Lord. He entered therein under the form of a young man bearing a scourge with three cords, which signified the work of our redemption: the first cord indicated the labours of His sacred body; the second, the devout intentions of His most holy Soul; the third, the excellent and incomparable virtue of His Divinity, which always co-operated together in Jesus Christ. Our Lord then touched her gently with the scourge, to remove from her all the stains and dust of human frailty and negligence. After this, He placed the scourge in the centre of her heart. The three cords appeared to form a throne for our Lord to rest upon; and as He seated Himself thereon, each of these little cords produced a green branch, which was covered with flowers. The first of these—that is, the virtue of His Divinity—grew up behind Him, and served as a shade for His Head; the others were on the right and left, and emitted a most agreeable fragrance.

As she chanted the words, *O Crux, ave, spes unica,** at

* "Hail, Cross, our only hope!" From the Hymn *Vexilla regis*, which was probably said then at Terce. Formerly the Hymn at Terce varied, now it is fixed, except on Whit Sunday.

Terce, St. Gertrude offered our Lord the devotions of all those who would salute Him that day while reciting it at the Canonical Hours. Then our Lord presented her devotion and zeal, in the form of a flower, to all those for whom she had made the offering; and this flower gave them great spiritual joy and beauty. "If this can be so advantageous to my sisters," said the Saint, "what wilt Thou give to those who apply themselves after the procession yet more fervently to serve Thee and adore Thee?" Our Lord replied: "As your sisters present Me with three different kinds of devotion, I will place these three flowers before them. Some of them desire to have devotion which they find they have not, and they offer me their exterior labours and exercises: to these I will present the flower that springs forth from the labours and exercises of My Body. Others abound in sweet devotion, and offer Me their fervent desires; and I will refresh them with the flower which proceeds from the pure intentions of My Divine Soul. Others, again, whose will is so united to Mine that they are one spirit with Me, offer themselves entirely to me, that I may do with them what I will; and to these I will present the noble flower of My Divinity."

After the procession, as the community made an inclination at the *Gloria, laus,** and prostrated at the *Fulgentibus palmis,* our Lord presented them with the flower of His bodily exercise, to console, fortify, and preserve them in His service, giving them to understand by this that He would ennoble their labours by the merit of His own. One

---

* "Glory and praise to Thee, Redeemer blest;" Hymn after the procession on Palm Sunday. This Hymn was composed by Theodolphus, Bishop of Orleans. The words *fulgentibus palmis* do not occur in it.

of the sisters then came to St. Gertrude to implore her to take some food, on account of her extreme weakness; but as she could not bear to take anything until she had heard the Passion,* according to her usual custom, she besought our Lord to tell her what she ought to do. He replied: "Refresh yourself, My beloved, in union with the love with which I refused the wine mingled with myrrh and gall when I had tasted it." As she returned thanks for the favour, our Lord presented His Heart to her, saying: "I present you therein with the desire which made Me refuse to drink, that I might give you to drink. Drink, then, freely what I, a skilful Physician, have prepared for you. This wine, mingled with gall and myrrh, was offered to Me that I might die more speedily; but the desire of suffering yet more for men prevented Me from drinking it. You, on the contrary, must take the food which is necessary for you, with the same love, that your life may be prolonged for My service. This wine and myrrh was mixed with gall; therefore you must also do three things in memory thereof. First: you must perform all your actions cheerfully for My glory; this is indicated by the wine. Secondly: you must use the conveniences of life, to enable you to suffer for My love; and this is indicated by the myrrh, which preserves from corruption. Thirdly: you must be very willing, for My love, to be deprived of the joys of heaven, and to remain in this valley of misery; and this is indicated by the gall. Each time that you use the necessaries of life with these intentions, I will regard you as you would a friend who had taken a bitter potion in order to leave you one which was sweet and palatable."

---

* The procession was then, as now, before Mass. The Passion according to St Matthew is read at Mass.

St. Gertrude, when eating, was always accustomed to repeat these words: "May the virtue of Thy Divine love incorporate me wholly into Thee, O most loving Jesus!" And when drinking, she said: "O most amiable Jesus, pour forth and preserve in my inmost being that Divine charity which reigns so powerfully in Thee, that it may penetrate me entirely, distilling itself into all the powers of my body and soul."

The Saint having inquired of our Lord how He would accept the same offering from others, He replied: "Those who use the same words as I have taught you will receive the same testimonies of affection from Me as I have shown to you." As the words of the Passion, *Emisit spiritum*, were read, St. Gertrude prostrated on the ground, saying: "Behold me, O Lord, prostrate on the earth in honour of Thy precious Death, beseeching Thee, by the excessive love which caused Thee to die, who art the life of all, that Thou wouldst destroy in me all that displeases Thee." Our Lord replied: "Cast from you all the vices which you desire should die in you, and draw into you, by the virtue of My spirit, those perfections of Mine which you desire to possess; and be assured that your sins will be pardoned, and that you shall feel the salutary effects of what you have thus drawn from Me into yourself; and each time that you endeavour to combat the vices which you have cast out, or to obtain the virtues with which I have inspired you, you will gain the double advantage—of obtaining the victory, and of feeling the fruit of My Passion."

After the mid-day meal, St. Gertrude retired to rest in a state of extreme lassitude and weakness—not to sleep, but rather to avoid the importunate visits with which she was overwhelmed, saying to our Lord: "I withdraw myself from the conversation of creatures, in memory of the salutary instruction which Thou didst give to-day, and to occupy myself with Thee, my Love and my all, beseeching Thee to speak to my soul." Our Lord replied : " As My Divinity reposed in My Humanity, so does My Divinity repose in your weariness." As the Saint perceived that those who came to her feared to interrupt her, thinking she slept, she asked our Lord if she should tell them that she was not sleeping, that they might do as they wished ; but He replied : " No ; let them merit by their exercises of charity the rewards which I desire and rejoice so much to give for it ; for there is nothing more useful to men than such exercises." Then He added : " I will propose two subjects on which you may meditate ; for there is nothing more useful in this life than for men to weary themselves in these labours, in which I take repose and delight, and to perform works of charity towards their neighbour."

On the evening of the day on which our Lord went to Martha and Mary in Bethania, as St. Gertrude ardently desired to entertain our Lord, she addressed herself to a crucifix, and, having kissed the Wound of our Lord's Side with the tenderest affection, she besought Him that He would vouchsafe to accept the hospitality of her heart, not-withstanding her unworthiness. The Lord, who hears those who cry to Him, presented Himself to her, and said to her caressingly : " Behold, here I am ; what will you give Me ?" The Saint replied : " My only Salvation, my true and only Good, alas ! I have nothing to present to Thy Divine magnificence, but I offer my whole being to Thy goodness, beseeching Thee to prepare within me all that Thou knowest to be pleasing to Thee." Our Lord replied : " If you desire that I should act as I will with you, give me the key of your heart, that I may leave or take away whatever I please." " And what is this key ?" inquired the Saint.   He answered : " It is your own will."

She understood by these words, that those who desire to entertain our Lord should give Him the key of their own will, abandoning themselves entirely to His good pleasure, with perfect confidence that His goodness will order all things for their salvation.   Then our Lord entered into her heart, and enjoyed therein all the Divine delights which He desired.

After this, St. Gertrude, being inspired by God, saluted the precious body of our Lord by repeating these words three hundred and sixty-five times : *Non mea, sed tua voluntas fiat, amantissime Jesu;* and she knew that He accepted this with great satisfaction.   She then inquired if our Lord would be pleased if certain persons, who desired to celebrate this Feast with devotion, should be guided by what she had written, taking Esther for her subject, and commencing with the words : *Egredimini, filiæ Jerusalem.* He replied : " I have this Feast so much at heart, that if any one takes pains to celebrate it with devotion, he shall have this honour—that, in the life eternal, besides the recompense of his other good works, I will prepare a feast for him which shall be worthy of the magnificence of My royal liberality."

CHAPTER XXIV.

For Wednesday in Holy Week.

ON Wednesday in Holy Week, at the words *In nomine Jesu*,* St. Gertrude bent her knees in honour of this most worthy name, to repair all the negligence which she had committed in this matter ; and, perceiving that our Lord was pleased with this, she knelt a second time at the word *cœlestium*, to supply for the negligence of the saints when in this life, in regard to the honour which they owed to God. When she had done this, the whole celestial court rose up with great sentiments of gratitude, thanking God for having given this grace to her, and praying for her. At the word *terrestrium*, she made another genuflexion, in satisfaction for the negligence of the faithful in praising God ; and then the Son of God imparted to her with singular joy the fruit of all the devotions which had been offered to Him throughout the whole Church. At the word *infernorum*, she also knelt to atone for the negligences of the damned. Then the Son of God arose, and stood before His Father, saying : " It is My right to condemn, since Thou hast given Me all power ; and by an equitable judgment I have consigned them to eternal flames. Therefore, I receive with such satisfaction the reparation which Gertrude has made for them, that the reward which I reserve until she is capable of the enjoyment of beatitude could not be comprehended by any mortal."

While the Passion was read, at the words, *Pater, ignosce illis*, St. Gertrude besought our Lord earnestly, by the love which made Him pray for those who crucified Him, that

---

* " In the name of Jesus, let every knee bow," &c. — Introit for Wednesday in Holy Week.

He would be pleased to pardon all those who had ever offended Him in anything. At this petition all the saints rose up in admiration, beseeching God to pardon her all the faults which she might have committed on their solemnities or festivals. Then the Son of God presented Himself also before His Father, offering the merit of His holy life, in satisfaction for all the faults which the Saint had committed in thought, word, or deed.

As they read the words, " To-day shalt thou be with Me in paradise," she knew in spirit that no one could obtain the grace of penitence in his last hour, if he had not rendered himself worthy of it by performing some good action during his life ; and that the good thief had obtained the favour of entering into glory the same day as our Lord, because, by the grace of God, he had seen and reprehended the injustice of his companion in crime, and could not bear to hear him pouring forth reproaches on One whom he knew to be innocent ; and had acknowledged himself deserving of the punishment which he suffered. Therefore God showed him mercy.

CHAPTER XXV.

For Holy Thursday.

Of offering the merits of Jesus Christ to obtain pardon for the sins of the Church— Of His love in the adorable Sacrament of the Altar.

On Holy Thursday, as the Lamentations were chanted at Matins, St. Gertrude wept before God the Father, in the bitterness of her heart, for all the sins which men had committed against the Divine Omnipotence. At the second Lamentation, she wept before God the Son for the sins which they had committed, through ignorance, against His ineffable wisdom. At the third Lamentation, she wept before the Holy Ghost for the sins committed, through malice, against His goodness. Then, at the verse *Jesu Christe*, when the *Kyrie eleison* was chanted, she approached the most sweet Heart of Jesus, and embracing it very devoutly on the part of the Church, she obtained the remission of all the sins which had been committed by thoughts, desires, or perverse will. At the *Christe eleison*, she embraced the blessed Mouth of our Lord, and asked pardon for all the sins of the tongue. Then, at the *Kyrie eleison*, she kissed our Lord's Hands, and obtained pardon of all the Church's sins of act. Lastly, when the people chanted the *Kyrie eleison* five times, after the hymn *Rex Christe*,* she kissed the Five Wounds of our Lord, to obtain pardon for all the sins of the five senses. While she did this she beheld five streams of grace gushing forth impetuously from the Five Wounds, and pouring themselves out over the whole Church, purifying it from all stains and impurities ; thus she knew that she had received the full fruit of what she had done at the Lamentations and at the *Kyrie eleison.*

This practice may be followed during the three last nights of Holy Week, with a perfect confidence of obtaining the same advantage thereby.

As the words, *Oblatus est quia voluit*,† were chanted at Lauds, our Lord said to St. Gertrude : " If you believe that I was offered on the cross to God My Father only because I willed it Myself, believe also that I now desire to offer

---

* The hymn *Rex Christe*, composed by St. Gregory, and the *Kyrie eleison*, were sung formerly at Tenebræ, after the Benedictus. **Gerbert**, p. ii. p. 232.

† " He was offered up because He Himself desired it ; and He Himself carried our sins." Ant. at Lauds for Maunday Thursday.

Myself for each sinner to God My Father, with the same love with which I offered Myself for all men in general. Therefore, there is no person, however sinful, who may not hope for pardon, by offering My Passion and Death to God My Father, provided that he believes firmly that he will obtain this grace, and that he is persuaded that the memory of My sufferings is the most powerful remedy against sin, when joined to a right faith and a true penance."

As St. Gertrude heard the words of the Gospel, *Cœpit lavare pedes discipulorum,** she said to our Lord : " O God ! since I do not merit that Thou shouldest wash me Thyself, how happy should I be if I might merit at least to be washed from my sins by one of Thy Apostles, that I might be more worthy to approach Thy precious Body and Blood." Our Lord replied : " I have washed away all your stains, and also those of all whom you have taught to ask for purification from seven worldly affections."   Then the Saint said: " Alas, Lord ! it is true that I have taught this to others, and have intended to do it myself ; but in teaching them, I have neglected it myself."   Our Lord replied : " I accept your good will for the act ; for My goodness is such, that when any one has the will to perform a good action, I count it as done, and recompense it as if it were accomplished, even if human frailty prevents its accomplishment."

Before communicating, she said to our Lord : " Behold, Lord, I offer Thee all the petitions of those who have been recommended to my unworthy prayers."   He replied : " You have enkindled as many flames in My Heart as there

---

* " He began to wash the feet of the disciples."   Gospel for Holy Thursday (St. John xiii. 1-15).

are persons for whom you pray." "Ah, Lord!" she said, "teach me how to enkindle this fire in Thy Divine Heart for every soul in the Church." "You will do this," He answered, "by practising four things : 1. By praising Me for all men whom I have created in My image and likeness. 2. By thanking Me for all the good which I have done for them, or which I may yet do for them. 3. By grieving for all the obstacles which they put to My grace. 4. By praying generally for all, that each may perfect himself in the state in which My providence has placed him, for his own good and for My honour and glory."

On another occasion, on the same solemnity, as Gertrude prayed with great recollection, our Lord appeared to her, even as He had appeared on earth on the same day. He seemed to pass this day in extreme anguish and bitterness, since all that He was about to suffer was continually present to Him ; for, being the tender Son of a tender mother,* He experienced beforehand the most lively and excessive suffering, anticipating death in all its terrors, and the inhuman cruelty and barbarity of His executioners.

As Gertrude felt this in spirit, she was so moved to compassion that she would have employed therein all the strength of her heart, had it been increased a thousand times ; but at last the violence of her love and her desire overpowered her, and she fainted away. Our Lord then said to her : "The same love which made Me suffer such extreme pains and affliction for the salvation of men, makes Me also suffer now in your heart, immortal and impassable as I am, by the intimate compassion with

---

* "Esset delicatæ virginis delicatissimus filius."

which it is penetrated for the salvation of My elect, in consideration of My afflictions and bitternesses.   Therefore,
in return for the compassion which you have had for My
sufferings, I give you the whole fruit of My Passion and
Death, to insure your eternal beatitude.   Further, your
heart shall have this honour, that whenever the Wood
of the Cross is adored, which was the instrument of My
sufferings, your soul shall feel the fruit and effects of
the compassion which is manifested to Me to-day; and
I will always grant you whatever you ask, and prosper
your wishes."   He added, " Whenever you desire to
obtain anything from Me, offer Me My Heart, which I
have so often given you as a token of our mutual friendship, in union with the love which made Me become
Man for the salvation of men; and I give you this
special mark of friendship, that this shall be presented to
whomsoever you pray for, as a rich man would present a
coffer to his friend to supply himself therefrom with all he
needed."   " I beseech Thee, O Lord," continued the Saint,
" to tell me what words Thou didst address to Thy Father
in Thine agony."   Our Lord replied : " The words I used
most frequently were these : 'O Entirety of My Substance !' " *

At Mass, whilst the secret prayers were being said,
before the religious had received Communion, the Lord
Jesus appeared to her in a state of extreme weakness, as if
He were about to give up the ghost; and this so touched her,
that she also felt as if about to expire.   She continued in
this state until the time for Communion, when she beheld
a marvellous vision ; for she saw the priest elevate a

* " O integritas substantiæ meæ ; " see 1 Thess. v. 23 : " That
your whole (integer) spirit," &c.

Body which was far larger than his own ; and by the virtue and power of his word, he bore Him who bears all things.

The Saint then understood that the strange feebleness which the Son of God appeared to suffer, indicated the excessive love with which He desired that we, who are as His Benjamins, His beloved ones, should be united to Him in holy communion ; that the ardour with which He desired this delight caused this weakness ; that He was reduced to this state by the violence of His love, so that He might be more easily touched and carried by the hands of the priest. She learned also on another occasion, that every time we look on the Host, which contains the body of Christ, with desire and love, we increase our eternal merit; and that our enjoyment in the other life will correspond with that which we have had in devoutly regarding this precious Body on earth.

CHAPTER XXVI.

For Good Friday.

The Saint is favoured with a rapture — Exercises on the Passion of our Lord.

THE memory of our Lord's Passion was so profoundly engraven on the soul of the Saint, that it became as honey to her lips, as music to her ears, and as a transport of joy to her heart. One Good Friday, as she heard the summons *

---

* *Sonitum tabulæ.* As the use of bells is forbidden from the *Gloria in excelsis* on Holy Thursday until the *Gloria in excelsis* on Holy Saturday, religious are summoned now, as then, to the Office and other conventual exercises by *sonitum tabulæ*, the sound of wooden clappers or pieces of wood struck on each other. Compline is the hour at which our Lord's burial is specially commemorated.

to Compline, she felt the same anguish in her heart as if she had been told that her dearest friend was even then about to expire, and she recollected herself to think yet more lovingly of the Passion of her Beloved. Her union with God became so intimate, that on this day and the following she was scarcely able to attend to anything exterior or sensible, unless obliged to do so by charity, of which she always made great account, and this that she might the more surely entertain Him within her who is love; for St. John said "God is charity. If we love one another, God abideth in us, and His charity is perfected in us" (1 John iv.)

She continued in this rapture the remainder of the day, and during the whole of the following day (Holy Saturday). What she experienced therein was such, that no human intellect could explain it; for she was so perfectly united to and absorbed in God, by the tenderness of her compassion, that she was entirely dissolved therein; and this was no imperfection, but rather the very height of perfection, as St. Bernard teaches when writing of the words of the Canticles : "We will make thee chains of gold : (Cant. i. 10). "When the soul is wrapt in contemplation, and a flash of heavenly light comes to illuminate it, the Divine infusion accommodates itself to sensible things, either to temper its brilliancy or to instruct in its doctrine, and thus shadows* the purity and splendour of its rays, to enable the soul to receive it, and to communicate it to others. I believe† that these images are produced in us by the holy angels. Therefore, let us attribute to God what is perfectly free from corporal images, and to the angels those which are more sensible."

We must not, therefore, consider that what God Him-

---

* " Adumbratus." † " Æstimo."

self infuses into the soul in secret is of less value. Nevertheless, we have passed over many things for this reason,
which might have been related here, and which are indeed
worthy of being recorded. Still, we have gathered up
some of the sparks of Divine love which flew forth from
the burning furnace of the Passion of Christ upon this
soul. On one Good Friday, at the hour of Prime, as the
Saint returned thanks to God for having appeared before a
Gentile and an idolator as His Judge, she beheld our Lord
enthroned in great majesty with God His Father, while
all the Saints prostrated before Him, thanking Him profoundly for having freed them from eternal death by His
own Death.

As the Passion was read, at the word *Sitio* (" I thirst"),
our Lord appeared to offer her a golden cup to receive the
tears of compassion which she had shed for His death.
And as the Saint felt her whole soul melting into tears,
and yet discretion obliged her to keep them back, she
asked our Lord what would be most pleasing to Him.
Then it appeared to her that a pure rivulet sprang from
her heart, and proceeded to our Lord's lips, and He said :
" These are the tears of devotion which you have restrained
from a pure intention."

At Terce, as she remembered our Lord's crowning
with thorns, His cruel scourging at the pillar, His weariness, and the agony of His shoulder, wounded by carrying the cross, she said to Him : " Behold, my sweetest
Love, I offer Thee my heart, desiring to suffer therein
all the bitterness and anguish of Thy dear Heart, in
return for Thy love in bearing the undeserved torments
of Thy Passion ; and I beseech Thee, whenever I forget
this offering through human frailty, to send me some sharp
bodily pain which may resemble Thine." He replied :

"Your desires are sufficient. But if you wish Me to have unbounded pleasure in your heart, let Me act as I please therein, and do not desire that I should give you either consolation or suffering."

Then, as the Passion was read, which says that Joseph took the Body of Jesus,* she said to our Lord : " That blessed Joseph was given Thy most holy Body ; but what share wilt Thou give of Thy Body to my unworthiness ? " Then our Lord gave her His Heart under the form of a golden thurible, from which as many perfumes ascended to the Father as there had been persons for whom the Lord died.

When the prayers were said after the Passion for the different Orders in the Church, according to the usual custom, as the priest knelt, saying *Oremus, delectissimi*, she saw all the prayers which had been made throughout the Church ascending together like fragrant incense from the thurible of the Divine Heart, so that each prayer by this union became marvellously sweet and beautiful.

Therefore we should pray for the Church on this day with great devotion, in union with the Passion of our Lord, which renders our prayers more efficacious before God.

On another occasion, on the same day, the Saint, ardently desiring to make some return to her Beloved for all His sufferings, said to Him : " O my only Hope, and Salvation of my soul ! teach me how to make some return to Thee for Thy most bitter Passion." Our Lord replied : " He who follows the will of another, and not his own, frees Me from the captivity which I endured when bound with chains on the morning of My Passion ; he who considers himself

---

* The Passion of our Lord according to St. John, which is read on Good Friday.

guilty, satisfies for my condemnation, at the hour of Prime, by false witnesses; he who renounces the pleasures of sense, consoles Me for the blows which I received at the hour of Terce; he who submits to pastors who try him,* consoles Me for the crowning with thorns; he who humbles himself first in a dispute, carries My cross; he who performs works of charity, consoles Me at the hour of Sext, when My limbs were cruelly fastened to the cross; he who spares himself neither pain nor labour to withdraw his neighbour from sin, consoles Me for My Death, which I endured at the hour of None for the salvation of the human race; he who replies gently when reproached, takes Me down from the cross; lastly, he who prefers his neighbour to himself, lays Me in the sepulchre."

On another Good Friday, as Gertrude besought our Lord to prepare her for a worthy Communion,† she received this reply: " I am hastening to you with such ardour that I can scarcely contain it; for I have gathered into My bosom all the good which My Church has done or said or thought to-day in memory of My Passion, to pour it forth into your soul at Communion for your eternal salvation." The Saint replied: " I give Thee thanks, O my Lord; but I desire greatly that this favour may be granted to me in such a manner that I may

---

* " Discolis."

† Formerly the faithful were admitted to Communion on this day. See Dom Gueranger's *Année Liturgique*, " Temps de la Passion," p. 549—a most valuable work, which is too little known in this country. See also Dom Martine, *De Ant. Ec. Ritibus*, tom. iii. The custom was gradually abolished, so that no exact time can be specified for the change. The Greeks celebrate Mass of the Presanctified every day during Lent, except Saturdays, Sundays, and the Feast of the Annunciation. The Milanese, or Ambrosian rite, prescribes the Mass of the Presanctified on the Fridays in Lent.

impart it to others when I wish to do so." He replied:
" And what will you give Me, My beloved, for such a
favour ? " Gertrude replied : " Alas, Lord ! I have nothing
worthy of Thee ; but, nevertheless, I have this desire,
that if I had all that Thou hast, I would give it to Thee,
so that Thou mightest dispose of it as Thou wouldest."
To this our Lord replied lovingly : " If you do indeed
desire to act thus towards Me, you cannot doubt that I
desire to act thus towards you ; and even more so, since
My goodness and love so far exceeds yours." " O God,"
she exclaimed, " how shall I come to Thee, when Thou
comest to me with such abundant goodness ? " He replied :
" I require nothing from you but to come to Me empty,
that I may fill you ; for it is from Me that you receive all
which makes you agreeable in My sight."

She understood tnat this emptiness was humility, which
made her consider herself destitute of merit, and made her
believe that without the grace of God she could do nothing,
and that what she did do was utterly worthless.

CHAPTER XXVII.

For Easter Sunday.

How the souls are freed from their pains—Of a good-will—How
to praise God in the Alleluia.

As St. Gertrude prayed fervently before Matins on the
blessed night of the Resurrection, the Lord Jesus appeared
to her, full of majesty and glory.   Then she cast herself at
His feet, to adore Him devoutly and humbly, saying : " O
glorious Spouse, joy of the angels, Thou who hast shown
me the favour of choosing me to be Thy Spouse, who am
the least of Thy creatures ! I ardently desire Thy glory,

and my only friends are those who love Thee ; therefore I beseech Thee to pardon the souls of Thy special friends * by the virtue of Thy most glorious Resurrection. And to obtain this grace from Thy goodness, I offer Thee, in union with Thy Passion, all the sufferings which my continual infirmities have caused me." Then our Lord, having favoured her with many caresses, showed her a great multitude of souls who were freed from their pains, saying : " Behold, I have given them to you as a recompense for your rare affection ; and through all eternity they will acknowledge that they have been delivered through your prayers, and you will be honoured and glorified for it." She replied : " How many are they ? " He answered : " This knowledge belongs to God alone." As she feared that these souls, though freed from their pains, were not yet admitted to glory, she offered to endure whatever God might please, either in body or soul, to obtain their entrance into that beatitude ; and our Lord, won by her fervour, granted her request immediately.

Some time after, as the Saint suffered most acute pain in her side, she made an inclination before a crucifix ; and our Lord freed her from the pain, and granted the merit of it to these souls, recommending them to make her a return by their prayers.

After this, the Saint, impelled by the fervour of her love, presented herself before her Spouse, and said to Him : " O my only Love ! as I have nothing which can render me worthy to appear before the King of kings, and as I cannot correspond in any degree to Thy love, all I can do is to give Thee all the life and strength of my body and soul as long as I live, to honour Thy glorious Resurrection." Our Lord replied : " I regard this offering of

---

* This seems to refer to the souls in purgatory.

your love for Me as a royal sceptre, which I will bear gloriously before the Most Holy Trinity, and in the sight of
all the saints." To this Gertrude answered : " Although
Thy grace has prompted me to make this offering, nevertheless I fear, on account of my own instability, lest I
should forget what I have promised Thee." But our
Lord replied : " And what will it matter if you do ? for I
will not allow what you have once given Me to escape from
My hand ; but I will always preserve it, as a proof of your
love for Me ; and whenever you renew your intention, this
sceptre will be adorned with flowers and precious stones."

When the *Alleluia* was chanted at the Invitatory, the
Saint animated all the powers of her body and soul to
recite the Matins of the Resurrection with devotion, saying to our Lord : " Teach me, I beseech Thee, O Master
full of sweetness, in what manner I can best praise Thee by
the ALLELUIA which is so often repeated on this Feast."
Our Lord replied : " You can praise Me by the *Alleluia*, by
uniting it to the praises which the saints and angels constantly offer Me in heaven. You will observe that all the
vowels, except the *o*, which signifies grief, are found in this
word ; and that instead of this *o*, the *a* is repeated twice.
At the first *a*, you will praise Me with the saints for the
glorious immortality by which the sufferings of My Humanity and the bitterness of My Passion were rewarded ;
at the *e*, praise Me for the sweet and ineffable joys which
gladden My eyes in gazing upon the Most Holy Trinity ;
at the *u*, unite yourself with the delight which I find in
hearing the concerts of praises in honour of the Blessed
Trinity which are sung by the saints and angels ; at the *i*,
enjoy the sweet perfumes and odours which I find in the
presence of the Most Holy Trinity ; at the second *a*, which
is put in place of the *o*, rejoice that My Humanity, which

was formerly passible and mortal, is now filled with the Divine immortality."

After this, as she continued to recite Matins, she was taught at each Psalm, each Response, and each Lesson, the sense which best corresponded with the solemnity of so great a day, and which best expressed the inconceivable pleasures which a soul enjoys when it is united to God.

CHAPTER XXVIII.

For Easter Monday.

That God takes an exact account of our merits ; and how they are enriched by the merits of Christ.

On Easter Monday, as St. Gertrude besought our Lord before communicating that He would be pleased to supply, by the merits of this august Sacrament, for her past negligences in religious observance, He presented her to His Father clothed in a religious habit, which appeared to be made of as many pieces as she had been years in the convent—the first piece representing the first year, the second the next year, and so on. The habit had no folds in it. The days and hours were noted in each year, with the thoughts, words, and actions, good or bad, even to the most trifling particulars ; and the end for which she had performed each action was also most carefully marked, whether for her own salvation, for the glory of God, or for the good of others. Her abstinences and her refreshments ; what she had done through obedience or of her own free will ; the little stratagems she had used that she might be told to do what she wished, or her address in extorting such obediences ;—all these were to be seen therein : these last actions appeared to be fastened to her habit by a little wet mud, and as if ready to fall from it. But when the Son of God had offered His holy and perfect life for her, she saw the habit covered with plates of transparent gold, pure and clear as crystal.

Her whole life, and all that had ever been defective in her conduct, even to the very least particular, now appeared in the light of truth, and was known to God and all His saints ; for not even the smallest stain or imperfection could be concealed. From this Gertrude understood that God forms, as it were, a representation of each person's life ; and that, while He remembers no more the sins which have been effaced by penance, according to the word of the Prophet, " I will not remember all his iniquities " (Ez. xviii. 22), there still remain some marks of our faults, that we may be reminded to praise His goodness for having pardoned them, and for having poured forth His favours upon us as if we had never offended Him ; so also the good works which we have done shine like beautiful flowers, that we may give glory to Him by whose help and assistance we have accomplished them, and that they may be a continual source of joy to us, that we may adore and love God, who, being One in Three Persons, lives, reigns, and works in us all the good we do.

CHAPTER XXIX.

For Easter Tuesday.

Of the renewal of spiritual espousals.

AT Communion on Easter Tuesday, St. Gertrude asked our Lord to renew the espousals which He had formed with her in spirit by faith, by religious profession, and by the entirety of her virginity.   Our Lord replied caressingly, that He would not fail to do what she asked : and inclining towards her, He embraced her soul, renewing therein all her devotion.   And as He thus embraced her, He gave her a brilliant necklace, adorned with precious stones, and thus reformed all her past negligences in her spiritual exercises.

CHAPTER XXX.

For Easter Wednesday.

That we can do nothing good without the Divine assistance.

ON Easter Wednesday, she besought our Lord that she might become fruitful in good actions, by virtue of His adorable Body.   He replied : " I will certainly make you fruitful in Myself, and I will use you to draw many to Me."   She replied : " How canst Thou draw others to Thee through me, since I am such an unworthy creature, and have almost lost the talent I once had of instructing and conversing with others ? "   Our Lord answered : " If you now had that facility of speaking, perhaps you would think that it was by this you won souls.   Therefore I have deprived you of it in part, that you may acknowledge that the grace which you possess of touching the hearts of others comes from My special grace, and not from the power and attractiveness of your words."

Our Lord then appeared to draw her towards Him inwardly, saying : " Even as I draw My breath, so will I draw to Myself all who submit lovingly and devoutly to you for My sake, and I will make them advance daily in perfection."

CHAPTER XXXI.

For Thursday in Easter Week.

Of offering our actions to God.

ON Thursday in Easter week, as the Gospel was read which relates how Magdalen " stooped down and looked into the sepulchre, and saw two angels," * St. Gertrude said to our Lord : " Into what sepulchre shall I look to find the consolation of my spirit ? " Our Lord then showed her the sacred Wound of His Side, where, instead of two angels, she heard two things : first, " You shall never be separated from My company ; " and secondly, " All your actions are perfectly agreeable to Me." † She was much surprised at this, and began to consider how it could be, since she thought her actions could not be pleasing to any one, and saw in them herself such great imperfections ; while the Divine light enabled her to discover a thousand faults where others could not see any ; but our Lord said to her : " The good and praiseworthy custom which you have of recommending your actions to Me so frequently, and of placing them in My hands, makes Me correct those which are defective, that they may please Me perfectly and all My celestial court."

* St. John xx. 11–18.
† " Omnia opera tua mihi perfectissimo modo placent."

CHAPTER XXXII.

For Low Sunday.

How we should dispose ourselves to receive the Holy Ghost.

ON the Sunday after Easter, as the Gospel was read * which says that our Lord breathed on His disciples, and gave them the Holy Ghost, St. Gertrude besought Him very earnestly that He would give her this grace also. "If you desire to receive the Holy Ghost," He replied, "you must touch My Side and My Hands, like My disciples." By this she understood that he who desires to receive the Holy Spirit must first touch the Side of our Lord—that is, he must acknowledge how much the Divine Heart has loved us in having predestinated us from eternity to be His children and heirs of His kingdom, and in pouring forth such benefits upon us daily, notwithstanding our ingratitude; that he must also touch the Hands of our Lord—that is, reflect with gratitude on all His labours for us during the three-and-thirty years of His mortal life, and on His Passion and Death, offering His Heart to God, in union with the love with which He said, " As the Father hath sent Me, I also send you " (St. John xx. 21), to fulfil His good pleasure in all things; for although men should desire and wish nothing but the good pleasure of God, they should seek even more ardently to do and to suffer what He wills—for he who acts thus cannot fail to receive the Holy Spirit, even as the disciples on whom the Son of God breathed. Our Lord then breathed on St. Gertrude, and said to her: "Receive the Holy Ghost. Whosoever sins

* St. John xx. 19-31.

you remit, shall be remitted." "How can this be, O Lord," inquired the Saint, "since the power of binding and loosing has only been conferred on Thy priests?" He replied : "Those whom you consider guilty, are so before Me ; and those whom you consider innocent, I also acquit, for I speak by your mouth." "O God, full of goodness!" replied the Saint, "since you have so often assured me of this gift, what advantage do I gain from receiving it again?" Our Lord replied : "When a deacon is made a priest, he does not cease to be a deacon, but rather he acquires a higher sacerdotal dignity ; and so when I give the same gift to your soul several times, I establish it more firmly therein, and thereby increase your beatitude."

CHAPTER XXXIII.

For the Feast of St. Mark, Evangelist.

Of the Litanies, and invocation of saints.

ON the Feast of St. Mark,* while the Litanies were recited at the procession, our Lord appeared to St. Gertrude, seated on a throne of majesty, adorned with precious stones, which formed as many brilliant mirrors † as there were saints in heaven. Each saint rose joyfully as he was named in the Litany to offer his prayers to God for those who had

---

* April 25. The origin of the custom of reciting the Litany of the Saints, or Great Litany, on this day is ascribed to St. Gregory the Great, who obtained thereby the extinction of a pestilence which devastated Rome in the year 590. The 25th of April was fixed for a yearly procession and chanting of Litanies before it was appointed for the Feast of St. Mark.

† "Speculorum lucidorum."

invoked him ; and the names of those who prayed to them appeared written on their hands : the names of those who had invoked them with fervour and purity were written in letters of gold ; the names of those who prayed only through custom were in black ; while the names of those who were careless and indifferent could scarcely be discerned at all.

St. Gertrude understood from this, that when the saints whom we have invoked pray for us, their prayers shine before God as a monument of the mercy which He has promised us, which obliges Him to have pity on us ; and when we invoke the saints with a pure and fervent devotion, they receive the brilliancy of the precious stones enchased in our Lord's robe, which are inscribed with the names of those who revere them and invoke their aid.

CHAPTER XXXIV.

For the Feast of St. John before the Latin Gate.

Of the sweet memory of St. John—How imperfections of which we forget to accuse ourselves in confession are pardoned by God.

On the Feast * of St. John *ante Portam Latinam,* he appeared to Gertrude ; and after having caressed and consoled her in a wonderful manner, he said to her : " Do not be troubled, O elect spouse of My Lord, at the failure of your bodily strength ; for what you suffer in this world is but little, and will last only for a moment, in comparison with the eternal delights which we now enjoy in heaven, and

---

* May 6.   The Feast is kept in commemoration of the miraculous deliverance of St. John from a caldron of boiling oil.

which you will soon possess with us when you enter therein ; for it is the nuptial couch of your Spouse, whom you love so ardently, whom you desire with such fervour, and whom you will at last possess as you desire." Then he added : " Remember that I, who was the beloved disciple of the Lord, was still more infirm in body than you are ; * and nevertheless I am now, as you see, the delight and devotion of the faithful ; so you also, after your death, will live in the hearts of many, and will draw many souls to God." Then she said complainingly to St. John, that she feared she had placed an obstacle to this, because she had forgotten to confess some little faults ; and when she remembered them, she could not have recourse to her confessor ; and that she could not always remember them when she went to confession, on account of her extreme debility. "Do not be troubled at this, my child," replied the Saint lovingly ; "for when you have prepared for a good and entire confession of your sins, and find that you cannot then have recourse to a confessor, if you forget anything in consequence of the delay, and omit to accuse yourself of it merely from a defect of memory, what you have forgotten will not fail to be effaced ; and the grief you have for the omission will adorn your soul as a precious jewel, which will render it pleasing to the heavenly court."

While Mass was being said, the Saint was occupied in reflecting on some writings which she had received from God by a special favour ; and as she heard the words, *Verbum Dei Deo natum*, at the Sequence, she recollected herself, that she might attend more devoutly to what was chanted in honour of St. John. But the Saint appeared

---

* " Multo plus defeceram viribus, et sensibus corporalibus quam tu."

at her side, and told her not to turn her mind from her first thoughts; obtaining for her from God, in a marvellous manner, the favour of being able to think of these writings and still to understand what was chanted in choir. At the words, *Audit in gyro sedis,* she said to St. John: "Oh, what joy must have filled thy soul when thou wert elevated so high!" He replied: "You speak truly; but know that I have a yet greater joy in the praises which you offer to God for me." He then remained seated near her until the words, *Iste custos Virginis,* when he took her up to the throne of God's glory, where, amid the most ineffable brightness, he was admired and praised by the whole celestial court, feeling the ineffable delights of the words, *Cœli qui palatium.* *

CHAPTER XXXV.

For the Ascension.

The manner of saluting our Lord's Five Wounds.

BEFORE the Feast of the Ascension of our Lord, St. Gertrude repeated this salutation five thousand four hundred and sixty-six times: "Glory be to Thee, most sweet, most gentle, most benign, most noble, most excellent, effulgent, and ever-peaceful Trinity, for the roseate wounds of my only Love!" As she repeated this salutation, our Lord Jesus appeared to her, more beautiful than the angels, bearing golden flowers on each Wound, and saluted her thus, with a serene countenance and the tenderest charity: "Behold in what glory I now appear to you. I will appear

---

* We have not been able to verify this sequence.

in the same manner to you at your death, and will cover all the stains of your sins, and of those also who salute **My** Wounds with the same devotion."

CHAPTER XXXVI.

For the Sunday before Ascension Thursday.

Of the merit of condescension and compassion for the infirm—And how we should desire contempt.

ON the Sunday before Ascension-day, the Saint rose very joyfully to recite Matins, hoping that our Lord would come to lodge in her heart for the four days preceding the Ascension, as she ardently besought Him to do; but after she had recited the Office as far as the fifth Lesson, she saw a religious who was ill, and who had no one to say Matins with her. The Saint, moved by the charity which always animated her, said to our Lord: "Thou knowest, O Lord, that I have almost exhausted the little strength I have in reciting my Office so far; nevertheless, as I ardently desire Thee to abide with me during these holy days, and as I have not a fitting abode prepared for Thee, I am willing, for Thy love, and in satisfaction for my faults, to commence Matins again." As she began the Office once more, our Lord verified the words He had said—"I was sick, and you visited Me;" and, "As you did it to one of these My least brethren, you did it to Me"*—by appearing to her, and overwhelming her with caresses, which could neither be explained nor understood.

It appeared to the Saint that our Lord was seated at a

---

* Matt. xxv. 40.

table in the most sublime glory, and that He was distributing ineffable gifts, graces, and joys to the souls in heaven,
on earth, and in purgatory—not only for each word, but
even for each letter which she had repeated; and she also
received an intelligence of the Psalms, Responses, and
Lessons, which filled her with inexpressible delight.

When the words, *Ad te, Domine, clamabo,* and *Salvum
fac populum tuum, Domine, et benedic hæreditati tuæ,* were
chanted, she besought our Lord to pour forth an abundant
grace and benediction on the whole Church. "What do
you desire that I should do, My beloved ?" He replied; "for
I give Myself up to you with the same love and resignation
as I abandoned Myself to My Father on the cross; for
even as I would not descend from the cross until He willed
it, so now I desire to do nothing but what you will. Distribute, then, in virtue of My Divinity, all that you desire,
and as abundantly as you desire."

After Matins, the Saint retired again to rest, and our
Lord said to her : " She who wearies herself in exercises
of charity has a right to repose peacefully on the couch
of charity ; " and as He said this, He soothed her soul so
tenderly, that it appeared to her as if she did indeed repose
on the bosom of this heavenly Bridegroom. Then she beheld a tree of charity, very high and very fair, covered with
fruit and flowers, and with leaves shining like stars, which
sprang forth from the Heart of Jesus, extending and lower-
ing its branches so as to surround and cover the nuptial
couch on which the soul of Gertrude reposed. And she
saw a spring of pure water gush forth from its roots, which
shot upwards, and then returned again to its source ; and
this refreshed her soul marvellously. By this she understood the Divinity of Jesus Christ sweetly reposing in His
Humanity, which imparts ineffable joys to the elect.

During Mass, at which she was to communicate, St Gertrude exposed the defects of her soul to God, as a friend might do to one from whom he expected every good ; and she besought Him earnestly to obtain pardon of all her sins and negligences, on the Feast of His Ascension, from His Father.   Then the Lord replied, with the greatest condescension : "You are that amiable Esther who pleases My eyes by your incredible beauty ; ask, then, what you will, and I will give it to you."

As she began to pray for all who were confided to her care, and for all her benefactors, our Lord approached her, and embraced her lovingly.   And by this embrace she understood that her heart had contracted some stain from having received a benefit in too human a manner on the preceding day.   "Ah, Lord !" she exclaimed, " why dost Thou suffer me to be revered as a saint, when Thou wert esteemed during Thy life as the very least of men, and since it is for Thy glory that Thy elect should be despised in this world ?"   He replied : " I have said by My Prophet, 'Shout with joy to God, all the earth, and give glory to His praise' (Ps. lxv. 1) ; therefore, I permit some persons to think well of you and to love you, for their sanctification and for My glory."   " But what will become of me," she replied, " if Thou dost sanctify them by my faults ?"   Our Lord answered : " I please myself by embellishing the gold of My grace which I have put in you, by making it appear sometimes black and sometimes shining."   By the word 'black' * she understood, that when one remembers having received a benefit in too human a manner, and repents humbly for their fault, they pleased God so much, that the dark colour enhances the beauty of the

---

* " Fusco."

shining gold. By the bright gold she understood, that when we receive benefits from God and men with thanksgiving, we render our souls still more capable of receiving and preserving the gifts of God.

CHAPTER XXXVII.

For the Rogation Days.

How we should pray for the just, for sinners, and for the souls in purgatory.

ON the Monday before the Ascension, St. Gertrude proposed to herself to do something to atone to God for the sins of the whole world; she then went to visit the sick person before mentioned, and having performed for her many services of charity which exceeded her strength, she offered them to God as an eternal thanksgiving and in satisfaction for all that His creatures had done, contrary to His will. When she had accomplished this, it appeared to her that a vast multitude of men and women were attached to her by a golden chain (which indicated charity), and that she led them to our Lord. He received them from her as a king would receive a prince who brought his enemies to his feet to swear obedience and inviolable fidelity to him.

On Tuesday, as she prayed before Mass for the perfection and sanctification of the just, in whatever manner might be most pleasing to her Spouse, our Lord extended His Hand, and blessed them with the victorious sign of the Cross; and this saving benediction descended into their hearts like dew, which made them flourish, strengthened them, and imparted new beauty to them.

On Wednesday, at the elevation of the Host, she besought our Lord for the souls of the faithful in purgatory, that He would free them from their pains by virtue of His admirable Ascension ; and she beheld our Lord descending into purgatory with a golden rod in His Hand, which had as many hooks * as there had been prayers for their souls ; by these He appeared to draw them into a place of repose. She understood by this, that whenever any one prays generally, from a motive of charity, for the souls in purgatory, the greater part of those who, during their lives, have exercised themselves in works of charity, are released.

Then the Saint repeated these words two hundred and twenty-five times, to salute our Lord's sacred Limbs : *" Ave, Jesu, Sponse floride, in jubilo quo ascendisti saluto et collaudo te ; "* † and it appeared to her that each salutation was presented to our Lord as an instrument of music which sounded most melodiously and in a manner most pleasing to Him, so that He testified how acceptable it was to Him. Those salutations which she had offered with the purest intention emitted the most sublime harmony ; while those she had recited less attentively, sounded mournfully, and were not so harmonious.

CHAPTER XXXVIII.

For Ascension-Day.

Of the renunciation of our own will—And certain exercises of piety for this Festival.

On the Feast of the Ascension, as the Saint prepared herself in the morning to offer the tenderest love and devotion

---

* "Uncus." This word is sometimes used poetically, by classical authors, for an anchor.

† " Hail, Jesus, beautiful Spouse ! I salute and praise Thee in Thy ascension joys."

to our Lord, at the hour of His Ascension, He said to her :
" Give Me now all the testimonies of joy which you are prepared to give Me at the hour of My Ascension ; for all the
joy which I then experienced will be renewed in Me, as I
am about to enter into you by the august and holy Sacrament of the Altar." " Ah, my only Love !" exclaimed the
Saint ; " teach me how to perform our usual procession
well, that I may fittingly honour the admirable procession
which Thou didst make when conducting Thy disciples to
Bethania." Our Lord replied : " As Bethania signifies the
' house of obedience,' you cannot make a better procession,
or one more pleasing to Me, than to offer Me the entirety
of your will, when you conduct Me within you, grieving
sincerely for having followed your own will on so many
occasions in preference to Mine, and determining firmly for
the future to perform My will perfectly in all things."

As she received Communion, our Lord said to her :
" Behold, I come to you, My Spouse, not to bid you farewell, but to take you with Me and present you to God My
Father." She understood by this, that when our Lord
enters into a soul by the holy Sacrament of His Body and
Blood, He attracts the desires and good-will of this soul
to Himself, as a seal makes an impression upon wax ; and
that He presents the representation of them thus formed
to His Father, to obtain from Him the graces which this
soul needs. The Saint then offered Him her prayers, and
those of some other persons, to serve as an ornament to His
sacred Wounds, for the day of His glorious Ascension.
Then the Lord Jesus appeared before His Father, adorned
with these prayers, as with so many precious stones ; and
His Father appeared to draw all these offerings of the
elect to Himself, by His almighty power, and then to
cause them to fall in rays of glory on the throne pre

pared from all eternity for those who had offered these prayers.

At the hour of None, as Gertrude was entirely absorbed in God, the Lord Jesus appeared to her again, more beautiful than the children of men, and clothed in a green tunic and a crimson mantle. The green tunic indicated the glorious and vivifying works of His adorable Humanity; the crimson mantle, the intense love which had compelled Him to endure such fearful sufferings, that His patience under these alone would have merited His glory. Our Lord then appeared to pass through the choir, accompanied by a multitude of angels, giving special testimonies of love to those who had communicated that day, and saying to them these sweet words: "I am with you unto the consummation of ages." * He also gave a golden ring to some in which a precious stone was set, saying: "I will not leave you orphans; I will come to you."

As the Saint was surprised at this, she inquired of our Lord if those to whom He had given the ring as a mark of special love would have more merit than others? Our Lord replied: "I have done this because, when they took their refection, they meditated on My goodness to My disciples, in eating and drinking with them before I ascended into heaven; and for each morsel that they took, saying, 'O most loving Jesus! may the virtue of Thy Divine love incorporate me entirely in Thee,' I have imparted a special brilliancy to the precious stones of their rings."

When the Antiphon *Elevatis manibus* † was chanted, our Lord rose up by His own Divine power, accompanied

---

* Matt. xxviii. 20.

† "He lifted up His hands and blessed them, and was taken up into heaven;" iii. Ant. at vespers.

by a troop of angels, who attended Him with the utmost vigilance and reverence, giving His benediction to the whole community, saying to them : " Peace I leave with you, My peace I give unto you." By which she understood that our Lord had poured forth His grace so effectually into the hearts of those who had celebrated this festival with singular devotion, that whatever trouble might happen to them, He would still leave some of His peace in their souls, even as sparks of fire are hidden under ashes.

CHAPTER XXXIX.

For the Sunday after Ascension.

How to prepare ourselves worthily to receive the Holy Ghost.

As the Feast of Pentecost was now approaching, St. Gertrude besought our Lord, at Communion on this day, to prepare her to receive these four virtues—purity of heart, humility, tranquillity, and concord. As she prayed for purity, she perceived that her heart was whiter than snow ; as she asked for humility, she saw our Lord prepare a cave in her soul to receive His graces ; when she asked for tranquillity, she saw Him surround her heart with a golden circle, to preserve it from the snares of her enemies ; then she said to Him : " Alas, my Lord ! I fear that I shall soon ruin this rampart of tranquillity : for as soon as I see anything which I know to be contrary to Thy will, I cannot conceal my resentment, and oppose it vehemently." To this our Lord replied : " This emotion will not disturb a holy tranquillity, but rather adorns it ; strengthening in you, as it were, so many barriers across which the burning love of the Holy Ghost breathes more efficaciously, and refreshes your soul more sweetly."

She then asked our Lord for the virtue of concord, and He crowned with this virtue all the other virtues which the Holy Spirit had imparted to her; but as she feared that if she suffered many contradictions on account of her zeal for regular observance, they would prove an occasion of losing this precious grace, the Lord replied: "The virtue of concord is not injured when men oppose injustice; and I Myself will restrain your zeal, so that you may be entirely conformed in all things to the operations of My Divine Spirit." Then she understood that whoever prays devoutly to God for the same virtues, in order to prepare a dwelling for the Holy Spirit, and tries to advance in them every day by practising them faithfully, will receive the same advantages.

CHAPTER XL.

For the Vigil and Feast of Pentecost.

Of the gifts of the Holy Ghost—And other exercises for this day.

As St. Gertrude prayed very devoutly, on the Vigil of Pentecost, that she might be prepared to receive the Holy Ghost, she heard our Lord saying these words to her interiorly with great love: "You will receive the virtue of the Holy Spirit, which is coming to you." But while she felt extreme joy and satisfaction at these words, she thought also of her utter unworthiness, and it appeared to her as if a cave was made in her heart, which became deeper and deeper as this sentiment of unworthiness increased in her soul. Then she saw a stream of honey coming forth from the Heart of Jesus, and distilling itself

into hers, until it was entirely filled.   By this she understood that it was the unction and grace of the Holy Ghost
which flowed thus sweetly from the Heart of the Son of
God into the hearts of the faithful.

Then the Son of God blessed this cave with His Divine
Hand, as the baptismal font * is blessed, so that each time
her soul entered therein it might be purified from every
stain.   As she rejoiced at this holy benediction, she said to
our Lord : " Alas, my Lord ! unworthy sinner that I am,
I confess with grief that, through my frailty, I have offended
in many ways against Thy Omnipotence, and that my
ignorance and malice have often offended against Thy
wisdom and goodness.   Therefore, O Father of Mercies,
have mercy on me, and give me strength from Thy
strength to resist all that is contrary to Thy will ; give me
grace from Thy inconceivable wisdom to avoid all that
may offend Thy pure Eyes, and enable me to adhere
faithfully to Thee by Thy superabundant mercy, so that
I may never depart from Thy will in the very least
degree."

As she said these words, she appeared to be plunged
into this cave to be regenerated therein, so that she came
forth purified from every stain, and whiter than snow ; and
being presented thus before the Divine Majesty, she put
herself under the protection of all the saints, as a newly
baptized person is placed in the care of their sponsors, that
they might pray to God for her.   Then all the saints offered
their merits to God very joyfully, in satisfaction for her
negligences and needs.   St. Gertrude, being thus adorned,
was placed by our Lord Himself before Him, so that His

---

* It will be remembered that the font is blessed on Whitsun-eve
as well as on Easter-eve.

Divine breath * entered into her soul, uniting her will efficaciously to His, and saying to her: "Such are the delights which I enjoy with the children of men;" for the respirations of her soul indicated her good-will, and the breath of our Lord His acceptance of her good intentions and desires. Thus Gertrude reposed sweetly in the arms of her Spouse, waiting until He should impart to her more perfect dispositions for the reception of the Holy Ghost.

As she offered some special prayers to obtain from God the gifts of the Holy Spirit, and first for the gift of fear, that it might keep her from evil, our Lord appeared to plant a very high tree in the centre of her heart, which extended its branches so as to cover it entirely. This tree had little spikes, from which grew very beautiful flowers. The spikes signified the gift of the fear of the Lord, which pricks the soul with compunction when it is inclined to evil; the flowers indicated the good-will which, joined to the fear of God, fortifies the soul against sin; and if man avoids evil and performs good actions, the tree produces fruit.

Then, as she asked for the other gifts, they were shown to her under the form of trees, differing in their fruits, according to the different virtues. A kind of dew distilled from the trees of knowledge and piety, from which she understood that those who apply themselves to these two virtues are watered by a gentle rain, which makes them flower and bear fruit. The trees of the gift of counsel and fortitude had little cords of gold, which signified that these gifts rendered the soul capable of compre-

---

* " Breathing thrice on the water, he proceeds," &c. ; see Blessing of the Font, in Missal.

hending spiritual things. Streams of delicious nectar flowed from the trees of wisdom and understanding; from which she learned that God pours Himself forth efficaciously on the soul by these gifts, and that it thus becomes satiated with the sweetness of His love.

That night, at Matins, as the Saint felt an extreme debility, which made her think that she could not live long, she said to our Lord : " What honour and what glory canst Thou gain from a miserable creature like me, who can only remain so short a time at the Office ? " Our Lord replied : " In order that sensible things may assist you to understand those which are spiritual, consider that a bridegroom finds the greatest pleasure in the most familiar intercourse with his bride ; and I assure you that no bride groom ever found more satisfaction in the endearments of his bride, than I do whenever My elect offer Me their hearts, purified from all sin, that I may take my delight therein." As she approached to receive Holy Communion, our Lord refreshed her heart by a Divine exhalation, which came forth from His sacred Limbs, and which gave her ineffable pleasure ; God making known to her that she had merited to receive the seven gifts of the Holy Spirit by her earnest prayers.

After she had communicated, she offered the whole life of Jesus Christ to God the Father, in satisfaction for her fault in never having made a sufficiently worthy preparation to receive Him into her heart, even from the hour of her regeneration in baptism. Then she saw the Holy Ghost in the form of a dove, descending from heaven upon the ador- able Sacrament, with an impetuous flight like that of an eagle ; and seeking the sweet Heart of Jesus, He appeared to enter therein, and find there a most agreeable abode.

As the hymn *Veni Creator* was chanted at Terce, our

Lord appeared to her, and opened His Heart, full of sweetness and tenderness, to her. Gertrude knelt before it, inclining so that her head rested in the centre of His Heart ; and her Spouse took her head and pressed it to Himself, uniting her will to His, and sanctifying it. At the second verse, *Qui, Paraclitus diciris,** she placed the hands of her soul,† that is, her actions, in the Heart of Jesus, and obtained consolations which so fortified her in her exercises of piety, that all which she performed henceforth could not fail to be most acceptable to God.

At the third verse, *Tu septiformis gratia* (*sic*), she placed the feet of her soul, that is, her desires, in the Sacred Heart, and thereby obtained their sanctification.

At the fourth verse, *Accende lumen sensibus,* she recommended her senses to God, and obtained this promise—that they should be so illuminated as to reflect their light upon the senses of others, who should be thereby excited to love God.

At the fifth verse, *Hostem repellas,* our Lord inclined towards her, and embraced her, to shield her against all the attacks of her enemies ; and in all this she experienced such satisfaction in her soul as to understand clearly what our Lord had said to her on the preceding day : " You shall receive the virtue of the Holy Ghost, which will come to you."

---

* So in Benedictine Breviary.   † " Manus animæ. "

CHAPTER XLI.

For Monday in Whitsun Week.

How the oblation of the Sacred Host supplies for our deficiencies—
Exercises for the *Agnus Dei.*

On Monday, at the Elevation, St Gertrude offered the
Sacred Host in satisfaction for her deficiencies in acquiring
spiritual goods, and even for extinguishing the light of the
Holy Spirit. It appeared to her that this Sacred Host
emitted a number of branches, which were collected by the
Holy Spirit and placed in the form of a hedge round the
throne of the Ever-Blessed Trinity. From this she understood that the excellence and dignity of this great Sacrament supplied fully for all her negligences. A voice also
came forth from the throne, which said : " Let her who has
given such rare flowers to her Spouse approach His Divine
and nuptial couch without fear." She understood by this
that God considered her perfect in habits of virtue, in consideration of the oblation which she had made to Him of
this Most Holy Sacrament.

At the first *Agnus Dei* she prayed for the whole Church,
as usual, beseeching God to govern it in all things as a true
Father. At the second *Agnus Dei* she prayed for the
faithful departed, that He might show mercy to them, and
release them from all their pains. At the third *Agnus Dei*
she asked for an increase of merit for all the saints and the
elect who should reign with Him in heaven. At the words
Dona nobis pacem our Lord inclined so lovingly towards her
that the sweetness of His embrace penetrated into the depth
of the hearts of all the saints, and they received thereby an
immense increase of grace and merit.

After this, as she approached the Holy Communion, the

saints rose up before her with honour and joy, and she saw that the light of their merits shone gloriously, even as a shield of gold shines when exposed to the rays of the sun ; and the reflection of this light shone into her soul.

St. Gertrude then remained in the presence of God, as if in expectation, because she had not yet obtained the grace of being united to Him. At last, after Communion, her soul was united to this Divine Spouse with such plenitude, that she enjoyed His presence in the most perfect manner possible in this world. Then the branches of which we have already spoken, with which the Holy Spirit had surrounded the throne of the Ever-Blessed Trinity, began to shoot forth green leaves and flowers, even as a plant flourishes after abundant rain, so that the ever-peaceful Trinity found ineffable pleasure therein, and all the saints experienced new delights.

CHAPTER XLII.

For the Tuesday in Whitsun Week.

How the Sacred Host supplies for all our negligences, and how the Holy Spirit unites Himself in Communion to holy souls.

On Tuesday in Whitsun week, St. Gertrude offered the Host to God, in satisfaction and reparation for her deficiency in gratitude for the favour which He had bestowed on her of uniting her more closely to Himself than others, and because she had not detached herself from everything else to attach herself entirely to Him. And as she did this with a perfect and full intention of suffering the penalty which she considered due to her negligence and weakness, our Lord—who is full of goodness, and who esteems a good

will even as an act *—appeared fully satisfied ; and the
Holy Spirit, concentrating all the virtues of this most
Holy Sacrament, entered with the Host into the soul of
Gertrude at the moment of Communion ; and God then
united Himself closely and inseparably to her.

CHAPTER XLIII.

For the Feast of the Blessed Trinity.

How we may glorify the Most Holy Trinity by our Lord Jesus
Christ—And what obstacles human affections place to our
advancement.

ON the Feast of the effulgent and ever-peaceful Trinity,
St. Gertrude recited this salutation : " Be Thou glorified,
O most mighty, most excellent, most noble, most sweet,
most benignant, ever-peaceful, and ineffable Trinity, who
art one God now and to endless ages ! " As she offered this
salutation to our Lord, He appeared to her in His Humanity, in which He is said to be less than His Father, and
stood in the presence of the adorable Trinity with all the
beauty and grace of a perfect man.   He had a most brilliant and beautiful flower on each part of His Body, to
which nothing material could be compared.   They indicated
by their brightness that, as our baseness and unworthiness
were utterly incapable of praising the adorable Trinity, our
Lord, by taking our nature, had so elevated it as to make
it worthy of being offered in sacrifice to this adorable
Trinity.

When Vespers commenced, our Lord offered His Heart
to the Blessed Trinity as a musical instrument, and by

---

* "Qui bonam voluntatem acceptat pro facto."

it every note and every word which was chanted in the Office on that day resounded most melodiously before God. But the chants of those who had little devotion emitted a low and unmelodious sound, like that which is heard on the large strings of a musical instrument. At the Antiphon *Osculetur me*, a voice came from the throne, singing: "Let My Divine Son, in whom is all My delight, approach Me, and give Me a sweet and loving embrace." Then the Son of God approached under His human form, embracing this incomprehensive Divinity, to which His Sacred Humanity alone has merited to be united so blessedly and so inseparably.

Then the Son of God said to His most pure Mother, in whose honour this Antiphon was chanted: "Do you also approach, My most dear Mother, and embrace Me." And at this embrace, the same flowers and the same beauty appeared on her as on our Lord, because it was from her He took human flesh. She learned also that whenever the Son is named on this most holy festival, the Father unites Himself in an ineffable manner with the Son, whose Humanity receives thereby a glory which reflects itself upon the Saints, giving them new knowledge of the incomprehensible Trinity.

In the morning, when the Antiphon *Te jure laudent* * was chanted at Lauds, St. Gertrude praised the Ever-Blessed Trinity with her whole soul, desiring to do the same at the moment of her death, if it were possible ; and it appeared to her that the effulgent and ever-peaceful Trinity inclined gently towards the Heart of Jesus, which resounded before

---

* This Antiphon is not in the present Office, but it may be found in an Office of the Blessed Trinity, v. Ant. at Lauds ; Res. et Ant. St. Gregorii.

it like a harp, and that three words therein were united to pay the homage which St. Gertrude had failed in rendering to the Blessed Trinity ; and these three words were —the omnipotence of the Father, the wisdom of the Son, and the love of the Holy Spirit. As she continued in sentiments of most fervent devotion all the morning, she began to consider whether it was her negligence which had prevented her from receiving as many lights as usual. But our Lord consoled her by these words : "Although My justice has deprived you of some lights and knowledge, on account of the human satisfaction which you have taken in chanting the Office, you may nevertheless be assured that the pains which you have chosen to endure in this service will not fail of their reward."

On another occasion also, and on the same high festival, St. Gertrude was vouchsafed the most sublime graces, particularly at the Church's offices, which are known to God alone.

CHAPTER XLIV.

For the Feast of St. John Baptist.

Apparition of the Saint—Effects of his intercession.

ON the Feast of St. John Baptist,* as the Saint assisted at Matins with all possible devotion, this Saint appeared to her, standing before the throne of God, in all the glory of his special prerogative of having baptized our Lord, and being the precursor of Christ. As the Saint considered him thus, she began to reflect why he was always represented as an aged man, and with a care-worn countenance. But

---

* June 24.

St. John informed her that this manner of representing him served to augment his glory, and that God had expressly permitted it, to teach men that the ardent desire which he had of serving Him would have led him to use every effort to combat the injustice and iniquity of men, and to attain to the highest perfection himself, even to old age ; and as he died in these sentiments, God had given him a very high reward for them.

As St. Gertrude inquired if his merits had been increased on account of his parents having been so perfect and holy, he replied : " Because I had holy parents, I was brought up to a greater love of justice, and therefore I was rendered more worthy of a place near the throne of God. But as for their rank and worldly advantages, I gained nothing by them except by despising them and by seeking to elevate my mind to heavenly knowledge ; so that I have gained a glory similar to that of a soldier, who, returning victorious from battle, rejoices all the more for having overcome more of the snares and surprises of his enemies than others."

During Mass, at which the religious communicated, St. John appeared to her again in crimson vestments, and his mantle was adorned with as many little golden lambs as there had been Communions received in his honour throughout the whole Church. Then she saw the Saint praying for all who had venerated him on that day ; and he specially sought to obtain for them the same grace which he had himself acquired—namely, his zeal and fidelity in the conversion of sinners.

CHAPTER XLV.

For the Feast of the Holy Apostles SS. Peter and Paul.

How we may feed Christ's sheep spiritually—Of the intercession **of** the Apostles---And the fruit of Holy Communion.

On the great Festival of the princes of the Apostles, **as the** second Response *Si diligis me,** was chanted at Matins, St. Gertrude asked our Lord what flock she should feed to testify her love for Him.   Our Lord replied : " Feed five lambs which are most dear to Me.   Feed your heart with Divine meditations, your lips with edifying words, **your** eyes with pious reading, your ears with charitable admonitions, and your hands with continual labour ; for **your** attachment and application to such things will be the greatest testimony of your affection which you can bestow on Me."

By these holy meditations she understood all thoughts for the glory of God, **for** the welfare of others, and for her own salvation ; the same was indicated by edifying discourses.   By pious reading, she understood all that could contribute to our salvation, as looking upon a crucifix, assisting the poor, giving good example.   By charitable admonitions, she understood receiving correction patiently. But as continual reading was inconsistent with manual labour, she understood that the desire of it was sufficient when the accomplishment was not possible.

At Mass, as she returned thanks for the special privileges bestowed on St. Peter, and particularly his having

---

* "If thou lovest Me, Simon Peter, feed My sheep.   Lord, Thou knowest that I love Thee, and that I would give my life for Thee ;" ii. Response, i. Nocturn.

heard these words from our Lord Himself, "Whatsoever thou shalt bind upon earth, it shall be bound also in heaven; and whatsoever thou shalt loose on earth, it shall be loosed also in heaven," * the Saint appeared to her, vested as a Pope,† and, extending his hands, he gave her his benediction, that it might work in her the same effects as it had worked in others, through the power which God had given him. As she approached the holy altar, and trembled for her unworthiness, St. Peter and St. Paul appeared to her, one on her right hand and the other on her left, as if to conduct her thither with great pomp; and when she had reached it, the Son of God received her Himself, saying to her : " I have brought you thither with the same arms with which I embrace you; but I have done this through the ministry of My Apostles, that your devotion might be fully satisfied."

Then, as she remembered she had not returned thanks for the graces bestowed on St. Paul, she besought our Lord to supply for her negligence. After Communion, as she prayed, she seemed to be seated, as a queen beside a king, on the same throne with our Divine Lord; before whom the Apostles knelt as soldiers receiving gifts from a prince; for her Communion had appeared to increase their merits. And as she was surprised at this, and thought that those Saints must have acquired sufficient merit for having offered the Adorable Sacrifice so frequently when on earth, she was told that the Saints took special delight in a soul when it has received Holy Communion with devotion and piety, even as a bride is congratulated on the day of her nuptials.

---

* Gospel for the Feast of SS. Peter and Paul (Matt. xvi. 13–19), in which our Lord specially addresses St. Peter.

† "In Papali gloria sacerdotalibus indutus."

CHAPTER XLVI.

For the Feast of St. Margaret, Virgin and Martyr.

The glory of this Saint, and of the recompense which God reserves for the least good action.

As St. Gertrude assisted at Vespers, on the Festival of the glorious virgin St. Margaret, she appeared to her in exceeding beauty, standing before the throne of God at the commencement of the Response *Virgo veneranda,* rays of light appeared to come forth from the King of Glory, which renewed and enhanced the merit of the virginity and beauty of the Saint, even as the touches of a painter enhance the perfection of his work. At the words *In magna stans constantia,* a ray from the light of the Passion increased the merits of her martyrdom. And as the words *Sponisque reddens præmia* * were chanted, our Lord turned to His spouse, the blessed Margaret, and said lovingly to her: " My daughter, have I not increased your merits to the highest degree ? and yet I am asked to increase them further." Then He united together all the devotions of those who had solemnised this Feast, to enhance the glory of this most blessed virgin.

---

* The Feast of St. Margaret, Virgin and Martyr, occurs on the 20th July. She obtained her crown at Antioch in the last general persecution. The Crusaders brought home glowing traditions of her virgin purity, her heroic constancy, and her sublime faith ; so that devotion to her was exceedingly propagated in England, France, and Germany during the Middle Ages. Her relics are now at Monte Fiascone, in Tuscany. We have not been able to verify the Antiphons, which are not in the present Office. The *Sponisque reddens* is from the hymn *Jesu, corona virginum;* Vespers, Com. of Virgins.

After this St. Margaret turned to Gertrude, and said to her: "Rejoice and be glad, O elect of my Lord! for assuredly, after the short term of your affliction on earth, you shall rejoice for all eternity in heaven, where the brief moments of temporal affliction and bitterness which you have endured shall be recompensed by endless years of sweetness and consolation: and all that you suffer now, either in body or soul, is an effect of the special love which God bears you, since you are daily more and more favoured with such sufferings, and you are thereby more prepared for the joys of eternity. Consider," she continued, "that on the day on which I obtained the glory which I now enjoy, instead of being honoured as I now am by the whole world, I was despised by all, and thought miserable and afflicted. Have, therefore, this firm confidence—that, when this life has ended, you will infallibly enjoy the eternal embraces of your Spouse, and those joys and delights which neither eye hath seen nor ear heard, and which it hath not entered into the heart of man to conceive "

CHAPTER XLVII.

For the Feast of St. Mary Magdalen.

Of true penance and good-will.

AT the first Vespers of the Feast of St. Mary Magdalen,[*] this blessed lover of Jesus appeared to Gertrude, adorned with as many precious stones and rare flowers as she had formerly committed sins. The Saint understood that the flowers signified the sovereign goodness of God in pardoning

---

* July 22.

her sins ; and the precious stones, the penance by which
the Divine grace had enabled her to expiate them.

At Matins, St. Gertrude besought this Saint to intercede
for her and for all who were committed to her care. Then
St. Mary Magdalen cast herself at the Feet of our Lord
and kissed them tenderly, raising them gently from the
ground, as if to invite all penitents to approach them.
Gertrude then approached, and kissing them devoutly,
said to Him : " I offer Thee now, O most loving Lord, the
sorrows of all those who are under my care, and with them
I water Thy blessed Feet with my tears." Our Lord
replied : " I accept your offering for them, and tell them
that they should wipe My Feet with their hair, kiss them,
and pour perfumes upon them."

From this she understood three things : first, that they
wiped our Lord's Feet with their hair, if they now endeavoured to expose themselves to every kind of adversity, to
efface any faults which they might have committed formerly by not bearing their sufferings patiently ; secondly,
that they kissed His Feet who confided fully in the goodness of God, who easily forgives all the sins for which we
are truly penitent : thirdly, that we anoint them when we
avoid carefully all that is displeasing to God.

Our Lord then said to her : " Pour forth this ointment
on Me with the same devotion as Magdalen opened the
alabaster box, and poured it upon My Head, so that the
odour perfumed the whole house. And know, that if you
defend the truth, you will act thus ; those who love and
defend the truth, and for its sake lose friends or any other
advantage, pour forth on My Head a box of precious ointment, the perfume of which fills My house ; for he who
corrects others, by giving good example, emits a sweet
odour. And if he fails in any way in the manner of

correcting or reprehending, either by negligence or by roughness, I will excuse him before God My Father and the whole court of heaven, even as I excused Magdalen."

To this Gertrude replied : " O Lord, since it is related of this loving penitent that she bought this ointment, can I not render Thee a similar service ? " He answered : " Whosoever desires that My glory may be promoted in all things, in preference to his own advantage or convenience, purchases a most precious ointment for Me ; although it may often happen that his good-will cannot be carried into effect."

CHAPTER XLVIII.

For the Feast of St. James.

Advantages of the pilgrimage to Compostella—And how we may honour the Saints by Communion.

ON the Feast of St. James the Great,* this Apostle appeared to Gertrude, adorned with the merits of those pilgrims who had visited his shrine. As the Saint was rapt in admiration thereat, she asked our Lord why this Apostle was so honoured by pilgrimages, that his relics appeared even more revered than those of the holy Apostles Peter and Paul. Our Lord replied : " The fervour of his

---

* It will be remembered that St. James the Great has received this appellation to distinguish him from St. James the Less, Bishop of Jerusalem. He was martyred eleven years after our Lord's Ascension at Jerusalem. His body was carried into Spain, where he had evangelised before his death. His relics were discovered in the ninth century, and translated to Compostella. The place was at first called " Ad S. Jacobum Apostolum," or Giacomo Postolo, and hence contracted into Compostella.

zeal for the salvation of souls has obtained this special privilege for him. And as I took him away from the world so soon, according to the decrees of My providence, that he was unable to convert many persons, which he most ardently desired to do, his desire still remains before Me fresh and flourishing, and what he was unable to do during his life I permit him to accomplish after his death, by bringing an immense number of pilgrims to his shrine, absolving them from their sins, and strengthening them in the Catholic faith."

Then, as she desired to obtain the remission of her sins through the merits of this Apostle, and as she could not undertake the pilgrimage, she approached the Holy Communion. As soon as she had accomplished her design, she beheld herself seated at a table with our Divine Lord, which was laden with various delicious viands. And as she offered our Lord His precious Body, which she had received, for the increase of the beatitude and glory of this Apostle, St. James presented himself before God as a prince, to thank Him for the favours which he had received through this Adorable Sacrament. He then asked that God would work in the soul of Gertrude all the good which He had ever deigned to work in any soul through his merits, because she had offered this Adorable Sacrament in his honour.

CHAPTER XLIX.

For the Vigil and Feast of the Assumption.

Of the manner of honouring and saluting the Blessed Virgin.

§ 1. *Of the prompt assistance which she affords to those who invoke her.*

As St. Gertrude was ill, on the solemnity of the Assumption, she was unable to fulfil her intention of saying as many *Ave Marias* as the Blessed Virgin had been years on earth; but she tried to supply for this devotion in some degree by the three aspirations—*Ave Maria, gratia plena, Dominus tecum.* As she offered them with great fervour for herself and those committed to her care, our Lady appeared to her in glory, clothed with a green mantle covered with golden flowers in the form of trefoils, and said to her: "Behold how I am adorned with as many flowers as those for whom you have prayed have uttered words in their petition to me; the brilliancy of these flowers corresponds to the fervour of their petitions; and I will turn this to their advantage, to render them more agreeable to my Son and all the celestial court."

St. Gertrude observed also that the Blessed Virgin had some roses with six leaves amongst the trefoils, and that three of these leaves were golden and enriched with precious stones; while the other three, which alternated with the former, were distinguished by an admirable variety of colours. The three golden leaves indicated the threefold division of the *Ave Maria* which she had made during her sickness; and the three other leaves were added by our Lord—the first, to reward her for the love with which she saluted and praised His most sweet Mother; the second, for her discretion and prudence in regulating her devotions during her illness; and the third, for the confidence which she had that the Lord and His loving Mother would accept the little she had done.

At *Prime* St. Gertrude besought our Lord to obtain His Blessed Mother's favour for her, as she feared she had never been sufficiently devout to her. Our Lord then, after bestowing many marks of tenderness and filial affection on His Divine Mother, said to her : " Remember, My beloved Mother, that for your sake I am indulgent to sinners, and regard My elect as if she had served you all her life with devotion."

At these words this most pure Mother gave herself entirely to Gertrude, for the sake of her Divine Son. As the Collect, *Deus, qui virginalem,** was read at Mass, our Lord appeared to renew in His Blessed Mother all the joys which she had experienced in His Conception, His Birth, and the other mysteries of His Humanity. At the words *Ut sua nos defensione munitos,*† which the Saint read with special devotion, she beheld the Mother of God extending her mantle as if to receive beneath its shelter all those who fled to her patronage. The holy angels then brought all who had prepared themselves very fervently for this Feast, and presented them to her as fair young virgins, who stood before her as before their mother ; while these good angels defended them from the snares of evil spirits, and carefully incited them to good actions.

The Saint understood that they had obtained this angelic protection by the words *Ut sua defensione,* &c. ; for at her command the angels never fail to protect and defend those who invoke this glorious Virgin.

---

* Collect for the Mass of the Assumption.
† " That defended by her protection," &c.

A number of little animals* appeared afterwards under
the mantle of the Blessed Virgin ; and this signified those
sinners who addressed themselves to her with devotion.
The Mother of Mercy received them with the greatest
charity, and covered them with her mantle ; thus manifesting with what affability she treats those who have recourse
to her ; how she protects them even during their wanderings ; and if they recognise their faults and return to her,
she reconciles them to her Son by a sincere penance.   At
the Elevation, St. Gertrude saw our Divine Lord imparting
Himself with all the joys of His Divinity and Humanity to
all those who had assisted at Mass with special devotion in
honour of His Blessed Mother, and who had desired to
serve her devoutly on the day of her Assumption ; so that,
being sustained by virtue of the Adorable Sacrament, they
were strengthened in their good desires, even as food
strengthens and invigorates the human frame.

After Mass the community proceeded to Chapter, and
the Saint saw a multitude of angels surrounding our Lord,
who appeared to wait with great joy for the arrival of the
religious.   Marvelling at this, she said to our Lord : " Why
hast Thou come to this Chapter, O most loving Lord, surrounded by such a multitude of angels, since we have not
the same devotion now as on the Vigil of Thy Divine
Birth ? "   Our Lord replied : " I come as the Father of a
family to receive those who have been invited to eat at
My house.   I come also from respect to My Mother, to
announce the solemn Festival of her eminent Assumption,
and to receive all who are prepared to celebrate this Feast
with holy disposition.   I come also to absolve, by the
virtue and authority of My Divinity, all those who humble

* " Diversi generis bestiolæ."

themselves for the negligences which they have committed concerning their Rule." He added : "I am present on all these Festivals, and see all that you do, although, on the Vigil of My Nativity, I assisted in an extraordinary manner."

§ 2. *Devotion for the hour of None.*

St. Gertrude recited None with special devotion, as the Office of the Assumption commences at that hour, according to the usages of the Order ; * and it was revealed to her that on the day previous to the Assumption of the Blessed Virgin she had been so absorbed in God, from the hour of None until the moment of her happy departure from this world, as to have nothing human in her, to live only by the Spirit of God, and to taste in anticipation all those celestial joys which she soon experienced perfectly and eternally in the bosom of God ; and that at the third hour of the night our Lord came for and took her to Himself with exceeding joy.

In the evening, at Vespers, the Saint beheld our Lord drawing into His Heart all the praises which had been chanted in honour of His Blessed Mother, and from thence pouring them forth upon her in an impetuous torrent. As the Antiphon *Ista pulchra es* was chanted, St. Gertrude offered the words to our Lord through His Sacred Heart, in memory of the sweet caresses He had bestowed on His Blessed Mother by the same words ; and this devotion, passing through the Heart of Jesus to the heart of Mary, encircled her like a cincture of stars, consoling her in a marvellous manner. Many of these stars appeared to fall

---

* The Office now commences at Vespers

to the ground ; * but the saints gathered them up, presenting them to our Lord with joy and admiration. This signified that all the saints obtain ineffable joy, glory, and beatitude from the superabundant merits of the Blessed Virgin.

When the Community chanted the Response, *Quæ est ista !* † the angels united with them in singing it. Our Lord Himself intoned the *Ista est speciosa*, the Holy Spirit animating His Divine Heart to praise and glorify the most excellent of all creatures.

At the hymn *Quem terra, pontus*, the Blessed Virgin seemed unable to contain the plenitude of her delights, and reclined on the bosom of her Son until the words *O gloriosa Domina.* ‡ Then she appeared as if aroused by the devotion of the faithful, and extended her hands over them to protect and console them by her maternal love. At the verse *Deo Patri* she rose again, and made three profound genuflexions, in honour of the Ever-Blessed Trinity ; and then she continued praying for the whole Church until the *Magnificat.* At the Antiphon *Virgo prudentissima*, she sent celestial light to all who invoked her devoutly.

§ 3. *Other revelations concerning the Blessed Virgin.*

On another occasion, at the Assumption, when St. Gertrude was so feeble as to be unable to assist at Matins, the Lord, the Orient from on high, visited her with ineffable goodness. It appeared to her at the sixth Response that she assisted in spirit at the moment when the Blessed

---

* "Pavimentum."

† iv. Ant. at Vespers, but worded differently now. The other responses are also in the present Office, and the hymn *Quem terra*, &c.

‡ "O Queen of all the virgin choir ; " Hymn at Lauds.

Virgin paid the last debt of nature, and entered heaven. Her rapture continued from this Response until the *Te Deum*, when she returned to herself once more; but during this rapture, she was favoured with a heavenly intelligence of all that was chanted, which filled her with ineffable joy.

At the Response *Super salutem*,* she saw the angels and apostles chanting in concert, as if to congratulate their Queen for her singular privileges. Meanwhile, as the soul of the Blessed Virgin left her body, it was received by her Divine Son into His arms. But our loving Jesus, who is the Father of orphans, recommended the needs and necessities of the Church, His Spouse, which are ever in His Heart, to her, while the seventh Response, *Sancta Deo dilecta*, was chanted. Then the Blessed Virgin advanced farther, while her Son united with the choirs of angels in singing the eighth Response, *Salve, Maria*, and the ninth, *Salve, pia mater Christianorum;* when our Lord, continuing in the person of His Church, added these words in a clear voice: *Virgo, solamen desolatorum.*

While the Queen of Heaven was being received therein, the Canticle *Audite me, Divini fructus*,† was sung with a transport of joy which no human words can express; and she appeared to enter a field adorned with the most exquisite flowers. At the words *Et fronde in gratiam*,‡ all these flowers became marvellously brilliant, and emitted a sweeter perfume, giving forth more melodious sounds than

---

* iv. Response, i. Nocturn.

† From Eccl. xxxix. 17. The first of the three Canticles, iii. Nocturn, Office of the Blessed Virgin; but it commences, *Obaudite me*—" Hear me, ye Divine offspring, and bud forth as the rose planted by the brooks of water."

‡ " Bring forth leaves in grace."

could be given by all the voices in the world united together
in the most exquisite harmony.

Then the Blessed Virgin, transported with joy because
of this incomparable beatitude, returned thanks to God
in these words, *Gaudens, gaudebo in Domine;* * and the
Eternal Father, as if pleased with the exalted perfection of
this excellent Virgin, blessed the Church Militant upon
earth with abundant sweetness, saying : *Non vocaberis
ultra derelicta.*† All the choirs of angels then chanted
these words : *Sexaginta sunt reginæ;* indicating by this
that the Virgin Mother was elevated above their orders.
The choirs of saints sang, *Et octoginta concubinæ,* declaring her elevation above them ; while both saints and
angels united their choirs in personating the Church
Triumphant, and chanted, *Et adolescentularum non est
numerus;* elevating the Mother of God above all, as she
merits to be elevated.

Then the Holy Spirit chanted the words, *Una est
columba mea;* her Divine Son adding, *Perfecta mea,* as if
to say that she was the most perfect of creatures. The
Eternal Father then said, *Una est matri suæ electa,* with
exceeding love, which indicated all that he desired to say
of her ; after this the whole celestial court chanted her
praise in the Versicle *Salve, nobilis.*

Then the Blessed Virgin was placed on a throne of

---

* "I will greatly rejoice in the Lord ;" ii. Response, iii. Nocturn,
from Isaias lxi.

† "Thou shalt no more be called forsaken" (Is. lxii.; iii.
Canticle). The quotations which follow are not in the present
Office. The quotation "sexaginta" is from Cant. vi. 7 : "There
are threescore queens, and fourscore concubines, and young maidens
without number. One is my dove, my perfect one is but one ; she
is the only one of her mother." The applicability of the first part of
this quotation is not very obvious.

glory on the right hand of her Son ; while all the citizens
of heaven assisted before the throne, employing themselves
in extolling her sovereign glory and the high and eminent
sanctity of her life, by which she had merited to obtain it ;
singing the Response, *Beata est virgo Maria;** to which the
Blessed Trinity added the words, *Ave Maria,* renewing in
her heart all the joy which she had formerly experienced
when saluted by the angel ; the choirs of saints chanting
the words, *Ecce exaltata est,* and recommending the Church
Militant to her intercession.

God the Father then chanted the words, *Ave, speciosa,*
to indicate the rare beauty of this most perfect of creatures ;
God the Son replying, *Sunamitis secundum cor summi
regis ;*† the Holy Ghost added, *Ave, mater Maria ;* and the
Son again replied, *Spiritu Sancto teste.* The saints then
knelt before her, in the person of the Church Militant,
chanting, *O sancta, O celsa ;* and the most Holy Trinity
chanted the third Response, *Quæ est ista ?*

The Blessed Virgin then chanted the *Te Deum* ‡ with
the whole celestial court, in honour of the Ever-Blessed
Trinity, adoring all the Persons in the first verse, the
Eternal Father in the second, the Son in the third, and
the Holy Ghost in the fourth. The Saint perceived that
each of the Divine Persons in particular was praised in
each verse except the seventh, *Tu Rex gloriæ, Christe,*
which refers particularly to the Son, and wherein He is
praised for all the holy affections of the Blessed Virgin,

---

* x. Response, iii. Nocturn ; and also *Ecce exaltata.*
† "The Sunamite according to the heart of the King." Probably
an allusion to 3 Kings i. 3, where Abisag the Sunamite is brought to
King David for her rare beauty, that she may minister to him. This
passage is not in the Office.
‡ The *Te Deum* is always chanted by Benedictines, unless the Office
is ferial.

which, by His assistance, she had always employed for the Divine glory. At the verse *Æterna fac*, she extolled each Person alternately, and perceived that nothing was attributed to the Father which belonged so exclusively to Him as to prevent its application to the Son and the Holy Ghost.

When St. Gertrude recovered from this ecstasy, she found her bodily health so strengthened, that she was even able to walk more quickly than her companions ; and this continued until after the High Mass.

§ 4. *Other revelations on the same subject.*

Three years after the occurrence of the favours just related, the Saint was confined to bed on the Vigil of the Assumption ; nevertheless she endeavoured to prepare herself for this great Festival with all possible fervour and devotion. While she was thus occupied, she beheld the Blessed Virgin in a beautiful garden, cultivated with the greatest care, and filled with rare flowers. Our Lady appeared to be in a rapture, caused by an excess of repose and joy, the serenity of her countenance and her gestures indicating that she was full of grace. In this garden there were roses without thorns, lilies white as snow, and fragrant violets, with many other flowers. But it seemed very marvellous that the farther these flowers were from the Blessed Virgin, the brighter was their colour and the sweeter their fragrance. Then she appeared to draw this odour to herself by inspiration, and to pour it forth into the Heart of her Son, which seemed to be opened for this purpose. A great number of angels were also in this garden, between these flowers and the Blessed Virgin, who served God by proclaiming her praises. St. John the Evangelist also remained near her, praying fervently, and she appeared to attract his prayers to herself like a sweet vapour.

As St. Gertrude took singular pleasure in this vision, she began to marvel what it might mean ; and our Lord taught her that the garden signified the chaste body of the Blessed Virgin ; that the flowers were her virtues ; that the beautiful roses which appeared so far from her were the actions which she had performed for the love of God and her neighbour, and which increased in merit as the love which prompted them was extended ; that the lilies signified her extreme purity ; and that the prayers of St. John, which she appeared to attract, signified the glory which she had received through him in consequence of the care which he had taken of her while on earth, that she might be enabled to spend more time in prayer.

Then she inquired what advantage St. John had gained from this ; and our Lord replied : " My Heart was drawn more towards him for each act of devotion which he offered to My Mother." Lastly, she understood that the vision of the Blessed Virgin which she had seen represented her soul, which always abounded in the fruits of virtue, and which she ever returned to God with the greatest thanksgiving.

At Matins she was again rapt in ecstasy, and beheld the Blessed Virgin reposing sweetly and peaceably upon her Divine Son, and the Son pouring forth into the heart of His Mother an ineffable joy, the fruit of the virtues which she had practised, and had returned to Him as their true and only Source. The Eternal Father seemed to chant the first Responsory, *Vidi speciosam*,* by which the whole

---

* *Vidi speciosam*, i. Response, i. Nocturn, Feast of the Assump-

celestial court understood that the Blessed Virgin had
indeed been a dove in purity and innocence ; that she
ascended above the rivers of waters by desire; that her
garment—that is, her holy life—was full of ineffable sweetness ; and that she was surrounded with roses and lilies—
that is with every virtue.

Then the Holy Ghost made known the holy life of the
Blessed Virgin by chanting the Response, *Sicut cedrus ;* the
saints, full of admiration and joy, adding the third Response,
Quæ est ista ? of which St. Gertrude received a marvellous
understanding ; but her infirmity caused her to forget it.
The saints then passed in procession round the throne of
the Blessed Virgin, chanting the fourth Response, *Gaude,
regina,* with profound respect and with a marvellous concord of voices, praising this mighty Queen on whom the
eternal light shone so gloriously ; so that she appeared to
all in heaven and earth as the most beautiful and accomplished Virgin in virtue and grace—as a Mother who provides for our wants, and who will increase our glory and
crown our joy and beatitude hereafter.

The choirs of angels then marched processionally, singing with a clear and melodious voice, *Fac nos lætari ;* and
the saints chanted the *Gloria Patri* in thanksgiving for
all the graces which the Blessed Virgin had obtained for
them ; both choirs then united together, singing all the
Antiphons and Psalms to the honour of God and the praise
of the Blessed Virgin. Meanwhile St. Gertrude was favoured
with a marvellous intelligence of all that was chanted.

tion : "I have seen thee, beautiful as a dove, ascending above the
rivers of waters ; the odour of thy garments was ineffable, and thou
wert encompassed with roses and lilies. Who is this that cometh up
from the desert like a cloud, perfumed with myrrh and incense ?"

At the fifth Response, the Blessed Virgin rose, and sang the words, *Beatam me dicent omnes generationes,* while her soul appeared as when it had been released from the body, reposing upon her Son, and immersed in an ocean of beatitude, being for ever united closely to the Ever-Blessed Trinity. The *Super salutem* was then chanted, the whole heavenly court rejoicing in her union with the King of kings. From this we may learn how God bestows favours on one person for the advantage of many ; and if we for our sins are hindered from entering this garden of delights, at least let us not fail to cull a few flowers from it.

§ 5. *Devotion for the Feast of the Assumption.*

On another occasion, as St. Gertrude assisted devoutly at Matins, she made three different meditations at each Nocturn. At the first, she reminded the Blessed Virgin of the ineffable consolations which she had received from her Divine Son and from the saints when expecting her death ; so that every word which she uttered appeared to encircle her like roses and lilies. At the second Nocturn, she reminded her of the ineffable delights which she had experienced when received into the arms of her Beloved at this happy moment. At the third Nocturn, she reminded her of the inconceivable glory with which she had been honoured at her entrance into heaven ; and at each word that she recited, she received a light and glory which could only be compared to the emission of the sweetest perfumes.

At Mass she said the *Laudate Dominum* (Ps. cxvi.) three times—first, beseeching the saints to offer their merits to our Lord, that she might make a worthy Communion ; secondly, saying it for the same intention in honour of the Blessed Virgin ; and thirdly, offering it to our Divine Lord.

The Blessed Virgin then rose at the prayer of the saints, and stood before the throne of the adorable Trinity, offering her merits and the favours which she had received on the day of her Assumption for St. Gertrude, whom she called to her, caressing her tenderly, and saying to her: "Come, elect one, and stand in my place, with all the perfection in virtue which caused the Blessed Trinity to incline towards me, that you may please the Blessed Trinity as far as possible in like manner." At this she was amazed, and replied: "Alas, O Queen of Glory! how can I merit so great a favour?" The Blessed Virgin replied: "Prepare yourself for it by three things: first, pray to be purified from every stain by the exceeding purity with which I prepared an abode within my virginal womb for my Divine Son; secondly, ask pardon for all your negligences by the profound humility by which I merited to be elevated above all the saints and the angels; thirdly, implore an abundant increase of merits through the incomprehensible love which united me to God in such a manner, that I can never be separated from Him."

St. Gertrude, having faithfully accomplished what the Blessed Virgin had directed, was rapt in ecstasy to the high degree of glory which the Queen of Heaven had merited; and being clothed in her merits, she pleased our Lord so surpassingly, that all the saints and angels came to honour her.

As the religious approached the Holy Communion, their glorious Queen stood on their right, covering them with her mantle, saying: "My dearest Son, look favourably upon all who have honoured my memory;" to this prayer He condescended very lovingly, treating them with the greatest tenderness. When the Saint communicated, she offered the Most Holy Sacrament to our Lord for His eternal praise,

and for the increase of the joy and glory of His Blessed
Mother, as a compensation for the merits with which she
had supplied her poverty. Our Lord then addressed Himself lovingly to His Mother, saying : " Behold, My Mother,
I return what you gave doubled, and I take nothing from
her of what you desired to bestow on her for My sake."
After the procession the community returned to the choir,
singing the Antiphon *Ave domina mundi Maria,* and it
appeared to St. Gertrude that heaven itself was full of joy
and triumph, the Blessed Virgin standing before the altar
at the right of her Son, and looking upon the religious.

As they sang *Ave cœlorum regina,* all the Saints prostrated before her, reverencing her as the Mother of their
Lord ; at the words *Ave virgo virginum,* she extended her
hand, and presented each with a white lily, engaging them
to follow the innocence and purity of her life. When they
sang *Per te venit redemptio nostra,* her maternal feelings
were so deeply moved, that she appeared unable to bear
the joy with which her heart was filled, and supported herself lovingly upon her Divine Son ; at the words *Pro nobis
rogamus, rogita,* the Blessed Virgin embraced her Son, respectfully offering each sister to Him, and praying for each.
When they commenced the Antiphon *Hodie beata Virgo,**
St. Gertrude beheld her surrounded with glory, and elevated
in the arms of her Son to the highest heavens, attended by
all the heavenly host with the greatest honour. In this
exalted position she blessed the community with the right
hand of her Divine Son ; and after this benediction, a

* These Antiphons are not in the present Office ; but the Antiphon
at *Magnificat* is like the above : "To-day the Virgin Mary ascends
into heaven ; let us rejoice, for she reigns with Christ for endless
ages."

golden cross appeared upon each religious, fastened by a green cord ; by which the Saint understood that a firm faith would render all who possessed it sharers in the same benediction of this Mother of Mercy.

CHAPTER L.

For the Feast of St. Bernard.

The merit and glory of this Saint.

As St. Gertrude reflected at Mass on the merits of St. Bernard,* to whom she had a particular devotion on account of his sweet eloquence, the illustrious abbot appeared to her, clothed in ineffable glory and in three different colours, each of which were equally brilliant—white, which indicated the integrity of his innocence and purity ; violet, his perfection as a religious ; and crimson, the fervour of his love ; and these three colours appeared to impart a special pleasure to all the saints. He had also golden bracelets, in which precious stones were interlaced with admirable skill : the gold indicated the inestimable value of his rare and admirable doctrine, and all that he had said or written for the good of souls ; the precious stones indicated his burning love of God. Our Lord drew into His Heart all the merits and advantages which had ever been gained by any person, either in heaven or on earth, from his words or writings, causing this to radiate from His Heart into that of St. Bernard, which resounded like a sweet instrument of music—his virtues, and above all his innocence and love, producing the sweetest melody imaginable.

* August 20.

The heart of the saint was also adorned with a brilliant diadem of many colours, on which appeared the profit which he had desired should be gained from his writings for the greater glory of God. St. Gertrude then repeated the *Laudate Dominum* two hundred and twenty-five times, in honour of the saint, returning thanks to God for all the graces with which He had favoured him. Then all that he said appeared on the vestments of the venerable father in the form of little shields, on which were engraven the virtues for which he had been specially distinguished when on earth ; and they shone also into the soul of Gertrude, who had returned thanks to God for them.

As the Saint prayed at Mass for all the religious of whom she had charge, and especially for those who were devout to St. Bernard, although they had not been recommended to her prayers, she beheld this venerable father again clothed in glory, the splendour of which appeared to pass from him to all those who desired to obtain the same fervent love of God as he had through his merits. As Gertrude marvelled at this, she inquired why those persons who had not practised the same virtues as he had done could appear thus enriched with his merits. He replied " A lady of noble birth is not less admired when clothed with the habits of another than when she wears her own, provided she is beautiful, and perfectly formed. Thus the virtues of the saints obtain the same advantages for those who praise God for their fervour in acquiring them."

St. Gertrude now observed, that those who had recommended themselves to her prayers with devotion appeared adorned with a singular brightness, which others did not obtain ; to show that the least action done with a right intention profits much, and that the least negligence, even in little things, may be a serious loss.

On the same day, as the Saint reflected on the glory of St. Augustine, to whom she had always been devout, and thanked God for the favours He had bestowed on him, he appeared to her with St. Bernard, as if equal to him in glory, as he had been equal to him in sanctity and doctrine. This great Bishop stood before the throne of the Divine Majesty, magnificently apparelled, while rays of ardent fire appeared to shoot forth from his heart, as also from the heart of St. Bernard, towards that of Jesus Christ; this indicated the eloquence by which the holy doctor had enkindled the fire of Divine love in the hearts of men. Rays of light, like sunbeams, proceeded from his lips, which filled the whole heavens, and figured the abundant and marvellous doctrines with which he had enlightened the Church. Beneath these rays there appeared arcades of light, of admirable clearness, which attracted the attention of all, and gave abundant pleasure and content to those who gazed upon them. As the Saint beheld this with joy and admiration, she learned from St. Bernard that these arcades represented the light of the doctrine of St. Augustine, and his immense labours in defence of the Catholic faith by his discourses, and by his writings and his ardent desires; having been brought, after so many wanderings, from the darkness of ignorance to the light of faith, that he might be able to close up the way of error to all men, and to open the way of the true faith.

St. Gertrude then inquired of St. Bernard if he had not had the same end in his writings. He replied : " I spoke, wrote, and acted under the impulse of an impetuous love of God ; but this illustrious doctor wrote from a principle of Divine love, and moved by the miseries which he had himself experienced."

Our Lord then drew to Himself from the blessed and

from the hearts of the faithful still on earth the faith, consolation, light, and love which the writings of St. Augustine had produced ; perfecting this, uniting it to His
Heart, and then pouring it forth into the heart of the Saint,
whose soul was penetrated by this Divine influence, and
became like a harp before God, emitting the most perfect and
the sweetest melody ; and as the virginity and love of God
had formed an admirable concert in the heart of St. Bernard, the penitence and fervent love of St. Augustine produced a similar effect, so that it was impossible to decide
which was the most melodious.   After this, St. Bernard
informed St. Gertrude that the melodies which she heard
were those which were spoken of in the words, *Omnis illa
Deo,* &c. ; * for the heart of each saint emits a melody which
corresponds to its virtues, and all are ever employed in the
Divine praises.

CHAPTER LI.

For the Feast of St. Augustine.

Of the glory and virtue of this Saint—Of the merits of St. Francis
and St. Dominic.

As the Antiphon *Vulneraverunt charitas* was sung at Vespers on the Feast of St. Augustine,✝ Gertrude beheld this

---

* From the hymn at Lauds for the Dedication of a Church.   The
hymns of this Office are very beautiful.   The hymn for Vespers in
the Roman Office differs from the Benedictine.   The former commences " Cœlestis urbs," the latter, " Urbs Jerusalem beata ; " but
the same idea is contained in each.

" Jerusalem, thou city blest,
Sweet vision of a peaceful land ! "

✝ August 28.   This Antiphon is from the Ursuline Breviary, v. at
Lauds.

great Bishop standing in glory, and unfolding his heart, which had been wounded with Divine love, like a beautiful rose before God, to present it to Him, and thereby recreating the citizens of heaven with a perfume of exceeding fragrance. The Saint then saluted him devoutly, praying for her community, and for all who were devoted to this saint. He then besought our Lord that the hearts of all those who desired to obtain a fervent love of God through his merits might be filled with it, as his had been, to the honour and glory of the effulgent and Ever-Blessed Trinity.

As St. Gertrude assisted at Matins with great fervour, she began to reflect what reward this great pastor of the Church had received for the delights and sweetness which he had found in contemplating the deep designs of God for the salvation of men, as he declares in his *Confessions.* As she reflected thus, he appeared to her in glory, bearing a globe on his head, enriched with an infinite variety of rare colours, and covered with brilliant stars, which indicated the reward that God had bestowed on him for his holy thoughts during life : such as the application of his mind to the things of God ; the contempt which he had for the pleasures of life, from his desire of finding pleasure only in God ; the care which he had taken to make his heart pleasing to God, who, as the Wise Man says, finds His delight in conversing with the children of men ; and all the occupations to which he had devoted himself with his whole soul, either by speaking, writing, or by promoting the love and glory of God by his example ; and the pleasures which he enjoyed were so great and so admirable, that he could pour them forth on all.

Then our Lord said to Gertrude : " Consider how perfect My beloved is in purity, humility, and fervent charity."

She replied, in great admiration : " O Lord, how can he be so pure, when he must have contracted so many stains in his wanderings from the faith before his conversion ?" He replied : "I permitted these wanderings, awaiting his return with patience and mercy, and then overwhelming him with My gratuitous favours."

After these words, as she examined the ornaments of this prelate very attentively, he appeared vested in a garment of crystalline purity, beneath which she saw three colours, which indicated his purity, humility, and charity ; and these shone forth as gold shines through crystal.

Then she said to our Lord : " My Lord, was not St. Bernard as devoted to Thee as St. Augustine, whose glory shines so resplendently ? and yet it seems to me that he does not enjoy the same delights." Our Lord replied : " Bernard, My chosen one, has received an immense recompense ; but your mind is not capable of discerning the glory of even the least of My saints : how, then, can it discern that of the greatest ? Nevertheless, to satisfy your devotion, to increase your love, and that you may know how many mansions there are in My Father's house, understand this : when the Church sings of any saint, *Non est inventus similis illi,** it means that, though all the saints possess the same glory, they do not possess it in the same degree, but each according to their merit." She replied : " O Lord God of truth, I beseech Thee, reveal to me something of the merits of the gentle Agnes and the glorious Catherine, to whom I have been singularly devoted from my infancy."

After God had granted her this favour, which we have

---

* " There was not found the like to him in glory " (Ecc. xliv. 20); i. Ant., Lauds, Com. of Conf. Pont.

recorded elsewhere, she desired to know something of the
merits of the holy Father's St. Dominic and St. Francis,*
who had been the chiefs of two Orders, and who had
laboured very ardently for the advancement of the
Church. Then these venerable Fathers appeared to her
in sublime glory, and equal in merit to the glorious Father
Benedict, adorned with garlands of roses similar to his,
and bearing sceptres. They appeared equal in merit to
the blessed Saints Augustine and Bernard, on account of
their devotion and preaching, by which they had given
such glory to God, and gained so many souls for Him.
But there was this difference : the blessed Father Francis
enjoyed special rewards for his profound humility, and the
glorious Father Dominic for the fervour and sublimity of
his desires.

At Mass, which the Saint heard with the greatest devotion, she was rapt to heaven before the throne of the Divine
Majesty. Then all the saints sang sweetly before the Virgin
the first six verses of the Sequence, *Interni festi gaudia,*
in memory of and in thanksgiving for the delights she had
enjoyed on the preceding night in contemplating the glory
of St. Augustine. When they had concluded, they indicated
to her that she should then chant the concluding verses in
their praise, as they had sung the preceding ones in her
honour. Then she chanted, by the organ of the sweetest
Heart of Jesus, the praises of the heavenly Jerusalem, commencing *Beata illa patria,* with the five following verses,
each of which appeared to fill the saints with ineffable
joy.

* The Feast of S⁺ Dominic occurs on the 4th of August ; that of
St. Francis on the 4th of October. It is remarkable that those who
were so united in life should have appeared together in glory to this
great Saint.

When she had concluded, our Lord, her loving Spouse, chanted the two Versicles, *Hoc in hac valle misera,* and *Quo post mundi exilia,* for her ; teaching her, as a kind master would teach his child, how she could merit eternal joys even in this exile. Then the choirs of angels chanted *Harum laudum præconia,* representing the prayers and desires of the Church ; and the saints united their voices to those of the angels to praise that admirable prelate of the Church, St. Augustine, while he poured forth ineffable light through heaven, imparting new joys and delights to all. At the last two verses, *Cujus sequi vestigia,* our Lord raised His Hand, and imparted an abundant benediction to all those who had praised the Saint devoutly.

CHAPTER LII.

For the Festival of the Nativity of the Blessed Virgin.

Exercises for celebrating this Feast devoutly –How powerfully the Blessed Virgin protects those who invoke her ; and how we may supply for our negligences in her service.

ON the glorious Feast of the Nativity of the Blessed Virgin,* St. Gertrude, having said as many *Ave Marias* as she had remained days in her mother's womb, offered them to her devoutly, and inquired what merit they would have who performed a like devotion. This benign Virgin replied : " They will merit a special share in the joys which I possess in heaven, which are continually renewed, and in the virtues with which the ever-blessed and glorious Trinity adorns me."

---

* September **8.**

At the Antiphon *Ave decus*, she beheld the heavens opening, while the angels descended and placed a magnifi- cent throne in the centre of the choir, whereon the Queen of Glory was seated, and manifested how lovingly she received the prayers and devotion of the religious on this Festival. The angels stood round this throne, attending the Mother of their God with the greatest respect and joy. The Saint also saw an angel standing by each of the religious, with a branch in his hand ; and this branch pro- duced different kinds of fruit and flowers, according to the devotion of the sister who was thus attended. At the conclusion of the Office, the angels brought these branches to the Blessed Virgin to adorn her throne. Then Gertrude exclaimed : " Alas, kind Mother ! I do not deserve to be thus united with the choirs of the blessed." She replied : " Your good-will suffices ; and the devout intention which you had at Vespers, of offering your prayers through the sweet Heart of my Son, in my honour, far exceeds any corporal work ; to assure you of this, I will present your branch of fruit and flowers to the adorable Trinity, as an oblation of the highest merit."

At Matins she beheld how the angels gathered the flowers and fruit of the different intentions of the religious, and presented them to the Virgin Mother. The flowers appeared more brilliant and beautiful in proportion to the earnestness of each ; and the sweetness of the fruit corres- ponded with the purity and fervour of their devotion.

At the *Gloria Patri* of the fourth Response,* as St. Gertrude praised the ineffable power of the Father, the

---

* It will be remembered that there are four Lessons in each Nocturn of the Benedictine Office. The *Gloria Patri* is said at the end of the fourth Response of each Nocturn.

incomprehensible wisdom of the Son, and the marvellous benignity of the Holy Ghost, in having given us a creature so full of grace to further our salvation, the Blessed Virgin stood before the Blessed Trinity, praying that the Divine Omnipotence, Wisdom, and Goodness would bestow as much grace on St. Gertrude as it was possible for any creature to receive ; and the Blessed Trinity poured forth an abundant benediction of grace upon her soul, which watered it like a gentle rain.

Then St. Gertrude chanted the Antiphon *Quam pulchra es*, in the person of the Son of God, in honour of His Father. This was accepted with great love by our Lord, who said to her : " I will reward you at a fitting time, according to My royal munificence, for the honour you have paid to My beloved Mother." *

At the Antiphon *Adest*, when the words *Ipsa intercedat pro peccatis nostris* were chanted, she saw the Blessed Virgin with a parchment in her hand, on which the words, " She will intercede," were written in letters of gold ; and this she presented to her Son by the ministry of angels. He replied lovingly : " I give thee full power, by My omnipotence, to be propitious to all who invoke thy aid, in whatever manner is most pleasing to thee."

As the Sequence *Ave præclara* † was chanted at Mass, at the words *Ora Virgo nos*, the Blessed Virgin turned towards her Son, and prayed for the community with her hands clasped. Then our Lord turned towards them, and blessed them with the sign of the cross, to prepare them to receive the adorable Sacrament of His Body and Blood.

At the words *Audi nos*, the Blessed Virgin appeared

---

* " Dulcissimæ genitrici."
† We have not been able to verify this Sequence.

seated on a high throne with her Divine Son ; and St. Gertrude addressed her thus : " Why do you not pray for us, O Mother of Mercy ?" She replied : " I speak for you to my Beloved, heart to heart." Then, when the same words were repeated again, the Virgin extended her royal hands over the convent, as if uniting herself to their desires, and praying as one with them to her Divine Son ; and this royal Son, at the following verse, *Salve nos, Jesu ;* turning towards the community, said to them : " I am ready to accomplish all your desires."

Then, as St. Gertrude reflected on the approaching Festival, and ardently desired that her heart might be prepared to solemnise it, she said to the Mother of God : " Since the glory of your Assumption moves the souls of those who meditate on it so deeply, I desire much to know what the angels think of the Feast of your Nativity in heaven, that our devotion may be increased thereby on earth." The Blessed Virgin replied : " The angels commemorate the ineffable joys which I experienced while in the womb of my mother when they offer me their homage with the deepest reverence. The archangels also contemplate in the mirror of the Blessed Trinity the eminent favours and graces which God bestowed on me above all creatures, and minister to me also ; while all the heavenly orders unite in serving and assisting me for the glory of God ; and for this they are now recompensed with special joys."

At Compline, as the *Salve Regina* * was chanted, St.

---

* Antiphon at Vespers from Trinity Sunday until Advent. It is generally believed that Adelmar, Bishop of Puy, composed this most touching devotion ; the last words, " O Clement," &c., were added by St. Bernard. Adelmar lived in the eleventh century, and the *Salve Regina* was introduced about that time into the services of the

Gertrude grieved before God that she had never served
His Mother with the veneration due to her ; and she
offered this Antiphon, through the Heart of Jesus, to
supply for her defects ; and our Lord supplied for her deficiencies by little tubes of gold, which passed from His
Heart to the heart of His Virgin Mother, and through
which He poured forth on her the tenderness of His filial
affection.   We may also supply for our negligences by the
following prayer, or any similar one :—

"O sweetest Jesus, I beseech Thee, by the love which
caused Thee to take flesh in the bosom of this most pure
Virgin, that Thou wouldst supply for our defects in the
service and honour of this most benign Mother, who is ever
ready to assist us, with maternal tenderness, in all our
necessities.   Offer her, O sweetest Jesus, the superabundant
beatitude of Thy sweetest Heart ; show her Thy Divine
predilection, which chose her from all eternity, before all
creatures, to be Thy Mother, adorning her with every
grace and virtue ; remind her of all the tenderness Thou
didst manifest to her when on earth, Thy filial obedience
to her in all things, and, above all, Thy care at the hour
of Thy Death, when Thou didst forget Thine own anguish
to solace hers, and didst provide her with a son ; remind
her, also, of the joys and glory of her Assumption, when
she was exalted above all the choirs of angels, and constituted Queen of heaven and earth.   Thus, O good Jesus, do
Thou make Thy mother propitious to us, that she may be
our advocate and protector in life and in death."

At the words *Eia ergo*, as St. Gertrude invoked this
most benign Mother, she saw her inclining towards her, as

Church.   Some authors attribute it to Hermann Contractus, a Benedictine monk of the same date.

if drawn by cords; by which she understood, that when we
invoke her devoutly as our *advocate*, her maternal tenderness is so moved, that she cannot fail to assist us.   At the
words *Illos tuos misericordes oculos*, the Blessed Virgin
inclined the eyes of her Son towards the earth, saying:
" These are my merciful eyes, which I incline towards all
who invoke me devoutly, and from them they obtain the
fruit of eternal salvation."   Then the Saint was taught by
our Lord to salute His Blessed Mother, at least daily, by
the words *Eia ergo*, and *Advocata nostra*, assuring her
that she would obtain great consolation thereby at the
hour of her death.

St. Gertrude then offered Our Lady a hundred and fifty
Ave Marias, beseeching her to assist her at the hour of her
death by her maternal tenderness; and each word which
she repeated appeared like a piece of gold, which our Lord
offered to His Mother, who used them for the help and
consolation of the Saint at the hour of her death.   Thus
she knew that when we recommend our end to any saint,
the prayers which are offered to them are presented before
the tribunal of the Judge, and the Saint to whom we have
recommended ourselves is appointed our advocate.

CHAPTER LIII.

For the Feast of the Exaltation of the Cross.

Of the exaltation of the Cross—Of the love of enemies—Of the observance of the regular fast – Of the true relics of Jesus Christ.

ON the Feast of the Exaltation of the Cross,* as St. Gertrude prostrated to reverence the relics, our Lord said to her : " Consider how I hung upon the Cross from Sext to Vespers, and that it is for this I am elevated to such sublime glory ; and understand thereby what benefits I will confer on the hearts of those in whom I have reposed for many years." She replied : " Alas, Lord ! how little pleasure Thou canst have had in my heart ! " He answered : " And what pleasure had I in the wood of the Cross ? I only honoured it because I willed to honour it, and so I reward those whom I will to reward."

During Mass our Lord gave her this instruction : " Consider the example I give to My elect in honouring this Cross ; and know that I honoured the instruments of My Passion, which caused Me suffering, more than those things which in My infancy were used for My convenience. If you desire to imitate my example, and to give Me glory and further your own salvation, you will love your enemies

---

* September 14. This Festival, it will be remembered, was first instituted to celebrate the finding of the Cross by St. Helen, after the miraculous vision of Constantine. It was kept at Jerusalem from the year 335, and by both the Greeks and Latins, as early as the fifth century, under the same title ; but since the eighth century, the Feast of the Discovery or Invention of the Cross has been transferred to May 3, and this day appointed for the commemoration of the recovery of this most venerable and ever-blessed relic from the Persians.

more than your friends ; and this will advance you marvellously in perfection.   Furthermore, if you neglect to do
this at first, but afterwards repent and overwhelm your
enemies with benefits, you will follow My example in
having concealed My Cross for a time, to exalt it triumph-
antly afterwards.   But the reason I so specially loved this
Cross was, that I obtained thereby the redemption of mankind, which I so ardently desired, even as devout persons
love the times and places where they have received special
favours from God."

As the Saint ardently desired to have some relics of the
wood of the Cross, that our Lord might look on her with
more love, He said to her : " If you desire to have relics
which will draw My Heart into yours, read My Passion, and
meditate attentively on every word contained therein, and
it will be to you a true relic, which will merit more graces
for you than any other ; and if you are not persuaded of this
by My inspirations, at least let your reason convince you
of it ; for when a friend wishes to renew his friendship with
his friend, he says, ' Remember what you felt in your heart
when I said such and such a word,' as if he would say,
' Remember what I did or said for you at such a time ; '
and thence you may know and be assured that the words
which I uttered when on earth are the most precious relics
which you can possess."

As she asked our Lord to enable her to keep the regular
fast of six months,* which commences on this day, he
replied : " Whoever observes the regular fast from zeal for
religious observance, and purely for My love, and who seeks
therein, not his own advantage, but Mine, I will accept it
from him, though I have no need of his goods, as an em-

---

* See Rule of St. Benedict, ch. xli.

peror wou..d accept the offer of a prince to furnish his table daily with every necessary. But if obedience and necessity obliges him to relax his fast against his will, and he submits in union with the humility with which I submitted to men when on earth for the glory of My Father, I will treat him as a friend would his dearest friend whom he had invited to his table."

On another occasion, on the same Festival, when St. Gertrude offered the annoyances which the community had suffered to our Lord, He replied : " I have drunk this chalice, which the fervour of your devotion has sweetened for Me ; and I will drink it as often as you offer it to Me, until, by inebriating Me with it, you render Me favourable to your desires." " But how, O Lord Jesus, can we give you this chalice to drink ? " she inquired. Then our Lord taught her that she could do this by reflecting on her unworthiness, by praising Him from the depth of her heart, by repenting sincerely for never having loved God as she ought, and by desiring to suffer for him, until the last moment of her life, even such sufferings as He had endured in His Divine Heart, were it possible ; and this He would accept as a chalice of the sweetest nectar.

Those who desire to make a similar offering can do so by saying the following prayer : " O vivifying Fount of sweetness ! O aromatic Sweetness of Divine delights ! O delicious Inebriation of all pleasure ! behold, I offer Thee, as far as I am able, a drop from my miserable indigence ; I grieve, and I will ever grieve, that my soul has so long fasted by abstaining from that celestial Food which never satiates. But now, O Creator and re-Creator of my substance, to whom nothing is impossible, for Thy glory so make my heart one with Thine, that I may truly say that I desire with my whole soul to suffer all that has been suffered by any human being, from the creation of the world until now, if I might thereby prepare an abode worthy of Thee within me, and satisfy Thy justice for all the opposition which I have offered to Thy inspirations and graces."

CHAPTER LIV.

For the Feast of St. Michael.

Of the faithful care which the angels have of us, and how we should honour them.

As the Feast of St. Michael * approached, St. Gertrude prepared herself for Holy Communion by meditating on the care which the angels had of her, by the Divine command, notwithstanding her unworthiness ; and as she desired to render some return to them, she offered in their honour the life-giving Body and Blood of Jesus in the Most Holy Sacrament, saying : " I offer Thee this most august Sacrament, O most loving Lord, for Thy eternal glory, in honour of the princes of Thy kingdom, and for the increase of their felicity and beatitude. Then our Lord drew this oblation to Himself in an ineffable manner, thereby causing the greatest joy to these angel spirits, who appeared even as if they had never before experienced such blessedness and superabounded in delights. Then each of the choirs of angels, according to their rank, inclined respectfully before St. Gertrude, saying : " Thou hast indeed honoured us by this oblation, and we will therefore guard thee with special care ; " the guardian angels adding : We will guard thee night and day with ineffable joy, and will prepare thee for thy Spouse with the utmost vigilance.

* September 29.

Then, as she returned thanks to God for this favour with great jubilation of spirit, she recognised her own angel guardian, and he appeared to her as a prince magnificently attired, standing between her soul and God, and endeavouring to unite and elevate her soul to God. She then offered some special devotion in his honour which he presented to the Ever-Blessed Trinity under the form of roses. The Archangels now saluted the Saint, saying to her : " O illustrious * spouse of Christ, we will discover to you the Divine secrets, according to your capacity of receiving them." The Virtues then said : " We will assist you in your labours, writings, and meditations for the glory of God." The Dominations said : " Since our Lord, the King of Glory, takes pleasure in your soul, and that you return Him love for love, we will offer for you the honour which you owe to His Sovereignty to supply for your deficiencies." The Principalities next addressed her, saying : " We will present you to the King of kings, adorned according to His Heart." The Powers added : " Since your Beloved is so blessedly united to you, we will continually remove every impediment, whether exterior or interior, which might interrupt His Divine communications, in imparting blessings to the Church, and rejoicing the heavenly court. For the prayers of one loving soul prevail more with God, both for the living and the dead, than the prayers of a thousand souls who love less."

Then St. Gertrude returned profound thanks to God for all these favours, and for many others which human frailty prevents us from relating ; but all are known to God.

---

* " Egregia."

CHAPTER LV.

For the Feast of the Eleven Thousand Virgins.

Of the fruits of thanksgiving—That God requires us to fructify His
gifts—And of the Response *Regnum mundi.*

As the words, *Ecce sponsus venit,* were chanted at the Office
of the Eleven Thousand Virgins,* St. Gertrude was deeply
moved, and said to our Lord : " O most desirable Spouse !
as I hear these words so frequently repeated, tell me how
Thou wilt come, and what Thou wilt bring † us ? " He
replied : " I will now work with you and in you.   Where
is your lamp ? "   She replied : " Behold, Lord, I will give
Thee my heart for a lamp."   He answered : " I will fill it
abundantly with oil—that is, with grace from My Heart."
She replied : " But where is the wick ‡ to light it ? "   Our
Lord replied : " Your pure intention of doing everything
for Me alone will be a wick, the light of which will be most
pleasing to Me."

---

* St. Ursula and her companions, martyrs : October 21st.   It is
believed that these holy martyrs came originally from Britain, and
that St. Ursula was their conductor.   There has been some question
as to the correctness of the number ; but modern researches, in
this as in many other instances, are tending to confirm the truth
of ancient traditions—though it is probable that the martyrs were
not all virgins.   St. Ursula was not the foundress of the Order
which bears her name : the humility of St. Angela, who instituted
the congregation, and a vision of St. Ursula, who encouraged her
holy undertaking, led her to conceal her imputed share in this
great work under the mantle of another.   One almost regrets that
the name of Angelines had not been given to an Order to which
it would have been so singularly appropriate as the guardians of
youth.

† " Allaturus."

‡ " Papyrus."   Wicks for lamps were made of this formerly.

At the Response *Verus pudicitiæ,* and at the words
Spes et corona virginum,* St. Gertrude returned thanks to
God for those virgins whom she beheld standing before
His throne : and He cast as many rays of glory on them
as she had made thanksgivings for them, which were then
reflected upon her ; by this she understood that those who
return thanks to God for the favours which He has bestowed
on any saint, share in the merits of that saint. As the
Response *Regnum mundi*† was chanted, at the words *Quem
vidi, quem amavi,* she remembered a person who was often
troubled by an ardent desire to see God, and she said to
our Lord : " When wilt Thou console her, that she may
sing this Response with joy ? " He replied : " To see Me,
to love Me, and to believe in Me, is a wish which none
can entertain without fruit ; therefore, when any soul has
this desire, and cannot obtain it because of human frailty,
My Humanity at once advances to My Divinity as a sister,
undertaking to do this favour as if by right of inheritance,
until that person has shaken off her carnal affections, and
is of herself able to undertake it, and thereby to attain
eternal joys."

On another occasion, when the words *Propter amoram
Domini mei* were chanted, the Divine Heart of our Brother‡
Jesus was so moved by these words, that He exclaimed
before His Father and the whole court of heaven, " I am
a debtor to My faithful servants for what they have now
done for Me." At the word *Jesus,* which signifies Saviour,
He acknowledged that He was their debtor for the fulfil-

---

* " Hope and crown of virgins."

† The *Regnum mundi* is from the x. Response, iii. Nocturn, Common of Widows : " The kingdoms of this world, and all their pomp,
I have despised for the love of my Lord Jesus Christ, whom I have
seen, whom I have loved, in whom I have believed."

‡ " Frater noster."

ment of the promises of salvation which He had made to them from their infancy, the accomplishment of which was deferred by His paternal providence until the appointed time. At the word *Christi*, which signifies Anointed, our Lord declared Himself obliged to recompense their good desires. At the words *Quem vidi, quem amavi*, He assured His Father and all the saints that they had rendered testimony to the Catholic faith by their good works ; and at the words *In quem credidi, quem dilexi*, He declared that they were united to Him by their firm faith and perfect charity.

Then St. Gertrude exclaimed : " Alas, Lord ! what wilt Thou do for those who are not in choir ? " He replied : " I have infused a devotion into all those who have been delighted with this Responsory, and have beatified all who are in this convent ; and those who have a similar devotion will receive a similar benefit." " But," she inquired, " if they can gain so much advantage by so little devotion, what harm can their negligence do them, when they can repair it so easily ? " Our Lord answered : " When an emperor bestows an estate and costly garments on one of his nobles, however little he may seem to value them, the emperor does not on that account deprive him of his liberality ; so, when I give great favours in return for a little devotion, those on whom I bestow them are obliged to profit by them, and if they fail to do so, they will lose the fruit thereof; but the ornament of My gratuitous goodness, in bestowing them, will always appear on them for My praise and glory." Then she inquired : " But how can they who have never been favoured with such revelations exercise themselves in such things ? " He answered : " They are bound to practise and to imitate them, according to the extent of the lights they are favoured with. I enlighten every one in such matters to a certain degree, and therefore they are bound to be grateful, and fulfil these obligations."

On another occasion, when the same Response was chanted, St. Gertrude saw a troop of demons, who surrounded the religious, showing them the pomps and vanities of the world. But at the words, *Regnum mundi . . . . contempsi*, the demons fled in confusion. By this she understood, that when any one contemns the world with great fervour, and casts from them all the temptations of the evil one, for the love of the Lord Jesus, that the devil immediately flies away, fearing to tempt them again, when he has met with such vigorous resistance.

CHAPTER LVI.

For the Feast of All Saints.

Of the different orders of the Church Militant—How to honour the Saints by thanksgivings, that we may participate in their merits.

ON the Feast of All Saints, St. Gertrude received some instructions on the mystery of the Blessed Trinity, and learned how the Trinity, which has neither commencement nor termination, and ever abounds in joy and beatitude, imparts eternal glory and blessedness to the saints. But human frailty is such, that she could not explain what she beheld in the clear mirror of the Divinity, so that she was obliged to explain it by images and comparisons. The King of Glory appeared to her as the Father of a great family, who was entertaining all His neighbours, the princes and powers ; so that the Church Militant and the Church Triumphant appeared to mingle together, and each took his

place according to his merit—those who lived holy lives
in the married state were with the Patriarchs, those who
merited to know the Divine secrets were with the Prophets,
those who laboured for the instruction and edification
of others were with the holy Apostles, and so on.   But
Gertrude observed that those religious who served God in
religious observance were joined to the choir of Martyrs ;
and as these were specially adorned in each member of
their body in which they had suffered for their Lord, so
the religious had some special reward for each act of self-
restraint which they had performed, whether in seeing,
hearing, tasting, walking, or speaking ; and they had
the same merit as the martyrs, and received the same
reward in heaven.   For as they had no persecutors to shed
their blood, they had offered themselves daily as a holo-
caust of sweetness to their God by their continued mortifications and restraints.

At Communion, as she prayed for the Church, but felt
a want of fervour,* she prayed to our Lord to give her
fervour, if her petitions were agreeable to Him ; and immediately she beheld a variety of colours : white, which indicated the purity of the virgins ; violet, which symbolised
confessors and religious ; red, which typified the martyrs ;
and other colours, according to the merits of the saints.
Then, as she feared to approach our Lord because she was
not adorned with any of these colours, she was inspired
by the Holy Ghost, "who teaches man wisdom," to return
thanks to God for all those who had been elevated to the
grace and state of virginity ; beseeching Him, by the love
which made Him be born of a Virgin for us, to preserve all
in the Church, to whom He had vouchsafed this favour

---

* " Sed sapore carens."

in most perfect purity of body and soul, for His own honour and glory; and immediately she beheld her soul adorned with the same shining whiteness as the souls of the virgins.

She then returned thanks to God for the sanctity and perfection of the confessors and religious who had pleased him from the beginning of the world, beseeching Him to bring all who were still militant in the Church to a happy end ; and immediately she beheld her soul adorned with violet; and as she continued to pray for the different states and orders in the Church, her soul was adorned with their respective virtues. As she returned most fervent thanks to God for these favours, she beheld herself clothed in a golden amice ; and standing thus marvellously adorned before our Lord, He turned to the saints, and exclaimed : "Behold her in garments of gold, clothed round about with varieties." * Then He opened His arms to receive her, as she was no longer able to support the torrent of Divine joys with which her soul was encompassed.

As the time for Communion approached, and her strength still failed her, she said to our Lord : " O my Beloved ! how can I rise to go to Thee, my Lord and my God, in this Sacrament, when my strength has failed me, and I have not asked any one to come to assist me ? " The Lord answered : " What need have you of human aid, when you are supported by My Divine arm ? I will give you strength to rise and approach Me." Then she arose, sustained by Divine grace ; and although she had not been able to walk without assistance for a long time before, she went in the strength of the Lord to receive His Body, and so became one spirit with Him.

* Psalm xliv. 14.

CHAPTER LVII.

For the Feast of St. Elizabeth.

How pleasing it is to the Saints that we should praise God on their account.

ON the Feast of St. Elizabeth,* as the words *Eia mater nos agnosce* were chanted, Gertrude saluted her very devoutly, beseeching her to remember her, though unworthy. Then St. Elizabeth said to her : "I know you in the mirror of eternal light, where the intention which you have in performing your actions shines with marvellous splendour." St. Gertrude then inquired : "Has my union with God, during the Office, rendered it less pleasing to you, as I thought less of you in consequence ?" She replied : "On the contrary, I accept it with infinite gratitude ; and it is as much more pleasing to me as a concert of music would be to the lowing of oxen."

CHAPTER LVIII.

For the Feast of St. Catherine.

Of the patronage and merits of this Saint.

WHEN our Lord explained the words, *Non est inventus similis illi,* to St. Gertrude, on the Feast of St. Augustine, He

---

* St. Elizabeth of Hungary ; Nov. 19. This Saint lived in the same century as St. Gertrude. She was born in 1207, died in 1231, and was canonised in 1235. The ardent devotion which her sanctity had excited was at its highest point of fervour at the close of the century, when St. Gertrude wrote.

The quotation *Eia mater*—"O Mother, acknowledge us for thy children"—is from the Prose, *Gaude, Sion, quod egressus,* Mass of St. Elizabeth, Nov. 19. *Missale Brixinense* showed her the merits of many saints, and, amongst others, those of the glorious virgin Catherine, to whom she had been singularly devoted from her infancy. To satisfy her desires, our Lord showed her this Saint, seated on a high throne, and in a state of great glory and magnificence, as if there were no queen in heaven whose glory equalled hers. The fifty philosophers, whom she had won by her wisdom and knowledge, appeared before her, and each held a golden sceptre in his hand, with which he touched the robe of the Saint, to indicate that their wisdom would have been useless had not this virgin taught them how to employ it for the honour and glory of their Creator. She observed also that our Lord bestowed the same caresses on this virgin as on St. Agnes, and that He drew into His Heart all that was said or done in her honour on earth, crowning her with it gloriously.

CHAPTER LIX.

For the Dedication of a Church.

§ 1. *Of patience under calumnies, of the oblation of our hearts in trouble, and of mutual charity.*

ON the Feast of the Dedication of the Church, as they chanted those words at Matins, *Regina Saba venit,* &c., at the words *Cum gemmis virtutum,** she said to God, with great compunction : " Alas, most kind Lord ! how shall I come to Thee, since I am not adorned with even the smallest garment of virtue ? " He replied : " Do you not

* From 3 Kings x. 1: "The queen of Saba came," &c., "and brought precious stones." The *Insinuationes,* however, have *virtutum,* as above.

know that you are sometimes annoyed by the calumnies which are said of you?" "Alas, Lord!" she answered. "my sins in this matter are often a stumbling-block to my neighbour." He replied: "Make each of these words which annoy you an ornament of virtue, and then come to Me, and I will be moved by My goodness, and receive you lovingly; the more you are blamed, the more My Heart will incline towards you, since you thus become more like Me; for I suffered contradictions continually."

At the Response *Benedic*,* our Lord introduced her into His Heart, which He adorned as a house, that she might celebrate the Dedication therein; but the exceeding delights which she found there so overcame her, that she said to our Lord: "My Lord, if Thou hadst permitted me to enter even where Thy Feet had once stood, it would have been more than enough for me; but what return shall I make to Thee for the stupendous favour which Thou hast now bestowed on me?" He replied: "As you give Me what is most precious to you—namely, your heart—I consider it only right to give you Mine, to take your delight therein; for I am a God to you in all things, in virtue, life, and knowledge."

Then she said: "If my heart has pleased Thee in anything, it has been by Thy grace." He answered: "Those whom I prevent with the sweetness of My benedictions, I reward with beatitude; and if any one co-operates with My grace, according to the good pleasure of My Heart, I conform Myself also to the good pleasure of his heart."

Our Lord then taught her the importance of mutual support and charity, by a vision of precious stones joined

---

* iii. Response, i. Nocturn: "Bless, O Lord, this house which I have built in Thy name."

together by plates of gold : and she learned that as the
jewels were united together by gold, so we should assist
and support each other by love and by a pure intention.

§ 2. *Of charity towards our enemies, and of the joy of our
Lord when a sinner is converted.*

On another occasion, on the Vigil of the Dedication,
St. Gertrude presented herself before God, who is the King
of kings, as another Esther, richly adorned, to plead for
her people—that is, for the Church—and she was received
by the true Assuerus with such tender charity, that He
admitted her into the sanctuary of His most sweet Heart,
saying to her : " Behold, I give you all the sweetness of
My Divine Heart, that you may pour it forth abundantly
on whomsoever you will." Then she poured forth abundant
graces on some enemies who had molested the convent *
a short time before ; and as soon as she had done this, she
perceived that all those on whom even the least drop had
fallen, repented of their faults, and were moved to true
compunction and desire of penance. Then, as she prayed
for another person, and drew forth largely from the Heart
of Jesus for him, she perceived that the grace poured on
him was immediately converted into gall. As she was
much amazed thereat, our Lord gave her this instruction :
" When a man gives money to his friends, they are at
liberty to purchase what they please with it ; and of those
who desire to purchase apples,† some might prefer sour
ones to sweet ones, as the former would keep longer. So it
is with My elect—when I bestow My grace on them, it

* " Villam ; " perhaps a grange or farm-house belonging to the
nonastery.
† " Poma."

operates in them in the way which will benefit them most. For example : it is better for some persons to have troubles in this life than consolations ; so, when I pour out My grace upon them, it increases their trials and afflictions, by which they receive more and more grace, according to the good pleasure of My Divine Heart ; and the consolation which they will enjoy hereafter is hidden from them now, that they may suffer more purely for My love."

As the Saint heard Matins, at the Response *Vidi civitatem*,* our Lord reminded her of certain words which she had often used to induce others to have more confidence in God ; and He said to her : " Know and be assured that I am always pleased when a soul repents of its faults, and resolves by My grace not to commit them again." When He said this, the Son of God proceeded to the throne of His Father, and chanted the Response *Vidi civitatem* with a loud and sonorous voice. She understood by this, that the Heart of Jesus is moved by the most ineffable tenderness, when a soul repents for the wanderings, the idle words, or the unprofitable works by which it has withdrawn itself from its God— who, by so many repeated favours, prevents and follows him—and earnestly begs to avoid a relapse for the future ; and as often as he falls as often does the Son of God chant the same words with ineffable joy.   By this she understood, that whoever purposes with sincere compunction to reform his life and to devote himself to good works, will indeed become the tabernacle of God, in which His Divine Majesty, who is blessed for evermore, will abide as a Spouse with His beloved.

God the Father then gave her His benediction, saying, *Ecce nova facio omnia* (" Behold, I make all things new ;")

---

* xii. Response, iii. Nocturn.

meaning thereby, that by compunction and the Divine benediction, united to the holy life of the Son of God, the faithful soul was perfectly renewed whereinsoever she had been deficient ; and hence there is joy before the angels for every sinner who repents, more than for the ninety and nine who needed no repentance, for the infinite goodness of God delights in seeing a soul truly penitent. Our Lord added : " When I lead a soul forth from this life by a marvellous way to the palaces of heaven, I sing this canticle for her, amongst the other joys with which I console her ' I saw the holy city, the new Jerusalem, ascending * from the earth ; ' and by these words I renew in her soul all the joys which I and all the celestial court have had, whenever she was sincerely sorry for her falls."

CHAPTER LX.

For the Dedication of a Chapel.

Of the presence and grace of God in holy places—And how the angels supply for our obligation of praising God.

AT the consecration of the church, as the Response *Vidi civitatem* † was chanted at Matins, our Lord appeared to St. Gertrude, clothed in pontificals, and enthroned near the altar, as if this was the place which he delighted to inhabit. As she beheld this, and considered how far our Lord was from the place where she prayed, she desired very ardently to draw Him nearer to her ; but He said : " Since I fill

---

* " Ascendentem de terra." This passage is partly a quotation from Rev. xxi. 2.

† " I saw the holy city, the new Jerusalem, descending from heaven ; " xii. Response, iii. Nocturn.

heaven and earth, why can I not fill this house? Do you not know that it is better to watch the place where the arrow falls than that where the bow is bent? and know that I do not act most effectively where I appear corporally, but rather where My treasure is, and where the Eye of My Divinity finds pleasure." Then He touched the altar as if it had been near Him, saying: "Whoever seeks for My grace, will find Me in My favours; and whoever seeks My love faithfully, will feel Me in interior sweetness." By these words she understood the great difference between those who endeavour to obtain health of body, and even of soul, according to their own will, and those who commit themselves with full confidence to Divine Providence.

As the words *Domus mea* * were repeated at Mass, our Lord touched the heart of Gertrude with His Right Hand, and exclaimed, as if He was deeply moved : " I will grant all you ask Me ;" at the same time extending His Hand to the centre of the church, as if to indicate that He would always be there, and ready to grant the favours which were asked of Him. While the Antiphon *Fundamenta templi ejus* was chanted at the Benedictus during the week, angelic spirits appeared around the walls, as if they had been deputed to guard the church, and to repel the attacks of all enemies. Their golden wings touched each other, and emitted a most exquisite melody. She observed also, that each descended in turn from the top to the bottom, to show with what vigilance they guarded their fellow-citizens, and preserved them from every evil.

On the Feast of the Dedication, as St. Gertrude was confined to bed, she reflected on the special favour our Lord had granted her at Matins, in the preceding year, by

---

* "Domus mea" is probably from a Collect.

telling her that the nine choirs of angels had made thanksgiving for her, which her infirmity had prevented her from making herself. Then she saw a river of pure and sparkling water flowing through heaven, in which the glory of God shone as the rising sun shines red upon the ocean; and as its little waves broke and glittered, it appeared as if a thousand suns were shining in heaven. This river signified the grace of devotion which she then enjoyed by the Divine favour, and the little waves signified the thoughts which she referred to God.

Then the King of Glory dipped a chalice in this river, and when he had filled it, He gave it to all the saints to drink; and as each obtained thereby new delights, they broke forth in praises and thanksgiving for all the graces which God had conferred on this soul. She also saw a little tube which came forth from the bottom of the chalice to all those whom she had inclined to serve God with great fervour, or who had been commended to her prayers : and they received great consolation thereby. Then she said to our Lord : "What advantage will these persons gain by what I have seen and heard, when they have neither seen nor heard them ?" He replied : " Is it not very advantageous for the head of a family to have his cellars well supplied with wine, although he does not constantly drink it ? Is it not sufficient for him to be able to partake of it whenever he desires ? Thus when I pour forth graces, in answer to the prayers of My elect, they do not immediately feel devotion ; but I will allow them to experience this sweetness whenever I consider it expedient for them."

CHAPTER LXI.

Of a marvellous vision, in which the Saint beheld our Lord celebrating Mass.

On *Gaudete* Sunday, as St. Gertrude prepared to communicate at the first Mass, which commences *Rorate*, she complained to our Lord that she could not hear Mass ; but our Lord, who compassionates the afflicted, consoled her, saying: " Do you wish, My beloved, that I should say Mass for you ? " Then, being suddenly rapt in spirit, she replied : " I do desire it, O beloved of my soul ; and I most ardently beseech Thee to grant me This favour." Our Lord then intoned the *Gaudete in Domino semper*, with a choir of saints, to incite this soul to praise and rejoice in Him ; and as He sat on His royal throne, St. Gertrude cast herself at His Feet, and embraced them. Then He chanted the *Kyrie eleison*, in a clear and loud voice, while two of the princes of the choir of Thrones took her soul and brought it before God the Father, where she remained prostrate.

At the first *Kyrie eleison*, He granted her the remission of all the sins which she had contracted through human frailty ; after which, the angels raised her up on her knees. At the second, He pardoned her sins of ignorance ; and she was raised up by these princes, so that she stood before God. Then two angels of the choir of Cherubim led her to the Son of God, who received her with great tenderness. At the first *Christe eleison*, the Saint offered our Lord all the sweetness of human affection, returning it to Him as to its Source ; and thus there was a wonderful influx of God into her soul, and of her soul into God, so that by the descending notes the ineffable delights of the Divine Heart flowed into her, and by the ascending notes the joys of

her soul flowed back to God.   At the second *Christe eleison*,
she experienced the most ineffable delights, which she offered
to our Lord.   At the third *Christe eleison*, the Son of God
extended His Hands, and bestowed on her all the fruit of
His most holy life and conversation.

Two angels of the choir of Seraphim then presented her
to the Holy Spirit, who penetrated the three powers of her
soul.   At the first *Kyrie eleison*, He illuminated her reason
with the glorious light of Divine knowledge, that she might
always know His will perfectly.   At the second *Kyrie
eleison*, He strengthened the irascible* part of her soul to
resist all the machinations of her enemies, and to conquer
every evil.   At the last *Kyrie eleison*, He inflamed her love,
that she might love God with her whole heart, with her
whole soul, and with her whole strength.   It was for
this reason that the choir of Seraphim, which is the
highest order in the heavenly hosts, presented her to the
Holy Ghost, who is the Third Person of the Most Holy
Trinity, and that the Thrones presented her to God the
Father, manifesting† that the Father, Son, and Holy Ghost
are One God, equal in glory, co-eternal in majesty, living
and reigning perfect Trinity through endless ages.

The Son of God then rose from His royal throne, and,
turning towards God the Father, intoned the *Gloria in
excelsis* in a clear and sonorous voice.   At the word *Gloria*,
He extolled the immense and incomprehensible omnipotence
of God the Father ; at the words *in excelsis*, He praised
His profound wisdom ; at *Deo*, He honoured ‡ the inestimable and indescribable sweetness of the Holy Ghost.   The
whole celestial court then continued in a most harmonious
voice, *Et in terra pax bonæ voluntatis.*   Our Lord being

---

* " Iracibilem."   † " Innuebatur."   ‡ " Reverebatur."

again seated on His throne, St. Gertrude sat at His feet
meditating on her own abjection, when He inclined towards
her lovingly. Then she rose and stood before Him, while
the Divine splendour illuminated her whole being. Two
angels from the choir of Thrones then brought a throne
magnificently adorned, which they placed before our Lord ;
two princes from the choir of Seraphim placed Gertrude
thereon, and supported her on each side, while two of the
choir of Cherubim stood before her bearing brilliant
torches ; and thus she remained before her Beloved, clothed
in royal purple. When the heavenly hosts came to the
words, *Domine Deus Rex cœlestis*, they paused, and the Son
of God continued alone chanting to the honour and glory
of His Father.

At the conclusion of the *Gloria in excelsis*, the Lord
Jesus, who is our true High Priest and Pontiff, turned to St.
Gertrude, saying, *Dominus vobiscum, dilecta*—" The Lord
be with you, beloved ; " and she replied : " *Et spiritus
meus tecum, prædilecta*—" And may my spirit be with Thee,
O my Beloved." After this she inclined towards the Lord,
to return Him thanks for His love in uniting her spirit
to His Divinity, whose delights are with the children of
men. The Lord then read the Collect, *Deus, qui hanc
sacratissimam noctem,* * which He concluded with the
words, *Per Jesum Christum filium tuum*, as if giving
thanks to God the Father for illuminating the soul of Gertrude, whose unworthiness † was indicated by the word
noctem (night), which was called most holy, because she
had become marvellously ennobled by the knowledge of
her own baseness.

St. John the Evangelist then rose, and stood between God

* Collect for Midnight Mass at Christmas.
† " Vilitas."

and her soul. He was adorned with a yellow garment, which was covered with golden eagles. He commenced the Epistle, *Hæc est sponsa*, and the celestial court concluded, *Ipsi gloria in sæcula*. Then all chanted the Gradual *Specia tua*,* adding the Versicle *Audi filia et vide*. After this they commenced the *Alleluia*. St. Paul, the great doctor of the Church, pointed to St. Gertrude, saying, *Æmulor enim vos* †—"For I am jealous of you" (2 Cor. xi. 2); and the heavenly choir sang the prose, *Filiæ Sion exultent*. At the words, *Dum non consentiret*, St. Gertrude remembered that she had been a little negligent in resisting temptations, and she hid her face in shame; but our Lord, who could not bear to behold the confusion of His chaste queen, covered her negligence with a collar of gold, so that she appeared as if she had gained a glorious victory over all her enemies.

Then another Evangelist commenced the Gospel *Exultavit Dominus Jesus;* and these words moved the Heart of Jesus so deeply, that He arose, and, extending His hands, exclaimed aloud, *Confiteor tibi Patre*,‡ manifesting the same thanksgiving and gratitude to His Father as He had done when He said the same words on earth, giving special thanks for the graces bestowed on this soul. After the Gospel He desired Gertrude to make a public profession of faith, by reciting the Creed in the name of the whole

* Gradual, Mass of Virgins; *Audi filia*, Gradual of St. Cecilia. This Mass appears to have been composed from several Masses.

† Epistle, Common of Virgins. We have not been able to verify the prose.

‡ "I confess to Thee, O Father, Lord of heaven and earth, because Thou hast hidden these things from the wise and prudent, and revealed them to little ones" (Matt. xi. 25); Gospel, Com. of Martyrs.

Church. When she had concluded, the choir chanted the offertory, *Domine Deus in simplicitate*, adding, *Sanctificavit* * *Moyses*. The Heart of Jesus then appeared as a golden altar, which shone with a marvellous brightness, on which the angel guardians offered the good works and prayers of those committed to their care. The saints then approached; and each offered his merits to the eternal praise of God, and for the salvation of St. Gertrude. The angelic princes, who had charge of the Saint, next approached, and offered a chalice of gold, which contained all the trials and afflictions which she had endured either in body or soul from her infancy; and the Lord blessed the chalice with the sign of the cross, as the priest blesses it before Consecration.†

He now intoned the words, *Sursum corda.* Then all the saints were summoned to come forward, and they applied their hearts, in the form of golden pipes, to the golden altar of the Divine Heart; and from the overflowings of this chalice, which our Lord had consecrated by His benediction, they received some drops for the increase of their merit, glory, and eternal beatitude.

The Son of God then chanted the *Gratius agimus*, to the glory and honour of His Eternal Father. At the Preface, He remained silent for an hour after the words *Per Jesum Christum*, while the heavenly hosts chanted the *Dominum nostrum* with ineffable jubilation, declaring that He was their Creator, Redeemer, and the liberal Re-

---

* *Domine Deus;* Offertory for Dedication of a Church. The continuation is taken from the Office for Dedication.

† " The priest, elevating his eyes towards heaven, &c., . . . makes the sign of the cross over the Host and Chalice, while he says: 'Come, O Sanctifier,' " &c. See Missal, Ordinary of the Mass.

warder of all their good works; and that He alone was
worthy of honour and glory, praise and exaltation, power
and dominion, from and over all creatures. At the
words *Laudant angeli,* all the angelic spirits ran hither and
thither, exciting the heavenly inhabitants to sing the Divine
praises. At the words *Adorant Dominationes,* the choir
of Dominations knelt to adore our Lord, declaring that to
Him alone every knee should bow, whether in heaven, on
earth, or under the earth. At the *Tremunt Potestatis,* the
Powers prostrated before Him to declare that He alone
should be adored ; and at the *Cœli cœlorumque,* they
praised God with all the angel choirs.

Then all the heavenly hosts sang together in harmonious concert the *Cum quibus et nostras ;* and the Virgin
Mary, the effulgent Rose of heaven, who is blessed above all
creatures, chanted the *Sanctus, sanctus, sanctus,* extolling
with the highest gratitude by these three words the incomprehensible omnipotence, the inscrutable wisdom, and the
ineffable goodness, of the Ever-Blessed Trinity, inciting all
the celestial choirs to praise God for having made her most
powerful after the Father, most wise after the Son, and
most benign after the Holy Ghost. The saints then continued the *Domine Deus Sabaoth.* When this was ended,
Gertrude saw our Lord rise from His royal throne, and
present His blessed Heart to His Father, elevating it with
His own hands, and immolating it in an ineffable manner
for the whole Church. At this moment the bell rang for
the Elevation of the Host in the church ; so that it appeared as if our Lord did in heaven what the priest did on
earth ; but the Saint was entirely ignorant of what was
passing in the church, or what the time was. As she
continued in amazement at so many marvels, our Lord
told her to recite the *Pater noster.* When she had finished,

He accepted it from her, and granted to all the saints and angels, for her sake, that, by this *Pater noster*, they should accomplish everything which had ever been accomplished for the salvation of the Church and for the souls in purgatory. Then He suggested to her to pray for the Church, which she did, for all in general and for each in particular, with the greatest fervour ; and the Lord united her prayer to those which He had offered Himself when in the flesh, to be applied to the Universal Church.

Then she exclaimed : " But, Lord, when shall I communicate ? " And our Lord communicated Himself to her with a love and tenderness which no human tongue could describe ; so that she received the perfect fruit of His most precious Body and Blood. After this He sang a canticle of love for her, and declared to her, that had this union of Himself with her been the sole fruit of His labours, sorrows, and Passion, He would have been fully satisfied. O inestimable sweetness of the Divine condescension, who so delights Himself in human hearts, that He considers His union with them a sufficient return for all the bitterness of His Passion ! and yet, what should we not owe Him had He only shed one drop of His precious Blood for us !

Our Lord then chanted *Gaudete justi*, and all the saints rejoiced with Gertrude. Then our Lord said, in the name of the Church Militant, *Refecti cibo,** &c. ; He then saluted all the saints lovingly, saying, *Dominus vobiscum*, and thereby increased the glory and joy of all the blessed. The saints and angels then sang, for the *Missa est*, *Te decet laus et honor Domine,* to the glory and praise of the effulgent and ever-peaceful Trinity. The Son of God extended His royal Hand, and blessed the Saint, saying :

---

* Communion, Com. of Conf. not Bishop ; Mass *Os Justi.*

" I bless thee, O daughter of eternal light, with this special blessing, granting you this favour, that whenever you desire to do good to any one from particular affection, they will be as much benefited above others as Isaac was above Esau when he received his father's blessing."

Then the Saint recovered from her rapture, and remained more closely united than ever to her Beloved.

PART V.

THE REVELATIONS OF ST. GERTRUDE.

COMPILED BY THE RELIGIOUS OF HER MONASTERY.

CHAPTER I.

How St. Mechtilde prepared for death, and received extreme unction.

WHEN Dame * Mechtilde, of happy memory, our chantress, who was full of good works, or rather full of God, was confined to bed in her last sickness, about a month before her death, she began to think of her end, and to reflect on some works which she had written. But on Sunday, as a person prayed for her, asking that she

---

* *Domina.* According to Bucelinus, *Aquila Imperii Benedictini,* p. 210, St. Mechtilde was the fourth and youngest child of the noble Count of Hackeborn. A few moments after her birth she appeared to be dying, and was at once carried to the Church to receive Holy Baptism. The priest who administered the Sacrament was a " holy and just man," who thus addressed the by-standers : "Why do you fear? this infant shall live and become a devoted spouse of Christ ; God will work many miracles through her ; and she shall finish her days in a good old age." Our Lord afterwards revealed to her that her baptism was thus hastened that she might at once become the temple of God and the possessor of His grace. She has mentioned this touching incident herself in

might have the grace of a happy death, under the protection of the Divine mercy, so that she might abandon herself to it with humble confidence when receiving the Body
and Blood of Christ, she knew in spirit that God had drawn

---

the first chapter of her Revelations, which are of scarcely less importance and interest than those of her saintly sister.

At seven years of age she was consecrated to God in the monastery
of Rodersdorf, where her sister had already been dedicated to
the Divine service, according to the ancient custom of the order;
which, however, as we observed before, has been abolished by
authority. It is probable that the two sisters removed at the same
time to Heldelfs. Here her life was a continual exercise of every
virtue. Notwithstanding her innocence of life, she practised the
severest corporal austerities, such as discipline and wearing hair-
cloth. Her love for Jesus Christ made her grieve over the sins
whereby men are continually offending Him, and a devotion to His
Sacred Passion and Death was especially dear to her. Such was
her fervour at the Divine Office, that she was often ravished into
an ecstasy; and so great was the purity of her soul, that our Lord
deigned to converse familiarly with her, and revealed His heavenly
secrets to her. She had also a most tender love for the souls in
purgatory; for whom she offered up penances and mortifications, and
sought by every means to procure their deliverance. St. Gertrude,
her Abbess, frequently consulted her, and received her advice as a
Divine oracle.

Though often visited with illness and sufferings, she endured
them with the most edifying patience and resignation, but yet, like
the Apostle, with a holy longing to be delivered from the prison of
flesh. Her loving desires were at length gratified, and she passed
to the embraces of her Spouse on the 19th November. It was the
Feast of St. Elizabeth of Hungary, and the religious interrupted
Matins in order to be present at her happy death. Chronologists
do not agree about the date of her birth and death, but she appears to have lived during part of the thirteenth and fourteenth
centuries.

Her Revelations are entitled, *Liber gratiæ spiritualis visionum et
Revelationum Beatæ Mechtildis Virginis devotissimæ*, and are divided
into five parts. The first part contains instructions for assisting at
Mass and the Divine Office on many Feasts of the year. Indeed,
the Divine Office was the special devotion of these saintly sisters,
and a devotion which appears to have been particularly acceptable

this soul to Himself entirely, and that He had only restored her for a brief space, that He might again abide in
her. Then she said to the Lord : " Lord, why dost Thou
wish her to continue on earth ?" He replied : " It is to
perfect the work which My Divine dispensation has de-
creed ; and she will contribute to this in three ways : by
the repose of humility, the table * of patience, and the joy†
of virtue. For example : in all that she sees or hears
from others, let her always humble herself and consider
herself the most unworthy of all. Thus will I rejoice in
the repose of her heart and soul. Secondly : let her
embrace patience joyfully, and suffer all her trials and
sicknesses willingly for love of Me ; thus she will prepare
Me a table of sumptuous delights. Thirdly : she will

---

to their Spouse. As true children of St. Benedict, it could not be
otherwise ; for he has said in his immortal Rule, " Let nothing be
preferred to the work of God " (ch. xliii.) ; therefore, in proportion
to the sanctity of his children, will be their devotion to the angelic
work of singing the praises of their King. Hence, where we find
the most exalted sanctity, we find also the greatest perfection in,
and love for, this work ; as in each Order in God's Church the
sanctity of its members will be characterised by a special devotion
to the special end for which Providence instituted its Rule and
observance.

The second part of these Revelations contains many facts relating to St. Mechtilde, and details of her communications with her
heavenly Spouse. The third and fourth parts are on the Divine
praise and on the salvation of men. The fifth part is devoted to the
souls in purgatory, with instructions how they may be assisted by
the Church Militant.

The Revelations of St. Mechtilde are becoming very scarce and
valuable. The principal editions are those of Paris, 1513 ; Cologne,
1536 ; Venice, 1522, 1558, and 1589. This Saint has been confounded
with St. Mechtild of Spanheim and St. Mechtild of Diessen by several
authors, amongst others by Alban Butler. Her name has never been
inserted in the Roman Martyrology.

    * " Mensam."   † " Lusum."

offer Me a joyful spectacle if she exercises herself in every kind of virtue."

On another occasion, when St. Mechtilde was ready to communicate, this person asked our Lord what He was about to do in her. He answered : " I am going to repose with her in this couch." By this she understood that the couch in which our Lord reposed with her was her perfect confidence, in all her afflictions, that God would order all that concerned her in the greatest love and mercy for the furtherance of her salvation ; so that she offered continual thanksgivings to Him, trusting entirely in His Providence.

When she was near her end, one evening at Vesper time, she was suddenly seized with such excruciating pain in the heart, that the sisters who stood round her could not restrain their tears ; but she consoled them, saying : " Do not weep for me, my beloved ones ; for I am so touched by your grief, that were it the will of my dearest Lord I would gladly bear this very pain all my life, if I could thereby obtain consolation for you."

On another occasion, when t ey urged her to take some medicine which they hoped would give her some relief, she yielded to their request ; but immediately after her sufferings increased greatly. On the following day the person before mentioned besought our Lord to reward her humble compliance. He replied : " From the suffering which My beloved endured on that occasion I have confected a most salutary remedy, which I have used to purify the souls of all sinners throughout the world."

On the Sunday *Si iniquitates*,* the Saint communicated

---

* " If Thou shalt observe iniquities, O Lord, Lord. who shall en-

for the last time before her death ; and this person prayed that she might be inspired to prepare for extreme unction, and that our Lord would keep her soul in His bosom, to preserve it from every stain, as an artist covers a newly-painted picture lest it should contract dust. When she told this to St. Mechtilde, who was always perfectly submissive to her superiors, she committed herself humbly to their good pleasure and to Divine Providence, which she hoped would never forsake her. However, her superior had such veneration for her, that she believed our Lord would make known the hour of her death to her ; and as she did not ask earnestly to receive this Sacrament, it was not administered that day.

But our Lord soon verified the words of the Gospel, "Heaven and earth shall pass away, but My words shall not pass away" (Matt. xxiv. 35) ; and he failed not to accomplish what He had promised to His chosen one. For on Monday * blessed Mechtilde became so ill, just before Matins, that we feared she had fallen into her agony, so that the priests were immediately sent for, and she received extreme unction. Thus, although the Sacrament was not administered on Sunday, it was administered the night of that day, as she received it before sunrise on Monday.

When her eyes were anointed by the priest, the religious who had prayed for her understood that our most loving Lord

---

lure it?" Introit, 22d Sunday after Pentecost. The date of St. Mechtilde's death admits of no dispute. The Feast of St. Elizabeth occurs on the 19th November, and, as it will be seen later, it was the fifth *feria* (Thursday) after this Sunday. The 22d Sunday after Pentecost, therefore, must have fallen on the 15th November.

* "Feria secunda,"

looked on her with Divine mercy, and, with a Heart **full of**
tenderness towards her, shed a ray of His Divine light into
her soul, imparting to her at the same time a share in the
merits which He had obtained when on earth by the glances
of His most holy Eyes ; and then she beheld the eyes of the
Saint, as if overflowing with the oil of divine compassion.
From this she understood that those who invoke this Saint
with confidence would feel abundant proof of the efficacy of
her intercession ; and that she had merited this favour with
God by her gentle, loving conduct towards others.   When
the other members of her body were anointed, our Lord
applied the merits of those parts of His own most sacred
Body to her also.   When her lips were anointed, this
zealous Lover * of our souls honoured her with marks of
the tenderest love, imparting to her the fruit of His most
holy lips.

When the Litanies were said, at the words *Omnes sancti
Seraphim et Cherubim, orate pro ea,*† she beheld the
hosts of seraphim and cherubim making way for her soul
to pass through their ranks, as if to give precedence to one
who had led so pure and virginal a life on earth ; who, like
the cherubim, had drawn spiritual knowledge so copiously
from the true Fount of all wisdom ; and, like the seraphim,
had been enkindled by Him who is a consuming fire (Heb.
xii. 29).

As the saints were named in the Litany, they offered
their merits for her with great joy, under the form of gifts,
which they presented to our Lord, who placed them in His
bosom for His beloved.   For two days after she had received extreme unction, she appeared to live only by

---

* " Ardentissimus animæ zelator."
† Not in the present Litany for the Dying.

union with her Lord, and to draw every grace from His Divine Heart. But the happy moment of her departure was at hand, and on Wednesday, which was the Vigil of St. Elizabeth, she fell into her agony, after None. The community, having assembled to assist their beloved sister in Christ by their fervent prayers for her happy passage to eternity, the person before mentioned beheld her soul under the form of a fair young girl, who applied her lips to the Wound of our Lord's Side, and drew thence streams of grace for the whole Church, and especially for those who were present. And she understood that she had prayed specially both for the living and the dead, and therefore our Lord had bestowed such abundant favours on her.

When they recited the *Salve Regina*, at the words *Eia ergo*, St. Mechtilde prayed very earnestly to the Blessed Virgin for the beloved sisters whom she was about to leave, beseeching her to have a special care of them ; as if she, who during her life had been so devoted to her community, so tender and helpful and loving, desired to secure an advocate for them after her death in the person of the Mother of Mercy. And this blessed Queen took the hand of the dying religious, as if she was accepting the charge of the community from her. Then, as they read the prayer *Ave Jesu Christe*, at the words *via dulcis*, she beheld the Lord Jesus showing His beloved spouse the way by which He purposed to draw her sweetly to Himself.

The Saint continued all day in her agony, without saying any other words than these, *Jesu bone ! Jesu bone !* as if to show how He dwelt in her heart, since His sweet Name was so constantly on her lips in the agonies of death. Then, as each of the sisters commended themselves to her prayers, beseeching her to intercede with God for their necessities, she immediately replied, "Willingly," although scarcely able to speak, as if she would say with what love she would pray for those who were committed to her care. St. Gertrude knew also that the great sufferings which her sister had endured with such patience had contributed much to her sanctification; and she beheld a certain vapour coming forth from those parts of her body which had suffered most; and this touched her soul, purifying it from its stains, sanctifying it, and preparing it for eternal beatitude.

Now Gertrude knew all these things in spirit, but she feared to declare them, lest it should be suspected that she had received these revelations; but this was contrary to the Divine will, whose glory it is to discover the truth (Tob. xii. 10), and who commanded His Apostles to preach on the house-tops what they heard in the ear (Matt. x. 27). As they said the Vespers of St. Elizabeth, St. Mechtilde's agony increased so evidently, that they feared she was about to expire; the sisters were, therefore, summoned from the choir, that they might redouble their prayers by her bedside.* As St. Gertrude assisted with the rest of the

---

* The Divine Office is the first and most solemn duty of all religious orders, who are bound to its recital. Yet now, as in the time of St. Gertrude, this great and solemn obligation gives way for the time when a soul is reaching the awful moment of its passage to eternity. Truly it may be said, "Charity never falleth away." The "prophecies" may cease, and there may be no Gertrude now hidden in the cloistered homes of her great Order; tongues may cease, for the language of those living under the same Rule may not be alike or understood in many lands; but charity never falleth away: and whether its exercise is needed by the bed of a dying religious in India or in Rome, in England or America, it is given with equal tenderness and promptitude. The religious dies surrounded by her sisters; their prayers for her

community, she found herself unable to understand or
attend to anything that was said : this occasioned her to
see her fault in concealing what God had revealed to
her.   But when she had promised our Lord to make
known these favours for His honour and glory and the
good of others, the use of her faculties was at once
restored.

After Compline the dying nun entered her third and
last agony ; and St. Gertrude was rapt in spirit, and
beheld her soul again under the form of a young girl, but
with new ornaments, the fruit of renewed sufferings.   She
observed also that this soul approached our Lord with
intense love, and began culling from His wounds—as a bee

---

may indeed be broken by sobs, and interrupted by tears; but are
not the tears and sighs also prayers, and the most moving prayers,
to His Heart who wept at the grave of Lazarus?   In the Order of
Poor Clares, with whose observances we are most familiar, it is
required that *two* sisters should remain night and day with the
religious from the moment there is the least apprehension of danger.
One is charged to summon the whole community, however engaged,
either by day or by night, the moment the agony commences ;
the other sister remains, so that the dying person may not be left
alone even for a moment.   And who can describe what must be
witnessed to be understood ?   Sometimes the loving adieu to each ;
sometimes the humble acknowledgment of faults, and the fervent
request for pardon of any disedification which may have been
given in a life which has perhaps been one of the highest edification ;
the kneeling sisters, unwearied in their prayers for hours, even
long after the soul so dear to them has heard her final doom ;
and the loving mother, who has forgotten her own weariness,
or it may be actual suffering, as she watches day and night by
the bed of her child, with such love as only a mother can offer,
and such consolations and helps as only a spiritual mother can
give ; whose absence, even during a prolonged sickness, is the
exception, and whose presence the rule.   Truly only those who
have witnessed such blessed deathbeds can estimate the grace of
a religious vocation.

from flowers—the sweet honey of the Divine delights. As they read this Response, amongst others, *Ave Sponsa*, the Blessed Virgin approached the soul of the dying nun to prepare it for enjoying the delights of the Divinity. Then our Lord Jesus—for the sake of His Blessed Mother, who alone merited to be called, and to be both a Virgin and a Mother—took a necklace of marvellous beauty, adorned with radiant gems, and placed it on the religious ; granting her the special privilege of being also called a virgin and mother, on account of the fervour and devotion with which she had guided her spiritual children.

CHAPTER II.

Of the happy death of St. Mechtilde, and her reward in heaven— Of the merits and intercession of the saints—And how to offer the Five Wounds of Christ to supply for our defects.

THE Matins of St. Elizabeth had already commenced, when it became apparent that St. Mechtilde was about to expire ; the community were therefore summoned again from the choir to assist at her happy death. Our Lord then appeared to the dying Saint as a Spouse radiant with beauty, crowned with honour and glory, and said to her tenderly : " Now, My beloved, I will honour you before your neighbours— that is, before this congregation, which is so dear to Me." Then He saluted her soul in an ineffable manner by each of His Wounds, so that each saluted her in four different manners : namely, by a melodious harmony, by an effica- cious vapour, by a fruitful dew, and by a marvellous light. Thus did our Lord call His elect one to Himself : the exquisite harmony indicated all the loving words which she had addressed to God, or uttered for the benefit of others; and these words were fructified exceedingly by passing through the Divine Heart. The vapour signified all her desires for the glory of God or the salvation of her neighbour; and these desires were marvellously increased by passing through the Wounds of Jesus. The dew which poured forth so abundantly represented the love which she had for God, or for any creature for His sake; and it was also greatly increased in sweetness by these sacred Wounds. The marvellous light signified all the sufferings which she had endured from her infancy, either in body or mind, which were ennobled beyond all human power of comprehension by union with the Passion of Christ; and that her soul was sanctified thereby, and impressed with the marks of Divine charity.

The enjoyment of these heavenly consolations restored even the bodily strength of the dying religious, as she continued aspiring after the joys on which she was so soon to enter. Our Lord then poured forth an abundant benediction on all who were present, saying: "Moved by the ardour of My love, I desire that each member of My beloved congregation should assist at this transfiguration, and that they should receive as much honour from the blessed in paradise as My chosen ones, Peter, James, and John, who assisted at My Transfiguration on the Mount, received from the other Apostles." Then the religious said: * "Lord, what benefit will they gain from these graces who do not

---

* This religious was probably the person who compiled the Revelations; the extreme care to conceal her name, and the abrupt way in which she is mentioned, are almost an evidence of this.

perceive them by any interior sweetness?" He replied :
" When a nobleman bestows an orchard on a friend, he
does not at once taste the fruit, as he must wait until they
ripen. Thus, when I pour forth precious gifts on a soul,
she does not perceive their sweetness until they are fructified by the exercise of exterior virtues ; but when the skin
of earthly pleasures and consolations is removed, then she
can taste the interior consolation."

The community now returned to the choir to say Matins. At the twelfth Response, *O lampas,** this soul appeared standing before the Blessed Trinity, praying devoutly for the Church. Then God the Father saluted her
lovingly by these words : " *Ave, electa mea* (Hail, My
elect one), who, by the example of your holy life, may
truly be called the lamp of the Church, abounding in oil—
that is, your prayers for the whole world." Then the Son
of God addressed her thus : " *Gaude, sponsa mea* (Rejoice, O My spouse), who may truly be called the medicament of grace, since by your prayers you have obtained
the restoration of so many to My favour." The Holy
Ghost added : " *Ave, immaculata mea* (Hail, My spotless
one), who may be called the nurse of the faithful, since
you have fed and nourished so many spiritually."

After this the Eternal Father conferred on her, by His

---

* This Response has evidently been adapted from the thirty-fourth
stanza of the hymn *Lætare Germania,* published in an Antiphonary of
the fifteenth century. It runs thus—
> " O lampas Ecclesiæ,
> Rivos profundens olei,
> Medicina gratiæ,
> Nutrimentum fidei."

The prose *Gaude Sion,* and the hymn *Lætare Germania,* are both in
honour of St. Elizabeth.

omnipotence, the grace of assisting those who, through human frailty, distrusted the Divine mercy, and of strengthening in them the gift of hope ; the Holy Spirit conferred on her the privilege of enkindling fervour and love in cold and tepid hearts ; lastly, the Son of God gave her, through the merit of His most precious Death and Passion, the grace of curing souls enfeebled by sin.

The celestial choirs then chanted, in a clear and sonorous voice, *Tu Dei saturitas, oliva fructifera, cujus lucet puritas, et resplendent opera.* * At the words *cujus lucet*, they honoured the sweet repose which our Lord had taken in her ; at the words *et resplendent*, they praised the pure intention which had animated all her actions ; in conclusion, all the saints chanted the Antiphon *Deus palim omnibus.*

During the Preface of the High Mass, our Lord appeared to St. Mechtilde, drawing her towards Him, and imparting new graces and favours to her soul, as if to prepare her for the enjoyment of eternal beatitude. At last the joyful moment came when she was to pass to the eternal embraces of her Spouse ; and the Lord of Glory, who is so great in His majesty and so tender in His love, invited her to Him, saying : "Come, blessed of My Father, possess the kingdom prepared for you" (Matt. xxv. 34). He reminded her also of the signal favour which He had conferred on her some years before, by giving her His Heart, as He said these words, to be her consolation and protection. Then He said : "And where is My gift?" In reply, she offered Him her heart, plunging it into His ; and our Lord touched her heart with His, absorbing her into Himself, and putting her in possession of eternal glory, where we hope she will obtain many favours for us by her intercession.

---

* "Delight of God, fruitful olive-tree, whose purity shines afar, whose works are glorious."

As the usual prayers were recited after her decease, our Lord appeared, enthroned in glory, and this soul reposed upon His bosom. As the words, *Subvenite sancti Dei, occurrite angeli*,* were read, the angels testified their reverence for her who had been thus honoured by their King; and they appeared as if adorned by the prayers of this soul, whom they had assisted by their prayers when she received the last anointing. The saints also acted in like manner.

Then the religious asked the deceased to pray for some persons in whom she had a special interest, that they might overcome their defects. She replied: "Now that I see all things in the light of truth, I know that all the affection which I entertained for any one when in the world was but as a drop in the ocean when compared to the love of the Divine Heart for them; and it is by a salutary providence that God permits their defects, that they may be humbled on account of them. Thus they daily attain greater perfection; and since I know this to be the will of God for them, I can desire and ask nothing else for them but what His wisdom ordains; and I continually adore this dispensation, and pray that it may be perfectly accomplished."

On the following day, at the Mass *Requiem æternam*,† St. Mechtilde appeared to place little golden tubes from the Heart of Jesus to those who had a special devotion to her, and thus obtained for them from the Heart of God whatever they desired. Each tube had a golden key, by which —that is, by the following or similar words—they could obtain whatever they desired: "O good Jesus, I beseech

---

* From the Commendation of the Departing Soul—one of the most touching and beautiful devotions which the Church uses.

† Introit, Mass for the Dead.

Thee to hear me, through the merits and prayers of St. Mechtilde and Thy other saints, by the mercy which disposed Thee to pour forth on them, and on other elect souls, Thy favours and graces ; " and we may be assured these words will incline the Divine mercy to comply with our desires.

At the Elevation of the Host, this soul appeared to offer herself with It to God for His glory and the salvation of mankind ; and the Son of God, who refuses nothing to His elect, grew her entirely into Himself, and offered Himself with her to His Father for all in heaven, on earth, and in purgatory. The soul of the deceased now appeared in glory to this religious, who asked her what advantage she had obtained from the recital of the Antiphon *Et quo omnia* * as many times as she had lived days on earth, and for having had as many Masses of the Blessed Trinity said as she had lived years, in thanksgiving for all the favours which had been conferred on her. She replied : " Our Lord has adorned me with a flower for each repetition of the Antiphon, and by which I draw into me the sweetness of the Divine Heart ; and for each Mass I have received a marvellous and inestimable delight, which affects all the senses of my soul."

On another occasion, when this religious kissed our Lord's Five Wounds in spirit, saying five *Pater nosters* for the negligences which she might have committed towards Dame Mechtilde in her last illness, because she feared she had not attended her with sufficient care when living, nor prayed for her with sufficient fervour when dead, she beheld five beautiful flowers springing forth from our Lord's

---

* v. Ant. Lauds, Office of the Blessed Trinity ; from Rom. xi. 36 : " Of Him, and by Him, and in Him are all things. To Him be glory for ever. Amen."

Wounds; and by the virtue which these Wounds communicated to them, they produced and poured forth a sweet and salutary balsam. The religious then said to St. Mechtilde: "O elect of my God, accept these flowers which the Divine goodness has produced to supply for my deficiencies; and may they be for thy glory, and serve to adorn thy triumph; but do not forget to pray for me, unworthy." She replied: "I prefer leaving these flowers where they are, that I may not be deprived of the honour of having them placed in the Wounds of my Lord; for I hope, whenever I touch them by my desires, that a healing stream will flow forth from them, for the salvation of sinners and the consolation of the just."

CHAPTER III.

Of the precious death of Sisters M. and L.—Of the exact account taken in purgatory of their faults, and of the reward of their merits.

Two ladies, more illustrious for their virtue than their distinguished birth—sisters in the flesh, but yet more closely united in the spirit by their equality in perfection—were called to the heavenly nuptials by their celestial Spouse, after having lived a most holy life from their very childhood. The first died on the glorious Feast of the Assumption, which was also the day of her profession; the other sister died thirty days after; but their deaths were so edifying and blessed, that we are about to relate some circumstances concerning them.

As Gertrude prayed for the eldest, who died on the Assumption, she appeared to her, surrounded with a glorious light and magnificently adorned, standing before the throne of Jesus Christ; but she seemed ashamed to lift up her eyes to Him, or to gaze upon His majestic countenance. When the Saint perceived this, she was moved to pity, and said to our Lord : " Alas, most loving Lord ! why dost Thou permit her to stand before Thee as a stranger, without manifesting any tokens of affection for her ? " Our Lord then extended His hand to her, as if to draw her to Himself ; but she drew back from Him with reverent fear.

As Gertrude marvelled much at this, she said to the soul: " Why do you thus fly from the embraces of your Spouse ? " She replied : " Because I am not yet perfectly purified from my defects, and am not in a condition to receive His favours. Even if Divine justice did not restrain me, I would deprive myself of these favours, of which I am not worthy." Gertrude then said : " How can this be, when I now see you standing before God in such glory ? " The soul answered : " Although all creatures are present to God, yet souls come near Him in proportion to their perfection in charity ; but none are worthy of this blessedness who are not perfectly purified from all the stains which they have contracted during their mortal lives."

A month after, when the second sister was in her agony, St. Gertrude prayed for her very earnestly. After her death, she appeared to her, surrounded with light, as a young virgin, clothed in a purple robe, that she might be presented to her Spouse. She also saw Jesus Christ, who stood near her, and who caused a certain consolation to proceed from His Wounds, to refresh and strengthen her five senses, so that the soul was exceedingly consoled thereby. St. Gertrude then said to our Lord : " Since Thou art the God of all consolation, why dost Thou permit this soul to appear so sad, as if troubled by some secret grief ? " He answered ; " I now manifest to her My Humanity, which does not perfectly console her; for thus I reward the special love which she manifested for My Passion in the last moments of her life. But when she is perfectly freed from all her stains, I will manifest the joys of My Divinity to her, and then she will have all she desires." "But, Lord," continued the Saint, "how is it that all her faults were not perfectly purified by the charity which she possessed at the last moment of her life, since Scripture teaches that man shall be judged according to the state in which he dies?" The Lord answered: "When a man loses his strength, he has no longer the power to execute his good designs, though he may have the will to do so. When, of My gratuitous goodness, I inspire these desires, and give this will, I do not always efface thereby the stains of past negligences, which would no doubt be accomplished if the person recovered health and strength, and then began to reform his life thoroughly." She replied: "Alas, Lord! cannot Thy abundant mercy remit the sins of this soul, who has loved Thee so ardently from her very childhood?" He answered: "I will indeed reward her love abundantly; but My justice must first be satisfied by the removal of her stains." Our Lord then turned lovingly to this soul, and said to her: "My spouse will consent willingly to what My justice requires; and when she is purified, she will enjoy My glory and consolation." As she consented, our Lord seemed to ascend into heaven, and to leave her after Him where she was; but she appeared as if ardently desiring to follow Him. The solitude was to purify her from the stains which she had contracted by conversing too freely with the other sex; and the efforts she made to ascend upwards purified her from some faults of indolence.

On another occasion, as St. Gertrude prayed for the same person at Mass, she said, at the Elevation of the Host:

" Holy Father, I offer this Host to Thee for this soul on the part of all in heaven, on earth, and in the deep ; " and she beheld his soul in the air, surrounded by a multitude of persons, who held representations of the Host in their hands, which they offered up on bended knees. The soul appeared to receive great assistance and inestimable joy from this devotion. Then the soul said : " I now experience the truth of what is said in Scripture, that no good action, however trifling, will fail to be rewarded ; and that no negligence, however trifling, will be unpunished ; * for this offering of the Sacrament of the altar procures the greatest consolation for me, on account of my former devotion in receiving It ; and the ardent charity which I had for others greatly enhances the prayers which are made for me ; while for both of these things I shall receive an eternal recompense."

The soul then appeared as if elevated higher and higher by the prayers of the Church ; and when her purification was accomplished, the Saint beheld our Lord coming for her to crown her as a queen, and to conduct her to eternal joys.

CHAPTER IV.

How a disobedience was expiated by an illness.

As Gertrude recited five *Pater nosters* for Dame S——, the eldest of the community, who had received Extreme Unction, and at last ended her prayer in the Wound of our Lord's Side—she besought Him to purify this soul with the water which flowed therefrom, and to adorn it

* Matthew x. 42, and xii. 36.

with the merits of His most precious Blood. She then saw this soul, under the form of a young virgin, crowned with a golden circlet, and supported by our Divine Lord, who imparted the graces she had asked to her soul. She understood by this, that the sister must remain longer on earth to be purified from a disobedience of which she had been guilty, in conversing * more than was right with a sick person : and this was accomplished. She suffered for five months in a manner which sufficiently manifested the fault from which she was being purified. On the day on which she was taken ill, she appeared very joyful, as if our Lord had granted her some great favour ; and she attempted to relate what had happened to her ; but as she had not the perfect use of her senses, she was unable to do so. But as she saw Gertrude standing by her, with some of the other religious, she called her by name, and said : "Do you speak for me, for you know all." St. Gertrude began to relate what had been revealed to her, and the invalid was then able to continue the recital herself. When the others made any observation, she at once refuted their assertions, declaring that our Lord had forgiven her sins, and bestowed many favours on her.

On the day before her death, St. Gertrude beheld our Lord preparing a place for her in His Divine arms ; but the soul appeared at His left, and separated from Him by a little cloud. She then said : "Lord, this place which Thou hast prepared will not be suitable for a soul covered with this cloud." He replied ; She will remain a little longer on earth, that she may become fit for it." And it was even so ; for the religious continued all that day and the following night in her agony. Next morning she be-

---

* "Communicans."

held our Lord coming towards the dying nun with marks of the greatest tenderness ; and she appeared to rise, as if to meet Him. Then St. Gertrude said : "Art Thou not come now to take this desolate soul to Thyself, as a merciful Father ? " and our Lord indicated by a sign that He had this intention.

Soon after her decease, she saw this soul again, under the form of a young virgin, adorned with roses, and advancing joyfully to her Spouse ; but when she came near Him, she fell at His feet as if almost deprived of life, until the words *Tibi supplicatio commendet Ecclesiæ* were repeated, when she arose, and cast herself into the Divine arms, where she is eternally replenished with the treasures of beatitude.

CHAPTER V.

Of the happy death of Sister* M.—The approbation of these Revelations—And the favours promised through her merits.

As Sister M., of happy memory, approached her end, St. Gertrude prayed for her with others, and said to the Lord : "Why dost Thou not hear our prayers for her, O most loving Lord ?" He replied : "Her soul is in such a different state from the souls of others, that she cannot be consoled by you in a human manner." She continued : "Is this a judgment ?" He answered : "I have now my secret in her, as I formerly had My secret with her." † Then, as Gertrude sought to understand these mysterious words

---

* "Sororis ; " the term "domina," however, which we have translated "dame," is generally used.

† "Secretum meum nunc habeo in ea, sicut olim habui cum eo."

our Lord said to her : " My majesty will enthrone itself in her." " But," she continued, " how will she die ?" He answered : " She will be absorbed by My Divinity, as a sunbeam absorbs a drop of dew." Then she inquired why the wandering of her exterior senses was permitted. He replied : " That you may know I am working in her interiorly, not exteriorly." She answered : " Our own hearts ought to teach us this." He replied : " And how can they receive this favour who rarely, if ever, enter into their interior, where grace alone is poured forth ?"

After this Gertrude besought our Lord to grant the grace of working miracles to Sister M. after her death, for the confirmation of the revelations which she had received, and to silence the incredulous. Our Lord replied, holding a book in His Hands : " Can I not gain a victory without fighting ?" He added : " When it is necessary, I subdue kings and nations by signs and wonders ; but now the experience of those who have tasted something of these celestial communications is sufficient to obtain credit for them. For the present, I bear with those who contradict them ; but I will at last silence their calumnies." St. Gertrude learned from this that our Lord is pleased with those who believe that He pours forth the effusions of His grace, not for their merit, but from the superabounding love of His Divine Heart.

As Sister M. was anointed, St. Gertrude saw our Lord touch her hand, saying : " When this blessed soul is freed from the chains of the flesh, I will pour forth the abundance of My mercy on all who are here present." As she continued in her agony, and the religious prayed for her still more fervently, she knew that our Lord would grant them three great favours : first, by accomplishing all their good desires ; second, by assisting them in overcoming their faults—and these two favours would be granted through her intercession ; the third benefit was, that He extended His Hand, and imparted His benediction to all who were present.

As Gertrude occupied herself in fervent thanksgivings, she beheld our Divine Lord, the King of Glory, whom the angels adore, standing at the head of the dying nun, whose breath appeared of a golden colour, and tended towards the Heart of her Spouse.   The Saint continued to gaze on this vision with great joy while the Psalm *Deus, Deus meus,* and the *Ad te levavi,** were recited, during which our Lord manifested the tenderest affection for religious.   After this the Suffrages were read, with the Antiphon *Ut te simus,* during which she beheld the Blessed Virgin, clothed in purple and adorned as a queen.   As she stood beside her Divine Son, she placed the head of this sister so that her breath might come more directly to the Heart of Jesus.   As they read the short prayer, *Ave, Jesu*—" Hail, Jesus, my Saviour, Word of the Father "—our Lord appeared encompassed with an increased splendour, like that of the sun at mid-day.   At first the Saint was overwhelmed by the magnificence of the vision ; but as she recovered herself a little, she beheld the effulgent rose of heaven, His Virgin Mother, who appeared to congratulate Him on having obtained a new spouse.

By this she understood that this happy union was then consummated, and the soul for ever immersed in the ocean of eternal beatitude.

* Psalm lxii. and cxxii.

CHAPTER VI.

Of the agony and death of M. B., and of her blessed soul—How
salutary it is to assist the souls in Purgatory.

WHEN M. B., of happy memory, was in her agony, Gertrude prayed for her most earnestly, and obtained a
knowledge of what was passing around her in this last
combat.   For a whole hour she beheld nothing but the
trouble which the soul endured for having sometimes taken
undue pleasure in exterior things ; such as, for having
had a coverlet of coloured cloth on her bed, embroidered
with gold.*   On the day of her decease, when Mass was
celebrated, Gertrude offered the Host for her ; although
she did not see her, she knew that she was present, and
addressed our Lord thus, as if seeking her, saying : " O
Lord, where is she ? "   He replied : " She will come to Me
pure and white."   From this she understood that the
prayers which were offered in charity had obtained great
grace for her in her last moments ; and that some persons,
moved by holy zeal, had offered their good works for her,
and charged themselves with the penalties due to her.

As Gertrude prayed for her again at the Mass which
preceded her interment, she beheld her seated at a festal
table beside our Lord, where the prayers which had been
offered were given to her under the form of different
kinds of food.   At the Elevation, as the Saint offered the

---

* " Quod lectus ipsius fuit depositus de picto panno," &c.   This,
doubtless, was before the religious had entered the monastery, as the
rule of poverty of every religious house would forbid such extrava-
gance.   The richly embroidered quilt was a very pitch of luxurious
refinement in that age, and hence indicated a habit of self-indulgence
or luxurious tastes, which probably caused the soul's suffering for an
act which was only its climax.

chalice for her, our Lord appeared to present it to her Himself. When she had tasted it, she immediately became penetrated with Divine sweetness, and rose up to pray for all who had ever injured her, either by thought, word, or act, rejoicing for the merit which they had obtained for her thereby. Then Gertrude inquired why she did not pray for her friends also ; but she replied : "I pray for them more efficaciously by speaking heart to heart to my Beloved."

On another occasion, as she remarked that she had offered all her merits for the deceased, she said to our Lord : * "I hope, O Lord, that Thou will frequently cast the eyes of Thy mercy on my indigence." He replied : " What can I do more for one who has thus deprived herself of all things through charity, than to cover her immediately with charity ? " She answered : " Whatever Thou mayest do, I shall always appear before Thee destitute of all merit, for I have renounced all I have gained or may gain." He replied : " Do you not know that a mother would allow a child who was well clothed to sit at her feet, but she would take one who was barely clad into her arms, and cover her with her own garment ? " He added : " And now, what advantage have you, who are seated on the shore of an ocean, over those who sit by a little rivulet ?" That is to say, those who keep their good works for themselves have the rivulet ; but those who renounce them in love and humility, possess God, who is an inexhaustible ocean of beatitude.

---

* The French translations have, "Elle resentit quelque espèce de tristesse "—a sentiment utterly unworthy of so generous and noble a soul, who could not regret what she had so freely and lovingly bestowed ; but it is not in any Latin edition which we have seen.

CHAPTER VII.

How the souls of G. and B. were purified for neglecting confession,
and for taking pleasure in earthly things.

As Scripture testifies that "By what things a man sinneth,
by the same also he is punished" (Wis. ii. 17), and, on
the contrary, that he will be rewarded in the things in
which he has suffered or done good, we give the following
examples for the benefit of our readers.

We had two persons with us, who were both ill at the
same time; one evidently suffered from a severe affection
of the chest, and hence she was attended more carefully.
The other, whose disease was not known, and who seemed
more likely to live, did not receive so much care; but, as
men are often deceived, the one for whom we feared the
least, died the first, and the other survived a month longer.
When the former approached her end, she had been
strengthened in grace by great patience and devotion, which
had purified her soul exceedingly; for the ardent love which
our Lord had for His spouse would not suffer Him to
permit the least stain to remain on her. Nevertheless, she
still needed some purification for having too easily omitted
confession; for sometimes when the priest came to her, she
feigned to be sleeping, not having any grave fault to accuse
herself of. As the hour approached when she was to be
received to the eternal embraces of her Spouse, He purified her from this stain. For when she asked for a confessor, she lost the power of speech when he came, and then
she feared exceedingly that she would suffer for her former
negligence after death, and so was purified from her fault
by this excessive fear.

Thus being entirely purified and freed from every

stain, she was released from the prison of the flesh, and received into eternal glory. Many revelations concerning this were made to Gertrude.

One of these was, that when she was brought to our Lord's throne of glory, He conferred this privilege on her, of seeming to soothe her, as a mother would a child when she wished her to take some bitter medicine ; and He did this to console her for some little inattention which had been shown her, in consequence of the religious being so much occupied in attending to her companion, whom they believed to be dangerously ill.

Our Lord then said to her : " Tell Me, My daughter, what you would wish Me to do for the soul of your companion ; and what consolation you desire Me to give her." She replied : " Give her the same gifts Thou hast bestowed on me, my dearest Lord ; for I cannot imagine any more consoling." And our Lord promised to comply with her request.

The other religious died a month later. The day after her death she was seen marvellously adorned, as a reward for the exceeding innocence and simplicity of her life, and her exactness in observing all the austerities of her Order ; but she had one stain from which she needed purification, and this was having received unnecessary consolations in her illness. She was purified in this manner : She stood at the gate of a palace, where our Lord was seated on a throne of glory, with a countenance so full of sweetness and love, that no human intellect could describe His beauty. He appeared anxious to receive His spouse ; but when she attempted to approach, she found herself withheld by nails, which fastened her garments to the ground ; and these nails were the imperfections she had committed in her sickness. But Gertrude, who was touched with compassion, prayed for her, and our Lord freed her from this impediment. Then the Saint said to our Lord : " Why was this soul freed by my prayers, and not restored by the prayers of those who loved her so much, and who prayed for her with such fervour and affection ? " He replied : " Their prayers have been of great service to her ; but they did not remove the impediment which I have revealed to you, and from which she has been released by your prayers." She continued : " How hast Thou fulfilled Thy promise to treat this person with the same goodness as Thou didst manifest to her who died first ? for she has lived longer in religion, and seemed to abound more in virtue, and yet the other appeared at once in Thy presence, and in greater glory." He answered : " My justice is immutable, for I reward each according to her works. She who has laboured least, cannot receive more than she who has laboured most, unless she has worked with a purer intention, a more fervent charity, or a more earnest strife ; but My mercy rewards works of supererogation, such as the prayers of the faithful ; and thus My rewards are not always proportioned to the person's actual merit."

Hence we may learn how carefully we should avoid taking pleasure in anything earthly, since this blessed soul was thus detained from happiness for this imperfection. This was even more fully manifested to St. Gertrude in another vision, in which she saw her before the throne of God, manifesting the same ardour as she had done at the gate ; not indeed desiring to approach, but appearing as if unable to move— and this was the second obstacle to her happiness ; and even when she was freed from this her happiness was not perfectly complete, until our Lord placed a magnificent crown on her head, which He

held in His hand, and which she received with **exceeding**
joy.

As St. Gertrude beheld this, she said to our Lord:
"Why has this soul been tormented so painfully, where
Thou art all-powerful?" He replied: "She has not been
tormented, but has waited with joy for the consummation
of her happiness: even as a young girl would wait for a
festival on which she was to be adorned with the ornaments which her mother had prepared for her."

After this, the soul thanked the Saint for the prayers
which she had offered for her; and Gertrude said to her:
"Why did you not receive willingly some admonition which
I gave you during your sickness, although you always
seemed so much attached to me?" The soul replied: "It
is for this reason that your prayers have now more power
with God, since they are offered more purely out of
charity."

CHAPTER VIII.

Of Sister G.'s happy preparation for death—Her fervent desires and her glory.

ANOTHER religious died with us who, from her childhood,
had shown the most entire aversion to the world and all its
attractions. When her agony came, she bade farewell to
all who were round her with great affection, and promised
to pray for them when she had attained eternal blessedness,
and the inexhaustible Source of all good. In the agonies of
her last moments, she said to God: "Lord, Thou knowest
the secrets of my heart, and how I have desired to persevere in Thy service, even to old age, and to devote all my
strength to Thee; but now, since it is Thy will, I come to

Thee : and all my desires are changed into a fervent longing to possess Thee, so that death has even become sweet to me ; yet, if it were pleasing to Thee that I should continue in my present state until the day of judgment, I would willingly do so, even were this the first day of the world's creation ; but as I know that Thou wilt give me rest to-day, I beseech Thee, of Thy mercy, and for the glory of Thy name, that I may continue to suffer until I have paid the debts of those souls whom Thou desirest most to release. And in this, O Lord, Thou knowest that I am not considering my merits, but purely Thy glory."

After this prayer and many others, the Infirmarian * asked the religious to allow her to arrange her feet before she died. She replied : " I will offer this sacrifice myself to my crucified Lord ; " and as she spoke, she extended her feet towards a crucifix,† saying: "I offer Thee all the movements of my feet, in union with the ardent love with which Thou didst commend Thy spirit into the hands of Thy Father with a great cry." Then she offered likewise the movements of her eyes, her lips, her hands, and her heart, with great fervour and devotion. After this she asked to have the Passion read for her, showing them herself where she wished them to commence : *Sublevitus Jesus*—" Jesus lifted up His eyes to heaven " (John xvii. 1) ; saying, if they commenced at the words, " Before the festival-day " (John xiii. 1), they would not have time to finish before her death. At the words, " And bowing His head, He gave up

---

* " Magistra infermorum."

† A crucifix is always placed at the foot of the bed when a religious has received the last Sacraments, and is not removed until after her decease. Thus her dying looks are most likely to rest on Him who died for her.

the ghost" (John xix. 30), she asked for the crucifix; then, kissing the Five Wounds with the tenderest devotion, she gave thanks to God with words of the most heavenly wisdom and devotion, most touching to all who were present; and then she lay back on her pallet, and slept sweetly in the Lord.

After her death, St. Gertrude saw her received by our Lord with the tenderest caresses, and specially rewarded for having renounced the world so generously for His love. She also heard the angelic choirs chanting the *Quæ est ista,** as they conducted her in triumphal procession to heaven. When she was brought before the throne of God, Jesus, the Spouse of virgins, turned towards her with great love, and said, "You are My glory." Then He crowned her as a queen, and enthroned her near Himself.

As Gertrude prayed for her at her interment on the following day, she beheld her in a state of joy and glory which exceeds all human comprehension. Then she inquired what reward she had received for certain virtues; and the soul obtained for her the grace of receiving some little share of her recompense, and then inquired: "What more do you desire to know of what I have received? The heavenly ark, which contains the plenitude of Divine sweetness, even the Heart of Jesus Christ, my Beloved, with all its treasures, is opened to me; with one exception, which I am deprived of because, when in life, I reserved to myself the secrets of my Spouse, and did not communicate them to others; and this treasure is open only to those who, giving freely, communicated to others all the gifts of God." "But," inquired Gertrude, "what reply shall I give to your friends

---

* "Who is she that goeth up by the desert, as a pillar of smoke of aromatic spices?" (Cant. iii. 6.)

and mine, when they ask me of your present state and reward, since no human words can express them?" The soul replied: "After you have smelt the perfume of many flowers, how can you make another person understand what you have experienced?—would you not content yourself with saying that the odour was very delicious? Thus, after you have known in spirit how great is the felicity with which God has rewarded me, you can only say that I have been rewarded beyond all my deserts for every good thought, word, or act by my faithful and beloved Jesus."

CHAPTER IX.

The rewards which Brother S. received for his fidelity and benevolence.

WHEN Brother Seq: (*sic*) was in his agony, Gertrude, being engrossed in some occupation, omitted to pray for him until she heard he was dead, and then began to reproach herself for her neglect of one who had always served the community so faithfully and affectionately as a lay brother; she therefore besought our Lord to reward his services abundantly, according to the multitude of His mercies. The Lord vouchsafed to reply thus to her: "I have rewarded him for his fidelity in three ways, in answer to the prayers of the congregation. From his natural benevolence, he took the greatest pleasure in conferring favours on others; and I have renewed in him all this pleasure for each act of kindness which he performed. I have also accumulated in his soul all the gratification and joy which he obtained for others by these acts of benevolence—such as giving a child a toy, a poor person a penny, a sick person some fruit, or any other relief; and, lastly, I have made him rejoice exceedingly, on account of the approbation which I have manifested for these actions; and I will soon supply all that he needs to attain perfect felicity."

CHAPTER X.

How Brother Hermann suffered for obstinacy—And of the assistance which may be obtained in the other life by the prayers of the Saints and the faithful.

As Gertrude prayed for the repose of the soul of Brother Hermann, a lay brother lately deceased, she inquired what his state was; and our Lord replied: "He is now present, and I have granted him this favour in return for the earnest prayers which have been made for him—I have invited him to assist at this feast." Then she saw our Lord, as the father of a family, seated at a table, on which were placed all the prayers, oblations, desires, &c., which had been offered for this brother. The soul stood sad and dejected at one end of the table, for he was not yet sufficiently purified to behold the loving countenance of our Lord; but he soon appeared exceedingly refreshed and comforted by what he beheld before him.

The Saint observed with some surprise that the effect of these offerings came to him directly from the offerings themselves, and not, as usual, through our Lord, who generally appeared to her to present the souls with the offerings made for them with great joy; but our Lord sometimes, of His own goodness, and in consideration of the merits of those who prayed for him, gave him some consolation Himself, which imparted great satisfaction to the soul.

The Blessed Virgin sat as a queen beside her Divine Son, and appeared also to place some gifts on the table, as a reward for the particular devotion which this soul had for her when on earth. The Saints to whom he had been devout also made offerings for him; and by these things, and the earnest love with which they were presented before God, the countenance of the brother became hourly more serene and joyful, and he slowly raised his eyes to gaze upon that blessed Light, which, when it is once beheld, imparts eternal joy, and causes all former sorrow to be forgotten.

As Gertrude observed that the soul still continued in the same position, she said to him : " For what fault have you suffered most ? " He replied : " For self-will and self-opiniatedness ; for when I did any kindness for others, I would not do as they wished, but as I wished myself ; and so much do I suffer for this, that if the mental agonies of all mankind were united in one person, he would not endure more than I do at present." She replied : " And what remedy will be most efficacious for you ? " He answered : " To perform acts of the contrary virtue, and to avoid committing the same fault." " But, in the meantime," inquired Gertrude, " what will afford you the greatest relief ? " He replied : " The fidelity which I practised towards others when on earth consoles me most. The prayers which are offered continually for me by my friends solace me as good news would solace a person in affliction. Each tone of the chant at Mass, or in the vigils which are said for me, seem to me as a most delicious refection. All that is done for me by others, with a pure intention for God's glory, such as working, and even sleeping or eating, affords me great relief and shortens my sufferings, on account of the fidelity with which I laboured for others."

" But," she continued, " what advantage do you gain from our desire to give you the merit of all the good works which God enables us to perform ? " He answered : " They are of great utility to me, for they adorn my soul." St. Gertrude replied : " But if any person deferred the prayer which they proposed to offer for you on account of sickness, would you suffer from it ? " The soul answered : " Delays, which are the result of prudence, do not harm us unless they are caused by negligence." She continued : " Were you not injured by our prayers during your sickness, as we asked more earnestly for your recovery than for the grace of a happy death ? " The soul replied : " This did not harm me, for I discovered therein the immense goodness of God, whose tender mercies are over all His works (Ps. cxliv. 9), as He was moved to do me even more good from beholding your affection for me." " But will tears shed for you through human affection do you harm ? " He answered : " These tears are to me as the kindness of a friend who consoles his friend when in affliction. And when I am in the enjoyment of perfect happiness, it will give me as much joy as the congratulations and applause of those I love; and I have merited this consolation by my faithfulness in your service, which has gained your affection for me."

On another occasion, when St. Gertrude recited the *Pater noster* for the same soul, she observed, to her extreme surprise, that his sufferings appeared greatly increased when she repeated the words : " Forgive us our trespasses, as we forgive those who trespass against us." As she inquired the reason of this suffering, he replied : " When I was in the world, I offended God frequently by my unwillingness to forgive those who injured me in any way ; and even when I had forgiven them, I showed my resentment by a grave manner when I met them ; and I suffer for this whenever these words are repeated for me." "And how long will you suffer thus?" inquired the Saint. The soul replied: "I shall suffer until I am entirely purified; but henceforward, by the mercy of God, whenever you say this prayer for me, I shall obtain great relief thereby."

When Mass was offered for this soul, he appeared radiant with light and transported with joy. Then Gertrude said to our Lord: "Is this soul now entirely freed from its sufferings?" Our Lord answered: "He is already free from much suffering, and no human being can form an idea of his glory; but he is not yet so perfectly purified as to be worthy to enjoy My presence, though he is approaching nearer and nearer to this purity by the prayers which are offered for him, and is more and more consoled and relieved." He added: "His obstinacy in following his own will, and his disinclination to submit to the will of others, have prevented him from obtaining relief from your prayers as speedily as he would otherwise have done."

CHAPTER XI.

How Brother John was rewarded for his labours and punished for his faults.

As it is but just that souls should be purified from their stains before they receive the reward of their good works, yet it sometimes appears that Mercy triumphs over Justice, as in the case of Brother John, the Procurator,* who worked so faithfully and laboriously for the good of the convent. His good works appeared in the form of steps, by which his soul ascended, after its separation from the body, satis-

---

* "Procurator curiæ."

fying for its imperfections by the pain which this exertion cost him ; but the higher he ascended, the less difficulty he experienced. However, as it is difficult to avoid all imperfcetions in this life, and as the justice of God punishes even the least negligence, when he came to certain steps he was seized with a sudden fear, which stupefied him, as if he expected that the next step would give way beneath him.

From this Gertrude understood that some of his good works had been tainted by some infidelity,* from which he was purified by this fear. When other members of the congregation prayed for him either mentally or vocally, she perceived that he was assisted in his ascent, as if they had extended their hands to help him upwards, and thus afforded him great consolation.

It was also revealed to her, that those who had served her community, when they expiated their faults after their death, were relieved in consideration of the services which they had rendered to them, and that this privilege would be continued as long as the religious continued in the same state of fervour.

CHAPTER XII.

How the soul of Brother The : was released by prayers in honour of the Five Wounds.

WHEN Brother The : (*sic*), the lay brother, died,who had laboured faithfully for the monastery for many years, St. Gertrude began to pray for him as soon as she heard of his decease. As she was thus occupied, she beheld him in spirit, and his soul appeared black and deformed, as if

---

* " Aliquam fraudem."

suffering intense anguish from some remorse of conscience
As she was exceedingly moved to compassion, she commenced reciting five *Pater nosters,* in honour of our Lord's
Five Wounds, which she embraced very tenderly. At the
fifth *Pater noster,* as she approached the Wound of our
Lord's Side, our Lord emitted blood and water from it, in
the form of a vapour; and she perceived that the soul was
exceedingly refreshed thereby interiorly, but that he suffered as if from exterior wounds, which caused him intense
pain. By the virtue of this blood and water the soul was
then transported into a garden of herbs, each of which
signified some good work which he had performed when in
the world; and on these our Lord conferred such virtue, in
answer to the prayers of the community, that each of these
plants became medicinal, and healed his wounds when
applied to them; and she understood that if the community persevered earnestly in their prayers, he would soon
be entirely cured. She knew also that there were some
herbs, which represented his imperfect actions; and when
he touched them, his sufferings were fearfully increased.

After his interment, as they chanted the *Media vita* as
usual, at the words, *Sancte Deus, sancte fortis, sancte et
immortalis,** when the religious prostrated † on the ground,
the soul elevated itself towards heaven with exceeding gratitude, appearing to prostrate with the community, thanking
God for having had the privilege of living in so holy a
convent, where his labours had been specially blessed and
accepted on account of the merits of those whom he served.
He declared also, wherever he had lived before he entered

---

* From the Reproaches chanted at the Adoration of the Cross
on Good Friday.

† " Venias faceret."

that house, he had been obliged to earn his bread by the labour of his hands, but that he had never gained thereby from all his exertions as much advantage as he had obtained in the monastery for his soul.

CHAPTER XIII.

What Brother F. suffered for indolence and want of submission—The efficacy of fervent prayer.

As Gertrude prayed for a lay brother lately deceased, she saw his soul under a hideous form,* as if consuming by a devouring fire. There appeared to be something under one of his arms which caused him excessive anguish, and he was bent down by an overpowering weight, so that he could not keep himself upright. She learned that he appeared in this horrible form because, although he wore a religious habit when on earth, he had failed to elevate himself to heavenly things. He was also suffering by fire for many other faults. The agony which he endured by what was concealed under his arm was a punishment for labouring to acquire temporal goods without the permission of his superior, and even concealing what he thus acquired. The weight which oppressed him so heavily was his disobedience to his superior.

On another occasion, as she read the Psalms and kept vigil, she asked our Lord what remedy could be applied to this soul. He replied : "Although the souls of the departed are much benefited by these vigils and other prayers, nevertheless a few words, said with affection and devotion,

---

* " In specie bufonis."

are of far more value to them." And this may easily be
explained by a familiar comparison; for it is much easier
to wash away the stains of mud or dirt from the hands by
rubbing them quickly in a little water, than by pouring a
quantity of water on them without using any friction; thus,
a single word, said with fervour and devotion, for the souls
of the departed, is of far more efficacy than many vigils and
prayers offered coldly and performed negligently.

CHAPTER XIV.

Those who have persevered long in sin are not easily benefited by the
prayers of the Church, and are liberated with difficulty.

ONCE, when a person was told that a relative had died, of
whose state she had great fear, Gertrude was so moved by
her affliction, that she offered to pray for the soul of the
deceased. Our Lord taught her, that the information had
been given in her presence by a special arrangement of His
providence. She replied: "Lord, couldst not Thou have
given me the compassion without this?" He answered:
"I take particular pleasure in prayers for the dead, when
they are addressed to Me from natural compassion, united
to a good will; thus a good work becomes perfected."

When Gertrude had prayed for this soul a long time,
he appeared to her under a horrible form, as if blackened
by fire, and contorted with pain. She saw no one near
him; but his sins, which he had not fully expiated, were
his executioners, and each member suffered for the sins
to which it had been accessory. Then St. Gertrude, desiring to intercede with her Spouse for him, said lovingly:
"My Lord, wilt Thou not relieve this soul, for my sake?"
He replied: "Not only would I deliver this soul, but thou-

sands of souls, for your love! How do you wish Me to show him mercy?—shall I release him at once from all his pains?" "Perhaps, Lord," she continued, "this would be contrary to the decrees of Thy justice." He answered: "It would not be contrary to it if you asked Me with faith; for, as I foresee the future, I prepared him for this when in his agony." She replied: "I beseech of Thee, Salvation of my soul, to perfect this work according to Thy mercy, in which I have the most perfect confidence."

When she had said this, the soul appeared under a human form and in great joy, but still bearing some marks of his former sins; however, the Saint knew that he must be purified further, and made as white as snow, before he would be fit to enter into the Divine presence; and to effect this, it was necessary for him to suffer as if from the blows of an iron hammer; furthermore, he had continued so long in sin, that the process of cleansing his soul was much prolonged, and he also suffered as if exposed for a year to the rays of a scorching sun. As the Saint marvelled at this, she was instructed that those who have committed many and grievous sins are not assisted by the ordinary suffrages of the Church until they are partly purified by Divine justice; and that they cannot avail themselves of the prayers of the faithful, which are constantly descending on the souls in purgatory like a gentle and refreshing dew, or like a sweet and soothing ointment.

Gertrude then returned thanks for this favour, and said to the Lord: "O my most loving Lord, tell me, I beseech Thee, what work or prayers will most easily obtain mercy from Thee for those sinners who have died in a state of grace, so that they may be delivered from this terrible impediment which prevents them from obtaining the benefit of the Church's prayers. For this soul appears to me now, when relieved from this burden, as if it had ascended from hell to heaven." Our Lord replied: "The only way to obtain such a favour is Divine love; neither prayers nor any other labours will avail without this, and it must be such a love as you now have for Me; and as none can have this grace unless I bestow it, so also none can obtain these advantages after death unless I have prepared them for it by some special grace during life. Know, however, that the prayers and labours of the faithful relieve the soul gradually from this heavy burden, and that they are delivered sooner or later, according to the fervour and pure intentions of those who thus serve them, and according to the merit which they have acquired for themselves when in this life."

Then the soul besought our Lord, by the love which had brought Him down from heaven to die upon the cross, that He would apply these remedies to his soul, and reward those who prayed for him abundantly; and our Lord appeared to take a piece of gold from him, and lay it by to recompense those who had assisted him by their prayers.

CHAPTER XV.

Of the oblation of the Host—And of prayers for the souls of deceased parents.

ON the Sunday on which the community prayed for the souls of deceased parents,* as St. Gertrude offered the Host

* In all conventual houses, the parents of each religious are considered the special charge of all. Mass, Communion, and the Office of the Dead are regularly offered for all deceased parents at stated periods throughout the year. Alas! what do not those

after she had received Holy Communion for the repose of their souls, she beheld an immense number coming forth from a place of darkness like sparks of fire; some in the form of stars, and others in other shapes. Then she inquired if this great multitude could be all composed of the souls of the deceased parents; and our Lord replied: " I am your nearest Relation,* your Father, your Brother, and your Spouse ; therefore, My special friends are also yours, and I could not exclude them from the commemoration of your parents ; therefore, you behold them all united together." From henceforward the Saint prayed constantly for those who were specially beloved by our Lord. On the following day at Mass, after the Elevation, she heard our Lord saying : " We have eaten with those who came and were ready ; we must now send to those who could not come to the feast." Another year, when the bell tolled for the Office of the Dead, she beheld a snow-white lamb, such as the paschal lamb is usually painted ; and, from a wound in its heart, a stream of blood flowed into a chalice, while it said : " I will now be a propitiation for those souls for whom a feast is prepared here to-day."

---

unhappy persons lose, both in time and in eternity, who hinder the consecration of their children to God ! and what gain is theirs who, by placing them in a holy and devoted community, secure the prayers of the most saintly souls for their own welfare both in this world and the next ! Perhaps only those who are inmates of the cloister know with what tender and fervent affection the relations of each member are prayed for by all.

* " Ego propinquissimus vester sum."

CHAPTER XVI.

Of the effect of the Great Psalter—Of the zeal of Christ for the
    salvation of souls—And how willing He is to hear the prayers of
    those who love Him.

As the community recited the Great Psalter * for the souls
of the faithful departed, which is believed to be of great
efficacy for them, St. Gertrude prepared herself for Holy
Communion, and prayed for these souls with great fervour.
She then inquired of our Lord why this Psalter was so acceptable to Him, and why it obtained such great relief for
the souls, since the immense number of Psalms which were
recited, and the long prayers after each, caused more
weariness than devotion. The Lord replied : " The desire
which I have for the deliverance of the souls makes it
acceptable to Me ; even as a prince who had been obliged

---

* The Great Psalter is explained in a succeeding chapter, and the
devotion of the Seven Masses, which is attributed to St. Gregory the
Great. He was also the institutor of the custom of celebrating Mass
for thirty days after the death or burial of the faithful. The origin
of this pious devotion is thus related by the Mère Blemer, in her
Année Benedictine : " A monk named Justine had kept some money
without permission. On his deathbed he acknowledged the fault to
one of the brethren, who at once informed St. Gregory. The Abbot
commanded that only one of the brethren should attend him, and
that he should be buried without holy rites. The severity of the
sentence convinced him of his fault, and he died sincerely penitent.
For thirty days after his decease no prayers were said for the repose
of his soul ; but at the expiration of that period, Gregory desired
Mass to be celebrated for him daily for thirty days. On the last day
Justin appeared to his brother, who knew nothing of the prayers
which had been offered for him, and declared that he was now released
from purgatory, after enduring intense torments. Hence the custom
of celebrating Mass thirty days for the departed was instituted by St.
Gregory.

to imprison one of his nobles to whom he was much attached, and was compelled by his justice to refuse him pardon, would most thankfully avail himself of the intercessions and satisfactions of others to release his friend. Thus do I act towards those whom I have redeemed by My Death and precious Blood, rejoicing in the opportunity of releasing them from their pains, and bring them to eternal joys."

" But," continued the Saint, " is the labour of those who recite this Psalter acceptable to Thee ? " He replied : " My love renders it most agreeable to Me ; and if a soul is released thereby, I accept it as if I had been Myself delivered from captivity, and I will assuredly reward it at a fitting time, according to the abundance of My mercy." Then she inquired : " How many souls are released by these prayers ? " He answered : " The number is proportioned to the zeal and fervour of those who pray for them." He added : " My love urges Me to release a great number of souls for the prayers of each religious ; and at each verse of the Psalm I release many."

As the devotion of the Saint was marvellously excited by this revelation, she immediately commenced the recital of the Psalter, though in a state of extreme weakness. When she had repeated one verse, she asked our Lord how many souls He had released ; and He replied : " I am so touched by the fervour of your love, that I have released a soul for each movement of your tongue." For which may sweet Jesus be praised and blessed for endless ages |

CHAPTER XVII.

Of the severe sufferings of a soldier—And the efficacy of the
Great Psalter.

ON another occasion, when Gertrude prayed for the faithful departed, she saw the soul of a certain soldier,[*] who,
as I believe, had been dead forty years, and who appeared
in a fearful state of suffering.   He suffered as if exposed
to the very fire of hell, and was unable to obtain the least
assistance from the prayers of the Church.   As the Saint
marvelled at this horrible apparition, she was instructed
that the soul had sinned exceedingly when in the world
by pride and haughtiness.   The effects of his sin were represented by horns, which covered his body ; and a slight
support, which appeared to prevent him from falling into
hell, indicated some little compunction he had manifested
for his crimes, which, by the Divine mercy, had led eventually to his repentance and salvation.

   As Gertrude felt great compassion for him, she began
to recite the Great Psalter, offering it for his soul's repose ;
and she had the satisfaction of knowing that her prayers
were answered.   The soul appeared to her freed from the
horrible shape in which he had been tormented, and in the
form of a young child, still bearing some marks of suffering,
but as joyful as if he had been delivered from hell and
taken up into heaven.   He was now placed with many other
souls, who seemed in the same condition.   She learned
also, that in this place he could benefit by the suffrages
of the Church, of which he had been deprived, until

---

[*] The French has " un certain gentilhomme ; " but this is incorrect
as the Latin rendering is " militis."

Gertrude obtained this deliverance. The souls received him with the tenderest affection, and appeared to prepare a place for him amongst themselves. This induced the Saint to pray very earnestly for them; and she perceived that our Lord removed them to a place of greater refreshment, whereby they were much consoled.

Then she said to the Lord : "What advantage will our community gain from reciting the Great Psalter?" Our Lord replied : "They will gain the advantage which the prophet has declared in these words : "My prayer shall be turned into my bosom (Ps. xxxiv. 13) ; My liberality and bounty will also grant them the favour of participating in the merit of this Psalter, whenever it is said, throughout the world."

On another occasion she said to our Lord : "O Father of Mercies ! if any one desires to recite this Psalter who cannot give the usual alms, nor obtain the celebration of the Masses which should accompany it, what offering can be substituted for them?" He replied : "He must communicate as often as Mass should have been said, and for each alms say a *Pater noster*, with the prayer *Deus, cui proprium est*,* for the conversion of sinners, doing an act of kindness also for the same intention." Then the Saint continued thus : "My God, let me speak once more to Thee, and allow me to ask if there is any shorter prayer which thou wouldst be pleased to receive as a substitution for the Great Psalter?" Our Lord replied : "The Psalter may be said by commencing with a prayer for pardon in these words : *In unione illius super cœlestis laudis*,†

---

* "O God, whose property is always to have mercy and to spare ;" first Collect after the Litany of Saints.

† See next chapter, the first prayer of which commences with these words.

and by adding the words, *Ave Jesu Christe splendor*, after each verse. The words of this prayer should be said in honour of the love by which I became Man to ransom men; then they should kneel in honour of My Passion, when repeating the words which refer to it, in union with the love with which I, the Creator of all things, submitted to be judged and to suffer by men; then they should stand when repeating the words which commemorate My Resurrection and Ascension, in union with that omnipotent power by which I conquered, rose victoriously, and ascended into heaven, to exalt human nature at the right hand of My Father. After this they should recite the Antiphon *Salvator mundi*, in union with the thanksgivings with which all the saints rejoiced in My Incarnation, Passion, and Resurrection. Lastly, they should receive the Sacrament of My Body for each Mass, and recite the *Pater noster* and the Collect *Deus cui* for each alms, adding an act of charity towards others. And I will accept this for the Great Psalter."

CHAPTER XVIII.

Explanation of the Great Psalter, and of the Seven Masses of St. Gregory.

As the Great Psalter has not been explained in the preceding pages, we subjoin an explanation of it, for the benefit of those who may read this work, taken from the *Exercises of St. Gertrude.*

First we must kneel to ask pardon of our sins, saying: "O most sweet Lord Jesus, in union with the celestial praises which the Ever-Blessed Trinity renders to Itself as alone worthy of praise, and which It imparts to Thy blessed Humanity, Thy glorious Mother, Thy Angels and Saints, and then returns to the abyss of Thy Divinity, from whence it had flowed forth, I offer this Psalter to Thy praise and glory. I adore Thee, praise Thee, bless Thee, and give Thee thanks, for the love of Thy Incarnation, Thy Birth, the hunger, thirst, labours, and griefs of Thy three-and-thirty years on earth, and for Thy love in giving Thyself to us in the Sacraments of the Altar; and I beseech Thee to unite the recital of this Psalter to the merit of Thy most holy life and conversation, which I offer for the living and the dead, for the souls of —— and of ——; and I pray Thee to supply for and repair all that they have neglected or omitted in praise, in thanksgiving, in prayer, in devotion, in good works, which by Thy grace they might have accomplished, and in which they have failed by their negligence."

Secondly, having again implored pardon, repeat this prayer: "O most sweet Lord Jesus Christ, I adore Thee and bless Thee, giving thanks to Thee for Thy love in redeeming us by Thy cruel sufferings, and because Thou, the Creator of the universe, wert taken prisoner, bound, betrayed, defamed, cast upon the ground, scourged, crowned with thorns, condemned, crucified, slain cruelly, and transfixed with a lance, for love of us. I offer Thee my petitions in union with the love with which Thou didst bear these outrages and indignities; beseeching Thee, by the merit of Thy most holy Passion and Death, to pardon the sins of those for whom I pray, whether they have offended against Thee by thought, word, or deed; and I implore Thee to offer to God the Father all Thy pains and griefs of body and soul, and the merit of each pain, for those who are still indebted to Thy justice."

Thirdly, repeat the following prayer standing up: "I

adore Thee, praise Thee, and bless Thee, O most sweet
Lord Jesus Christ, giving Thee thanks for the victorious
love by which Thou didst elevate our nature to the right
hand of God the Father, after raising it up victoriously from
the tomb ; and I beseech Thee to grant the souls for whom
I pray a participation in Thy victory and triumphs."

Fourthly, after imploring the mercy of God, say :
" Saviour of the world, save us all : Mary, holy Mother of
God and ever Virgin, pray for us. We beseech Thee, by the
intercession of all Thy holy apostles, martyrs, confessors,
and holy virgins, to keep us from evil, and to lead us to the
perfection of all good. O most sweet Lord Jesus, I adore
Thee, praise Thee, and bless Thee, for all the favours Thou
hast conferred on Thy blessed Mother and on Thy elect, in
union with that gratitude with which Thy saints rejoice in
Thy blessed Incarnation, Passion, and Resurrection ; beseeching Thee, by the prayers of Thy glorious Virgin Mother
and all the saints, to supply the needs of these souls."

Fifthly, recite the hundred and fifty Psalms of the
Psalter devoutly and consecutively, saying, after each verse :
" Hail, Jesus Christ, Splendour of the Father, Prince of
peace, Gate of heaven, Bread of life, Son of a Virgin,
Vessel of the Divinity ! " At the conclusion of each Psalm,
repeat the following words kneeling : " Eternal rest give to
them, O Lord, and let perpetual light shine upon them."
Then say a hundred and fifty Masses, or have them said,
or offer as many Communions, or at least fifty or thirty.
Give alms also a hundred and fifty times, or, if this is
impossible, say the *Pater noster* and the Collect *Deus cui*,
performing the same number of acts of charity. In these
acts of charity may be included the least kindness done to
another for the love of God—such as a kind word, or a
kind act, or even a fervent prayer.

We also consider it right to say something of the Seven Masses which, according to our tradition, were divinely revealed to St. Gregory, as we believe that they will contribute greatly to the relief of the holy souls, through the merit and efficacy of the intercession of Christ. If possible, seven lights should be burned at each Mass, in honour of the Passion of our Lord, and each day fifteen* *Pater nosters* and *Ave Marias* should be recited, and seven alms given. The Office of the Dead must also be said.

The first Mass is the *Domine ne longe*, with the entire Passion, as on Palm Sunday ; and we should beseech our Lord, by the contempts which He freely suffered when bound and betrayed in the hands of sinners, that He would deliver those captive souls who, of their own will, enslaved themselves.

The second Mass should be *Nos autem gloriari*, as on the third feria after Palm Sunday (Tuesday in Holy Week), in which we must beseech our Lord, by His unjust condemnation to death, to deliver the souls justly condemned to punishment by their own act.

The third Mass should be *In nomine Domine*, as on the fourth feria after Palm Sunday ; and by this we must implore our Lord, by His guiltless suffering when attached to the cross, to deliver these souls from the punishment which they have deserved by attaching themselves to unworthy pleasures.

The fourth Mass will be *Nos autem gloriari*, with the Passion *Egressus est Jesus*, as on Good Friday,† when we must beseech our Lord, by His most bitter Death and the-

---

* "Quindecim." The Italian translations also have "quindeci ;" but the French has " sept," though otherwise tolerably correct in the rendering of this chapter.

† Probably the Mass of the Presanctified was not said then. The

piercing of His Heart, to heal these souls from the wounds and punishments of sin.

The fifth Mass is the *Requiem,* at which we must pray our Lord, by His holy burial, and by the tomb in which He, the Lord of heaven and earth, was enclosed, to deliver these souls from the fate to which they have condemned themselves by their sins.

At the sixth Mass, *Resurrexi,** we must pray that the souls may be freed from every stain, and made worthy to participate in His glory by the merits of His joyful Resurrection.

And at the seventh Mass, *Gaudiamus,* as on the Assumption of the Blessed Virgin, let us beseech our Lord and His most holy Mother, by the joy which she felt on the day of her Assumption, that by her merits and mediation these souls may be freed from every restraint, and associated for ever to the company of their heavenly Spouse.

If you act thus towards others, be assured that your prayer will return into your own bosom, with abundant fruit, at the hour of your death.   But it will be far more advantageous for you to perform this devotion for yourself while you are able, than to trust to others after your decease ; and God, who is faithful to His promises, will keep it for you, and return it to you in good time, through the bowels of His mercy, who has visited us as the Orient from on high (Luke i. 78).

Introit is that now used on Holy Thursday ; but the same Passion is read on Good Friday.

  * Introit for Easter Sunday.

CHAPTER XIX.

The reward of praying for the dead—And the punishment of
disobedience and detractions.

ON one occasion, while Mass was celebrating for a poor
woman who had died lately, St. Gertrude recited five *Pater
nosters*, in honour of our Lord's Five Wounds for the repose
of her soul; and, moved by Divine inspiration, she offered
all her good works for the increase of the beatitude of this
person. When she had made this offering, she immediately
beheld the soul in heaven, in the place destined for her;
and the throne prepared for her was elevated as far above
the place where she had been, as the highest throne of the
seraphim is above that of the lowest angel. The Saint then
asked our Lord how this soul had been worthy to obtain
such advantage from her prayers, and He replied : "She
has merited this grace in three ways: first, because she
always had a sincere will and perfect desire of serving Me
in religion, if it had been possible ; secondly, because she
especially loved all religious and all good people ; thirdly,
because she was always ready to honour Me by performing
any service she could for them." He added : You may
judge, by the sublime rank to which she is elevated, how
agreeable these practices are to Me."

A certain religious died who had always been accustomed to pray very fervently for the souls of the faithful
departed ; but she had failed in the perfection of obedience,
preferring her own will to that of her superior in her fasts
and vigils. After her decease she appeared adorned with
rich ornaments, but so weighed down by a heavy burden,
which she was obliged to carry, that she could not approach
to God, though many persons were endeavouring to lead
her to Him.

As Gertrude marvelled at this vision, she was taught that the persons who endeavoured to conduct the soul to God were those whom she had released by her prayers; but this heavy burden indicated the faults she had committed against obedience. Then our Lord said: "Behold how those grateful souls endeavour to free her from the requirements of My justice, and show these ornaments; nevertheless, she must suffer for her faults of disobedience and self-will." The Saint replied: "But, Lord, did she not repent when admonished of these faults before her death? did she not perform penance for them? and does not Scripture say, 'when man confesses, God pardons?'"* Our Lord answered: "If she had not acted thus, the burden of her faults would have been so heavy, that she could scarcely ever have come to Me."

Then the Saint beheld her ornament, which appeared like a vessel of boiling water containing a hard stone, which must be completetly dissolved therein before she could obtain relief from this torment; but in these sufferings she was much consoled and assisted by these souls, and by the prayers of the faithful. After this our Lord showed St. Gertrude the path by which the souls ascend to heaven. It resembled a straight plank, a little inclined; so that those who ascended did so with difficulty. They were assisted and supported by hands on either side, which indicated the prayers offered for them. Those who were assisted by the angels had a great advantage, as they repelled the dragons who flew round it, endeavouring to prevent their prayers. The religious who have lived under obedience were assisted by a kind of railing, placed at each side of this plank, so that they were both supported and protected from falling.

---

* "Cum homo agnoscit, Deus ignoscit."

In some places these railings were removed, as a punishment to those superiors who had failed to govern their subjects by the rules of obedience. But all the souls who had been truly obedient were assisted and supported by the angels, who removed every impediment from their path.

A religious, who had listened to murmurs and detractions, appeared to the Saint also under a human form, and was punished by having her ears closed with a hard substance, which she could only remove with great difficulty and by slow degrees; her mouth also was covered with a kind of bridle, for having uttered some detractions, so that she could not taste the Divine sweetness. It was revealed to St. Gertrude that this person had sinned through inadvertence and ignorance, and had repented for her fault; but that those who persisted habitually in this sin would be punished far more severely, and their sufferings would be so intense and horrible as to make them objects of aversion to the citizens of heaven.

" Alas, Lord!" exclaimed the Saint with tears; "formerly Thou didst show me the merit of the saints, and now I only see the punishments of these souls." He replied: " Men were then more easily won by gifts of grace; now they must be terrified by threats and judgments."

We will now relate how the Divine mercy prepared Gertrude for her last end.

CHAPTER XX.

Of the ardent desire of death which our Lord enkindled in **the**
soul of Gertrude.

On the Feast of Blessed Martin,* at the Response *Beatus Martinus*, the Saint cried out to the Lord with burning desire : O Lord, when wilt Thou show me a like favour ? " He replied : " I will soon take you to Myself." These words excited an exceeding desire in her soul to be dissolved and to be with Christ, although she had never felt the same desire before.   On the fourth feria (Wednesday) after Easter Sunday, when she had received Communion, she heard our Lord saying to her : " Come, my chosen one, that I may enthrone Myself in thee." And she knew that the hour was approaching of which our Lord had already spoken to her on St. Martin's Day, saying, " I will soon take you to Myself." Our Lord then added : " Do not live for yourself during the short time which remains for you, but employ yourself entirely in promoting My glory, according to your own desires." The time of her death was deferred, that she might have a longer preparation for it, according to this instruction. For as Scripture tells us that delay increases our desires, so also does it increase our merit.

Once, when Gertrude was occupied with these thoughts, on a Sunday, our Lord said to her : " If I granted you at the moment of your death the accomplishment of all the holy desires which you have entertained, it would be little in comparison with the grace I am about to confer on you. Choose," He continued, " whether you will die now, or

---

* November 11. This was probably the year before the Saint died. The Response is the vi. Response, ii. Nocturn.

suffer a long sickness first, that you may know something of the infirmities of a protracted illness." The Saint replied : " Lord, do Thou Thy holy will." He answered : " You do right to submit to My decision ; and if you consent, for My love, to remain longer in the body, I will establish My abode in your heart, as a dove in its nest ; and at the same time I will hide you in My Heart, from whence I will lead you forth to eternal joys."

From this moment her desire of departing this life was moderated, and she heard these words continually whispered in her soul : " My dove, in the clifts of the rock " (Cant. ii. 14). But her desire returned after a time, and our Lord said to her : " What bride would complain of the time spent in adorning herself for her bridegroom, or regret occasions of increasing his love ? For after death the soul cannot merit, neither can it suffer anything for God."

CHAPTER XXI.

How Gertrude prayed for death.

ONCE, as Gertrude received Holy Communion, she found herself so weak that she inquired of the Lord if her end was near. He replied : " When a bride hears that there are many messages from her betrothed, treating of the conclusion of their alliance, she begins to prepare herself for it. In like manner, when you feel inward suffering and illness, you should begin to prepare for death." " But how shall I know when that desirable hour will come which will release me from the prison of the flesh ? " Our Lord answered : " Two of the noblest angels of the celestial court shall whisper in your ears, through golden trumpets, this

melodious song : ' Behold, the Bridegroom cometh ; go ye
forth to meet him.' " She replied : " And, my Lord, in
what chariot shall I be taken to behold Thy blessed Face ? "
He said : " My love will pour itself forth on you, and
bring you to My kingdom." " And whereon shall I repose
in this chariot ? " Our Lord answered : " Your seat will
be, confidence in My mercy, from which you must expect
every good." " Shall I have reins to guide this chariot ? "
she inquired. He replied : " Your fervent love will supply
this need." The Saint continued : " As I know what will
be necessary for the journey, I will not inquire further ;
but I ardently desire to travel on this road." Our Lord
answered : " Your joys will exceed all you can hope or
desire ; for whatever may be imagined by My elect as to
their future blessedness, will be far exceeded by the
reality."

CHAPTER XXII.

Of the wounds of Divine love with which the Saint was transfixed.

THE Saint heard a brother who preached in the chapel
saying, amongst other things, that love was a golden arrow,
which obtained all that it touched ; and that he was a fool
who used this arrow to hunt after earthly pleasures, when
he might use it to obtain eternal joys. Then Gertrude exclaimed, in an ardour of love : " Oh, how happy I should be
if I possessed this golden arrow ! for I would transfix Thee
with it, my Beloved, that I might possess Thee eternally."
As she said these words, she beheld our Lord holding a
golden arrow in His hand, and He said to her : " You desire
to wound Me ; but I will to pierce you, so that your wound

may never be healed." As He said this, the arrow appeared bent in three places. By this she understood that the arrow of Divine love wounds in three ways : first, by rendering all earthly pleasures distasteful, so that nothing in this world can afford the soul pleasure or consolation ; secondly, by exciting an ardent desire in the soul to be united to God, finding that it cannot breathe or live apart from Him ; thirdly, the soul is so transfixed as to be almost separate from the body, and overwhelmed with the torrent of Divine delights.

After this revelation St. Gertrude desired, with a merely human desire, to die then in the church where this favour had been vouchsafed to her ; as if the holiness of the place where the body ceased to live would have profited the soul. And as she repeatedly asked to obtain this grace, our Lord said to her : " When your soul goes forth from your body, I will hide you under My paternal care, as a mother would cover and caress her beloved child when terrified by fear of shipwreck. And as the mother would rejoice in the joy of her child when they had reached land in safety, so will I rejoice in your joy when you are safe in paradise."

Then the Saint gave thanks to God for all His love, and renounced her former desires, confiding herself entirely to His Divine Providence.

CHAPTER XXIII.

Our preparations for death are not forgotten before God.

ONCE, as the Saint implored our Lord to show her mercy at the hour of death, He replied : " How can I fail to

accomplish what I have already commenced ? " She replied :
" If Thou hadst taken me out of the world when I thought,
by Thy Divine communications, that my end was near, I
should have supposed that I was better prepared to die ;
but now I think that my negligences have rendered me
less worthy." Our Lord answered : " All things are ordered
by the wisdom of My providence ; whatever you have once
done is always before Me, and whatever you may add
thereto will not be lost."

From this she understood that preparation for death
may be made long before the event ; as a prince prepares
for a long time when about to celebrate his nuptials. In
the preceding harvest the grain and the grape are stored
up in his cellars, so that there may be an abundant supply
when they are needed for use ; then the event may not
be spoken of again until the time approaches, although
the preparations are made. Thus God incites His elect
to prepare for death, though He may not take them out
of the world for some time.

CHAPTER XXIV.

Exercises in preparation for death — And devotion to the Blessed Virgin.

The following instructions were written by St. Gertrude
as a yearly preparation for death :—

The first day should be employed in considering our
state in our last sickness ; the second day, in preparation
for our last confession ; the third, in meditating on extreme
unction ; the fourth, in preparing for the Holy Viaticum ;
the fifth, in reflections on death.

This preparation for death, which the Saint taught

others, was used also by herself ; and she communicated
on the preceding Sunday, to obtain grace to perform this
exercise devoutly, singing the 41st Psalm, *Quemadmodum,*
for this intention, with the Hymn *Jesu nostra redemptio,*
that her soul might be perfectly united to our Lord.   Then
our Lord said to her : " Unite yourself to Me, as the prophet Eliseus united himself to the child † whom he raised
to life." " But, Lord, how shall I accomplish this ? " inquired
the saint.   Our Lord replied : " Join your hands to Mine ;
that is, recommend to me all the works of your hands :
place your eyes on Mine ; that, is unite the movements of
your body to the movements of Mine.   Thus your members will become one with Mine, and will participate in
their innocence and sanctity, so that henceforth they will
move only for My glory."   And this alliance, which the
Saint formed with our Lord, was like a golden zone, which
united her soul indissolubly to her Beloved.

When Gertrude approached the Holy Communion, she
remembered that she had not been able to confess on the
preceding day, though she had ardently desired to do so ;
and she besought our Lord to pardon her sins and negligences.   And as she prayed thus, she beheld our Lord
uniting her to Himself with chains of gold, so that her soul
appeared, as it were, enclosed in His Divinity, as a precious
stone would be in a golden casket.

The next day, as she found her illness increasing, she
read the Psalm *Quemadmodum* twice, with the Hymn *Jesu
nostra redemptio,* in honour of the union of the Divinity

---

* " As the hart panteth after the fountains of water, so my soul
panteth after Thee, O God " (Ps. xli.)

† " And Eliseus went up and lay upon the child, and he put his
mouth upon his mouth, and his eyes upon his eyes, and his hands
upon his hands " (4 Kings iv. 34).

and Humanity in the person of Christ for our salvation.
At the same time, these chains appeared to unite her still
more closely to her Lord. The third feria she repeated
these devotions three times, in honour of the union of
Christ Jesus with the Ever-Blessed Trinity, by which
human nature is so glorified. On the fourth feria—the day
appointed in her exercises for meditation on death—she
beheld her soul fastened to the crucifix, like a jewel incased
in gold; and she perceived that golden vine-leaves came
forth from the cross, the beauty of which was reflected on
the gold. From this she understood how pleasing the Passion of Christ, in union with which she had offered her
sufferings to our Lord, had rendered her soul to the Blessed
Trinity. On the fifth feria, as she confessed her sins to
her Spouse in the bitterness of her heart, she knew that He
pardoned them, for she beheld a number of precious stones
in the golden vine-leaves. On the sixth feria (Friday), as
she meditated on extreme unction, our Lord appeared to
her, and anointed her eyes, ears, and lips with a liquor
which came from His inmost Heart; and this precious
liquor also communicated to the different members of her
body the merits of the deified Body of Christ.

On Saturday, as she prepared in anticipation for the
Holy Viaticum, at the Adorable Sacrifice of the Mass, she
saw four angelic princes surrounding the throne of the
Divine Majesty. Two of these angels placed themselves at
each side of our Divine Lord, and the other two came to
the Saint and conducted her to her Spouse. Our Lord received her with the greatest tenderness, and then united her
to Himself by the life-giving Sacrament of the Altar. The
Saint occupied herself on Sunday by repeating the prayers
which she had composed as a preparation for death, offering our Lord each member of her body as dead to the

world, and desiring henceforth to exist only for His eternal praise and love. After this He blessed her with His own Hand, and marked the sign of the cross upon each member of her body, which appeared to glorify them marvellously, and to free them from every stain.

At the Elevation of the Host she offered her heart to our Lord, that He might make it die to the world ; beseeching Him, by the innocence of His most holy life, to free it from every stain of sin, and, by the incomprehensible love which united God to Man in the Divine Person, that He would prepare her to receive His gifts. Our Lord then appeared to her, and opened His Heart with both hands, from which so ardent a fire poured forth that the soul of the Saint was completely dissolved thereby. From this union of her heart with the Heart of her Spouse, a tree sprang forth, adorned with gold and silver leaves ; and our Lord said to her : " This tree proceeds from My union with you ; My Divinity is figured by the golden leaves, and your soul by the silver leaves, which are enclosed therein." As the Saint prayed for those who were committed to her care, she saw the tree producing ripe and beautiful fruit ; and the branches hung down in such a manner, that these persons could gather this fruit as they pleased.

After this, feeling much exhausted, she lay back on her pallet, saying : " I offer this rest to Thee as if it were given to Thy sacred Humanity." He replied : " And I will supply by My mercy for all your sins of human frailty."

Then she inquired if her present weakness would be the means of bringing her to eternal rest ; and our Lord replied : " I am leading you nearer to Me by this infirmity. For when a king is about to espouse a princess who lives in a distant land, he sends his officers and courtiers to conduct her to him with all possible pomp and magnificence; and they are charged to spare neither pains nor expense to render the journey easy and agreeable to her. When she has arrived at her destination, he places her in one of his royal palaces, and gives her a ring as a pledge of espousals. Here she remains, attended with all honour, until the nuptial day, when the king comes for her himself, and conducts her to his imperial throne.

"Now I, your Lord and your God, am the true and faithful Lover of your soul; and I share in all the pains of body or soul with which you are afflicted, and send My saints to attend you and congratulate you on this royal road which leads you to Me. The instruments of music and rejoicings are your sufferings, which resound in My ears as an harmonious concert, moving Me to compassionate you, and inclining My Heart more and more towards you. Then, when you arrive at your journey's end, I will meet you and espouse you before all My saints with a holy embrace, in the Sacrament of Extreme Unction. The sooner you receive this Sacrament, the greater will be your happiness; for then I will approach you nearer and nearer, so that your whole being will be enraptured with the blessedness of My embrace; and I will convey you Myself across the dark river Death, immersing you in the ocean of My Divinity, where you will become one spirit with Me, and reign with Me for endless ages. Then you will be consoled for all the trials and sufferings you have borne when on earth, with the same harmonious music and the same delights as those which now enrapture My deified Humanity."

Our Lord then continued thus: "If any one desires a similar visit in his last moments, let him endeavour daily to clothe himself with My perfect life, and to imitate it continually; let him learn to subdue his flesh, and to renounce his own will entirely into My hands; let him live by the Spirit, and believe that I will seek his good in all things by My paternal providence. Let him offer Me every adversity and contradiction, and for each I will reward him with rich jewels and precious gifts. If, through human frailty, he seeks himself in anything, let him immediately do penance, and once more resign himself to My will, and I will receive him with the right hand of My mercy, and lead him with ineffable honour and glory to the kingdom of eternal light."

On the following Sunday, as Gertrude solemnised the feast of her eternal joy, and the happy moment when she should appear before the Ever-Blessed Trinity released from exile, she was ravished in ecstasy, and beheld all the merits and joys of each choir of angels and of the different saints; and as her heart overflowed with joy in considering their blessedness, she returned the most fervent thanks to God for it. She also thanked Him for all the graces, gifts, and glory which He had bestowed on the Blessed Virgin His Mother; beseeching her, for the love of her Son, to offer her virtues for her to the King of virtues.

Then the Queen of Heaven, moved by her prayers, offered her virginal purity for her, as a white garment; her peaceful humility, as a green tunic; and her unfading charity, as a purple mantle. When our Lord had clothed her in these robes, the saints, rejoicing in her beauty, prayed that she might be adorned with their graces and virtues also. And He placed a necklace on her, adorned with precious stones. each of which seemed to attract the different graces which had been asked for her. But it must not be understood from this that any one can receive from others what they have failed to obtain for themselves;

nevertheless, some souls may receive for their gratitude
what others fail to obtain.

CHAPTER XXV.

How our Lord Jesus and all the Saints console the souls of the just
in their last moments—And with what love our Lord communicates Himself to His elect in the Sacrament of the Altar.

As Gertrude reflected on death, she exclaimed to our Lord :
" How happy and how honoured are they who merit to be
consoled and strengthened by Thy saints in their last moments ! I am unworthy of this consolation, for I have never
honoured Thy saints worthily ; therefore I cannot expect
consolation from any saint, save from Thee alone, the Sanctifier of all the saints." Our Lord replied : " You will not
be deprived of this consolation because you expect all from
Me ; on the contrary, My saints will love and minister to
you all the more for it, and at the moment when men
usually feel most fear and anxiety, I will send My Saints to
assist you, and I will come to you Myself in all the glory
and beauty of My Divinity and Humanity." She replied :
" And when wilt thou accomplish Thy promise, and bring
me from this land of exile to the land of rest ? " Our Lord
answered : " Will a royal bride complain of the applause of
the populace if it only increases the love of her bridegroom
for her ? " " But, Lord," continued the Saint, " how can
this apply to me, who am the vilest of Thy creatures ? "
He replied : " Know that I communicate Myself to you
entirely in the Sacrament of the Altar, which after this life
cannot be ; and in this union there is more blessedness and
delight than in any human love, for that is often vile and

transitory ; but the sweetness of this union ennobles and dignifies the soul."

Our Lord had often incited the Saint to desire her deliverance from the flesh ; and now she became seriously ill, so that the physicians had no hope of her recovery. This intelligence filled her with joy, and she said to our Lord : " Although I desire, above all things, to be delivered from the prison of the flesh, and united to Thee, nevertheless, if it pleases Thee, I would willingly remain on earth and endure the severest suffering, even until the day of judgment." Our Lord replied : " Your good-will so moves My Divine benignity, that I accept it as if you had accomplished what you offer." As He said this, a marvellous joy appeared in His Divine countenance, which imparted a new and ineffable gladness and consolation to all the saints. Then He continued : " In that hour when I draw you entirely to Myself, the mountains—that is, the saints—shall drop sweetness ; the heavens shall pour forth honey on the earth, from the abundance of your beatitude ; the hills shall flow with milk and honey—that is, I will attract carnal and earthly souls by My grace, for your sake."

Then she began to make fervent thanksgiving for these favours, and to excite her gratitude further by reflecting on many graces which our Divine Lord had promised her. And these favours were : first,* a promise that she should die of Divine love, and that her death should be caused thereby, even as love caused the Death of the Son of God on the cross ; second, that in the adorable counsels of the Ever-Blessed Trinity the Holy Spirit had prepared to preside at her death, and order all that passed within her ; third, that all who assisted her in her last illness, or even

* " Item."

desired to do so, should themselves be assisted and protected by Divine love in their last moments ; fourth, that our Lord would bestow as many graces on them as it was possible for men to receive ; fifth, that in the hour of her happy departure an immense number of sinners should be converted to true penance by the infinite and gratuitous mercy of God ; sixth, that an infinite number of souls should be delivered from suffering, and obtain an increase of merit and beatitude, and enter with her into the celestial kingdom ; seventh, that whoever besought our Lord to bestow any grace on her should be rewarded by receiving the same grace themselves ; eighth, that whoever returned thanks to God for the graces bestowed on her should receive, sooner or later, according to the decrees of His providence, all they desired for their salvation, if they observed the following conditions—(1) to praise the eternal love of God, who chose her from all eternity ; (2) to thank Him for having drawn her so sweetly to Himself ; (3) for having united her to Himself so intimately and familiarly ; (4) for having blessedly consummated His work in her, and for having granted all her petitions ;—ninth, that our Lord had sworn to Gertrude by the truth of His Passion, and confirmed His promise by the seal of His Death, that whoever prayed for her during her life, at her death, or after her death, should receive the most abundant graces and favours, if they had also the intention of including in this prayer all for whom God wished them to pray, if they commenced their petition by offering it through the merit of the infinite love which drew Him down from heaven to earth to accomplish the work of our salvation, and concluded it by offering it in union with His Death, and the glory and triumph with which He presented His adorable Humanity to the Father on the day of His glorious Ascension.   Futher, He promised that those who prayed thus for her should receive all the graces which they had asked for her, as if they had made themselves worthy of obtaining them.

CHAPTER XXVI.

Of the sweet repose which the Saint enjoyed ; and how she satisfied for her negligences.

SOME time after this our Lord Jesus appeared to her, and seemed as if He was preparing a couch on which she might repose ; but, instead of a soft bed of feathers, He displayed before her, as it were, all the sufferings which He had endured on the cross for the salvation of men, that its salutary fruit might prepare her soul for eternal life.   The pillow which He offered to support her head was the dolours of His most sweet Heart when He hung upon the cross, and remembered how unavailing all His sufferings would be for so many souls.   As a mattress for this couch, He offered her His abandonment and contempt in His Passion, the infidelity of His friends towards One who was of all friends the most faithful, His cruel binding, mocking, and contempt. Lastly, He offered her the merits of His most precious Death as a coverlet, that she might be sanctified thereby, according to the good pleasure of His Divine mercy.

As Gertrude reposed therein sweetly, the Heart of our Lord, in which all treasures are hidden, appeared to her as a mystical garden of exceeding beauty, in which all the desires of His holy Humanity were represented under the figure of an exquisite verdure, and all His thoughts as violets and lilies.   The virtues of our Divine Lord were figured by a fruitful vine, like that of Engaddi, whose grapes were of so delicious a sweetness.   This vine extended its branches and leaves round the Saint, affording her the most agreeable shade and refreshment; and our Lord gave her fruit, that is, His virtues, from the different branches of this tree, causing her also to drink the delicious wine which it produced.

Then she beheld three pure fountains springing forth in the Divine Heart, which emptied themselves miraculously into each other; and our Lord said to her: " You will drink from these rivulets so efficaciously at the hour of your death, that your soul will attain such perfect health and such consummate perfection as to be unable to remain longer in the body; in the meantime, let this delightful vision serve for your spiritual adornment." Then she besought the Eternal Father to look upon her for the sake of the holy Humanity of our Lord Jesus Christ, to purify her from all sin, and to adorn her with His Divine virtues; and she knew that her prayers were heard. After this she prayed thus : " O most loving Father, give me Thy most loving benediction ; " and the Lord extended His omnipotent Hand, and blessed her with the sign of the Cross. Then this benediction appeared like a golden tent, which covered the couch already mentioned ; and she saw also many instruments of music placed therein, which signified the joys she obtained through the Passion of Jesus Christ.

These heavenly delights changed her sufferings into joy, and as she now occupied herself entirely with her own perfection, she began to compose some short and fervent prayers, to supply for her negligences in reciting the Canonical Hours, the Office of the Blessed Virgin, and the Office of the Dead. She also desired to supply for her deficiencies in certain virtues, such as the love of God and her neighbour, humility, chastity, obedience, consideration for others, thanksgiving, rejoicing or grieving with others,

&c. Then she endeavoured to supply for the negligences
of which she believed herself guilty in the Divine praises,
in thanksgiving, in prayers, and in reparation, not only for
herself, but also for the whole Church.

Nor was she satisfied with this reparation ; for she
desired for each fault, and for each member of her body, to
recite twenty-five short prayers, adding at the end of every
petition the *Pater noster* and *Ave Maria*, for which she
had a special devotion ; and these prayers not only moved
the heart of man, but even touched the very King of Glory,
who rejoiced thereat exceedingly ; and although the Saint
had a most perfect confidence in the promises related above,
which our Divine Lord had made to her, nevertheless her
humility urged her to labour for their fulfilment, by her
own earnest coöperation with Divine grace. She also
perused her holy Rule with extreme diligence, seeking to
supply for her omissions in its observance by her prayers,
sighs, and tears ; so that she not only satisfied for any fault
she might have committed therein, but obtained also new
ornaments and graces from God. Then she applied all
the powers of her soul and body to higher things, praying
with exceeding fervour, ardently desiring a perfect and
eternal union with her God, uniting her devotion to the
mutual love and ineffable gratulations of the Ever-Blessed
Trinity, and repeating the verse, " When wilt Thou come ?
my soul thirsteth for Thee," with the words, " O most
loving Father." (The last words she had learned in a
marvellous manner, and she knew that they were most
acceptable to God.)

She repeated these prayers continually, unless her
bodily weakness was so great as to prevent it ; and she
offered the reparation also, if her soul was not attracted
to a more sublime prayer. The consolations vouchsafed to

her were so abundant, that they were imparted even to those who attended her ; so that many sought to be near her to obtain her instructions, and to learn these prayers from her. Hence, most fervent prayer was made for her recovery, or even that her death might be retarded ; and God, who hears the desires of the humble, granted this favour, and spared her a little longer to those who loved her so tenderly ; affording her also an opportunity of increasing her merit.

The verse abovementioned is here subjoined—

" Amongst a thousand still desired,
 When wilt Thou come, O Jesus mine?
When wilt thou fill my soul with Thee,
 Which knows no joy on earth but Thine?

" Oh, come! oh, come! most mighty King;
 Father of boundless power and praise:
Thy joy is light, Thy light is joy.
 Oh, hasten, Lord, life's passing days.

" Thou thinkest thoughts of tenderest love,
 Sparing our sins, and giving place
To mercy ; sweetest, dearest Lord,
 Oh, come ; I long to see Thy Face." *

---

* " Desiderate millies,
 Mi Jesu, quando venies ?
 Me lætam quando facies ?
 De te me quando saties ?
 Veni, veni, Rex optime !
 Pater immensæ gloriæ,
 Effulge clarè lætius,
 Jam expectamus sæpius.

" Tua te cogat pietas, ut mala nostra superis parcendo : et voti compotos nos tuo vultu saties."

CHAPTER XXVII.

How the Saint supplied for her negligences in the service of the Blessed Virgin Mary.

As the Saint occupied herself in making these reparations, she grieved exceedingly for her omissions in devotion to the Blessed Virgin, and she besought our Lord to offer her prayers Himself to His Blessed Mother. Then the King of Glory arose and offered her His deified Heart, saying : " Behold, My beloved Mother, I present you My Heart, which abounds in all beatitude, and I offer you all the Divine affections by which I predestinated, created, and sanctified you from all eternity to be My Mother ; with a the love and tenderness which I manifested to you on earth, when you carried Me in your bosom and nourished Me with your milk, and the fidelity with which I subjected Myself to you, as a Son to a Mother ; and especially My tenderness towards you in the hour of death, when I pro- vided you with a faithful guardian, forgetting My own sorrows. I offer you the glory and honour to which I elevated you on the day of your Assumption into heaven, when you were exalted above all the choirs of saints and angels, and proclaimed Queen and mistress of heaven and earth. I offer you once more all these tokens of My love, as if I presented them to you anew, in favour of My spouse, that you may overlook her negligences in your regard, and assist her at the hour of her death with all the tenderness of a mother."

Then the Blessed Virgin accepted this charge with the greatest pleasure, saying : " Grant, my beloved Son, when I receive Thy chosen spouse, according to Thy Divine good pleasure, that she may receive some of the overflowing delights which I enjoy." The goodness of the Lord towards her moved Gertrude deeply, and she exclaimed: "Alas, my most loving Lord! I am grieved that I have not satisfied for my negligences in reciting the Canonical Hours in like manner, since Thy inconceivable goodness receives so graciously my poorest efforts." Our Lord replied: "Do not be grieved, My beloved; for I have renewed all your desires, in union with that love which prompted My Divine Heart to infuse into you these noble and loving aspirations; and I have united to this the most devout and pure intention which any human heart could offer Me, presenting it to My Father in satisfaction for all your negligences, so that His paternal goodness inclines towards you with the tenderest affection."

CHAPTER XXVIII.

How Gertrude prepared for death.

EVERY Friday, at the hour of None, St. Gertrude retired apart from all creatures, in order to devote herself to preparation for death, and especially to recite the prayers for the agonising. After she had practised this devotion for some time, our Lord rewarded her by a special grace. On one of these occasions she was rapt in ecstasy, and our Lord manifested to her the manner of her death. She beheld herself reposing in the arms of our Lord, under the form of a fair young maiden, in her agony; and at the same time she saw an immense number of saints and angels surrounding her, with censers in their hands, in which they offered the prayers of the Church with great joy to the King of Glory. When they invoked the Blessed Virgin by the Antiphon *Salve Maria,* our Lord made a sign to His Blessed Mother to console His elect; and the Queen of Virgins appeared in marvellous radiance, and supported the head of the dying person. Her guardian angel also appeared under the figure of an illustrious prince, who came to congratulate her on her happiness.

As she invoked the archangel St. Michael, she beheld the glorious chief of the angelic hosts, with a multitude of angels, all prepared to assist her and to combat the demons, whom she also saw under hideous forms, but so weak and powerless that they could not do her the slightest injury; and this afforded her the greatest consolation. A column of light appeared to proceed from the lips of the dying person to the very throne of God; and this had such virtue, that it was apparent even the angelic guard was not needed to defend her against the demons, for it caused them such terror that they endeavoured to fly and conceal themselves.

As each of the saints was invoked in the Litany of the Dying, he appeared ready to assist her. The Patriarchs had branches in their hands, from which their good works were suspended in place of fruit; and these they placed round her. The Prophets bore golden mirrors, on which were depicted the sublime revelations which God had imparted to them; and these they also offered for her assistance, placing them opposite to her. The beloved disciple St. John came next, and presented her with two golden rings; each Apostle who followed presented one also: and these rings represented the fidelity which the soul had towards our Divine Lord.

The Martyrs followed, holding golden palms in their hands, which shone radiantly with all their sufferings. The Confessors had golden flowers, which represented their virtues: and these they also presented to her. The Virgins offered her roses, the stalks of which had little crooks of gold, which signified the close union with the Lord which they enjoyed on account of their purity ; and the Lord Jesus, the King and Spouse of virgins, was adorned with a robe covered with the same number of roses as there were virgins, who appeared to communicate in His merits by these golden crooks, which fastened the flowers to His robe; these crooks also represented the particular virtues of each virgin.

Then the Lord, seeing that Gertrude was adorned with the flowers of each virgin, inclined towards her, to bestow on her as many graces as there were ties which attached her to Him ; and thus she experienced something of the happiness of these blessed souls. The Widows and the other saints then brought their offerings in the form of golden caskets ; and all the merits which had been offered for her, by an admirable communication, became her own, so that her soul shone resplendently before God.

The holy Innocents also had their share in this festival, to honour the Lord who had purchased them with His precious Blood, and made them heirs of His kingdom. They seemed, however, to have less merit of their own, but their souls were marvellously adorned by the union of their innocence with the innocence of Jesus Christ. Then the Son of God inclined towards Gertrude and embraced her lovingly, absorbing her into Himself as the sun, in its meridian splendour, absorbs a dewdrop ; so that her soul was, as it were, received into the Heart of her Spouse with all the virtues and merits which had been conferred on her, and she was surrounded and penetrated by Him as fire inflames iron.

CHAPTER XXIX.

How our Lord authorised this work.

AFTER this work was finished, our Lord Jesus appeared to her who had completed it, holding it in His Hand ; and pressing it to His Heart, He said to her : " I have placed this book thus upon My Heart, that every word contained therein may be penetrated with Divine sweetness, even as honey penetrates bread. Therefore, whoever reads this book devoutly will receive great profit for his salvation." Then she besought our Lord to preserve this book from all error for His own glory, and He extended His adorable Hand, signing it with the sign of the Cross, saying : " I consecrate by My benediction all that is written in this book, that it may promote the salvation of those who read it with humble devotion." He added : " The labour of those who have written this book is also most agreeable to Me, particularly in three things : first, I taste therein the sweetness of My Divine love, by which all that is related therein has been effected ; second, I am exceedingly pleased with the good-will of those who wrote it ; third, I contemplate with singular pleasure My gratuitous mercy, which appears in all that is written in this book. I desire, therefore, that this work should be fructified by My most holy Life and My Five Wounds ; and the seven gifts of the Holy Ghost shall be the seven seals of Divine mercy with which it sl all be sealed, so that none may be able to take it out of My Hand."

On another occasion, when the compiler * of this book communicated, she had it hidden in the sleeve of her habit, under her mantle, to offer it to our Lord for His eternal

* " Compilatrix."

praise and glory. As she prostrated before receiving the Body of the Lord, one of the religious saw our Lord approaching her with great manifestations of joy and tenderness ; and He addressed her thus : " I will penetrate with My Divine sweetness and fertilise every word of this book which you have offered Me, and which you have written by the direction of My Spirit : and I will manifest to whoever reads this book with humble love what will be most useful for him, and will take him into My bosom, breathing into his soul life and truth. But if any one reads it through vain curiosity, and a desire to pry into My secrets to censure and mock them, I will assuredly humble and cast him down shamefully."

CHAPTER XXX.

Oblation of this work to the Divine glory—Conclusion.

I OFFER Thee this work, O Lord Jesus Christ, Fount of eternal light, in union with that ineffable charity which moved Thee, the Only-begotten of the Father, in the plenitude of the Divinity, to take upon Thee our nature, and to become Man. I offer it to Thee on the part of all Thy creatures, because it is Thine ineffable tenderness for mankind which caused Thee to pour forth those sweet and efficacious graces on the heart of Thy chosen spouse, to fructify them, to draw her to Thyself, and to unite her to Thee eternally.

I beseech Thee to take this work into Thy Divine keeping, that it may glorify the omnipotence of the Father, the wisdom of the Son, and the love of the Holy Ghost. I offer it to Thee in fervent thanksgiving for all the graces which Thou hast communicated or wilt communicate through this work, even to the end of time. And as I am an utterly vile and unworthy creature, I offer Thee, in satisfaction for all my deficiencies and omissions, my blindness and ignorance, Thy own sweetest Heart, ever full of Divine thanksgiving and eternal beatitude. Amen.

Deo gratias.

INDEX OF SUBJECTS.